Households of God

HOUSEHOLDS OF GOD

The regular canons and canonesses of St Augustine and of Prémontré in medieval Ireland

Martin Browne OSB and Colmán Ó Clabaigh OSB

EDITORS

FOUR COURTS PRESS

Typeset in 10pt on 12.5pt BemboPro by
Carrigboy Typesetting Services for
FOUR COURTS PRESS LTD
7 Malpas Street, Dublin 8, Ireland
www.fourcourtspress.ie
and in North America for
FOUR COURTS PRESS
c/o IPG, 814 N Franklin St, Chicago, IL 60610.

A catalogue record for this title is available
from the British Library.

ISBN 978-1-84682-788-4

Printed in England
by CPI Antony Rowe, Chippenham, Wilts.

Contents

Illustrations

FIGURES

COLOUR PLATES
(*between pages 140 and 141*)

Abbreviations

AC	*Annála Connacht: The Annals of Connacht*, ed. A.M. Freeman (Dublin, 1944)
AFM	*Annála ríoghachta Éireann: Annals of the Four Masters from the earliest period to the year 1616*, ed. John O'Donovan, 7 vols (Dublin, 1851)
AH	*Archivium Hibernicum*
AI	*The Annals of Inisfallen*, ed. Seán Mac Airt (Dublin, 1951)
ALC	*The Annals of Loch Cé: a chronicle of Irish affairs, 1014–1590*, ed. W.M. Hennessy, 2 vols (London, 1871)
Anal. Hib.	*Analecta Hibernica*
Ann. Conn.	*Annála Connacht (AD1224–1544)*, ed. A.M. Freeman (Dublin, 1951)
ATig.	Annals of Tigernach
AU	*Annála Uladh, Annals of Ulster; otherwise Annála Senait: a chronicle of Irish affairs, 431–1131, 1155–1541*, ed. W.M. Hennessy and B. MacCarthy, 4 vols (Dublin, 1887–1901)
bar.	barony
BL	British Library, London
BL Add. MSS	British Library Additional MSS
Bodl.	Bodleian Library, Oxford
Burton and Stöber, *Canons*	Janet Burton and Karen Stöber (eds), *The regular canons in the medieval British Isles* (Turnhout, 2011)
Cal. Pat. rolls Ire., Hen VIII–Eliz.	*Calendar of patent and close rolls of chancery in Ireland, Henry VIII to 18th Elizabeth*, ed. James Morrin (Dublin, 1861)
CDI	*Calendar of documents relating to Ireland, 1171–1307*, ed. H.S. Sweetman, 5 vols (London, 1875–86)
CLAHJ	*County Louth Archaeological and Historical Journal*
Colker, *Latin MSS*	M.L. Colker, *Trinity College Library Dublin: descriptive catalogue of the medieval and Renaissance Latin manuscripts*, 2 vols (Dublin, 1991)
CPL, 1 [etc.]	*Calendar of entries in the papal registers relating to Great Britain and Ireland: papal letters* (London & Dublin, 1893–)
d.	denarius
DIB	*Dictionary of Irish biography*
ed.	editor(s); edition; edited by
EHR	*English Historical Review*
EIMP	*Extents of Irish monastic possessions, 1540–1541, from manuscripts in the Public Record Office, London*, ed. N.B. White (Dublin, 1943)
Feiss and Mosseau, *Saint Victor*	Hugh Feiss and Juliet Mosseau (eds), *A companion to the Abbey of Saint Victor in Paris* (Leiden & Boston, 2018)
Flanagan, *Charters*	Marie Therese Flanagan, *Irish royal charters: texts and contexts* (Oxford, 2005)

Flanagan, 'Louth'	Marie Therese Flanagan, 'St Mary's Abbey, Louth, and the introduction of the Arrouasian observance into Ireland', *Clogher Record*, 10 (1980), 223–34
Flanagan, *Transformation*	Marie Therese Flanagan, *The transformation of the Irish church in the twelfth century* (Woodbridge, 2010)
Gillespie and Refaussé, Med. MSS	Raymond Gillespie and Raymond Refaussé (eds), *The medieval manuscripts of Christ Church Cathedral, Dublin* (Dublin, 2006)
HBS	Henry Bradshaw Society
Hogan, *Llanthony*	Arlene Hogan, *The priory of Llanthony Prima and Secunda in Ireland, 1172–1541: lands, patronage and politics* (Dublin, 2007)
IHS	*Irish Historical Studies: the Joint Journal of the Irish Historical Society and the Ulster Society for Irish Historical Studies*
IMC	Irish Manuscripts Commission
JCHAS	*Journal of the Cork Historical and Archaeological Society*
JGAHS	*Journal of the Galway Archaeological and Historical Society*
JRSAI	*Journal of the Royal Society of Antiquaries of Ireland*
L. & P. Hen. VIII	*Letters and papers, foreign and domestic, Henry VIII*, 21 vols (London, 1862–1932)
Milne, *CCCD*	Kenneth Milne (ed.), *Christ Church Cathedral Dublin: a history* (Dublin, 2000)
MRHI	A. Gwynn & R.N. Hadcock, *Medieval religious houses: Ireland* (Dublin, 1970 [repr. Dublin, 1988])
NLI	National Library of Ireland, Dublin
NUI	National University of Ireland
ODNB	*Oxford dictionary of national biography* (Oxford, 2004)
Ó Riain, *Dictionary*	P. Ó Riain, *Dictionary of Irish saints* (Dublin, 2011)
Ormond deeds	E. Curtis (ed.), *Calendar of Ormond deeds*, 6 vols (Dublin, 1932–43)
PRIA	*Proceedings of the Royal Irish Academy*
Rot. pat. Hib.	*Rotulorum patentium et clausorum cancellariae Hiberniae calendarium*, ed. Edward Tresham (Dublin, 1828)
s.a.	*sub anno*, under the year
Sheehy, *Pont. Hib.*	Maurice P. Sheehy (ed.), *Pontificia Hibernica. Medieval papal chancery documents concerning Ireland, 640–1261* (2 vols, Dublin, 1962)
Ss	Saints
TCD	Trinity College Dublin
trans.	translation/translated by
VCH Glouc.	*The Victoria history of the county of Gloucester*, ed. William Page, vol. ii (London, 1907)

Contributors

EDEL BHREATHNACH was CEO of The Discovery Programme from 2013 to 2019 and is a medieval historian whose current interests are in early medieval kingship and landscape and in medieval monasticism. She is the author of *Ireland and the medieval world, AD 400–1200* (Dublin, 2014).

MARTIN BROWNE is a monk of Glenstal and currently serves as Headmaster of the Abbey secondary school. He is the co-editor (with Colmán Ó Clabaigh OSB) of *The Irish Benedictines: a history* (Dublin, 2005) and *Soldiers of Christ: the Knights Hospitaller and the Knights Templar in medieval Ireland* (Dublin, 2015); and (with Luke Macnamara OSB) of *The Glenstal companion to the Easter Vigil* (Dublin, 2019).

MIRIAM CLYNE is an archaeologist and a Visiting Research Fellow at the Department of History of Art and Architecture, Trinity College Dublin. Her research focuses on the Premonstratensian and Augustinian canons in medieval Ireland. She is author of *Kells Priory, Co. Kilkenny: archaeological excavations by T. Fanning and M. Clyne* (Dublin, 2007).

TRACY COLLINS is a professional archaeologist, and co-director of Aegis Archaeology Ltd, with a special research interest in medieval female monasticism. She has published on the subject, and has directed archaeological excavations at St Catherine's Old Abbey, Co. Limerick, arguably the best-preserved later medieval Augustinian nunnery in the country.

CHRISTY CUNNIFFE works as a Community Archaeologist for Galway County Council. He specializes in the archaeology and architecture of the medieval Irish church, particularly the interpretation of ecclesiastical iconography and funerary art. He is engaged in an on-going study of the medieval parish churches of Clonfert diocese.

ADRIAN EMPEY is a Visiting Research Fellow in the Department of History, Trinity College Dublin. He has written widely on themes relating to Anglo-Norman settlement in Ireland, the evolution of the parochial system, and more recently on aspects of legal history. He is the author of *Gowran, Co. Kilkenny, 1190–1610: custom and conflict in a baronial town* (Dublin, 2015).

MARIE THERESE FLANAGAN is Professor Emerita of Medieval History at Queen's University Belfast and a historian of twelfth-century Ireland spanning the conventional periodization between pre-invasion and post-invasion Ireland. Her books include *Irish royal charters: texts and contexts* (Oxford, 2005) and *The transformation of the Irish church in the twelfth century* (Woodbridge, 2010).

CLEMENS GALBAN is a Canon Regular of St Augustine of Stift Klosterneuburg in Austria. Originally from the United States, he is a doctoral candidate in church history at the Pontifical University of the Holy Cross in Rome. The title of his dissertation is 'Provost Georg Muestinger and the introduction of the Raudnitz reform into Stift Klosterneuburg, 1418–*c*.1421'.

ARLENE HOGAN is an art historian and medievalist. She established the Friends of the National Gallery of Ireland. Her publications include *Kilmallock Dominican Priory: an architectural perspective, 1291–1991* (Limerick, 1991) and *The priory of Llanthony Prima and Secunda in Ireland, 1172–1541: lands, patrons and politics* (Dublin, 2008).

RACHEL MOSS is Associate Professor in the History of Art and Architecture at Trinity College Dublin, specializing in Irish medieval material culture. She was editor and principal author of *Art and architecture of Ireland, volume 1, medieval, c.400–1600AD* (London, New Haven and Dublin, 2014).

LOUISE NUGENT is a professional archaeologist, with a research interest in Irish medieval and modern pilgrimage and material culture. She has published on the subject, and is engaged in an on-going study of modern pilgrimage at holy well sites in Ireland.

COLMÁN Ó CLABAIGH is a monk of Glenstal and a medievalist specializing in the history of monastic and religious orders in late medieval Ireland. He is the author of *The Friars in Ireland, 1224–1540* (Dublin, 2012) and co-editor (with Martin Browne OSB) of *Soldiers of Christ: the Knights Hospitaller and the Knights Templar in medieval Ireland* (Dublin, 2015).

TADHG O'KEEFFE is Full Professor of Archaeology in University College Dublin. His most recent book is *Tristernagh Priory, Co. Westmeath: colonial monasticism in medieval Ireland* (Dublin, 2018).

PÁDRAIG Ó RIAIN is Professor Emeritus of Early and Medieval Irish at University College Cork and a former president of The Irish Texts Society. He is the author of numerous publications on Irish hagiography, place-names and textual transmission including *Feastdays of the saints: a history of Irish martyrologies* (2006) and *A dictionary of Irish saints* (Dublin, 2011).

BRENDAN SCOTT holds a PhD in early modern Irish history from NUI Galway and has published widely on the Reformation and the dissolution of the monasteries in Ireland.

Acknowledgments

We are grateful first and foremost to the contributors for the speed and good humour with which they delivered their chapters and to Martin Fanning and the team at Four Courts Press for producing this volume to their customary high standard. Thanks are also due to Abbot Brendan and our confreres at Glenstal for their support and particularly to Br Emmaus O'Herlihy OSB who designed the cover.

The publication of this volume was made possible by generous subventions from various institutions and individuals. We gratefully acknowledge the financial and moral support of Aegis Archaeology Ltd, Limerick; the Abbot and Community of Daylesford Abbey, Pennsylvania; the Burns Library and the Center for Irish Programs, Boston College; the Prior and Community of St Saviour's Dominican Priory, Dublin; the Mayo Arthroplasty Conference and the Centre for Norbertine Studies, St Norbert's College, Wisconsin. We are likewise grateful to Derek and Helen Bennett; Francesca Caraballese; Fr Andrew Ciferni, OPraem; Dr Tracy Collins; Frank Coyne; Fr James Dollard; Dr Eugene Duffy; Dr Christian Dupont; Fr Hugh Feiss OSB; Theresa Hyland; Artie and Mena Kenny; Professor Eamonn O'Donoghue; Fr Henry O'Shea OSB and Ken and Joanna Phelan for their support.

Ut in omnibus glorificetur Deus

Martin Browne & Colmán Ó Clabaigh
Glenstal Abbey
The Assumption of the Blessed Virgin Mary
2019

Introduction

If history is written by the victors, then monastic history has, until recently, largely been the preserve of the survivors. This partly explains why the regular canons and canonesses of St Augustine, in their various guises, have received so little attention in Irish monastic historiography, despite being the most widespread of all the medieval religious orders. Unlike the Cistercian monks and the mendicant friars and nuns, the canonical movement had a miniscule presence in early modern Ireland and was largely untouched by the monastic revivals and refoundations of the nineteenth and twentieth centuries. In consequence there were few structures to preserve institutional records and even fewer members with the inclination and opportunity to examine them. It seemed timely then, in July 2017, to redress this by devoting the Fourth Glenstal History Conference to exploring the canonical movement in Ireland and this volume represents the proceedings of that gathering. As what follows demonstrates, the neglect of the past has been succeeded by a vigorous, multidisciplinary research impetus that augurs well for the future.

The regular canons and canonesses emerged in the context of the twelfth-century transformation of the Irish church and of the colonization process that ensued from the Norman invasion of 1169. Although the primary sources at first seem meagre, when viewed synoptically they provide a comprehensive insight on all aspects of their lives and ministry.[1] Recent archaeological investigations have also shed light on their activities in Ireland.[2] The upsurge of interest in the canonical movement elsewhere in Europe, particularly in Great Britain, provides valuable comparative perspectives on the Irish material as many of the contributions to this volume demonstrate.[3] Similarly, some important studies of individual foundations have appeared in local historical and archaeological journals and these are listed in the bibliography. The unpublished 1996 TCD PhD thesis of Dr Sarah Preston remains a fundamental starting point for any study of the movement in Ireland.[4]

The surviving primary sources include a small number of original charters relating to Kells Priory, Co. Kilkenny, Holy Trinity Priory, Dublin and Clare

---

1 P. Connolly, *Medieval record sources* (Dublin, 2002), pp 14–37 is the essential introduction to this material. **2** In addition to the contributions to this volume by Collins, Clyne, Cunniffe and O'Keeffe, see also T. Fanning, M. Dolley and G. Roche, 'Excavations at Clontuskert Priory', *PRIA*, 76 (1976), 97–169; M. Clyne, *Kells Priory, Co. Kilkenny: archaeological excavations by T. Fanning and M. Clyne* (Dublin, 2007); Margaret Quinlan Architects, *Conservation plan: Athassel Augustinian Priory, County Tipperary* (Dublin, 2009). **3** J. Burton and K. Stöber (eds), *The regular canons in the medieval British Isles* (Turnhout, 2011). **4** Sarah M. Preston, 'The canons regular of St Augustine in medieval Ireland: an overview', PhD thesis, University of Dublin, 1996. **5** N.B. White (ed.), *Irish monastic and episcopal deeds AD 1200–1600* (Dublin, 1936). M.J. McEnery and R. Refaussé (eds), *Christ Church deeds* (Dublin, 2001); R. Gillespie, 'The Christ Church deeds' in

Abbey, Co. Clare.[5] The ephemeral nature of these documents led many communities to transcribe them into cartularies such as those surviving from Tristernagh Priory, Co. Westmeath, All Hallows Priory, St Thomas' Abbey and the hospital of St John at the New Gate in Dublin, as well as those detailing the Irish possessions of the English and Welsh houses of Llanthony Prima and Secunda.[6] Charters and rental material relating to the houses at Cong and Ballintubber, both in Co. Mayo, and Kells, Co. Kilkenny, survive in seventeenth-century copies made for Sir James Ware.[7] Both the *Liber Niger* and the *Liber Albus* of Holy Trinity Priory, Dublin contain administrative material from the thirteenth through the sixteenth centuries.[8] Miriam Clyne has published a recently discovered rental of the Premonstratensian community at Lough Key that sheds valuable light on how the canons administered their property in a Gaelic milieu.[9] Little survives to illustrate the routine expenditure of the communities with the exception of some household and manorial accounts relating to Holy Trinity Priory, Dublin and a set of kitchen receipts from Kells, Co. Kilkenny.[10]

Unlike the situation in England, no library catalogue or book list survives from an Irish Augustinian or Premonstratensian foundation and none of the surviving manuscript material originated in a nunnery.[11] Despite this, the intellectual and spiritual interests of some of the male communities are evident in what survives.[12] The manuscripts associated with Dublin's Holy Trinity Priory have been the subject of a recent study and are discussed further below.[13] Liturgical texts include missals from St Thomas's Abbey, Dublin, and Duleek, Co. Meath, an elaborately ornamented psalter from Holy Trinity Priory, Dublin and a breviary from St Mary's Abbey, Trim.[14] Martyrologies and hagiographical material survive from the houses at Clogher, Clonard, Holy Trinity Priory and St Thomas's Abbey, Dublin,

Gillespie and Refaussé, *Medieval MSS*, pp 103–28. See also M.T. Flanagan, *Irish royal charters: texts and contexts* (Oxford, 2005), pp 325–31. **6** R. Butler (ed.), *Registrum prioratus omnium sanctorum juxta Dublin* (Dublin, 1845); J.T. Gilbert (ed.), *Register of the abbey of St Thomas, Dublin* (London, 1889); E. St. John Brooks, *Register of the hospital of St John the Baptist without the New Gate, Dublin* (Dublin, 1936); M.V. Clarke (ed.), *Register of the priory of Tristernagh* (Dublin, 1941); E. St. John Brooks (ed.), *The Irish cartularies of Llanthony Prima and Secunda* (Dublin, 1953); A. Hogan, *The priory of Llanthony Prima and Secunda in Ireland, 1172–1541: lands, patronage and politics* (Dublin, 2007). An unpublished sixteenth-century cartulary of St Thomas's Abbey survives in two portions, Oxford Bodleian MS Rawlinson B. 499 and Dublin, RIA MS 12 D 2. **7** M.J. Blake, 'Ballintubber Abbey, Co. Mayo: notes on its history', *JGHAS*, 3 (1904), 68–71; M.J. Blake, 'An old rental of Cong Abbey', *JRSAI* 35 (1905), 130–5; White, *Irish episcopal and monastic deeds*, pp 300–13; D. Ó Murchadha, 'Gill Abbey and the "Rental of Cong"', *JCHAS*, 90 (1985), 31–45. **8** C. Ó Clabaigh, 'The *Liber Niger* of Christ Church Cathedral, Dublin' in Gillespie and Refaussé, *Medieval MSS*, pp 60–80. A.J. Fletcher, 'The *Liber Albus* of Christ Church Cathedral, Dublin, in Gillespie and Refaussé, *Medieval MSS*, pp 129–62. **9** Miriam Clyne, 'The rental of Holy Trinity Abbey, Lough Cé' in Thomas Finan (ed.), *Medieval Lough Cé: history, archaeology and landscape* (Dublin, 2010), pp 67–96. **10** J. Mills (ed.), *Account roll of the priory of the Holy Trinity, Dublin, 1337–1346* (Dublin, 1891); Clyne, *Kells Priory*, pp 10–11. **11** T. Webber and A.G. Watson (eds), *The libraries of the Augustinian canons* (London, 1998). **12** Unless otherwise stated, what follows summarises Preston, 'Augustinian canons', 237–54. **13** Gillespie and Refaussé, *Medieval MSS*. **14** BL Add. MS 24,198; Bodl. MS Corpus Christi College 282; Bodl. MS Rawl. G. 185; TCD

Navan, Co. Meath, Knock Abbey, Co. Louth and Saints Island, Co. Longford.[15] The survival of a copy of *The ecclesiastical history of Eusebius* from Greatconnell Priory and a copy of Vincent of Beauvais' *Speculum historiale* from Inistioge Priory, Co. Kilkenny, indicate an interest in history on the part of these communities.[16]

As significant landholders the canons and canonesses often came into conflict over their rights and privileges and this is reflected in the surviving crown, judicial and exchequer records.[17] Likewise, as possessors of extensive ecclesiastical benefices, they are frequently mentioned in episcopal and papal sources.[18] The survival of two canon law texts from Duleek, Co. Meath, and Lorrha, Co. Tipperary, and the administrative material preserved in the *Liber Niger* of Holy Trinity Priory, Dublin, demonstrate due diligence in the preservation of their privileges and administration of their properties.[19] The valuation of Irish dioceses for papal taxation purposes undertaken in the early fourteenth century provides much information on the income the canons and canonesses derived from their benefices.[20] Likewise the extents of monastic possessions taken during the campaign to dissolve the Irish monasteries enumerate the possessions of many Augustinian and Premonstratensian houses as well as the Irish properties belonging to English foundations.[21]

In the opening chapter of this volume Edel Bhreathnach situates the Irish canonical movement in both Irish and contintental contexts and exposes its complexity as an expression of the *vita apostolica* that animated many contemporary reform movements. She draws on the experience of male and female monasticism to caution against preoccupation with formal structures in ascertaining what constituted the canonical life in Ireland. Marie Therese Flanagan provides a comprehensive account of the origins and expansion of the Victorine canons in Ireland whose principal foundation was St Thomas's Abbey in Dublin. Drawing on a thorough analysis of surviving cartularies and other contemporary sources she demonstrates how the Victorines consolidated and administered their estates in the twelfth and thirteenth centuries and oversaw the parishes from which they derived tithes. She also demonstrates the predominantly Anglo-centric character of the order, closely associated with the elite of the Anglo-Norman colony and with Victorine communities in England. In contrast, the predominantly Gaelic character and outlook of the regular canons of Prémontré forms the subject of Miriam Clyne's chapter. Although the foundations at Carrickfergus and White

---

MS 84. See the contribution by Moss below.   **15** K. Nicholls, 'The register of Clogher' in *Clogher Record*, 7:3 (1971/1972), 361–431; Brussels Bibliotheque Royale MS 8590–8, ff 176v–81v; Lambeth Palace MS 213, f. 230; TCD MS 576; TCD MS 97; Bodl. MS Rawl. B. 486, ff 16–23; Bodl. MS Rawl. B. 485; Bodl. MS Rawl. B. 505. See the contributions to this volume by Ó Riain and Ó Clabaigh.   **16** Hereford Cathedral Library MS, p. 4; TCD MS 188.   **17** For editions and calendars see Connolly, *Medieval record sources*, pp 14–37. P. Connolly (ed.), *Irish exchequer payments 1270–1446* (2 vols, Dublin, 1998). Many of these records can be accessed online at the Irish chancery project website CIRCLE http://chancery.tcd.ie/   **18** Connolly, *Medieval record sources*, pp 38–49.   **19** London, Lambeth Palace MSS 46, 60.   **20** H.S. Sweetman and G.F. Handcock (eds), *Calendar of documents relating to Ireland*, vol. 5, 1302–7 (London, 1886), pp 202–323. But see the cautionary note in Connolly, *Medieval record sources*, pp 40–1.   **21** White, *EIMP*; Connolly, *Medieval record sources*, p. 46.

Abbey in the north-east of Ireland formed part of John de Courcy's colonization of his newly conquered territory in Ulster, it was the Gaelic foundations centred on Holy Trinity Abbey, Lough Key, that came to dominate in Ireland. She provides an illuminating account of the communities from their origins to their ultimate disappearance in the seventeenth centuries based on recent archaeological excavations, historical material and the order's internal legislation.

Extensive archaeological research also informs Tracy Collins's ground-breaking work on Augustinian nuns, their monasteries and their estates in medieval Ireland. She shows how the fluidity of the Augustinian Rule was reflected architecturally with most nunneries deviating from what is typically regarded as the normal claustral arrangement. Christy Cunniffe's case study of the co-located male and female foundations at Clonfert, Co. Galway, confirms many of Bhreathnach's and Collins's insights. Drawing on historical sources and recent archaeological work, he illustrates how such communities operated in a Gaelic context. In contrast, Adrian Empey's contribution shows the predominant role that the regular canons had in establishing the parochial system in Anglo-Norman territories. The erection of parishes was a prerequisite for the successful implantation of the twelfth-century reform programme, while the establishment of manors, often co-extensive with the parish, was fundamental to the process of colonisation. The willingness of the regular canons to undertake parochial work explains their popularity both with reforming Gaelic bishops and Anglo-Norman patrons. It also resulted in the canons gaining a near monopoly of tithe income in many parts of the Anglo-Norman colony. Arlene Hogan's case study of how the canons of Llanthony Prima and Secunda exploited their endowments in Ireland provides a case study of this colonisation in action. She shows how their administration of the lands and incomes granted them by Hugh de Lacy and other Anglo-Norman lords helped to consolidate the Anglo-Norman presence in Meath and Louth. She also demonstrates how the communities' representatives in Ireland remitted grain to the motherhouses in Wales and England and discharged their charitable, pastoral and hospitaller obligations in Ireland.

The next four chapters examine the influence of the canonical movement on medieval Irish architecture, art, hagiography and pilgrimage. Tadhg O'Keeffe presents a comparative analysis of the transeptal churches at some early Augustinian sites. He argues that this architectural form gave a distinctive identity to some of these early Anglo-Norman foundations and provides a perceptive analysis of one of the most important of these, the priory of St Edmund the Martyr at Athassel, Co. Tipperary. Rachel Moss argues that Augustinian art and material culture constituted a visual means of conveying a sense of antiquity, continuity and authority. Pádraig Ó Riain futher develops this theme in his chapter on the canons' contribution to medieval Irish hagiography. In addition to producing several influential liturgical texts and martyrologies, the canons were the pre-eminent composers of saints' lives in Ireland in the twelfth and thirteenth centuries. Here they often recast the *vitae* of their subjects to consolidate their own position within a shifting ecclesiastical context. The canons served as the custodians of many of the shrines in Ireland and Louise Nugent explores their role in promoting pilgrimage. Many of these, like the shrine of St Radegund at Rathkeale, Co. Limerick, were local affairs. Some, like the Holy Rood of Ballyboggan or the shrine of Our Lady of Trim, were of regional significance while Ireland's only international pilgrimage destination, St Patrick's Purgatory, Lough Derg, was also served by the regular canons.

Colmán Ó Clabaigh examines the chapter books and necrologies that survive from Trim and Dublin to gain an impression of the *mentalité* and inner workings of these communities and of their relationships with their patrons and benefactors. Brendan Scott demonstrates how the dissolution campaigns of the 1530s and 1540s impacted the male and female communities of Dublin and the Pale. He argues that though the communities were relatively small, the redistribution of their land brought little benefit to anyone other than those who received them. In an insightful concluding contribution Clemens Galban traces the survival of the canonical movement from the upheavals of the sixteenth and seventeenth centuries through the vicissitudes and conflicts of the eighteenth century until its eventual disappearance with the death of the last Irish regular canon, Abbot Patrick Prendergast, in 1829. The determination of the tiny band of Irishmen who adopted the canonical lifestyle in this period at times bordered on obduracy and their defence of real and imagined privileges often brought them into conflict with the Irish Catholic hierarchy. Nevertheless, the discovery of one of the icons of twelfth-century Irish art, the Cross of Cong, amongst Abbot Prendergast's possessions completes the cycle and touchingly illustrates the contribution that the regular canons and canonesses made to Irish church and society.

Martin Browne & Colmán Ó Clabaigh

The *Vita Apostolica* and the origin of the Augustinian canons and canonesses in medieval Ireland

EDEL BHREATHNACH

One must believe that many of the 'new' Augustinians were traditional Irish clergy of the old order in a new and trendy black habit, and that they maintained many of their old concerns and practices including an interest in scholarship, at least on the part of some. At several of the houses coarbs and erenaghs continue to be recorded in the annals and, if the officer class remained, many more humbler members survived the changes.[1]

THE STANDARD NARRATIVE

The opening quote of this essay is taken from Donnchadh Ó Corráin's commentary on the Irish church during the twelfth century. In these few sentences, Professor Ó Corráin captures both the certainty of scholars that the Augustinian canons spread throughout Ireland easily and quickly at this time, and the niggling sense that there is a problem with this interpretation: if the canons had been so successful, why then did the existing ecclesiastical order survive until at least the fifteenth century? When did the concept of the *vita apostolica* or a form of the *ordo canonicus* originally arrive in Ireland? Gwynn and Hadcock, whose volume *Medieval religious Houses Ireland* has been so influential in the study of the canons in Ireland, were themselves unsure of this early phase. They noted, for example, that Abbot Gualterus of Arrouaise, when writing of Malachy of Armagh's visit to his monastery sometime around 1140, 'does not explain how Malachy managed to introduce the Arrouaisians at so many places in Ireland. There are no records of Irishmen training in France, nor of canons being sent from Arrouaise to teach their Rule in Ireland'.[2] And later they admitted that no 'authentic records exist of the dates when certain early Irish monasteries became Augustinian, nor for new foundations in that order ... In many cases, such monasteries are *presumed* [my italics] to date from after 1140, and the foundation date "+1140" in the following list does not necessarily mean that they became Augustinian during Malachy's lifetime'.[3] Despite their cautious comments, Gwynn and Hadcock's list has been

---

1 D. Ó Corráin, *The Irish church, its reform and the English invasion* (Dublin, 2017), p. 88.   2 *MRHI*, p. 150.   3 *MRHI*, p. 151.

read in many subsequent studies as a definite list of houses of Augustinian canons, even though many of them are annotated with the '+1140' marker. Marie Therese Flanagan points to the problems caused by this reading of the *MRHI* list:

> It cannot be emphasized too strongly that the possible use of the Augustinian Rule or its route of transmission to Ireland, before Malachy's visit to Arrouaise, remains unknown, and that most of the dates proposed by Aubrey Gwynn and Neville Hancock in their *MRHI* relied on secondary sources, often derived from seventeenth- and eighteenth-century antiquarian scholars such as Sir James Ware and Mervyn Archdall, whose works need to be subjected to modern scholarly scrutiny.[4]

The aim of this essay is to open up a debate on a number of fronts: to survey current observations on the origins of the Augustinian canons elsewhere; to establish the extent to which any form of *ordo canonicus* – or even concepts deriving from such a tradition – existed in pre-Norman Ireland; and, to review the reality of the rapid advance of Augustinian canons through the 'old' foundations of pre-Norman Ireland during the twelfth and thirteenth centuries. Foundations associated with the Anglo-Normans such as Llanthony Prima and Secunda, discussed below by Arlene Hogan, are mentioned only insofar as they impinged on pre-Norman churches and their lands.

Dealing with canons is never straightforward and tracing a community following an Augustinian rule is not always easy unless communities were regular canons following the Arrouaisian or Premonstratensian constitutions.[5] Some regular canons, as in Christ Church, Dublin, served in cathedral chapters; others simply had their own houses. The existence and function of secular canons is an additional complication that needs to be kept in mind. In Ireland the picture is even more difficult due to the lack of sources, the dominance of the Gwynn and Hadcock narrative among scholars, and above all, the continuing major questions relating to the organization and operation of the church between the eleventh and thirteenth centuries.

THE COMPARATIVE APPROACH

The study of the canons highlights some of the fault lines that persist in scholarship of the medieval church in Ireland: the perspective tends to be insular, viewing the Irish situation as particularly different from elsewhere. The twelfth-century Irish church, and especially regular communal life (monastic or canonical), is too often mediated through the works of influential outsiders such as Bernard of Clairvaux,

---

4 Flanagan, *Transformation*, p. 137.   5 For a standard and fair description of medieval canons, see C.H. Lawrence, *Medieval monasticism: forms of religious life in Western Europe in the Middle Ages* (3rd ed., London & New York, 2001), pp 160–8.

whose main witness was Malachy of Armagh, and Giraldus Cambrensis, who vilifies the Welsh church much as he does the Irish.[6] The ever-present chronological divide between the pre-Norman and Anglo-Norman era distorts the narrative in that it creates a false chasm between what came before and the different culture that followed the twelfth-century 'reform' movement and the establishment of an Anglo-Norman dominated church in parts of the island.

What if another approach is adopted to rethink the Irish narrative and that the *vita apostolica* and the canons are taken as an illustration? A comparative review of debates concerning the nature and existence of an Augustinian rule elsewhere might inform our own discourse, and especially assist in tracing elements of any form of the *ordo canonicus* in Ireland before Malachy and Lorcán Ua Tuathail, among others, became active in the twelfth century. From the outset, the most important conclusion deduced from such a comparative review is that attempts to normalize the institution of canons in Western Christendom prior to the eleventh century were not overwhelmingly successful. Despite codifications such as Chrodegang's eighth-century *Regula canonicorum* or the *Institutio canonicorum*, ascribed to Amalarius of Metz but more likely compiled by Benedict of Aniane in parallel with the *Concordia regularum* (the normalization of the monastic *Regula Benedicti*) for the Council of Aachen in 816,[7] there was no standard rule of Augustine. There was a consistent debate regarding the distinction between monks and canons as expressed in *Regula canonicorum*:

> It is permissible for canons to wear linen, to eat meat, to give and receive private property and to possess church property in humility and righteousness, since we do not find that the sacred canons prohibit these things; on the other hand they are strictly forbidden for monks, who lead a stricter life according to the provisions of their rule. Nevertheless, the life of canons and monks should not differ when it comes to avoiding vice and cultivating virtue.[8]

Apart from the crucial matter of ownership of private property and possessions, the physical environment of monks and all forms of canons was at issue: were they enclosed or not? Chrodegang distinguished between canons who were inside a cloister within their own community (*intra claustra in ipsa congregatione*) or operating in the world outside (*extra claustra in civitate*).[9] The question of *cura animarum*, who had the right to care for the souls of the laity and to preach, was also at the heart of the role of canons in society. Could monks take on a pastoral role or was this a function solely for canons? By emphasizing the importance of the *vita apostolica*, a

6 H.J. Lawlor (ed.), *St Bernard of Clairvaux's Life of St Malachy of Armagh* (London, 1920); J.F. Dimock (ed.), *Itinerarium Kambriæ et descriptio Kambriæ*. Giraldi Cambrensis opera, vol. 6 (London, 1868), pp 120–1. **7** J. Bertram, *The Chrodegang Rules: the rules for the common life of the secular clergy from the eighth and ninth centuries: critical texts from the eighth and ninth centuries* (Burlington, 2005). **8** Ibid., p. 144, para. 115. **9** Ibid., Section CXLIV, *Ut claustra canonicorum diligenter custodiantur.*

reflection of the apostolic church handed down from the Acts of the Apostles, it has been argued that Chrodegang as bishop of Metz regarded reforming the canons of his cathedral as a step towards reforming the laity in general.[10] Despite the best efforts of reformers such as Chrodegang and Benedict of Aniane, these debates continued for centuries afterwards.

Why did it take so long to form an Augustinian rule? First, there was no agreed text of an Augustinian rule as such, and even the association with Augustine developed only gradually. During the eleventh and twelfth centuries three of Augustine's texts that related to living a *vita apostolica* or *vita communis* came to form the basis for a rule for regular canons: Augustine's *Præceptum*, his *Præceptum longius* and *Regula recepta*. The difficulty of implementing a normalized rule where so many variant customs existed was exacerbated where no one central authority (especially the papacy) had the capacity to enforce codified rules or control a proliferation of communities with their own interpretations of Augustinian and other texts.[11] The ideal of living together as a community according to an Augustinian vision of apostolic community at this time 'generated a particularly wide variety of partly experimental and sometimes only temporary new forms of spiritual life'.[12]

The complexity of understanding how the medieval church worked on the ground is best illustrated by practices in various regions. In England, the debate has centred on the origins of the minsters, who serviced them and what function they played in the pastoral care of the laity, in developing a parochial system, and in their relations with bishops and monasteries. John Blair, who has led much of the debate on the nature of minsters since the 1990s, has commented that these churches housed religious communities that varied in size, wealth and religious complexion, and that they exercised rights over defined territories, later mother-parishes, for which they provided pastoral care.[13] Private manorial churches, new Benedictine and collegiate foundations came to absorb or vie with the minsters post-AD 950. We should be mindful in the Irish context that when the regular and secular canons took hold in England between the late eleventh and mid-thirteenth centuries, they often moved into the minsters and replaced the existing regime (*forma vitae*).[14] Indeed, regular canons were instrumental in the survival of Anglo-

10 M.A. Claussen, 'Practical exegesis: the Acts of the Apostles, Chrodegang's *Regula canonicorum*, and the early Carolingian reform' in D. Blanks, M. Frasetto and A. Livingstone (eds), *Medieval monks and their world: ideas and realities. Studies in honor of Richard E. Sullivan* (Leiden/Boston, 2006), pp 119–46 at 122–4.   11 Y. Veyrenche, '*Quia vos estis qui sanctorum patrum vitam probabilem renovatis* … naissance des chanoines réguliers, jusqu'à Urbain II' in M. Parisse (ed.), *Les chanoines réguliers. Émergence et expansion (XIe–XIIIe siècles)* (Publications de l'Université de Sainte-Étienne, 2009), pp 29–70 at 37 (following L. Verheijen, *La Règle de St Augustin*).   12 C. Lutter, 'Vita communis in Central European monastic landscapes' in E. Hovden, C. Lutter and W. Pohl (eds), *Meanings of community across medieval Eurasia: comparative approaches* (Leiden, 2016), pp 362–87 at 368 (noting G. Constable, 'Religious communities, 1024–1215' in D. Luscombe and Jonathan Riley-Smith (eds), *The new Cambridge medieval history*, vol. 4 (Cambridge, 2004), pp 335–67.   13 J. Blair, 'Debate: ecclesiastical organization and pastoral care in Anglo-Saxon England', *Early Medieval Europe*, 4:2 (1995), 193–212.   14 J. Burton, 'Les chanoines réguliers en Grande-Bretagne' in Parisse, *Les chanoines réguliers*, pp 477–98 at 487–9.

Saxon saints' cults: in the diocese of Coventry and Lichfield, for example, minsters with active cults were taken over by canons at Runcorn, Rochester, Stone (Ss Wulfad and Rufinus), Repton (Ss Wystan and Guthlac), Trentham (Ss Werburgh and Wulfere) and Mobberly (St Wilfrid).[15] Rather than viewing this apparent takeover as an attempt at asset-stripping by the canons or by bishops, Andrew Abram's conclusions in his essay on this topic are worth considering in relation to similar transformations in Ireland:

> The concept of memory in terms of the use and encouragement of cults by the black canons, with their continued significance to patrons and benefactors in a local context, is evidenced by dynastic and individual burials at houses such as Stone, Trentham, Repton … the example of Stone Priory illustrates the continuing promotion and utilization of earlier cult centres by Augustinian communities and their supporters in terms of political, cultural, and social identity, and as lasting centres of devotion.[16]

This was also the case in so many Irish churches and with so many Irish saints into the late medieval period where the canons more than any other order promoted early cults and contributed to the compilation of the lives of Irish saints, as Pádraig Ó Riain demonstrates below.

Looking beyond England to the Continent, it is instructive, considering that there was direct influence from there with regard to the introduction of the canons to Ireland, to examine medieval Flanders, from which the Arrouaisian and Premonstratensian Rules originated. In her study of *l'espace flamand* (modern Belgium, Flanders and also the French departments of le Nord and Pas-de-Calais), Brigitte Meijns has tracked the changes in the canonical infrastructure from an ecclesiastical landscape dominated by secular collegiate canons and those in cathedral chapters, who nominally followed the Council of Aachen's *Institutio canonicorum*, to one in which the *vita apostolica* followed by regular canons intruded significantly into their way of life between 1070 and 1155.[17] Existing collegiate or cathedral chapters accepted the regular life, in many cases under the direction of a zealous bishop, with a small number (17 out of 87) affiliating themselves to the Arrouaisian or Premonstratensian Rules. As in England, the experience in *l'espace flamand* provides pointers as to how we should read the contemporary – and it is contemporary – situation in Ireland. Meijns demonstrates how bishops used this transformation to weaken the aristocratic grip on many churches, and while in many instances they succeeded, in others they did not. Among those churches were the important pilgrimage centres of Notre-Dame in Bruges and Notre-Dame in Saint-Omer whose patrons were the counts of Flanders and whose attraction for nobles and laity were their important relics.[18] Others remained secular and

---

15 A. Abram, 'Augustinian canons and the survival of cult centres in medieval England' in Burton and Stöber, *Canons*, pp 79–95.   **16** Ibid., pp 94–5.   **17** B. Meijns, 'Les chanoines réguliers dans l'espace flamand' in Parisse, *Les chanoines réguliers*, pp 456–76.   **18** Ibid., p. 475.

continued somehow to follow the Aachen Rule, which after all allowed canons to nominally live in community but to hold possessions, while celibacy was an option. Flouting the precept of celibacy was not in the spirit of Aachen, but nevertheless many canons lived with women, had children and passed their prebends on to their sons. A transitional arrangement was attempted – as so often happens with such fundamental changes in the church – whereby canons who resisted regular life were allowed to continue as they were, but that on their deaths their prebends reverted to the regular canons.[19] A key to measuring the success, or even the reality, of the canons in Ireland must lie in examining in detail the familial connections (pre- and post-Norman) of canons and other officials associated with churches reputed to have adopted some form of Augustinian rule.

In sum, a comparative approach offers important lessons as to how the Irish evidence is approached. The church was a complicated organization everywhere and composed of a multitude of strands, many of which reflected the cultures of particular societies, but as an international organization common issues and even common resolutions come to the fore and were applied. The narrative of the Augustinian canons and canonesses in Ireland needs to be placed within such a context.

RECOGNIZING THE 'VITA APOSTOLICA' IN PRE-TWELFTH-CENTURY IRELAND

The task of assessing if any form of canonical community existed here before the twelfth century, and if it did, how it fitted into the native ecclesiastical landscape, is problematic. It is difficult, as the Irish sources are unique and are primarily in the vernacular. This factor has so often led scholars to view Ireland as at odds with elsewhere. Rather than lamenting the lack of 'standard' sources, a more abstract approach might enable us to read the Irish sources comparatively rather than in isolation. We should also continually keep in mind that a definitive Rule of St Augustine for regular communities did not consolidate anywhere until the twelfth century, so that the idea that Ireland lagged behind is not accurate.

For the purposes of this chapter I want to look at three aspects that permeate the general literature on monks and canons and that enable us to navigate the diverse strands of the pre-twelfth-century Irish church. These are: the sacerdotal state, pastoral duties and ownership of property. This discussion does not include the *manaig* 'lay tenants' of the church. It concerns the distinction between those living communally and following some form of *vita contemplativa* within the larger ecclesiastical settlements or in more remote places (monks in the religious sense), and the *vita activa*, priests active among the laity, normally under the jurisdiction of a bishop. In her paper 'Early Irish priests within their own localities', Cathy Swift brings our attention to the ordinary working priest who 'lived on farms not

19 Ibid., p. 471.

very different from those of their neighbours and in houses which, like their neighbours, had servants and, on occasion at least, other family members in residence'.[20] Swift concludes further: 'Their duties included not just the performance of sacraments for their congregations, for they also had an important role as judges, being respected for their ability to identify suitable penalties with due regard for the specific context of a particular case and the true remorse of a perpetrator'.[21] This description is not that distinct from the priests functioning in Anglo-Saxon minsters or indeed Wendy Davies's characterization of the church in rural Iberia (apart from Catalonia) which bears a remarkable resemblance – up to AD 1000 at least – to the structure of the Irish church in which there were different kinds of local priests operating in the community:

> the single priest (or small group), serving a church and local community; priests who were members of lay religious households, where the leader of the community was often a lay person … priests in aristocratic households … The first and second of these groups are in practice difficult to differentiate from very small monasteries, that is monasteries with no more than five or six members … Small monasteries, and other communities of this kind should be differentiated from the medium-sized and great monasteries of northern Iberia – communities with 30 or 60 or 200 members, living a regulated day, with formalized commitment, following a known Rule.[22]

The Irish annals have little to say about the local, rural priest: they are virtually invisible in all the major collections. The priests whose deaths are recorded are confined primarily to Armagh, and then to Kildare, Clonmacnoise and a scattering of other medium-sized monasteries (Aghaboe, Clonenagh etc.). As to normative legislation, apart from the *Collectio canonum Hibernensis*, the eighth-century *Ríagail Phátraic* ('Rule of Patrick') provides a fairly detailed picture of the preparation of young men for the priesthood, their role in the community and their relations with bishops and other church officials.[23] The tenth-century composite version of the Rule of the Céli Dé and the Rule of Patrick is particularly interesting in that it reflects precisely what I see as a key division in the pre-twelfth-century Irish church, not unlike the Iberian model. In summary, this consisted of communities following some form of monastic discipline and liturgical routine, varying from foundation to foundation especially in relation to ascetic practices. The Céli Dé were to the fore in these foundations.[24] Then there was the church, primarily

20 C. Swift, 'Early Irish priests within their own localities' in F. Edmonds and P. Russell (eds), *Tome: studies in medieval Celtic history and law in honour of Thomas Charles-Edwards* (Woodbridge, 2011), pp 29–40 at 39–40.   **21** Swift, 'Early Irish priests', p. 40.   **22** W. Davies, 'Local priests in Iberia' in S. Patzold and A.C. van Rhijn (eds), *Local priests in early medieval Europe* (Berlin, 2016), pp 125–44.   **23** E. Gwynn (ed.), 'The Rule of Tallaght', *Hermathena 44, supplemental volume* (Dublin and London, 1927); W. Follett, *Céli Dé in Ireland: monastic writing and identity in the early Middle Ages* (Woodbridge, 2006), pp 114–16, 142–3.   **24** Follett, *Céli Dé*, pp 212–5.

bishops and priests, who served the majority of the laity and who worked with those holding other ecclesiastical offices that dealt with the administration of ecclesiastical estates and tenants (*manaig*), maintenance of relics and relations with the aristocracy. In the Rule of Patrick's section on what might be termed the 'secular church', the legislators' concerns are with the administration of the sacraments and the offering of the Mass. One particular task delegated to priests that occurs elsewhere, and is often associated with secular canons, is the care of liturgical vessels.[25] As to property, the ordained priest serving minor churches of the *tuatha* (small local units equated to the smallest kingdoms) has claim to *tuarastal a uird* ('the stipend of his orders'), a house, garden, bed, habit, a sack of seed-corn, a cow in milk. In return, he administers the rites of baptism, communion, intercessory prayers for the living and the dead, Mass every Sunday and every chief festival. Most importantly, he is expected to celebrate all the canonical hours, chant the standard 150 psalms, with the significant caveat 'unless hindered by teaching or hearing confessions' (*acht mina thoirmesci forcetul no amnchairdius*).[26] In a sense this is what distinguished monks in a regulated community (whatever their rule) from priests working among the laity, a fundamental distinction that influenced how either prayed correctly. Renie Choy, in an article on legislating intercessory prayer in the Carolingian monastic reform, taking the description of the *Concordia regularum* (based on Ezekiel 34:3–4) for monks as 'feeble sheep', addresses the question of the quality of prayer for the clergy (the shepherds) and monks:

> For clergy (the shepherds) charged with the task of praying correctly and teaching their sheep how to pray correctly … could learn the meaning of the Lord's Prayer and be able to teach it to their congregations. For monks, the 'feeble sheep', however, the problem of 'how to pray correctly' was much more complicated, so much so that it gave a fundamental impetus to the development of liturgical codes of monastic rules.[27]

That latter concern for monks is clear from the section in the Rule of the Céli Dé dealing with a monastic community which contains far more provisions for liturgy and prayer than the Rule of Patrick's section on the secular clergy.

Turning to the hierarchical organization of the church, – a vast topic that has been addressed in detail over the decades by among others Kathleen Hughes, Richard Sharpe, Thomas Charles-Edwards and Colmán Etchingham[28] – it seems

---

25 Gwynn, 'The Rule of Tallaght', p. 81, para. 57 ('and every altar [has] its complete furniture (*aidme*)').   **26** Ibid., p. 81, para. 58.   **27** R. Choy, 'Praying by the rules: legislating intercessory prayer in Carolingian monastic reform' in K. Pansters and A. Plunkett-Latimer, *Shaping stability: the normation and formation of religious life in the Middle Ages* (Turnhout, 2016), pp 69–87 at 73.   **28** K. Hughes, *The church in early Irish society* (London, 1966); R. Sharpe, 'Churches and communities in early medieval Ireland: towards a pastoral model' in J. Blair and R. Sharpe (eds), *Pastoral care before the parish* (Leicester, 1992), pp 81–109; T. Charles-Edwards, 'The pastoral role of the church in early Irish laws' in Blair and Sharpe, *Pastoral care before the parish*, pp 63–80; C. Etchingham, *Church organizaton in Ireland, AD 650 to 1000* (Maynooth, 1999).

relevant to concentrate on what the Rule of St Patrick says about the education of boys for ordination. The text is particularly concerned with offering boys to God and Patrick to study for ordination: 'If anyone therefore shall offer the tithe of his body to God for the purposes of study, it will be the same as if he renovated the churches of Ireland [Gwynn 'Erin'] and restored its belief after it had vanished.'[29] And further, anyone who taught boys who were offered to God and Patrick 'the Psalms with their hymns, canticles and lections, and the rites of baptism and communion and intercession, together with the knowledge of the ritual generally, till the student be capable of receiving Orders' was due a living. Once the student was educated, there was an examination in public: one proficient in ecclesiastical learning (*suí*) or a bishop 'before whom proof in the Psalms has been made is entitled to a collation of beer and food for five persons the same night.'[30] Perhaps we have not recognized sufficiently the role of priests, bishops and those proficient in ecclesiastical learning in preparing men for ordination in the early Irish church, and in doing so have missed a vital infrastructure that existed and was directed primarily from Armagh?[31] As noted earlier, relatively few priests are mentioned in the annals and most of them are associated with Armagh and Clonmacnoise, with a scattering in Kildare, Aghaboe, Glendalough, Louth and Kells. Certain references suggest that Armagh and less so Clonmacnoise housed a community of priests, perhaps some form of nascent community of canons. For example, the death of Máel Brigte mac Doilgen, 'noble priest of Ard Macha, and senior of the priests of Ireland' in the fiftieth year of his priesthood (which means that he had been ordained around 1080) occurred in 1132,[32] the same year as Malachy became the successor of Patrick. The terms *prímshacart* or *ardshacart* 'chief priest' is used occasionally. *AFM* 948 refers to Rechtabra mac Máenaig, chief priest of Clonmacnoise, followed by Óengus mac Brain priest and learned senior (*sruith shenóir*), also of Clonmacnoise.[33] Some form of community of priests may have existed in Armagh, and if it did, then the foundation dedicated to Ss Peter and Paul may have formalized into a community of regular canons under the direction of Ímar úa hÁedacáin, Malachy's mentor, who had instituted the building of a stone church there in the 1120s.[34] Malachy's brother, Gilla Críst (Christianus), bishop of Clogher (d. 1138), who was most likely a regular canon, was buried in the church of Ss Peter and Paul in Armagh.[35] It might be noted in passing that the complexity of Armagh during this period might be compared with similar complex communities in St Andrews in Scotland and in Iona.[36]

From this very superficial and brief overview of the pre-twelfth-century Irish church we can identify a church of diverse elements, similar to elsewhere: a

---

29 Gwynn, 'The Rule of Tallaght', p. 83, para. 61.   **30** Ibid., p. 83, para. 62.   **31** Follett, *Céli Dé*, pp 114–16.   **32** *AFM*.   **33** As these references are recorded in *AFM*, there is a need for a note of caution as this might reflect later terminology reflected back into the pre-Norman period. **34** Flanagan, *Transformation*, pp 43–4.   **35** *AFM*.   **36** K. Veitch, 'A study of the extent to which existing native religious society helped to shape Scotland's monastic community 1070–1286' (PhD, University of Edinburgh), accessed on https://www.era.lib.ed.ac.uk/handle/1842/6905 on 20 March 2017.

genuine coenobitic tradition with a strong eremitical component; a clergy with a pastoral remit and subject to bishops with sufficient education to ordain; an embryonic episcopal infrastructure and possibly communities of priests in major churches; a scholarly community versed in ecclesiastical and secular learning; and a hugely powerful and wealthy class, many of them lay people whose main responsibility was to maintain their churches' estates, tenants and economies.

THE CANONS AND CANONESSES IN IRELAND: THE ORIGINS AND THEIR PROGRESS

We now come to the narrative of the regular Augustinian canons and canonesses in Ireland and in particular their interaction with the existing Irish church. Rather than cover all the churches reputed to have adopted an Augustinian rule in twelfth-century Ireland, this section will examine a number of churches for which contemporary or at least near contemporary sources have survived. A chronological narrative is well-nigh impossible to establish. Instead, I propose to look at a number of strands with the aim of explaining how the canons emerge in the sources, what their functions were and if the existing church absorbed them or changed because of them. These strands consist of canons and the establishment of a *sedes episcopalis*; canons, kings and nobles; canons transforming existing monasteries and island hermitages; and women and the Augustinian Rule.

Canons and the establishment of a 'sedes episcopalis'

It has been observed generally that a key component of the administrative reorganization of the Western church in the eleventh and twelfth centuries involved a partnership between bishops and canons, regular and secular. Ireland was no exception. One of the best examples of this phenomenon, and a very complex example, is the cluster of houses in the kingdom of Airgialla that stretched from modern counties Tyrone to Louth: St Mary's Priory, Louth; the abbey of Ss Peter and Paul, Knock, Co. Louth; and the male and female houses at Termonfeckin, Co. Louth.[37] The narrative of these houses bears a resemblance to narratives elsewhere. They were founded on the initiative of bishops who were particularly influential, Malachy and Áed Ua Cáellaide, bishop of Airgialla, both of whom along with Malachy's brother, Gilla Críst, spearheaded a programme of diocesan transformation during the 1130s and 1140s. This was an experiment that they may have seen as offering a model for the whole island but that greater expectation was not realized, since established interests often won out, as witnessed in the demarcation of dioceses at the synod of Kells in 1152.

What was the model preferred by Malachy and his inner circle? The original seat of the diocese of Airgialla at Clogher was moved to Louth and the canons of

37 Flanagan, 'Louth', 223–34.

St Mary's Priory, Louth, seem to have serviced the cathedral chapter, assuming that the contents of a late twelfth-century charter reflect this earlier period.[38] The secular patron involved, Donnchad Ua Cerbaill, king of Airgialla, was instrumental in supporting this episcopal programme and actually resided occasionally at Louth.[39] A pattern of the co-location of royal residence, 'cathedral'[40] and Augustinian chapter, abbey or priory in the twelfth century can be detected at other Irish locations such as Ferns, Co. Wexford, possibly Clonard, Co. Meath, and Tuam, Co. Galway. The other significant pattern, noted in relation to Augustinian houses in England and Wales,[41] was their attachment to early saints and to shrines and relics. The church of Louth is a prime example of the use of existing relics by canons. Louth (Lugbad) was an important early monastery with a special link to Armagh, as it was the resting-place of Mochta, Patrick's disciple. The stone shrine-chapel at Louth, likely to date to the twelfth century,[42] probably housed the relics of Mochta, which prior to the changeover to canonical rule was presided over by a hereditary family, the Uí Duibinnsi,[43] on the eve of Malachy's transformation of the church. Mochta was not forgotten, however, as in 1242, 'A great chapter was held by the primate of Armagh and the abbots of the canons regular of Ireland, at Louth, on which occasion many of the relics which Mochta had collected, and brought from Rome, were taken up'.[44]

The language of this entry, as it is recorded in *AFM*, may reflect later terminology, but it does point to the continuation of older saints' cults and veneration of their relics by the canons. The location of the abbey of Ss Peter and Paul at Knock, Co. Louth, of which little survives,[45] should be noted in passing. The site is located on a height a distance away from the *sedes episcopalis* (4.4 km to the SW of Louth village). Presumably this was deliberate and reflects the desire of a regular community of regular canons, possibly following the Arrouaisian Rule, to distance themselves from the busy hub that was Louth village during the twelfth century. If Lorcán Ua Tuathail, abbot of Glendalough and later archbishop of Dublin, founded St Saviour's Glendalough for regular canons in the 1150s/60s, it was similarly located at a distance from the centre of the Glendalough settlement. Apart from following the Divine Office and liturgy, what were these regular canons doing? As noted by Flanagan, with the compilation of a martyrology by Máel Muire Ua Gormáin (?d. 1181), abbot of Knock, 'it is evident that the regular canons at Knock were engaged in the production of liturgical manuscripts.'[46] Furthermore, Ua Gormáin's work suggests that no more than their brethren in Louth who were memorializing Mochta and his relics, the canons at Knock memorialized

---

38 H.J. Lawlor, 'A charter of Cristin, bishop of Louth', *PRIA*, 32C (1914–16), 28–40. **39** Flanagan, *Transformation*, p. 151. His house mentioned in *AFM* 1164. **40** *Pace* Kenneth Nicholls' comment 'indeed it might be queried whether any Irish bishop possessed a cathedral – in the strict sense – before that date [1169]'. Nicholls, 'Mediæval Irish cathedral chapters', *AH*, 31 (1973), 102–11 at 102. **41** Abram, 'Augustinian canons and the survival of cult centres'. **42** T. Ó Carragáin, *Churches in early medieval Ireland* (London, 2010), pp 280–2. **43** *AFM* 1123, 1133. **44** *AFM*. **45** V.M. Buckley, *Archaeological inventory of County Louth* (Dublin, 1986), p. 80: SMR 11:81 (Thomastown). **46** Flanagan, *Transformation*, p. 149. **47** Ó Riain, *Dictionary*,

the early saint's cult, as Pádraig Ó Riain has suggested,[47] by compiling the Latin Life of Mochta, now preserved in the Codex Salmanticensis,[48] as well as commemorating saints' feast days both of the universal church and the Irish tradition in the Martyrology of Gormán.[49]

Canons, kings and nobles

Bishops were instrumental in handing churches over to canons or in establishing new foundations. As seen in the case of Louth, however, kings and nobles were also an essential part of the canons' network of patrons, the most obvious example elsewhere being Henry I of England.[50] There is some evidence that the same happened in Ireland, although very few 'royal' foundations are corroborated by contemporary sources. St Mary's Abbey, Ferns, Co. Wexford is an exception as there is a strong case to accept the surviving copy as the text of the original charter.[51] Ferns was an episcopal seat included in the list of dioceses that resulted from the synod of Ráith Bresail in 1111. This was a diocese that was coterminous with the core kingdom of the Uí Chennselaig, to whom the founder of St Mary's Abbey, Diarmait Mac Murchada, also king of Leinster, belonged. By the mid-twelfth century at least, the Uí Chennselaig's main *caput* was at Ferns: the annals record that in 1166 Diarmait mac Murchada's enemies, Tigernán Ua Ruairc and Diarmait Ua Máelsechlainn, demolished his stone house at Ferns, burnt his camp and banished him overseas to England.[52] This is the context of the granting of a charter to Augustinian regular canons *c.*1160/2. The strong hand of the new ecclesiastical status quo is also evident as the charter was witnessed by the bishops of Lismore (as papal legate), Leighlin, Ferns, Ossory, Kildare, Glendalough and by Lorcán Ua Tuathail, then abbot of Glendalough and Diarmait mac Murchada's brother-in-law.

The charter contains a number of notable elements.[53] This is a royal foundation to which Diarmait grants the canons the tithes and first fruits of his mensal lands (*dominicum*) throughout his kingdom, along with ale or mead from his *villa* in Ferns for the welfare of his soul and those of his ancestors and successors.[54] Diarmait also guaranteed that his heirs would not interfere in the election or installation of the abbot, but that 'he who is chosen according to the Rule of St Augustine with the consent of the entire convent, or its wiser part, should freely be instituted and, after his election and before installation in the abbacy by archbishop or bishop, he will be presented to me and my heirs or their seneschal by reason of lordship, so that he may be blessed by the bishop through us.'[55] Diarmait's dynasty, the Uí

pp 465–7. **48** W.W. Heist (ed.), *Vitae sanctorum Hiberniae: ex codice olim Salmanticensi, nunc Bruxellensi. Lives of the saints of Ireland, from the Salamanca manuscript now of Brussels*, Subsidia Hagiographica 28. Société des Bollandistes (Brussels, 1965), pp 394–400. **49** W. Stokes (ed.), *Félire Húi Gormáin: The martyrology of Gorman* (HBS, London, 1895). **50** J.C. Dickinson, *The origins of the Austin canons and their introduction into England* (London, 1950), p. 108. **51** Flanagan, *Charters*, pp 283–90. **52** ATig. 1166. **53** For the text and translation see Flanagan, *Charters*, pp 284–5. **54** Ibid., p. 285. **55** Flanagan, *Charters* pp 284–5.

Chennselaig, had a long tradition of intruding candidates into offices in Ferns, and this caused tension, so much so that it is mentioned as a concern in the lives of the founder saint Máedóc.[56] The lands of St Mary's Abbey, Ferns were not confined to the *caput* at Ferns itself. The charter notes that Diarmait Mac Murchada granted the canons the tithes and first fruits *de dominico per Hukenselich* 'of my demesne throughout Uí Chennselaig'. Flanagan interprets this grant as Diarmait providing discrete units from his own mensal lands to his new foundation rather than granting them one consolidated estate.[57] Her interpretation is borne out by detailed examination of the parcels of land granted – where they can be identified – and their associations with the Mac Murchada dynasty and with Anglo-Normans, especially Strongbow, who were Diarmait's closest allies. These lands were mainly quite separate from the episcopal manor and lands of Ferns and with one or two possible exceptions were not parishes. What of the fate of St Mary's after Diarmait Mac Murchada and Strongbow? The provision in its original charter that the election of the abbot was subject to the consent of the bishop of Ferns and also of the Mac Murchada dynasty immediately brought St Mary's under the control of two external authorities. Records suggest that from an early stage, the regular canons were in competition with the bishop and what seems to have been a separate community of canons attached to the episcopal household, which amounted to a small cathedral chapter similar to others established in the late twelfth and early thirteenth centuries.[58] The community of St Mary's appears in the records during the late medieval period as small in numbers, poor and constantly disorderly and, yet for all that, they held onto the lands granted to them in the original charter until the sixteenth-century dissolution.[59]

Unlike the abbey of Ss Peter and Paul at Knock, St Mary's, Ferns was physically located in the precincts of the existing episcopal church. The layout of Ferns is worth noting: the current cathedral church, which is a much reduced version of the medieval church, lies at a centre-point encircled by large enclosures often regarded as a pattern common to many pre-Norman sites. St Mary's is to the SW at an angle to the cathedral and, most significantly, situated on the line of the outer enclosure. This suggests that the earlier enclosure was redundant at the time or that there was a deliberate policy to re-shape the ecclesiastical landscape of Ferns, a feature that is beginning to emerge elsewhere in Ireland, as at Kilmacduagh, Clonmacnoise, Glendalough and Durrow. At these sites later foundations were located either on or outside the original enclosure and by the twelfth century smaller churches were dispersed at a distance from a cathedral or mother church.

Irish kings and bishops were not alone in presiding over the introduction of regular canons to Ireland. From the outset of their settling in Ireland, Anglo-

56 Ibid., pp 101–2.   **57** Ibid., pp 92–3.   **58** Nicholls, 'Mediæval Irish cathedral chapters', 102–11.   **59** For recent studies of Ferns see T. O'Keeffe and R. Carey Bates, 'The abbey and cathedral of Ferns, 1111–1253' in I. Doyle and B. Browne (eds), *Medieval Wexford: essays in memory of Billy Colfer* (Dublin, 2016), pp 73–96; E. Bhreathnach and G. Dowling, 'The lands and settlements of Augustinian canons, bishops and lords of medieval Ferns, Co. Wexford' (in preparation).

Norman lords and bishops were also patrons of the canons, and their support was often based on considerations similar to their Irish counterparts. One strategy involved the consolidation of new settlements. Such was the case of St Thomas's Priory at Ballybeg, Co. Cork, outside the walls of the de Barry borough of Buttevant, endowed in the early thirteenth century by Philip and David de Barri as part of their development of the borough, although, as often happened during the thirteenth century, their significance was usurped by the mendicant Franciscans.[60] The canons of Llanthony Prima and Secunda benefitted from endowments made in the east and the midlands by the de Lacys and their knights, Anglo-Norman bishops and King John.[61] The Llanthony cartularies and other contemporary sources such as papal documents[62] provide crucial evidence, not often acknowledged, as to the character of pre-Norman local churches and also their reaction to the transformation of the Irish church during the twelfth and thirteenth centuries. Significant urban foundations including Holy Trinity Priory (Christ Church), Dublin, founded originally for the canons by Lorcán Ua Tuathail as archbishop of Dublin, benefited from its relationship with Dublin's cathedral and as a result took control of many small churches around the city and its hinterland.[63] This is also true of the Victorine house of St Thomas in Dublin, and interestingly, the female convents of Clonard, Co. Meath, and Kilcreevanty, Co. Galway, swept up among their possessions dozens of existing smaller churches. While there were clear economic benefits to the canons and canonesses from papal confirmation of their extensive possessions, this was not simply 'asset stripping'. They also brought these small churches within the orbit of the organized episcopal administrations of the archbishops of Dublin and Tuam and the bishop of Meath. Relations were not always stable, however, as is evident from the disputes that arose between the nuns of Kilcreevanty and the archbishop of Tuam in the early thirteenth century.[64]

In her study of the Llanthony cartularies, Arlene Hogan observes that many of the churches referred to as coming into the possession of the Augustinian canons were religious foundations established before the advent of the Anglo-Normans and that it was part of Llanthony's policy – and indeed that of their episcopal and noble patrons – to establish a firmer grip on the land over which they now held sway.[65] Two specific policies are noteworthy in the context of the canons' treatment of pre-Norman foundations as they provide some insight into practical changes to church administration that the canons implemented on their lands. They placed canons in smaller churches and where necessary built churches and houses for themselves, as explained in a charter of William Petit to the Llanthony canons *c.*1205–10: '… two chapels should be built in the parish of Dunboyne, one of them beyond the wood towards Rathbeggan and the other on this side of the wood on the other side from Dunboyne … and the parishioners who use these chapels must build them at their own expense …'.[66]

60 E. Cotter (ed.), *Buttevant: a medieval Anglo-French town in Ireland* (2013).   **61** Hogan, *Llanthony.* **62** Sheehy, *Pont. Hib.*   **63** Ibid., i, pp 41–2, no. 13.   **64** Ibid., i, pp 239–41, no. 154.   **65** Hogan, *Llanthony*, p. 80. See also her contribution to this volume.   **66** Ibid., pp 56–7; 259.

Another grant was made by William Messet, *c.*1177–91, concerning the church of Kilcooly (barony of Upper Navan, Co. Meath). Clearly there was an existing church and cemetery there and in providing for the canons, Messet also gave them 'a certain land which is next to the cemetery on the northern side of the church to make a dwelling house for themselves.'[67] There are many other instances of the same process that explains how so many pre-Norman churches remained the focal points of parishes established on a formal basis during this period. This process has echoes of the takeover of minsters in England alluded to earlier. On a grander scale, and probably closer to the comparison with minsters, was the treatment of the pre-Norman ecclesiastical settlement of Duleek, Co. Meath, by the Llanthony canons. Not unlike Glendalough, although in a completely different landscape, Duleek was one of the region's main churches, and was also the place of residence of the regional kings, the Uí Chellaig of Brega/eastern Mide and their over-kings, the Uí Máelsechlainn. In 1123, for example, Murchad Ua Máelsechlainn, king of Tara, was attacked in a house in Duleek by the Gailenga, a sept subject to him. He managed to escape but the annals record that the Gailenga killed many people and burned eighty houses around Duleek in the raid.[68] No doubt because of its royal connections and for other political reasons, Duleek was included in the list of dioceses at the synod of Ráith Bresail in 1111 but was unstable from the very beginning and was later subsumed into the diocese of Meath. The obit of one twelfth-century Irish bishop of Duleek, Gilla Mo-Chua mac Camchuairt, is recorded in 1117.[69] The Llanthony charters are significant in that they sketch out the existing ecclesiastical landscape of a proto-diocesan centre and describe how the Llanthony canons used it as their own initial settlement.[70] They took over the reliquary church of the founder St Cianán, whose remains 'lie on the northern side of the chancel, which same church the aforesaid canons obtained and possessed peacefully without disturbance'.[71] The oratory of St Cairbre was situated next to the cemetery of St Cianán,[72] while the church of St Michael at Duleek, which may have also been in existence when the canons arrived, and its grange, became an integral part of the Llanthony settlement.[73] St Patrick's church, also in the vicinity of St Cianán's, was an early foundation reflecting Duleek's association with Armagh as Cianán was regarded as Patrick's disciple.[74] In addition to these three churches was St Mary's, Duleek, reputedly founded as an Augustinian house by one of the Uí Chellaig kings. No contemporary evidence exists but the church's inclusion as *ecclesia Sancte Marie de Damliag* in a list of possessions confirmed in 1196 to Agnes, abbess of St Mary's, Clonard, the Augustinian female foundation of the Uí Máelsechlainn dynasty, hints at the existence of a pre-Norman house.[75] Beyond

67 Ibid., pp 59; 234–5.   **68** *AU, AFM.*   **69** *AU, AFM.*   **70** A. Simms, 'The geography of Irish manors: the example of the Llanthony cells of Duleek and Colp, Co. Meath' (with appendix by John Bradley), in J. Bradley (ed.), *Settlement and society in medieval Ireland* (Kilkenny, 1988), pp 291–326.   **71** Hogan, *Llanthony*, p. 351.   **72** Ibid., p. 358.   **73** Ibid., p. 136.   **74** J. Bradley, 'St Patrick's Church, Duleek', *Ríocht na Midhe*, 7 (1980–1), 40–51. See also www.archaeology.ie, accessed 11 April 2018.   **75** Sheehy, *Pont. Hib.*, i, p. 84, no. 29.

that, there is no proof that this community followed an Augustinian rule. It would appear from the evidence that the Llanthony canons found in Duleek on their arrival in the late twelfth century an ecclesiastical landscape not unlike other similar places throughout Ireland. It was located strategically on the River Boyne and probably on an important routeway and consisted of a cluster of small churches dedicated to different saints, including to the founder saint whose relics were kept in that church. Albert Suerbeer of Armagh *c.*1242 commended the Llanthony canons for following the Rule of St Augustine, fulfilling 'the order of its profession in a praiseworthy manner' and being caught in a vortex of hatred between the two nations on the island 'you stretch forth your hands in charity to both ... so that you seem to embrace all your neighbours and foster them by your charity'.[76]

If the German archbishop of Armagh wondered at the ability of the Llanthony canons to stretch forth their hands to both Irish and Anglo-Normans, he was in fact alluding to the capacity of canons following an Augustinian rule to be flexible and to adapt easily to what awaited them in a new environment. Ireland was no exception. The canons could move into an area with small numbers using existing churches and live off relatively small endowments. But the question remains as to how far and how quickly did they progress throughout the island?

Canons in hereditary churches and island hermitages

The impression that Augustinian canons took wholesale control of of pre-Norman 'monasteries',[77] underpinned by Gwynn and Hadcock's volume, requires an extensive, detailed re-assessment. As noted above, Flanagan has made the point that references to twelfth-century associations between existing churches and canons are insecure and mainly based on late sources such as Archdall and Ware. Twelfth- and thirteenth-century papal documents offer some idea of the spread of Augustinian canons throughout the country. Other than at Cistercian houses, dedications to St Mary among smaller churches granted to larger Augustinian houses may indicate the presence of canons. The possessions of the Augustinian canonesses of Clonard, confirmed in 1196, included churches dedicated to St Mary at Duleek, Termonfeckin, Skreen, Kells, Fore, Durrow, Clonmacnoise and Annaghdown.[78] The papal taxation list of 1302–7 is another text against which the spread of canons into existing churches might be measured: about thirty houses may have been Augustinian houses in the early fourteenth century.[79] Ten of these were Anglo-Norman foundations, seven have fairly secure Irish origins (Armagh, Clones, Holy Trinity Dublin, All Saints Dublin, St Mary de Hogges in Dublin, Glendalough and possibly Clare Abbey) while the foundation histories of the remaining houses is unclear. It is significant that some of the latter were located in

---

76 Hogan, *Llanthony*, p. 308.   **77** It is a misnomer to designate all the pre-Norman churches listed in *MRHI* as monasteries. A major review of all these churches is required to establish their functions and structures.   **78** Sheehy, *Pont. Hib.*, i, no. 29. Notably, vills associated with a number of these foundations reflect links with the canonesses as they retain the place-name Calliaghstown 'the vill of the nuns (*caillech*)'.   **79** H.S. Sweetman and G.F. Handcock (eds), *Papal*

diocesan centres (Clogher, Kells, Clonfert, Elphin, Annaghdown, Tuam, Duleek and Clonard) and as such may have had canons *in situ* from at least the thirteenth century as Christy Cunniffe demonstates below with reference to Clonfert. Contemporary references to priors and canons in the majority of houses listed by Gwynn and Hadcock only begin to occur in the sources from the mid-fourteenth century onwards.[80]

A further category examined briefly in this essay are two churches that had known traditional functions associated with relics, hereditary families and hermitages and are listed in *MRHI* as churches of Augustinian canons. The first example is Drumlane, Co. Cavan, a church that was twinned with Ferns as they shared the same patron saint, Máedóc, and were ruled by Conaing Ua Fairchellaig, *airchinnech* (hereditary administrator) of Drumlane in the mid-eleventh century.[81] Drumlane had the upper hand with regard to the saint's cult as it was in the possession of the eleventh-century reliquary known as the *Breac Máedóc*.[82] While the lives of Máedóc are a palimpsest of different periods and different churches, they were probably compiled at Drumlane and not at Ferns.[83] The Uí Fhairchellaigh remained in charge of the church until the fifteenth century but the relationship between them, the Augustinian house and the bishop of Kilmore is far from clear. In his study of the coarb in the medieval Irish church St John D. Seymour traced the records of the Uí Fhaircheallaigh's hold on Drumlane from 1298 to 1438, mainly through petitions recorded in the Calendar of Papal Letters.[84] They consistently claimed their rights to what is described in a petition of 1401 as a *dominium* (the office of coarb). In that same record David Ó Faircheallaigh, clerk, wanted his cousin, Maurice, a priest, removed from the office as he contended that the latter's family had intruded unlawfully into the office. David was successful in his petition.[85] The Uí Fhaircheallaigh managed to hold on to their lands and of course maintained their position as keepers of the *Breac Máedóc*.[86] If Maurice Ó Faircheallaigh was a priest, the annals record that other members of the family were canons: in 1484 John Ua Fairchellaigh, canon of the community of Druim-lethan, died and Brian Mór Ua Fairchellaigh, 'he that began to build the anchorite's cell at the great church of Druim-lethan', died in the same year.[87] The bishops of Kilmore also intervened at times as is evident from the following complicated extract from the Calendar of Papal Registers:

taxation calendar of documents relating to Ireland, vol. 5 (1302–7).   **80** Part of any future re-assessment of the Augustinian canons in medieval Ireland would have to include an up to date archaeological and art historical evaluation of existing remains which in many instances appear to suggest that these sites were subject to constant re-building. See www.archaeology.ie (religious houses – Augustinian canons), accessed 16 April 2018.   **81** *AFM*.   **82** G. Murray, 'The Breac Maodhóg: a unique Irish medieval reliquary' in J. Cherry and B. Scott (eds), *Cavan: history and society* (Dublin, 2014), pp 83–125.   **83** C. Doherty, 'The transmission of the cult of St Máedhóg' in P. Ní Chatháin and M. Richter (eds), *Ireland and Europe in the early Middle Ages: texts and transmission* (Dublin, 2002), pp 268–83.   **84** St John D. Seymour, 'The coarb in the medieval Irish church (circa 1200–1550)', *PRIA*, 41C (1932–4), 219–31 at 225–6.   **85** *CPL*, 7, pp 398, 452.   **86** Seymour, 'Coarb in medieval Irish church', 226, 229.   **87** *AU, AFM*.

Confirmation – at the recent petition of the Augustinian prior and convent of St Mary's Drumleachan, in the diocese of Kilmore, containing that although from ancient times they held to their own uses the perpetual vicarage of St Medocius's, Drumlechen, and [that although] afterwards a number of secular priests were instituted by the bishops, nevertheless bishop Nicholas has, on its voidance, restored them to possession of the said vicarage, whose value does not exceed 8 marks, and has given it to them anew; and adding that since their restoration they have been wont to cause it to be served, now by their canons, now by secular priests – of the said restoration and gift.[88]

It was no surprise that tensions existed at Drumlane as a number of the known priors of St Mary's named in the fourteenth century belonged to the Mág Shamhradháin (McGovern) family, who also laid claim to ownership of the cult of St Máedóc.[89] Among them was Cormac Mág Shamhradháin, bishop of Ardagh (d. ?1476), for whom a bardic praise poem was composed.[90] The extensive physical remains at Drumlane consist of a round tower and a church that appear to date to various periods from the thirteenth to the fifteenth centuries, but mainly to the later period. Oliver Davies conjectured that this building phase is reflected in the petitions of 1431 and 1436 requesting to build a cloister and refectory and to repair the parish church and the priory church.[91] This indeed may have coincided with Cormac Mág Shamhradháin's period as prior, although his position was challenged by one Patrick Ó Faircheallaigh.[92]

What can be said of the canons of Drumlane? The Augustinian canons may have established themselves in Drumlane by the late twelfth or early thirteenth century as a Prior de Drumlechan is mentioned in the 1302–7 papal taxation.[93] However, the bishop of Kilmore often intervened in the affairs of Drumlane, and two rival hereditary ecclesiastical families held onto their rights, and on occasion appear to have vied with one another to control the priory. It is unclear if any constant form of *vita apostolica* prevailed in medieval Drumlane: the sources suggest not, while the architecture of the place tends to support the existence of a regular community especially by the fifteenth century.

The second case study deals with a pre-twelfth-century church on an island, which is reputed to have adopted an Augustinian rule. Once more the association with canons prior to the fifteenth century is tenuous, while traditional functions and structures survived into the late medieval period. Inis Clothrann (Inchcleraun), Co. Longford, on Lough Ree, is a truly splendid site consisting of an extensive early enclosure, six churches (variously dating from the tenth to the fifteenth

88 *CPL*, 13, p. 298.   **89** *CPL*, 11, p. 307.   **90** G. Mac Niocaill (ed.), 'Dán do Chormac Mág Shamhradháin Easpag Ardachaidh 1444–?1476', *Seanchas Ard Mhacha*, 4 (1960–1), 141–6.   **91** O. Davies, 'The churches of County Cavan', *JRSAI*, 78 (1948), 73–118 at 91. This article includes a detailed survey of the architectural remains at Drumlane. See also L. Kelly, *The diocese of Kilmore, c.1100–1800* (Dublin, 2017), pp 35–41.   **92** *CPL*, 8, p. 585.   **93** *Papal taxation*, p. 213, no. 698.

century, the largest of which is reputedly the Augustinian house) and *leachta* ('saints' beds').[94] The oldest church, possibly dating to as early as the tenth century, is St Diarmait's shrine chapel, which resembles Temple Ciarán in Clonmacnoise.[95] Con Manning has identified two building phases in Templemore church, the remains of an eleventh-century church embedded into a later phase. It is not certain if this second phase coincided with the addition of claustral buildings including a sacristy, chapter house, possibly a refectory, a cloister garth and ambulatory to the church. References to this island complex suggest that it fulfilled a number of functions. Like many island churches on the Shannon, it was subject to attacks by warring Irish kings, especially the fleets of Munster (1015, 1050, 1089).[96] But it also attracted senior ecclesiastics and important nobles as a place of retreat or burial: these included Áed Ua Finn, bishop of Bréifne (d. 1136), Gilla na Náem Ua Ferghaile, lord of Muintir Ainghile, 'the most prosperous man in Ireland' (d. 1141), and his son Murchad (d. 1150), Gilla na Náem Ua Duind, a leading man of learning who collaborated with the compiler of the Book of Leinster (d. 1160), and Dubchoblaigh wife of Mac Carrghamna (d. 1168). Diarmait Ua Braein, former coarb of Commán (of Roscommon) and *aird-shenóir* of Connacht (d. 1170),[97] died on the island. Diarmait Ua Braein's relative Tipraide O'Breen, also coarb of Commán, 'learned in theology, history, and law', died on Inis Clothrann, 'on his pilgrimage' (d. 1232). In 1244, Donnchad mac Fingein, a member of the O'Conors of Connacht and bishop of Elphin, died there but was buried in the Cistercian monastery at Boyle. There are few references to 'officials' associated with the churches on the island and mention of it as a priory, St Mary's, does not occur until the fifteenth century.[98] Inis Clothrann would have been attractive to the regular canons: an island hermitage, the location of an early saint's cult (Diarmait), a possible destination for pilgrims and the burial place of notable people. In her assessment of the small number of houses of regular canons in Wales, Karen Stöber notes that similar places, 'ancient' churches known as *clasau* such as Beddgelert and the pilgrim site of Bardsey Island, were Augustinian houses probably from the thirteenth century, although the evidence is as hazy as the Irish evidence.[99] She and Janet Burton suggest that some *clasau*, the equivalent of many Irish pre-Norman houses, had a pre-Augustinian phase 'not Augustinian from the outset … it [Beddgelert] belonged to no fixed order'.[100] The conundrum we are faced with is what was the function of Inis Clothrann between the twelfth and fifteenth centuries? Once more the sources do not provide the evidence for a foundation of regular canons. Perhaps it went through a pre-Augustinian phase inhabited by a

---

94 For the only detailed survey of this site, see F.J. Bigger, 'Inis Chlothrann (Inis Cleraun), Lough Ree: its history and antiquities', *JRSAI*, 10 (5th series) (1900), 69–90.   **95** C. Manning, 'Remains of a second pre-Romanesque church at Inchcleraun on Lough Ree', *Archaeology Ireland*, 26 (Summer 2012), 28–9.   **96** All dates referred to in this section are recorded in *AFM*.   **97** This was the same year as the *translatio* of Commán and his relics were enshrined.   **98** *CPL*, 9, p. 429; *CPL*, 10, p. 672; *CPL*, 12 p. 40.   **99** K. Stöber, 'The regular canons in Wales' in Burton and Stöber, *Canons*, pp 97–113.   **100** Ibid., p. 108.

community that formalized into an official community of regular canons towards the fifteenth century? The answer may lie in the archaeology and architecture of the island, and in particular, the church of Templemore and its claustral buildings. A full survey might establish if these buildings belonged to the thirteenth century or later, and by doing so, confirm or otherwise the chronology of the presence of canons on the island.

Women and the Augustinian Rule in Ireland

The nature of female religious life in pre-Norman Ireland has yet to be studied in a manner that includes consideration of all forms of sources and their implication for our understanding of the subject (Fig. 1.1).[101] The tendency to use hagiography and the annals as the primary sources for this topic has skewed the narrative to some extent, as they, of course, deal primarily with major churches such as Kildare, Clonbroney and Killeavy and often have been re-worked in later periods by men who were members of religious orders themselves. As Pádraig Ó Riain shows elsewhere in this volume, among the most active in such revisions of saints' lives were the fifteenth-century Augustinian, Augustine Mac Graidín of All Saints' Island on Lough Ree and the seventeenth-century Franciscan friar, Mícheál Ó Cléirigh. One might note also, for example, that the single source for the Life of Monenna of Killeavy by Conchubranus, BL MS Cotton Cleopatra A.ii.3b–56b, was compiled by Geoffrey, abbot of the English Benedictine monastery of Burton-on-Trent some time during the first half of the twelfth century. Geoffrey used this text as a source for his own Life of the British saint, Modwenna.[102] The annals provide lists of abbesses for the larger female foundations, but give no information about their way of life. One dominant theme in hagiography is that female founders and their communities were often subject to bishops. Of Monenna, her life relates that 'having returned from Saint Brigid to Bishop Ibor she lived in Airtschonis. Many virgins of Christ had gathered together there at that time, and they lived under the authority of the bishop (*sub potestate episcopi*), their number increasing daily.'[103] This situation was common throughout Christendom and as Conchubranus probably wrote the life in the late eleventh or early twelfth century, it may reflect the situation in Ireland at the time. On the other hand, the earlier Irish law *Córus Bésgnai* lays down that male ecclesiastics and religious women were bound by law and rule (*co racht 7 ríagail*) according to the proper legal order of the

101 C. Harrington attempts to cover the subject in her volume *Women in a Celtic church: Ireland, 450–1150* (Oxford, 2002). A detailed examination of the sources is required similar to S. Foot's two volumes on Anglo-Saxon female religious: *Veiled women: the disappearance of nuns from Anglo-Saxon England* and *Veiled women: female religious communities in England, 871–1066* (Aldershot, 2000). For a consideration of the archaeology of medieval Irish nunneries see the contribution by Tracy Collins below. **102** M. Esposito, 'The sources of Conchubranus' Life of St Monenna', *English Historical Review*, 35 (1920), 71–8 at 71. **103** 'The Life of Saint Monenna by Conchubranus: Part 11', ed. by Ulster Society for Medieval Studies, *Seanchas Ard Mhacha*, 10 (1980–1), 117–41: 122–3, §4. **104** Etchingham, *Church organizaton in early Ireland*, p. 80.

1.1 An Augustinian regular canoness from Mervyn Archdall, *Monasticon Hibernicum* (Dublin, 1786).

church (*fri córus rachtge ecalsa*) under the direction of an abbot along with a proper confessor (*anmchara*).[104]

A feature of female communities in Ireland, as portrayed particularly in genealogical texts and saints' pedigrees, is that most were familial churches, and very few survived beyond one or two early generations, possibly because of restrictions relating to women's inheritance, although this conclusion needs further examination. A fine illustration of these early family foundations survives in the secular Leinster genealogies, one section of which unusually records in detail the noble women of the prominent dynasty of Uí Dúnlainge [my translation]:

> The daughters of Ailill son of Dúnlaing, namely, Mumain (Mugain) and Feidelm in Cill ingen Aililla [the church of the daughters of Ailill in parish of Lyons, Co. Kildare]. The daughters of Cormac son of Ailill, namely, Eithne and Darcárthain in Tulach meic Feilmeda [Tullow, Co. Carlow] where their relics (*taiseda*) are kept. The daughters of Cairpre son of Cormac, namely, Cumna and Sodealb in Cill Náis [Naas, Co. Kildare].[105]

If historical at all, and their personal names suggest ties with non-Christian deities, these women were merely noted in genealogies and martyrologies: any female community, if they existed at all, probably did not last beyond the seventh or eighth centuries. When interpreting such early sources, we should be mindful of Sarah Foot's reluctance to impose the vocabulary of later medieval institutional arrangements relating to nuns, their *forma vitae* and cloisters on female religious in Anglo-Saxon England.[106] No rule for female religious is known from pre-Norman Ireland and the concept of double monasteries, possibly confined to Armagh and Kildare, has yet to be understood. In his study of the organization of the early church, Etchingham suggests that there was a constant anxiety about contact between ecclesiastics and female religious lest the former's chastity be compromised. He quotes a single intriguing reference to the *les caillech* 'enclosure of the veiled women' within the *faitche* 'precinct' of the *Céli Dé* foundation at Finglas (Co. Dublin) as a potential example of a place where rigorous monasticism prevailed that included a distinct female community.[107] One glimpse of religious women participating in ceremonies, often overlooked due to the glittering description of Kildare in Cogitosus's Life of Brigid, is that preserved in the seventh-century Latin *Liber Angeli*. It describes Armagh as a city (*urbs*) in which Christians of both sexes lived together in religion, consisting of three orders, *uirgines et poenitentes (et) in matrimonio ligitimo aeclessiae seruientes* ('virgins, penitents and those serving the church in legitimate matrimony'). 'These three orders are allowed to hear the word of preaching in the church of the northern district on Sunday always; in the southern basilica, however, bishops and priests and anchorites and

---

105 M.A. O'Brien (ed.), *Corpus genealogiarum Hiberniae* (Dublin, repr. 1976), p. 340: 316r46 fn. (f). 106 S. Foot, *Monastic life in Anglo-Saxon England, c.600–900* (Cambridge, 2006), pp 9–10. 107 Etchingham, *Church organizaton in early Ireland*, pp 349–50.

other religious offer pleasing praises'. This image of female religious subject to some form of regulated life and enclosure differs considerably from heroine-saints such as Brigid and Monenna who are depicted as travelling freely, and although subject to abbots or bishops, interacting with all levels in society, from kings to the lowliest poor.

It is difficult to extrapolate from the sources if this was the type of female religious life that existed in Ireland on the eve of the arrival of the orders to Ireland. A notable practice evident from the eleventh century onwards is of noble women dying in important ecclesiastical foundations, among them, Armagh, Emly, Derry, Glendalough, Clonmacnoise, Cork, Ardfert and Lismore. Going on pilgrimage to die or retreating *in clericatu* was a practice resorted to by Irish kings since the seventh century,[108] but the phenomenon of women retreating to such places was later and possibly reflects the custom of widows and other women becoming vowesses in later life. Some were probably patrons of the church during their often turbulent lives, none of greater fame than Derbforgaill wife of Tigernán Ua Ruairc, king of Bréifne who was taken by Tigernán's arch-rival Diarmait Mac Murchada, king of Leinster. Whatever about the complexity of her relationships with both kings, Derbforgaill was an important patron, apparently endowing the newly founded Cistercian monastery of Mellifont in 1157 and a female foundation at Clonmacnoise in 1167, going on a pilgrimage to Mellifont in 1186, and dying there in 1193. Significantly, Derbforgaill was the daughter of Murchad Ua Máelsechlainn, king of Mide, reputedly one of the most important royal patrons of new order foundations during the twelfth century, perhaps including a female Arrouaisian foundation at Clonard (Co. Meath).

The history of Augustinian female foundations throughout Europe is no different from that of their male counterparts. The nature of each foundation and their relationships with Augustinian canons, bishops and dignitaries depended on local circumstances. Piecing together their histories can be problematic due to the lack of source material, and has often to be deciphered through the lens of sources originating in male foundations.[109] Ireland is no different and the situation is again best dealt with by adopting a comparative approach. Religious institutions that were private or 'family' monasteries, founded and controlled by lay aristocratic families, were common, for example, in parts of Spain. These functioned as a means through which the sacred legitimized power, as family mausolea and as protectors of family estates. Female monasticism was an essential part of this system, and noblewomen (*dominae*) were instrumental in transforming many houses to following the Benedictine, Cluniac, and occasionally, Augustinian Rules during

108 E. Bhreathnach, 'Abbesses, minor dynasties and kings *in clericatu*: perspectives of Ireland, 700–850' in M.P. Brown and C.A. Fahr (eds), *Mercia: an Anglo-Saxon kingdom in Europe*, Studies in the Early History of Europe (Leicester, 2001), pp 113–25. 109 A. Grélois, 'Les chanoines réguliers et la conversion des femmes au XIIe siècle' in Parisse (ed.), *Les chanoines réguliers*, pp 233–63 at 234. 110 G. Cavero Domínguez, 'Spanish female monasticism: "family" monasteries and their transformation (eleventh to twelfth centuries)' in J. Burton and K. Stöber (eds), *Women in the medieval world* (Turnhout, 2015), pp 15–52.

the eleventh and twelfth centuries.[110] In Ireland, the female Augustinian house at Clonard may offer a similar model. Clonard was a dynastic family foundation controlled by the midland dynasty of Uí Máelsechlainn that appears to have been 'transformed' by female members of the extended dynastic family. By the twelfth century the Uí Máelsechlainn were a very fractious dynasty riven by internal rivalries, whose kingdom, which technically stretched from the eastern coast (modern Co. Meath) into modern Co. Westmeath, was constantly under pressure from competing provincial kings. These kings favoured one Uí Máelsechlainn faction over another and having divided the kingdom between east and west Mide, attempted to control the Uí Máelsechlainn kingship.

The church was implicated in this complex dynastic rivalry. This is most clearly reflected in the fluctuation of the diocesan divisions of the kingdom of Mide, from the two sees of Duleek and Clonard of the synod of Ráith Bresail in 1111 to the two sees of Clonard and Clonmacnoise of the rival synod of Uisnech, convened by Murchad Ua Máelsechlainn and the abbot of Clonmacnoise in 1111 to 'correct' the Ráith Bresail synod's decision. This was despite the best efforts of the early 'reforming' bishop Máel Muire Ua Dúnáin (d. 1117), who had strong personal links with Clonard and Mide but who became an advisor to Muirchertach Ua Briain, king of Munster, in his attempts at establishing an agreed diocesan structure in Ireland in the early twelfth century.[111] In addition, Murchad's wife was Mór, daughter of Muirchertach Ua Briain.[112] Understanding Murchad Ua Máelsechlainn and the ecclesiastical and political connections of the Uí Máelsechlainn women is essential to explaining the background to the endowment of a female Arrouasian foundation in Clonard. During his career, Murchad, who was always had a precarious hold on his kingship, was both protected and censured by the church. In 1144, he was protected from Toirdelbach Ua Conchobair, king of Connacht, by 'an extensive array of relics and ecclesiastical guarantors', but was censured in 1150 by the 'successor of Patrick', Gilla Meic Liac, archbishop of Armagh.[113] On that occasion, the kingdom of Mide was divided in three parts by more powerful regional kings. If Murchad endowed the Cistercian foundation at Bective, Co. Meath, the first daughter house of Mellifont – and this is not certain – he may have done so in the mid-to-late 1140s while under the protection of leading ecclesiastics, or as reparation for his misdeeds in 1150. He died in Durrow, Co. Offaly in 1153. His wife Mór also died in Durrow in 1137, as did his son Máelsechlainn, by poisoning in 1155.[114]

Durrow was both a royal *caput* and an eminent church. Clonard also held this status as annalistic entries record the deaths there of nobles such as Ben Mide, daughter of Conchobar Ua Máelsechlainn, in 1137 and notably in 1139, Cú

111 D. Ó Corráin, 'Mael Muire Ua Dúnáin (1040–1117), reformer' in P. de Brún, S. Ó Coileáin and P. Ó Riain (eds), *Folia Gadelica; essays presented by former students to R.A. Breatnach* (Cork, 1983), pp 47–53 at p. 50. Máel Muire Ua Dúnáin finally died in retirement in Clonard in 1117. 112 M. Dobbs (ed.), 'The Ban-shenchus', *Revue celtique*, 48 (1931), 163–234 at 232. 113 Flanagan, *Transformation*, pp 181–3. 114 *AFM* entries *sub anno*.

Chonnacht, chief *ollam* in poetry. Turning to the Uí Máelsechlainn women, their patronage of the church was equally as complex as that of their male relatives, and there is no indication that they lived cloistered lives in any new foundation. In 1167, Derbail, daughter of Donnchad Ua Máelsechlainn, died in Clonmacnoise 'after a victory of will and confession', suggesting that like many other noble women she retreated to an ecclesiastical settlement at the end of her life. In the same year her kinswoman Derbforgaill, daughter of Murchad Ua Máelsechlainn, was involved in the completion or furnishing of the 'Nuns' Church' at Clonmacnoise.[115] She had already donated gold, a chalice and altar-cloths to Mellifont in 1157, and it was to Mellifont that she retired and died in 1193.[116] The most notorious episode in Derbforgaill's life was her kidnapping (voluntarily or otherwise) in 1152 by Diarmait Mac Murchada, king of Leinster and arch-rival of her husband, Tigernán Ua Ruairc, king of Bréifne. Notwithstanding her father Murchad's role in endowing new foundations, her association with Mac Murchada and Ua Ruairc, two royal patrons of the church, must have had an influence on her. Ua Ruairc granted lands to the community of Kells, Co. Meath,[117] as well as apparently endowing lands to an Augustinian community at Navan, Co. Meath.[118] Mac Murchada endowed one of the earliest houses of women following the Arrouaisian observance, St Mary de Hogges in Dublin. Confirmation of grants made by him to the convent were endorsed by the papal legate to Ireland Cardinal John Paparo in 1152,[119] suggesting that this foundation was the first Augustinian house endowed by Mac Murchada. He may have been influenced in his choice of order by his kinsman through fosterage, Áed Ua Cáellaide, bishop of Louth (d. 1182), who completed the Augustinian foundation at Knock, Co. Louth, in 1148 and who, as noted by Flanagan, is described in the necrology of Santo Savino of Piacenza as 'prior of the canons, nuns, and holy women throughout Ireland'.[120] Flanagan has also suggested on the basis of the prior of Louth having first say in the election of the abbess of Odder – the site to which the Clonard convent transferred *c.*1380 – that the abbess of Clonard may have been dependent on St Mary's, Louth.[121]

A further vital connection between Diamait Mac Murchada and the Uí Máelsechlainn dynasty was that his sister Dubcablach was wife of Muirchertach Ua Máelsechlainn and, more significantly, mother of Agnes 'the great abbess' (d. 1196)[122] of the Arrouaisian convent of Clonard, who is also described in the twelfth-century *Banshenchas* ('Lore of Women') as *ceand caillech Erend* ('head of the nuns of Ireland').[123] She was related to Derbforgaill, probably a first cousin. It was from within this network that the Augustinian convent at Clonard was founded.

---

115 *AFM*. For a detailed consideration of the date of this impressive Romanesque building and Derbforgaill's involvement in its construction, see J. Ní Ghrádaigh, '"But what exactly did she give?": Derbforgaill and the Nuns' Church at Clonmacnoise' in H. King (ed.), *Clonmacnoise studies* 2 (Dublin, 2003), pp 175–207.   **116** *AU, ALC, AFM*; Flanagan, *Transformation*, p. 201.   **117** G. Mac Niocaill, *Notitiæ as Leabhar Cheanannais 1033–1161* (Cló Morainn, 1961), pp 24–6 (VII). **118** E. St John Brooks, 'A charter of John de Courcy to the abbey of Navan', *JRSAI*, 63 (1933), 38–45 at 39.   **119** Flanagan, *Charters*, pp 384–5.   **120** Ibid., pp 73–4; Flanagan, *Transformation*, pp 148–9.   **121** Flanagan, 'Louth', 231–3.   **122** *ALC*.   **123** Dobbs, 'The Ban-shenchus', 234.

Who were the female religious of Clonard and what was their *forma vitae*? We have no evidence regarding their *forma vitae* except that they were somehow affiliated to the Arrouaisian observance, which if genuinely followed could have meant a strict observance of the Divine Office and rules concerning their habits, their food and their work. Evidence from elsewhere suggests that some women, the *sorores*, were involved in manual labour or worked in hospitals, while others, possibly the wealthier women, produced items such as altar-cloths and vestments.[124] In light of this, Derbforgaill's gift of cloth for the nine altars in the church at Mellifont could have been made in a female foundation, possibly even Clonard. If the list of Clonard's possessions confirmed in the papal confirmation of 1195 is a genuine reflection of the lands and churches for which the foundation was responsible,[125] it raises issues about the role of women such as Agnes Ua Máelsechnaill as both ecclesiastical administrators and the head of a community of holy women. Was she, *In Caillech Mór* or 'the great abbess', similar to the pre-Norman abbesses in Kildare, because of her secular or spiritual authority? Certainly, she and her cousin Derbforgaill lived through a violent era during which fierce dynastic and regional wars were fought, while at the same time those involved in these wars contributed hugely to a church in the process of transformation. And notably, both women seem to have outlasted their menfolk and lived long lives. And if there was transformation, existing practices did not end. The Uí Máelsechlainn and families subject to them kept the Clonard community in their grasp until the late fourteenth century when the last abbess of a 'Mide' family died. Thereafter, the office was held by local Anglo-Norman women until the dissolution.[126]

CONCLUSION

This chapter is unsatisfactory in that it has raised far more questions than it has answered. Nevertheless, it may also have opened up areas of research and substantial themes relating to the origins and spread of the Augustinian canons and canonesses in Ireland that require considerably more analysis. There is a clear need to undertake far more detailed archaeological and architectural studies to determine the date of buildings and other features on sites reputed to be associated with Augustinian canons and canonesses. This might go towards resolving the problem of the lack of documentary evidence for their presence on some of these sites until the fifteenth century. The complex nature of canons, between secular and regular canons in cathedral chapters, in regular communities or ministering among the laity in very small numbers, bedevils any study of the Augustinians, and this is the case for Ireland as for elsewhere. Any more detailed study of the canons and

124 Grélois, 'Les chanoines réguliers et la conversion des femmes', pp 245–6.   **125** Sheehy, *Pont. Hib.*, i, pp 83–6, no. 29.   **126** D. Hall, 'Towards a prosopography of nuns in medieval Ireland', *AH*, 53 (1999), 3–15 at 4–5. The community transferred to Odder, Co. Meath, *c*.1380.

canonesses in Ireland, particularly during the twelfth and thirteenth centuries, would have to build on the discussion in this chapter of their use of existing pre-Norman churches to stabilize an emerging diocesan and parochial infrastructure. The evidence suggests that in certain regions they were an instrumental component of this mission, and that their activities had started prior to the coming of the Normans as part of a movement spearheaded by a generation of zealous bishops and dominant Irish kings. And finally, to return to Donnchadh Ó Corráin's observations at the beginning of this chapter, there is no doubt that the status quo survived in many churches at least until the fifteenth century and that many of these churches in Ireland reputed to have adopted an Augustinian rule during the twelfth century remained firmly in the hands of traditional hereditary families, who throughout the medieval period maintained their privileges and lands. Some of these families, or others who intruded into their churches, adopted a *vita apostolica*, but this was not consistent, and in many instances happened as late as the fifteenth century.

Victorine canons in medieval Ireland

MARIE THERESE FLANAGAN

This contribution focuses on those Augustinian canons in medieval Ireland who followed the *ordo*, that is, the daily routines or in-house customs of the abbey of Saint-Victor in Paris. Saint-Victor had been founded as a reformist community by 1111, possibly as early as 1108, and it became one of the most important monasteries in medieval Paris, enjoying royal patronage, and noted especially for its scholarship and production of manuscripts.[1] The Victorines were one of several types of Augustinian regular canons who emerged in the course of the twelfth century in the context of a European-wide reform movement. One can distinguish between canons who relied on the Rule of St Augustine and those who augmented that rule with more detailed written observances based on a particular house, such as Saint-Victor (Fig. 2.1).

Augustinian canons who adopted the customs of the monastery of St Nicholas in Arrouaise in Picardy had been introduced into Ireland by St Malachy in 1142;[2] and Arrouasian houses were among the most numerous of those Augustinian canons in Ireland who followed the customs of a particular house.[3] However, the precise date and agency of transmission of the Victorine observance to Ireland is less clear. Victorine customs are attested at St Thomas's Abbey, Dublin, by no later than 1192. As so often with Augustinian communities in Ireland, it can be difficult to ascertain when precisely the Rule of Augustine was first adopted and whether a particular *ordo* was followed from that time, or approved subsequently. This is certainly the case with the introduction of Victorine observances into medieval Ireland. Not even the exact number of Victorine houses at any one time is assured.[4] What is clear is that all were Anglo-Norman, or English, foundations, of which St

1 See J. Longère (ed.), *L'abbaye Parisienne de Saint-Victor au moyen âge: communications présentés au XIIIe colloque d'humanisme médiéval de Paris (1986–1988)*, Bibliotheca Victorina, 1 (Turnhout, 1991), and earlier works there cited; M.E. Fassler, *Gothic song: Victorine sequences and Augustinian reform in twelfth-century Paris* (2nd ed., Notre Dame, IN, 2011); E.A. Matter and L. Smith (eds), *From knowledge to beatitude: St Victor, twelfth-century scholars and beyond: essays in honour of Grover A. Zinn Jr* (Notre Dame, IN, 2013); Feiss and Mousseau *Saint Victor*. For the customs of Saint-Victor, see L. Jocqué and L. Milis (eds), *Liber ordinis Sancti Victoris Parisiensis*, Corpus Christianorum Continuatio Medievalis, 61 (Turnhout, 1984). For the Victorines in Ireland the only study to date has been that of H.B. Feiss, 'The order of St Victor in Ireland' in *Ordo canonicus: studia canonicalia cura confoederationis canonicorum regularium S. Augustini edita*, series altera, 4 (1988), pp 56–87. I am grateful to Colmán Ó Clabaigh OSB for providing me with a copy of this article. 2 Flanagan, 'Louth', 223–34; Flanagan, *Transformation* (Woodbridge, 2010), pp 136–54. 3 These houses are listed in *MRHI*, pp 153–6. However, as Bhreathnach notes above, much more work remains to be done on when precisely Arrouaisian customs were adopted by individual communities. 4 The main listing is in *MRHI*, pp 153–6.

2.1 Eighteenth-century depiction of the abbey of St Victor, Paris. Image courtesy of Hugh Feiss OSB.

Thomas's Abbey in Dublin was to be the first and to become the wealthiest and most influential. It was the only Victorine community to acquire abbatial status and it is also the house for which there is by far the most surviving evidence. Victorine observances therefore were introduced following English intervention in Ireland and remained confined to the colony. Despite initial enthusiastic support from many native Irish bishops, Victorine communities were to develop no sustained contacts with native Irish houses; rather, they can be said to have acted as a mediator and instrument of colonization with their canons drawn exclusively from the colonial population.

ST THOMAS'S ABBEY, DUBLIN

The most important Victorine community in Ireland had its origins in a foundation initiated in 1177 in Dublin on behalf of King Henry II, which was to remain the only English royal monastic foundation in post-invasion Ireland.[5] As a royal foundation, it may be expected to have had a close connection with the English

---

5 For the view that royal foundations of mendicants by the English kings cannot be convincingly identified in Ireland, see C. Ó Clabaigh, *The friars in Ireland, 1224–1540* (Dublin, 2012), pp 88–9.

kings; added to which it was located just outside the west gate of the city of Dublin, which Henry II, during his time in Ireland in 1171–2, had determined to retain as royal demesne. Dublin was to become the capital of English royal government with canons, certainly from the fourteenth century onwards, exercising important offices in the English administration in Ireland. In March 1177, Henry II's agent in the recently established Angevin lordship of Ireland, William fitz Aldelin, 'on the king's behalf (*ex parte domini regis*)', granted land at Donore, south of the walled city, to the 'church of St Thomas, martyr of Christ'.[6] Fitz Aldelin's charter was issued in the presence of a visiting papal legate, Vivianus, cardinal priest of the church of Santo Stefano on the Coelian Hill, Laurentius (Lorcán Ua Tuathail), archbishop of Dublin, and 'many bishops of Ireland'; on the basis of that description and of individual bishops named in the witness list, its drafting most likely coincided with a synod convened in Dublin by the papal legate on the first Sunday of Lent which fell on 2 March in 1177.[7]

The dedication to 'Thomas, martyr of Christ' referred to Thomas Becket, archbishop of Canterbury, who had been murdered on 29 December 1170 by four knights of King Henry II.[8] In one of the speediest of canonizations, certainly in the medieval period, Pope Alexander III declared Thomas Becket to be a martyr saint on 21 February 1173. The murder of Becket, following a bitter conflict with Henry II, which had resulted in Becket's exile for a period of six years, impacted adversely on Henry's reputation since the king was considered to have been implicated in, even if he had not directly ordered, the killing. In particular, it had serious repercussions for Henry's relations with Pope Alexander III. In the wake of the murder, two cardinal legates, Albertus and Theodwinus, had been dispatched to meet with the king but, in advance of their arrival, Henry had removed himself to Ireland: one of the reasons offered by the Canterbury chronicler, Gervase of Canterbury, for Henry's departure for Ireland in the autumn of 1171 was that the king was deliberately seeking to avoid having to meet the legates.[9] When, however,

---

6 *Calendar of charter rolls, 1257–1300* (London, 1906), pp 386–7 (recited in an inspeximus of King Edward I, issued on 14 January 1291); *Calendar of documents relating to Ireland, 1285–92*; ed. H.S. Sweetman (London, 1879), pp 380–1, no. 839. Among the named witnesses to the charter are Eugenius, bishop of Clonard, Nemias, bishop of Kildare, and Augustine, bishop of Waterford. Fitz Aldelin's authority to act on behalf of Henry II is emphasized by the letter of credence whereby Henry commanded the clergy and lay magnates of Ireland to be attentive to fitz Aldelin if they wished to have the king's love, which is invariably recited alongside later royal confirmations of William fitz Aldelin's charter for St Thomas's. In addition to Edward I's confirmation, cf. those of Edward III in 1330 and Richard II in 1379: *Calendar of charter rolls, 1327–41* (London, 1912), p. 192; *Calender of patent rolls, Richard II, 1377–81* (London, 1895), p. 354. The foundation did not at first have abbatial status. See further below, pp 39–40.   7 For the synod, see *Expugnatio Hibernica: the conquest of Ireland by Giraldus Cambrensis*, ed. A.B. Scott and F.X. Martin (Dublin, 1978), pp 180–3 (hereafter *Expugnatio*); *AU*, *AFM* s.a. 1177.   8 Literature on the Becket controversy is vast, among which the writings of Frank Barlow and Anne Duggan are of especial importance. See F. Barlow, *Thomas Becket* (2nd ed., London, 1997); A.J. Duggan, *Thomas Becket* (London, 2004).   9 Gervase of Canterbury, *Historical works*, ed. W. Stubbs, 2 vols, Rolls Series (London, 1879–80), i, pp 234–5, ii, p. 79. A similar claim is made in a letter by Becket's

his eldest son, the young King Henry, rebelled against him in collusion with King Louis VII of France, with potentially very serious repercussions for instability in Henry's continental dominions, he judged a speedy negotiation with the papacy to be politically expedient. Leaving Ireland as soon as weather permitted,[10] Henry hastened to meet the pope's legates at Avranches in Normandy, where negotiations took place over 17–18 May 1172 and which led on 21 May to a formal public reconciliation in the cathedral. This was to be followed on 30 May by a yet larger assembly of ecclesiastics and nobles at Caen, the capital of Normandy, with another public solemn oath sworn by Henry on the Gospels that he had not been involved in the murder, the aim of the second occasion being to ensure even greater publicity.

Henry vowed that, in reparation for Becket's murder, he would personally take the cross and depart for the Holy Land in the summer of 1173. In 1175, however, he secured a release from that crusading vow from another papal legate, Hugo Pierleone, on a mission to England in that year, the commutation being that the king would instead undertake to found three monasteries.[11] This was reported favourably by the chronicler, Roger of Howden, at that time close to the royal court.[12] But, according to more hostile assessments of two other contemporary chroniclers, Ralph Niger and Gerald de Barri (also known as Giraldus Cambrensis or Gerald of Wales), the king effected the commutation of his vow in a very niggardly fashion. Henry had an existing religious community at the church of the Holy Cross in Waltham (Essex) converted from secular to regular canons; he re-founded a nunnery at Amesbury (Wiltshire), expelling Benedictine nuns in favour of a community drawn from Fontevraud in Anjou, and he made a small new foundation for Carthusian monks at Witham (Somerset), the first house of that order to be established in England.[13] In the case of Waltham and Amesbury, there

clerk and confidant, Herbert of Bosham, presumably writing to Cardinals Albertus and Theodwinus while Henry was in Ireland, that the king 'had fled to the ends of the earth': C. Ó Clabaigh and M. Staunton, 'Thomas Becket and Ireland' in E. Mullins and D. Scully (eds), *Listen, O isles onto me: studies in medieval word and image in honour of Jennifer O'Reilly* (Cork, 2011), pp 87–101 at p. 88.   **10** Gerald de Barri depicted Henry waiting impatiently at Wexford for storms to abate and adverse winds to change direction: *Expugnatio*, pp 102–3.   **11** *Gesta Henrici secundi Benedicti abbatis*, ed. W. Stubbs, 2 vols, Rolls Series (London, 1867), i, pp 134–6; cf. pp 165, 173–4. In his revised version Roger refrained from linking the re-foundation at Waltham with reparation by Henry for Becket's murder: *Chronica Magistri Rogeri de Houedone*, ed. W. Stubbs, 4 vols, Rolls Series (London, 1868–1), ii, pp 118–19. According to Ralph de Diceto, Henry promised to maintain 200 knights in defence of Jerusalem for a year: *Radulfi de Diceto opera*, ed. W. Stubbs, 2 vols, Rolls Series (London, 1876), i, p. 352. Ralph subsequently recorded the installation of canons at Waltham on 11 June 1177 without linking it to Henry's penance: ibid., p. 420. For discussion, see J.T. Appleby, 'The ecclesiastical foundations of Henry II', *Catholic Historical Review*, 48 (1962), 205–15. For Henry's ecclesiastical patronage more generally, see E.M. Hallam, 'Henry II as a founder of monasteries', *Journal of Ecclesiastical History*, 28 (1977), 113–32; M. Chibnall, 'Changing expectations of a royal benefactor: the religious patronage of Henry II' in E. Jamroziak and J. Burton (eds), *Religious and laity in Western Europe, 1000–1400* (Turnhout, 2006), pp 8–21.   **12** For Roger, see now M. Staunton, *The historians of Angevin England* (Oxford, 2017), pp 51–66.   **13** *Radulphi Nigri chronica: the chronicles of Ralph Niger*, ed. R. Anstruther,

was no change of existing dedications: Waltham remained dedicated to the Holy Cross, Amesbury to St Mary and St Mellor, and the Witham foundation, like all Carthusian houses, was dedicated to the Virgin. In general, Henry was not an extravagant monastic patron and he established few new religious foundations throughout his long reign. Nonetheless, his outlay in relation to the three houses that he endowed in England in reparation for the murder of Becket was not as slight as his critics, Gerald de Barri and Ralph Niger, implied.[14] At Waltham the rebuilt church was substantially enlarged, with a sum of £1,200 expended for the building work, while a further £373 8s. 5d. was spent on timber and transport.[15] At Amesbury around £1,000 was spent between 1178–9 and 1184.[16] In the case of Witham, the king supplied the sum of £466.[17] None of these three religious houses was dedicated to St Thomas, even though they resulted from the peace settlement agreed with the papal legates and the subsequent release from Henry's penitential vow to go on pilgrimage to the Holy Land.

In 1174, Henry also made his peace with the monks of Canterbury. On his own initiative, over 13–14 July 1174, he undertook a very public penitential pilgrimage to Canterbury, dismounting at first sight of the cathedral and progressing through the streets barefoot and in penitential garb, wearing only a hair shirt and shift. Having spent the night at Becket's shrine, he confessed his culpability in the murder and, prostrating himself before the monks, begged to be subjected to the discipline of more than 200 strokes of a rod. Then placing four marks of gold on Becket's tomb, he assigned an annual income of £40 to Christ Church Canterbury; and he promised to build a monastery (*cenobium*) in the martyr's honour, therewith securing the monks' absolution.[18] That monastery was to be St Thomas's Abbey in Dublin.

Caxton Society, 13 (London, 1851), p. 168; *Giraldi Cambrensis opera*, ed. J.S. Brewer, J.F. Dimock and G.F. Warner, 8 vols, Rolls Series (London, 1862–91), viii, pp 169–72; W.L. Warren, *Henry II* (2nd ed., London, 2000), pp 212–14.   **14** A.J. Duggan, 'Diplomacy, status, and conscience: Henry II's penance for Becket's murder' in K. Borchardt and E. Bünz (eds), *Forschungen zur Reichs-Papst- und Landesgeschichte: Peter Herde zum 65. Geburtstag von Freunden, Schülern und Kollegen dargebracht*, 2 vols (Stuttgart, 1998), i, pp 265–90 at pp 286–7; reprinted in A.J. Duggan, *Thomas Becket: friends, networks, texts and cult* (London, 2007), vii.   **15** In the financial year 1176–7 alone the king expended £100 on the church at Waltham: *Pipe roll 23 Henry II, 1176–1177*, Pipe Roll Society, 26 (London 1905), p. 201. At Amesbury nuns were brought from Fontevraud and from its priory at Westwood, though those who were expelled nonetheless received a grant of wine from the king and an annuity of ten marks for their abbess: ibid., pp 64, 166, 177, 179.   **16** Around November 1186 Henry II visited Amesbury in person to install the nuns of Fontevraud there when casks of red and white French wine were purchased at a cost of 100 shillings, while 100 marks from the issues of the vacant see of Salisbury were allotted to the nuns to be spent on the church: *Pipe roll 33 Henry II, 1186–1187*, Pipe Roll Society, 37 (London, 1915), pp 187, 203–4.   **17** H.M. Colvin, *The history of king's works*, 8 vols (London, 1963–82), i, pp 88–9, 90.   **18** William of Canterbury, 'Miracula S. Thomae', 6.93 in *Materials for the history of Thomas Becket*, ed. J.C. Robertson and J.B. Sheppard, 7 vols, Rolls Series (London, 1875–85), i, pp 487–8; cf. Roger of Howden, *Gesta Henrici*, i, p. 72; *Chronica*, ii, pp 61–2; F. Barlow, *Thomas Becket* (London, 1986), pp 269–70. For perceptive comments on the royal display of humility by Henry II, see N. Vincent, 'Pilgrimages of the Angevin kings of England' in C. Morris (ed.), *Pilgrimage:*

The only house founded by Henry II in reparation for Becket's murder that was dedicated to the saint therefore would be that in Dublin. It, however, went unnamed by contemporary English chroniclers and does not figure in primary, or indeed either much in secondary accounts of the aftermath of the Becket controversy, despite the vast literature on that subject. This is chiefly because the Dublin foundation resulted from Henry's vow made at Canterbury in 1174 rather than from the terms of his reconciliation with the papal legates. Gerald de Barri, for example, the principal chronicler of the English invasion of Ireland, recorded nothing of its foundation, even though he well knew of it from his personal visits to Ireland. His silence is the more noteworthy in that his relatives, his uncle, Robert fitz Stephen, his cousin, Raymond le Gros, and his brothers, Philip and Robert de Barri, who were all afforded prominent roles in his *Expugnatio Hibernica*, were among the earliest donors of land to the new foundation.[19] Yet the reporting of this foundation and its benefactions would not have suited Gerald's argument advanced in his *Expugnatio* that both the earliest settlers and Henry II were insufficiently generous to the church in Ireland with, as Gerald saw it, inevitably negative consequences for the success of the English advance.[20] Gerald also included an account of the martyrdom of Becket in his *Expugnatio*, describing it has having been carried out by four 'dogs of the palace';[21] and he grew ever more hostile to Henry II and his sons in his later writings.[22] On his first visit to Ireland in 1183 Gerald actually witnessed a grant to the '*fratres* of the church of St Thomas of Dublin' of lands in Cork made by his brother, Philip de Barri, while on a later visit between 1204 and 1206 Gerald witnessed a charter of Simon, abbot of St Thomas's, so his silence may hardly be construed as an oversight.[23]

It can be argued that Henry was indeed less generous to the Dublin foundation than he had been in the case of the Waltham, Amesbury and Witham endowments.

the English experience from Becket to Bunyan (Cambridge, 2002), pp 12–45 at pp 16–17. For the view that the king's piety did not notably increase in the aftermath of Becket's death, see ibid., p. 29. **19** J.T. Gilbert (ed.), *Register of the abbey of St Thomas, Dublin*, Rolls Series (London, 1889), pp 113–14, 205, 214–15 (hereafter *RST*). The *terminus post quem* for the compilation of this cartulary is the commission of Pope Gregory X to the bishop of Meath and the abbot of St Thomas on 21 July 1272, empowering them to use ecclesiastical censure to protect the possessions of the Lord Edward in Ireland. This document on the final page of the manuscript was omitted by Gilbert in his edition but is printed by C. McNeill, 'Rawlinson manuscripts, class B', *Analecta Hibernica*, 1 (1930), 111–78 at 164–7. Gilbert's edition took no account of the gatherings in the manuscript which are complex, nor did he identify later insertions by other hands. These are partially outlined in the important article by A. Gwynn, 'The early history of St Thomas's Abbey, Dublin', *JRSAI*, 84 (1954), 1–35. Gwynn plausibly surmised that the cartulary was compiled during the abbacy of William Le Walleis (1270–89). **20** *Expugnatio*, pp 242–3; he reiterated this view in the dedicatory letter addressed to King John on the eve of his expedition to Ireland, arguing that 'exalting the church' had been replaced by 'despoiling churches': ibid., p. 264. **21** Ibid., pp 72–5. **22** The most recent discussion is in Staunton, *Historians of Angevin England*, pp 95–107. **23** *RST*, pp 205, 323–5; C. McNeill (ed.), *Calendar of Archbishop Alen's register, c.1172–1534* (Dublin, 1950), p. 27 (hereafter *CAAR*). For Gerald's visits to Ireland, see R. Bartlett, 'Gerald of Wales' (*c.*1146–1220×23) in *Oxford dictionary of national biography*, ed. H.C.G. Matthew and B. Harrison, 60 vols (Oxford, 2004), 21, pp 925–7 (hereafter *ODNB*).

William fitz Aldelin's charter, issued on behalf of the king, granted no more than one carucate of land at Donore with a mill and meadow outside the city; this provided the demesne or home farm for the new community.[24] In terms of landed endowment, this was a meagre grant. It was rather the series of benefactions from the earliest colonists that enabled the rapid growth of the new community in Dublin. These endowments were determined, in part, by the chronological coincidence of the arrangements for the foundation of St Thomas's made at Dublin in March 1177 that were confirmed by Henry II two months later, at a council in Oxford in May at which Henry put new administrative arrangements for Ireland in place, designating his youngest son, John, as lord of Ireland.[25] Among the earliest benefactors to the new community was Gerald de Barri's uncle, Robert fitz Stephen, to whom he was especially close, and Milo de Cogan, who together were granted the 'kingdom of Cork', that is, the Mac Carthaig kingdom of Desmond, by Henry II at the council of Oxford to hold as tenants-in-chief of the king and who each made some of the earliest endowments to the 'church of St Thomas' from their new acquisitions in Munster.[26] Both these men had not only witnessed William fitz Aldelin's charter issued at Dublin in March 1177, they were also present at Oxford in May when Henry II confirmed the terms of fitz Aldelin's charter and on the same occasion made a speculative grant to them of lands in south Munster.[27]

King Henry's May 1177 confirmation of fitz Aldelin's charter was to be the only document issued in his own name in favour of the Dublin foundation. This could be interpreted as indicating that the king did not take a sustained interest in the project. In his testament, for example, drawn up in February 1182 and sent to the pope for endorsement, Henry listed very detailed bequests to be made from his personal treasure at the time of his death to religious houses in England, Normandy and Anjou, to the Hospitallers and Templars as well as to the mother houses of Grandmont, Cîteaux, Cluny, Arrouaise and Premontré, but there was no mention of his foundation in Dublin.[28] Up to his death in 1189, Henry II cannot be said to have made much effort to provide a secure revenue base for his new foundation in Dublin or to strengthen its economic position. There was notably little outlay on Henry's part; and he certainly did not expend the substantial sums of money that he had in relation to the three English houses that he endowed in reparation for Becket's murder.

24 The paucity of lands held by St Thomas's Abbey in Dublin at the dissolution is evidenced in A.J. Otway-Ruthven, 'The mediaeval church lands of Co. Dublin' in J.A. Watt, J.B. Morrall and F.X. Martin (eds), *Medieval studies presented to Aubrey Gwynn SJ* (Dublin, 1961), pp 54–73 at pp 70–1. Much land in and around Dublin was already in ecclesiastical possession by 1172. The name form 'Donoure' suggests a pre-existing landed estate. 25 Henry's confirmation charter is recited alongside that of William fitz Aldelin in the inspeximus of King Edward I issued on 14 January 1291: above, note 6. 26 *RST*, pp 201–4, 214–16. 27 For Henry II's grant of the 'kingdom of Cork', see *Expugnatio*, pp 184–5. The text of Henry's charter is in J. Ware, *De Hibernia et antiquitatibus eius disquisitiones* (London, 1654), pp 237–9; G. Lyttelton, *History of the life of King Henry II*, 6 vols (3rd ed., London, 1773), vi, pp 406–8. 28 Gervase of Canterbury, *Historical*

It is not immediately apparent why Dublin should have been chosen as the location for Henry's foundation dedicated to the English martyr, Thomas Becket. There is very clear evidence, however, that Becket's cult spread early to Ireland and some suggestive evidence that by 1177 there may already have been a chapel associated with Becket just outside the walls of the city of Dublin, which may have formed the nucleus for the royal foundation.[29] Following Becket's murder, Becket's cult rapidly gained wide currency, in part owing to its assiduous propagation by the monks of Christ Church Canterbury, who immediately began compiling a series of miracle collections and arranging to have copies sent out to contacts and churches in Latin Christendom.[30] Thomas's early biographer, William fitz Stephen, referred as early as 1173 to the existence of a book of miracles at Canterbury, adding that there were other collections of miracles, including in Ireland, which were committed to memory but not written down.[31] Almost directly following Becket's canonization on 21 February 1173, pilgrims from Ireland, both Irish and Anglo-Norman incomers, began travelling to Canterbury. A series of miracles relating to native Irish pilgrims at Canterbury was included in one of the earliest miracle collections, that of the monk, William of Canterbury, which was compiled between mid-1172 and 1176–7.[32] William recounted a story of an Irish pilgrim leper named Sitricius whom the saint especially favoured by addressing him in the Irish language, telling him that he had been healed. While the forename, Sitric, might suggest an individual of Hiberno-Norse origins, he is described as *de media regione Hiberniae*.[33] Another anecdote concerned Cocubur, described as a kinsman (*cognatus*) of Theodericus, king of Conatia, presumably a reference to Toirdelbach Ua Conchobair, who died in 1156; Conchobar, who was of sufficiently high status to have travelled with *comites* and 'a monk as interpreter', suffered from elephantiasis, and made at least two pilgrimages to Canterbury on the advice of a certain Abbot Marianus.[34] It has tentatively been suggested that he may have been in the party of the Irish delegation that negotiated the Treaty of Windsor on behalf of Ruaidrí Ua Conchobair, king of Connacht, in October 1175.[35] Another miracle related how an Irish youth named Colonius (Columus/Colum?), who begged silver from the

---

works, i, pp 297–300; L. Delisle and E. Berger (eds), *Recueil des actes de Henri II*, 4 vols (Paris, 1909–27) ii, pp 219–21. **29** Ó Clabaigh and Staunton, 'Thomas Becket and Ireland', pp 87–101. **30** For the Canterbury collections, see R. Koopmans, *Wonderful to relate: miracle stories and miracle collecting in high medieval England* (Philadelphia, PA, 2011). On the growth of the cult, see also P. Webster and M.P. Gelin, *The cult of St Thomas Becket in the Plantagenet world, c.1170–c.1220* (Woodbridge, 2016). **31** Ó Clabaigh and Staunton, 'Thomas Becket and Ireland', p. 91. **32** For these dates, see Koopmans, *Wonderful to relate*, p. 140. Books 1–6.90 were compiled between mid-1172–c.1175, with chapters 6.91–168 added *c*.1176–7. **33** *Miracula S. Thomae*, 2.59, in *Materials*, i, p. 221. **34** *Theodorici regis cognatus de Conatia: Miracula S. Thomae*, 1.19, in *Materials*, i, p. 431. He is identified by Robertson as 'Roderick, king of Connaught', but Theodoricus more usually equates with Toirdelbach. Cf. the twelfth-century *Vita Flannani* where Toirdelbach is latinized as Theodricus: W.W. Heist (ed.), *Vitae sanctorum Hiberniae* (Brussels, 1962), pp 281–2, 284, 286–92, 298, 413. By contrast, Ruaidrí is Latinized as Rodericus in the text of the treaty of Windsor: Roger of Howden, *Gesta*, i, pp 102–3; *Chronica*, ii, pp 84–5. **35** M. Bull, 'Criticism of Henry II's expedition to Ireland in William of Canterbury's miracles of St Thomas Becket',

monks of Canterbury to buy an ampulla for Thomas water at the shrine in Canterbury – water reputedly mixed with the saint's blood, 'that most fashionable and sought-after of secondary relics' in the late twelfth century[36] – but instead stole one that he found on the ground and was punished by the growth of a tumour on his neck which, however, was cured when he confessed to an Irish deacon and did penance to the saint.[37] There was also Daniel *natum in Hybernia civitate Duvelina*, who had been sent by his father on business to France where, on detecting signs of leprosy, he entered a monastery and subsequently made a pilgrimage to Canterbury and was cured.[38]

The native Irish pilgrims are especially important testimony to the rapid dissemination of the cult, which may also contextualize, in part, the early support offered by native Irish bishops to the new foundation. Two early thirteenth-century pilgrims' flasks from St Thomas's shrine at Canterbury were found in excavations at John's Lane and Wood Quay in Dublin, as well as one in Waterford, material witness to pilgrim traffic from Ireland to the shrine.[39] The topicality of Becket's murder in Ireland is evidenced also in the account by Gerald de Barri of a conversation that he had with Mauricius (Muirges Ua hÉnna), archbishop of Cashel, around 1185, during which it had been remarked that no one in Ireland had ever won the crown of martyrdom in defence of their faith, to which the archbishop wryly responded that there was now a people come to Ireland who well knew how to create martyrs.[40]

The early miracle collection of William of Canterbury also included anecdotes relating to Anglo-Norman, or English, adventurers in Ireland. One of these concerned a soldier named Walter who was serving in Ireland under Earl Richard and had left two horses that he had worn out in plundering expeditions 'within the enclosure of the chapel of the martyr Thomas, near the city of Dublin'; when these were then stolen Walter enquired of the *capellanus*, 'the chaplain', as to the whereabouts of his horses. The thief, through a miracle of Thomas and because of Walter's devotion to the saint, was led back with the horses to the spot from which he had taken them.[41] Richard, earl of Strigoil, more popularly known as Strongbow, died in April 1176; and although it is well-nigh impossible to rely on the chronology of a miracle story, which implies that Strongbow was alive when the incident occurred, it may nonetheless suggest that before Strongbow's death there was already a chapel *prope Dubliniam* dedicated to St Thomas, with a chaplain

---

Journal of Medieval History, 33 (2007), 108–29 at 121.   **36** Vincent, 'Pilgrimages', p. 34. **37** *Miracula S. Thomae*, 3.54 in *Materials*, i, pp 308–9.   **38** *Miracula S. Thomae*, 2.57, in *Materials*, i, pp 219–20.   **39** B. Spencer, 'Pilgrim souvenirs' in P.F. Wallace (ed.), *Miscellanea I: medieval Dublin excavations, 1962–1981*, ser. B, 2, fasc. 1–5 (Dublin, 1988), pp 33–48 at pp 35–9.   **40** *Giraldi Cambrensis opera*, v, pp 178–9. For Muirges's use of the Latinized forename, Matthaeus, see below p. 38.   **41** *Miracula S. Thomae*, 6.128 in *Materials*, i, pp 545–6. A thief being compelled by a saint to return goods to the place from which they had been stolen was not a miracle unique to Becket. Cf. R. Bartlett, *Why can saints do such great things? Saints and worshippers from the martyrs to the Reformation* (Princeton, NJ, 2013), p. 402.

2.2 A regular canon of St Victor from Mervyn Archdall, *Monasticon Hibernicum* (Dublin, 1786).

and a demarcated precinct.[42] It may have been that chapel which was chosen for the site of Henry II's endowment in March 1177. As to by whom the chapel was built, a charter of Reginaldus, archdeacon of Cork, 1177–82, claimed that oratories in honour of St Thomas had been constructed in many places and that specifically in the city of Dublin 'an oratory had been erected by certain citizens for the veneration of the martyr in whose name it is built in which religious men serve God night and day'.[43] A papal privilege issued to Archbishop Lorcán Ua Tuathail on 20 April 1179, confirming the possessions, rights and privileges of the see of Dublin, listed, among parochial churches, that of St Thomas.[44] This appears to be the church that subsequently became the site of St Thomas's Abbey, from which it may be inferred that it took some time to achieve the establishment of a community of canons. That there was a church, but not an organized religious community at the site, is suggested also by a clause in William fitz Aldelin's charter, ordering that 'whoever by the will of the lord king of England shall be custodian (*custos*) of the said tenement in honour of God and the holy martyr, Thomas, should possess all of the said tenement as freely and fully as any other church holds any tenement freely in England and Ireland'.[45] This suggests that a regular community was not yet *in situ*, but also that the king expected to have a role in the appointment of the head of such a community, as indeed the English crown did subsequently invariably have in St Thomas's Abbey.

How much interest, or input, did Henry II have in his new foundation? Was it he who determined that its religious community should adopt the Rule of St Augustine and the *ordo Sancti Victoris*, that is, the daily customs, of the house of Saint-Victor in Paris? (Fig. 2.2) In the broader context of Henry II's monastic patronage, it is the case that from 1170 onwards Augustinians benefitted more from Henry's patronage than either Benedictines or Cistercians. It is not possible to be definitive, since the earliest evidence for an association between the Dublin community and the customs of Saint-Victor dates from a charter issued around 1192 by John Cumin, first Anglo-Norman archbishop of Dublin, confirming the parochial church of St James within the city to St Thomas's, and in a confirmation of that grant around the same time issued by Mattaeus (Muirges Ua hÉnna), archbishop of Cashel, in his capacity as *legatus natus*, or native papal legate, in Ireland.[46] The eminent ecclesiastical historian, Aubrey Gwynn, surmised that it was

---

42 Internal evidence in Book 6 of William of Canterbury's *Miracula S. Thomae* places the composition of the miracles from chapter 99 onwards *c.*1176–7: Koopmans, *Wonderful to relate*, p. 140.   **43** *In civitate Dublinie a quibusdam civibus oratorium in predicti venerandi martiris nomine est edificatum in quo quia viri religiosi Deo nocte dieque serviunt: RST*, p. 219. William of Canterbury recorded a miracle linked to a chapel that had been built in honour of St Thomas at Waterford by a number of the city's citizens (described as *Angli, Franci and Normanni*): when fire broke out in the city the straw houses of those who had built the chapel were spared: *Miracula S. Thomae*, 6.80 in *Materials*, i, p. 477; Ó Clabaigh and Staunton, 'Thomas Becket and Ireland', p. 92.   **44** Sheehy, *Pont. Hib.*, i, no. 9.   **45** As in note 6 above.   **46** *RST*, pp 236, 284 (*in ecclesia beati martiris Thome extra Dubliniam in ordine Sancti Victoris instituta*); p. 317 (*ad justum peticionem virorum religiosorum canonicorum ecclesie Sancti Thome martiris exoratos esse decernentes ipso canonicos ipsamque*

under the influence of Archbishop Cumin that St Thomas's adopted the customs of Saint-Victor, with its status being raised at the same time from priory to that of abbey.[47] This would broadly coincide with a series of other significant developments in Dublin in 1192, such as the dedication on St Patrick's Day, 17 March, of the new collegiate church of St Patrick established by John Cumin that would later become a second cathedral church for the city of Dublin.[48] It may not be coincidental that it was also a few weeks later on 15 May 1192 that John, son of Henry II, and lord of Ireland since 1185, granted a charter of liberties to the city of Dublin, which freed it from its dependent status 'as a colonial adjunct of Bristol' to whose citizens Henry II had so high-handedly granted Dublin in 1172.[49] John's 1192 charter established the separate identity of Dublin's citizens from its former mother-town and there are other indications for reorganization in the city around that time.[50] It is more likely to have been the archbishop, whose role as an administrator on behalf of the English crown in the nascent colony is well attested, who initiated the enhancement of the status of St Thomas's from priory to abbey

ecclesiam cum ordine Sancti Victoris in ea instituto). As native papal legate, Muirges Ua hÉnna held a legatine synod in Dublin in 1192: *Annals of Inisfallen*, ed. S. Mac Airt (Dublin, 1951), *s.a.* 1192.3. He was present at the consecration of the new collegiate church of St Patrick on 17 March 1192: G.J. Hand, 'The rivalry of the cathedral chapters in medieval Dublin', *JRSAI*, 92 (1962), 193–206 at 195, note 15, citing the manuscript of Dudley Loftus's collection of annals in Marsh's Library, Dublin. Muirges's charter for St Thomas's most likely dates from around that time, though it should be noted that he is also attested in Meath in 1195 when, alongside John Cumin, archbishop of Dublin, he presided over the solemn reburial of Hugh de Lacy (d. 1186) at Bective Abbey, the body having been recovered from the Irish: J.T. Gilbert (ed.), *Chartularies of St Mary's Abbey, Dublin*, 2 vols, Rolls Series (London, 1884–6), ii, p. 276. **47** Gwynn, 'Early history', 13–19. The likelihood of Henry II having determined the choice of the Victorine observance is suggested by V. Davis, 'Relations between the abbey of St Thomas the martyr and the municipality of Dublin, *c.*1176–1527', *Dublin Historical Record*, 40 (1987), 57–65. It could be said to correspond chronologically with the relatively brief period in the 1170s when the Victorine observance was in fashion in England, as evidenced by the foundation of Keynsham (Som.) as a Victorine house, *c.*1172×3, the re-foundation of Shobdon at Wigmore in 1172 and the entry of Victorine canons at St Augustine's, Bristol. See N. Vincent, 'The early years of Keynsham Abbey', *Transactions of the Bristol and Gloucestershire Archaeological Society*, 111 (1993), 95–113 at 100. **48** See H.B. Clarke, 'Cult, church and collegiate church before *c.*1220' in J. Crawford and R. Gillespie (eds), *St Patrick's Cathedral, Dublin: a history* (Dublin, 2009), pp 23–44. The college of canons may have been organized by Cumin during his initial period of residence in Dublin in 1184–6. **49** See G. Mac Niocaill, *Na Buirgéisí, XII–XV aois*, 2 vols (Dublin, 1964), i, pp 78–81; J.T. Gilbert, *Historical and municipal documents of Ireland, AD 1170–1320*, Rolls Series (London, 1870), p. 1; H.B. Clarke, 'The 1192 charter of liberties and the beginnings of Dublin's municipal life', *Dublin Historical Record*, 46 (1993), 5–14 at 9. The draft of the charter could have been produced before the occasion of its sealing. **50** In his capacity as papal legate Muirges Ua hÉnna, probably also in 1192, issued a confirmation of a settlement over disputed lands between John Cumin as archbishop of Dublin and the monks of St Mary's Abbey which had been settled 'before the justiciar of the lord count [John] and the entire *comitatus* of Dublin by writ of Count John and by oath of twelve jurors', Muirges, having received a mandate both from the pope and Count John instructing him to protect the interests of the monks: *Chartularies of St Mary's, Dublin*, i, p. 145. This may be said to attest to organizational activity in Dublin in 1192, including the earliest reference to a county court at Dublin.

and concurrently its adoption of the customs of Saint-Victor, especially since there is otherwise so little evidence after 1177 of Henry II's interest in his new foundation.[51]

This would still leave unresolved the issue of from where the earliest canons for St Thomas's were recruited. The only other Augustinian community within the city walls in 1192 was the cathedral priory of Holy Trinity, Dublin, and it followed the customs of Arrouaise. Outside the eastern perimeter lay the priory of All Hallows, or All Saints, which also followed the observances of Arrouaise. Archbishop Cumin may have wished to promote the status of St Thomas's vis-à-vis these other Augustinian houses by elevating it to an abbey and by introducing an *ordo* that differentiated it from that of Arrouaise. Certainly, in a general protection issued by Pope Innocent III to St Thomas's Abbey on 21 March 1216, the introduction of the *ordo canonicus* according to the Rule of Augustine was attributed to 'J[ohn], of blessed memory archbishop of Dublin', that is, John Cumin (1181–*c*.1212).[52] If this was indeed the case it could hardly have happened before Cumin's arrival in Dublin in August 1184 and the adoption of the Victorine *ordo* could have been later still. This is not to rule out that Cumin may have done so with the interest and encouragement of John as lord of Ireland pursuing an intention of Henry II. The earliest charters refer simply to the 'church of St Thomas' and to *fratres* serving God there, a neutral term that need not even signify canons, to be followed by references to 'canons' and 'regular canons' serving God there.[53] The first mention of the Rule of St Augustine occurs in a papal privilege of Pope Gregory VIII on 9 December 1187, which does not conflict with a chronology of John Cumin having introduced the Rule of St Augustine to St Thomas's.[54] One has to bear in mind that the processes of foundation could be quite slow and involve different stages. While the most important pre-invasion Augustinian foundations in Ireland, notably Armagh, Glendalough, Knock and Termonfeckin, were led by abbots, the majority of post-invasion Augustinian foundations in Ireland, as was also the case in England, were ruled by priors. The precedence of St Thomas's over other Augustinian houses in Dublin may therefore be said to have been emphasized by its abbatial rank.

Might, however, the introduction of the Victorine *ordo* at St Thomas's predate its first attestation around 1192 and have been chosen at the specific instigation of Henry II in 1177, or at some time before the king's death in 1189?[55] The Victorine

---

51 Although consecrated to the see of Dublin in 1181 'through the king's influence', Gerald de Barri described Cumin first being sent to Ireland by Henry II in the autumn of 1184 in advance of John's expedition of 1185 'to prepare the way for his son's arrival there': *Expugnatio*, pp 198–9. 52 Sheehy, *Pont. Hib.*, i, no. 95. 53 Cf. *RST*, pp 13–14, 26–36, 75–7, 210–11, 292. 54 Sheehy, *Pont. Hib.*, i, no. 17. 55 Only one other charter, that of William Aguillun, a tenant of Philip of Worcester, granting ecclesiastical benefices in Kilmallock (Co. Limerick), with a date-range *c*.1192–*c*.1207, referred to the canons as *de ordine Sancti Victoris*: *RST*, p. 236; cf. above, note 46. It too may date more narrowly to around 1192. Among approximately 970 surviving documents relating to St Thomas's, there are only three references to the *ordo Sancti Victoris*, all assignable to around 1192. This may be said to support Gwynn's view that the *ordo* was adopted around that

observance had been introduced into England in 1140, though there were relatively few English houses that adopted it and all were located in the south-west. The largest Victorine community was that of St Augustine's Abbey, Bristol, a city that had long-standing links with Dublin predating Anglo-Norman intrusion into Ireland.[56] The foundation of a house at Bristol was begun around 1140 by Robert fitz Harding, a Bristol urban landholder, close associate of the future King Henry II and supporter of the Angevin cause during the civil war of King Stephen's reign when the city of Bristol had been an Angevin stronghold.[57] Indeed, according to the anonymous Anglo-Norman rhymed history variously referred to as the *Song of Dermot and the Earl, La geste des Engleis en Yrlande* and *The deeds of the Normans in Ireland* it was in the house of Robert fitz Harding 'near to St Augustine's' that Diarmait Mac Murchada, exiled king of Leinster, stayed while in Bristol in the autumn of 1166.[58] At some unknown point Fitz Harding arranged for canons of Saint-Victor in Paris to occupy St Augustine's, a step that was almost certainly inspired by the introduction of canons drawn directly from Saint-Victor in or around 1140 at Shobdon (Herefordshire), the community ultimately settling at Wigmore (Herefordshire).[59] From the 1150s onwards endowments to the Bristol house increased under the patronage of Robert fitz Harding and the future King Henry II,[60] and it may have been as early as 1153 that St Augustine's acquired

---

time. If the supposition that the priory of St John, Clonard, was founded by Hugh de Lacy between 1183 and 1186 and was colonized from St Thomas's, as argued in *MRHI*, p. 163, this would lend further weight to the view that St Thomas's did not at that time follow the Victorine *ordo*, since there is no evidence for its use at Clonard. For the number of 970 documents, see below, p. 46. **56** See A. Gwynn, 'Medieval Bristol and Dublin', *IHS*, 5 (1947), 275–86; J. Bradley, 'A tale of three cities: Bristol, Chester, Dublin and "the coming of the Normans"' in H.B. Clarke and J.R.S. Phillips (eds), *Ireland, England and the Continent in the Middle Ages and beyond: essays in memory of a turbulent friar, F.X. Martin, OSA* (Dublin, 2006), pp 51–66. **57** See R.B. Patterson, 'Robert fitz Harding of Bristol: profile of an early Angevin burgess-baron patrician and his family's urban involvement', *Haskins Society Journal*, 1 (1989), 109–22, who details the several houses owned by fitz Harding in Bristol; idem, 'Bristol: an Angevin baronial caput under royal siege', *Haskins Society Journal*, 3 (1991), 171–81 at 174, for Henry's contacts with Bristol before his accession as king. **58** G.H. Orpen, *Song of Dermot and the earl* (Oxford, 1892), ll 231–5, pp 18–21; E. Mullally, *The deeds of the Normans in Ireland: la geste des Engleis en Yrlande* (Dublin, 2002), ll. 231–5, p. 59. At some point during the financial year 1170–1, Robert became a canon of St Augustine's, Bristol, where he died on 5 February 1171; R.B. Patterson, 'Robert fitz Harding' in *ODNB*, 47, p. 119; D. Walker (ed.), *The cartulary of St Augustine's Abbey, Bristol*, Gloucestershire Record Series, 10 (Bristol, 1998), p. xiv. He is commemorated in the necrology of Saint-Victor under 5 February: *Obiit Robertus filius Herdic ecclesie Sancti Augustini de Bristo canonicus et fundator, de cuius beneficio habuimus x. marcas argenti: Necrologium abbatiae Sancti Victoris Parisiensis*, ed. U. Vones-Liebenstein, M. Seifert and R. Berndt, Corpus Victorinum, Opera ad fidem codicum recollecta, 1 (Münster, 2012), p. 101.9–10. See further below, note 112. **59** See J.C. Dickinson, 'The origins of St Augustine's, Bristol' in P. McGrath and J. Cannon (eds), *Essays in Bristol and Gloucestershire history* (Bristol, 1976), pp 109–26; J.C. Dickinson, 'English regular canons and the Continent in the twelfth century', *Transactions of the Royal Historical Society*, 1 (1951), 71–89 at 73–9. There is no reference to the *ordo Sancti Victoris* among approximately 500 charters of St Augustine's Abbey, Bristol: Walker, *Cartulary of St Augustine's Abbey*, passim. **60** Charters in Walker, *Cartulary of St Augustine's Abbey*, nos 2–15, 66–73.

abbatial status. By 1152 it was in receipt of a confirmation charter from Henry while still count of Anjou. Henry's mother, Matilda, had been responsible for the re-founding of a house of secular canons at St Mary de Voto (Notre Dame du Voeu) at Cherbourg in Normandy, drawing canons from Saint-Victor.[61] John Cumin's charter for St Thomas's *c*.1192, which contains the first reference to the *ordo Sancti Victoris*, was witnessed by Gilbert, a canon of St Augustine's, that is, of Bristol.[62] There is a possibility therefore that Henry may have intended from the outset that his new foundation in Dublin should adopt Victorine observances and be linked institutionally with St Augustine's, Bristol, bearing in mind that in 1172 the king had granted the city of Dublin to his men of Bristol. However, there is no evidence for a formal institutional link between St Thomas's and the Bristol house and, in any case, if there ever was such a plan it may have been abandoned when the city of Dublin secured its freedom from Bristol in 1192. There is certainly evidence for continuing contacts between St Thomas's, Dublin and St Augustine's, Bristol from *c*.1192 and into the second decade of the thirteenth century.[63]

Was there more than a pious intention to Henry II's foundation? Whether or not intentional, the establishment of a monastic community just outside the west gate of the city of Dublin provided a stimulus to the development of the western suburb. The 'West Gate' near which St Thomas's was located, as specified in early charters, was also described as the 'New Gate', the name by which it eventually became permanently known.[64] The expanse to the west of the city was the only area immediately outside the city walls that did not already have a major religious house at the time of the Anglo-Norman intrusion.[65] On the north side across the

---

61 M. Chibnall, *The Empress Matilda: queen consort, queen mother and lady of the English* (Oxford, 1991), pp 179–80.   **62** *RST*, p. 285. Gilbert also witnessed a charter of John, bishop of Leighlin, which cannot be earlier than 1192, since Simon (de Rochfort), bishop of Meath, was also a witness: *RST*, p. 307. One Robert, 'canon of St Augustine', witnessed a charter of Henry de Rochfort which was also witnessed by Simon (de Rochfort), bishop of Meath: *RST*, p. 130. No significance need attach to the fact that four Bristollians, Gilbert La Warre, Thomas Le Martre, and Aelelm and Roger, brothers of Haim of Bristol, witnessed William fitz Aldelin's charter in March 1177, since they constitute but three of fifteen lay witnesses. The context for their occurrence is the grant by Henry II to his men of Bristol in 1171–2 of the city of Dublin *ad inhabitandum*: Mac Niocaill, *Na Buirgéisi*, i, pp 75–6; Gilbert, *Historical and municipal documents*, p. 1. For these Bristol families, see G. O'Keeffe, 'The merchant conquistadors: medieval Bristolians in Dublin' in S. Duffy (ed.), *Medieval Dublin XIII* (Dublin, 2013), pp 116–38. Only Thomas le Martre made a small grant to St Thomas's: *RST*, p. 418; the others patronized St Mary's Abbey, Dublin, the hospital of St John the Baptist, Dublin and the Hospitallers in Kilmainham.   **63** Below, pp 47–9.   **64** Cf. the description *c*.1192 of the bounds of the parish of St James as *a porta nova occidentali Dublin*: *RST*, p. 284.   **65** On the development of the Dublin suburbs, see H.B. Clarke, '*Urbs et suburbium*: beyond the walls of medieval Dublin' in C. Manning (ed.), *Dublin and beyond the Pale: studies in honour of Patrick Healy*, Rathmichael Historical Society (Bray, 1998), pp 45–58; idem, *The four parts of the city: high life and low life in the suburbs of medieval Dublin*, The Sir John T. Gilbert Commemorative Lecture, 2001 (Dublin, 2003); C. Duddy, 'The western suburb of medieval Dublin: its first century', *Irish Geography*, 34 (2001), 157–75 (renders in pence sterling have been mistakenly translated as rents in 'grain', pp 162–3); idem, 'The role of St Thomas's Abbey in the early development of Dublin's western suburb' in S. Duffy (ed.), *Medieval Dublin IV*

Liffey lay St Mary's Abbey, founded in 1139. Located to the east was All Hallows Priory and the convent of St Mary de Hogges, both foundations associated with Diarmait Mac Murchada, while on the south, in what Howard Clarke has described as the 'ecclesiastical suburb', there was a series of pre-invasion churches and precincts, including churches dedicated to Saints Michael, Paul, Peter and Kevin.[66] The street pattern of the western suburb developed linearly along its main artery, that of the present day Thomas Street and continuing on to St James's Street. In the earliest charters in the chartulary of St Thomas's, what would become known as Thomas Street is referred to with relational descriptors, such as 'the great street', the 'great new street', and 'the great street leading to Kilmainham',[67] suggesting, as Clarke has argued, that it was a new route. Did Henry II or his agent, William fitz Aldelin, intend that the new foundation should stimulate development of a western suburb, the area which afforded the most ready access to the hinterland and was also potentially vulnerable to attack? The foundation for Hospitallers at Kilmainham *c.*1174 might similarly be construed as assisting in affording protection to the city on its western approach.

Although Henry II himself gave a relatively small grant of land for the foundation of St Thomas's, from 1185 onwards, when Henry II's son, John, assumed Angevin lordship of Ireland, it acquired a series of privileges within the royal demesne of Dublin or its vicinity. Eight texts of charters that were issued by John as lord of Ireland for St Thomas's between 1185 and 1199 have survived. On his visit to Ireland in 1185 John granted 'the church of St Thomas the martyr beside Dublin and the canons' a carucate of land at Wicklow.[68] Between 1185 and 1189 he granted them first a tenth of beer and then the full customary render of beer and mead due to him from the taverns of Dublin, later to be known as the 'tolboll'.[69] At some time between 1189 and 1199 he gave them a tithe of all rents due to him in the city.[70] On 25 July 1192, John issued a general confirmation of all grants that had, or would be, given to the church of the canons of St Thomas's (this may have been occasioned by its elevation from priory to abbey).[71] On 18 October 1197, he confirmed the church of Kilsallaghan (bar. Nethercross, Co. Dublin) and granted the right to have a boat on the water at Dublin, and a tithe of salmon from the kitchen at Dublin Castle and forbade pleas against the canons to

(Dublin, 2003), pp 79–97.   **66** Clarke, 'Urbs et suburbium', pp 51–4.   **67** E. St J. Brooks (ed.), *Register of the hospital of St John the Baptist without the Newgate, Dublin* (IMC, Dublin, 1936), pp 8, 22 (*c.*1190); *a magno novo vico: RST*, p. 404 (*c.*1195).   **68** *Chartae, privilegia et immunitates* (printed for the Irish Record Commission, Dublin, 1829–30, published 1889), p. 5. See also 'Charta Johannis Dom. Hib. pro protegendo canonicos S. Thomae martyris Dublin. Ex Rot. Ant. penes comitem Midiae 21 H. II. Teste me ipso apud Donour', which implies that John issued a letter of protection at Donore: C. McNeill, 'Harris: collectanea de rebus Hibernicis', *Analecta Hibernica*, 6 (1934), 248–450 at 253. It should, however, read Dovour, that is, Dover.   **69** Gilbert, *Historical and municipal documents*, pp 50–1; *Chartae, privilegia et immunitates*, pp 4–5; cf. H.F. Berry, 'Proceedings in the matter of the custom called tolboll, 1308 and 1385. St Thomas' Abbey v. some early Dublin brewers', *PRIA*, 28C (1910), 169–73.   **70** Gilbert, *Historical and municipal documents*, p. 55; *Chartae, privilegia et immunitates*, p. 9.   **71** *Chartae, privilegia et immunitates*, p. 6.

be heard in any court other than his own and granted them the right to have their own court.[72] A day later, he granted a burgage within the city free from all customs except those pertaining to the crown.[73] As king, on 21 April 1202 he confirmed all endowments and the privilege of their own court of their men and of all plaints and pleas excepting those pertaining to the crown.[74] This was the origin of what became known as the liberty of St Thomas. Nonetheless, the amount of specifically land or ecclesiastical benefices granted by John as lord of Ireland or king remained, as in the case of his father, Henry II, relatively meagre. It was rather the early Anglo-Norman colonists who endowed the house with substantial lands and ecclesiastical benefices in Meath, Leinster and Munster, with an outlying grant from John de Courcy of a church outside the *civitas* of Downpatrick and three carucates of land.[75]

Notable is the support that St Thomas's received from native Irish bishops for the impropriation of churches and ecclesiastical benefices in their dioceses, bishops who had been appointed in the pre-invasion period and whose episcopate spanned the period of the invasion. Among the earliest episcopal charters are confirmations from Lorcán Ua Tuathail (Laurentius), archbishop of Dublin (1162–80),[76] Máel Calann Ua Cléirchén (Macrobius), bishop of Glendalough (a.1176–86),[77] Echtighern Mac Máel Chiaráin (Eugenius), bishop of Clonard (a.March 1177–91),[78] Gregorius Ua hÁeda, bishop of Cork (fl. 1173×7–1182),[79] Matthaeus Ua Mongaig, bishop of Cloyne (fl. 1173×7–1192),[80] Echmílid (Malachias), bishop of Down

---

[72] *Chartae, privilegia et immunitates*, p. 8. The church of St David of Kilsallaghan had been granted by Albert Locart *Deo et operi Sancti Thome de Dublin* and confirmed by Laurentius (Lorcán Ua Tuathail), archbishop of Dublin (d. 14 Nov. 1180): *RST*, pp 166, 285–6.   [73] *Calendar of charter rolls, 1257–1300*, p. 387; *Calendar of documents relating to Ireland, 1285–92*, pp 380–1, no. 839; *Chartae, privilegia et immunitates*, p. 8.   [74] *Chartae, privilegia et immunitates*, p. 131; *Calendar of charter rolls, 1257–1300*, pp 386–8; *Calendar of documents relating to Ireland, 1285–92*, pp 380–1, no. 839. The abbot had made a fine of 15 ounces of gold for the confirmation of his charters with two terms of payment set as the feast of St Michael and Easter, but it was cancelled on the fine rolls because he had letters of quittance from the king which were recorded on the close rolls: *Rotuli de oblatis et finibus*, ed. T.D. Hardy (London, 1835), p. 188; *Calendar of documents relating to Ireland, 1171–1251*, ed. H.S. Sweetman (London, 1875), no. 172. The close rolls for the regnal years 1–5 John have not survived. In 1215, in the context of the restoration of the lordship of Meath to Walter de Lacy, King John confirmed to St Thomas's all their churches in the diocese of Meath: *RST*, pp 6–7.   [75] *RST*, pp 221–3 and passim.   [76] *RST*, pp 285–6 (church of Kilsallaghan granted by Adam Locart; cf. above, note 72).   [77] *RST*, pp 291–2 (church of 'Rathkartin' on the presentation of Hugh de Breskir, tenant of Thomas of Flanders, and ten acres of land and a messuage and all ecclesiastical benefices; cf. p. 168).   [78] *RST*, pp 252–60, 280–1 (ecclesiastical benefices of the lands of Leonisius de Bromiarde; churches of Dunshaughlin, Donaghmore, Killegland, Greenoge, Moyglare, tithes and ecclesiastical benefices of Ratoath).   [79] *RST*, pp 210–11, 220 (all ecclesiastical benefices granted to the *fratres* in the diocese of Cork; also the church of St Nessan).   [80] *RST*, pp 319–20 (ecclesiastical benefices of all the lands of Robert de Altaribus); M.T. Flanagan, '*Conquestus and adquisicio*: some early charters relating to St Thomas' Abbey, Dublin' in E. Purcell et al. (eds), *Clerics, kings and Vikings: essays on medieval Ireland in honour of Donnchadh Ó Corráin* (Dublin, 2014), pp 127–46 at p. 140 (confirmation of all churches and tithes given or to be granted in his diocese; the brothers of St Thomas's to render two *sextarii* of wine or monetary equivalent annually at Christmas for the celebration of the Divine Office in

(*c.*1176–1202),[81] Felix, bishop of Lismore (*c.*1179–res. 1202),[82] Felix Ua Duib Sláine, bishop of Ossory (*a.*1180–1202)[83] and Gilla Críst Ua Mucaráin (Cristianus), bishop of Louth (*c.*1187–93).[84] Episcopal support for communities of canons is well attested elsewhere, notably in France and in England: bishops took particular interest in regular canons because canons undertook pastoral roles within lay society, especially in parishes in their care. St Malachy (d. 1148) provides an earlier example of episcopal promotion of regular canons in the pre-invasion context. One might therefore extrapolate that the Irish bishops who confirmed churches to St Thomas's envisaged that the canons would play a material role in parish organization, if not indeed formation in circumstances where geographically delimited parochial structures were still in the process of formation.

Some of the bishops' charters have a reserving clause, saving episcopal rights. A charter of Gregorius, bishop of Cork, stipulated an annual payment of a *sextarius* of wine on the feast of St Finbarr for the celebration of the Divine Office.[85] Felix, bishop of Lismore, granted the church of St John in Lismore *in mercato ville* in return for an annual render of two wax candles, each two pounds in weight, to be paid on the feast of St Mochuta, patron of Lismore.[86] These are very likely customary episcopal dues that predated the invasion period. Mentions of Irish saints date from the 1170s and 1180s, but noteworthy is how quickly Irish saints disappear from the documents in the registers in dating clauses, to be replaced not only by universal feasts or saints, but also by those with a strong English accent, such as St Augustine of Canterbury, St Alphege, the first martyred archbishop of Canterbury, St Dunstan, St Edmund king and martyr, St Edward the confessor.[87] It emphasizes the colonial dimension of St Thomas's. With the exception of a single instance of St Patrick, no Irish saints occur among feast days in subsequent documents, although an extant martyrology from St Thomas's does include more Irish saints.[88]

---

the church of Cloyne). **81** *RST*, p. 222 (church beside St Patrick's well in Down and three carucates of land and a tithe of all John de Courcy's table). At the dissolution, St Thomas's no longer held the church in Downpatrick. **82** *RST*, p. 213 (church of St John in the vill of Lismore *pro salute domini mei regis Anglie et Johannis filii sui*). **83** *RST*, pp 311–13 (all ecclesiastical benefices in the 'tuatha of Sillethe and Comesehthe and Clonmunehri' and the installation of Arnold, cleric of Thomas de Druhull, *domini fundi*, in the church of Holy Trinity, Balimuchin/ Baligilemucki and the church of St Brigit of Killached). For the identification of Ballimuchin as Dunmore (bar. Fassadinin, Co. Kilkenny) and Killached as Killahy (bar. Crannagh, Co. Kilkenny), see E. St J. Brooks, *Knights' fees in counties Wexford, Carlow and Kilkenny* (IMC, Dublin, 1950), pp 210–11. **84** *RST*, pp 267–8 (confirmation of all ecclesiastical benefices of the vill of 'Macubalother' with tithes of the fee of Osbert [de Clinton] of Coleshill); cf. ibid., pp 49–50. **85** *RST*, pp 209, 211. His successor Murchad Ua hÁeda (*c.*1192–1206) reserved an annual tribute of a pound of wax to be rendered on the feast of St Thomas: ibid., p. 220. **86** *RST*, p. 213. For Mochuta, see P. Ó Riain, *A dictionary of Irish saints* (Dublin, 2011), pp 470–3. Two charters of Thomas, abbot of Glendalough, mention the feast of St Kevin for payment of renders: *RST*, pp 167, 293. **87** Details are derived from the unpublished registers of St Thomas's. **88** These examples are drawn from the unpublished registers of St Thomas's. For discussion of the martyrology in TCD MS 97, see P. Ó Riain, *Feastdays of the saints: a history of Irish martyrologies*, Subsidia Hagiographica, 86 (Brussels, 2006), pp 250–4, 325. Many of the pre-invasion churches appropriated to St Thomas's had dedications to Irish saints.

The most substantial body of evidence for St Thomas's, Dublin, comprises three cartularies or registers, the earliest of which dates from the third quarter of the thirteenth century,[89] and two unpublished early sixteenth-century registers transcribed in 1526.[90] Together, these three registers contain around 1400 documents, but allowing for overlap of texts across the three registers, there are approximately 970 charters and other property deeds that shed light on the abbey's ecclesiastical benefices and landholdings. By comparison, there is much less evidence relating to either the internal organization of the house, its interior religious life, or scholarly activities. The important composite manuscript, TCD MS 97, in various hands of thirteenth–fourteenth-century dates, formerly belonging to St Thomas's Abbey, which came to Trinity College Dublin via the collection of manuscripts belonging to Archbishop James Ussher, is discussed elsewhere in this volume.[91] It includes a copy of the *Liber ordinis* of Saint-Victor, commentaries of Hugh of Saint-Victor and Richard of Saint-Victor[92] on the Rule of St Augustine, various versions of monastic rules, a necrology, and a martryology that has rubrications for the feast of St Thomas and of his Translation, and for St Victor.[93] Although it is not certain whether the manuscript was actually written

---

89 Oxford, Bodleian Library MS Rawl. B. 500, edited by J.T. Gilbert as in note 19 above. **90** Oxford, Bodleian Library MS Rawl. B. 499; Dublin. Royal Irish Academy, MS 12 D 2 (olim MS 98). These registers were transcribed by William Copinger of Cork about whose career little else is known. To the 495 documents in *RST* can be added a further 235 documents in Oxford, Bodl. MS Rawl. B. 499 and a further 238 documents in RIA MS 12 D 2. No original charters from St Thomas's have survived. The earl of Meath, to whose ancestors most of the property of St Thomas's passed at the dissolution of the monasteries, possessed a parchment roll of charters of probable sixteenth-century date that was last seen in 1843: Gwynn, 'Early history', p. 11. In 1876 an imperfect seal matrix of the communal seal of St Thomas's, attributed to the early thirteenth century, was in the possession of Patrick Francis Moran, then bishop of Ossory: M. Archdall, *Monasticon Hibernicum*, ed. P.F. Moran, 2 vols (Dublin, 1873–6), ii, p. 56. **91** See pp 235–51. See also C. Ó Clabaigh, 'Formed by word and example: the training of novices in fourteenth-century Dublin' in K. Stöber, J. Kerr and E. Jamroziak (eds), *Monastic life in the medieval British Isles: essays in honour of Janet Burton* (Cardiff, 2018), pp 41–52. **92** For Richard of Saint-Victor and his probable English origins, see M. Haren, 'St Victor, Richard of (d. 1173?)' in *ODNB*, 48, pp 672–4. **93** Dublin. Trinity College Library, MS 97 (olim B.3.5). For a description, see Colker, *Latin MSS*, i, pp 183–95. This manuscript was used for the edition of the *Liber ordinis* by Jocqué and Milis, as in note 1 above, who also list the contents of the manuscript, pp xxi–xxii. The section on 111 different signs to be deployed in times of silence was translated by H.F. Berry, 'On the use of signs in the ancient monasteries, with special reference to a code used by the Victorine canons at St Thomas's Abbey, Dublin', *JRSAI*, 22 (1892), 107–25; reprinted in *English historical documents, volume 3, 1189–1327*, ed. D. Rothwell (London, 1975), pp 751–5. It corresponds to Jocqué and Milis, *Liber ordinis*, pp 116–34, cap. 25. The only other extant manuscript from St Thomas's is an early fourteenth-century missal with additions of the fifteenth century, now British Library MS Add. 24,198. An entry on f. 54v records *Jacobus Cottrell abas Sancti Thome me possidet*. See *Catalogue of additions to the manuscripts in the British Museum* (London, 1877), p. 21; W. Hawkes, 'The liturgy in Dublin, 1200–1500', *Reportorium Novum*, 2 (1958), 33–67 at 58–62. Two pages are reproduced in colour in *Facsimiles of national manuscripts of Ireland*, ed. J.T. Gilbert, 4 vols, Public Record Office of Ireland (Dublin, 1874–84), iii, plate XVI (the text is the commencement of the ceremonial for the blessing of an abbot of St Thomas's).

in Dublin, it is nonetheless an important witness to scholarly activity within St Thomas's. A number of the texts have glosses and marginalia, some of which have been described by Marvin Colker, who produced the modern detailed catalogue of Trinity's medieval manuscripts, as having an 'an Irish flavour'.[94]

Scholarship and teaching was a distinctive feature of the Saint-Victor community in Paris and in that context it may be noted that around 1365 St Thomas's claimed that it had operated an institution known as the king's alms house, where between twenty-four and sixty *pauperes et scolares*[95] were housed. It had been rebuilt in 1345 but had collapsed by 1365 when the abbey petitioned the king for additional alms.[96] This bears comparison with the almonry boys who are attested at a number of English Augustinian houses from the late thirteenth century.[97] Almonries were buildings established by monasteries, usually at the edge of their precincts, which provided an education for youths who were not novices in the community. The boys received meals, accommodation and education without any requirements to serve in the religious community. The original motive in the case of the English examples appears to have been primarily charitable, as is suggested also in the case of St Thomas's by the coupling of *scolares* with *pauperes*. It is worth noting, in light of attested links between St Thomas's and St Augustine's Abbey, Bristol, that it had such an almonry.[98]

Although there is no indication that Victorine houses in Ireland attended the annual chapter at Saint-Victor in Paris,[99] TCD MS 97 demonstrates awareness of its decrees. A note on the daily meeting in chapter in the *Liber ordinis*, titled *Qualiter fratres mane surgant*, is introduced by the rubric *Istud corrigitur per capitulum generale in domo Sancti Victoris Parisius sic.*[100] While they may not have attended the general chapter, there is, nonetheless, evidence that the Victorines in Ireland maintained a

---

94 Colker, *Trinity College Library, Dublin: descriptive catalogue*, p. 194. **95** Oxford, Bodleian Library MS Rawl. B. 499, ff 23r, 26r–27v. **96** See H.F. Berry, 'Proceedings in the matter of the custom called tolboll, 1308 and 1385', *PRIA*, 28C (1910), 169–73. On 26 May 1363, the king ordered Thomas de Dale and Richard Vynegre to make inquisition concerning the alleged withdrawal of alms and other works of piety in St Thomas's Abbey 'founded by the king's progenitors and of the king's patronage': *Calendar of patent rolls, Edward III, 1361–1364* (London, 1912), p. 368. **97** See N. Orme, 'The Augustinian canons and education' in Burton and Stöber, *Canons*, pp 213–32 at pp 226–9. **98** Ibid., p. 228. **99** Evidence relating to the attendance of English houses is also scant. Nevertheless, David, abbot of Bristol (1216–34), sometime before 1222, along with the abbots of Wigmore and Keynsham, wrote to the abbot and general chapter of Saint-Victor requesting that the English houses should not be excluded from the chapter, and sending the sub-prior of Wigmore as their proctor. A second letter, thanking the abbot and general chapter for their kind treatment of their envoy, highlighted the difficulty that the canons needed to secure permission from the king before they could travel: R. Hill, 'A letter-book of S. Augustine's Bristol', *Transactions of the Bristol and Gloucestershire Archaeological Society*, 65 (1944), 141–56 at 142–3, 155, nos 42–3. It is possible that links were compromised consequent on the loss by King John of large portions of the Plantagenet continental dominions after 1204. A description of how the general chapter of *ordo Sancti Victoris Parisiensis* was conducted is contained in the cartulary of St Augustine's, Bristol: Walker, *Cartulary of St Augustine's Abbey*, pp 403–5. It is independent of the description of the chapter given in the *Liber ordinis*, pp 153–63. **100** Colker, *Latin MSS*, p. 188; *Liber ordinis*, p. 232, l. 16.

relationship of fraternity with other Victorine houses both in Ireland and in England. It has already been noted that a canon of St Augustine's, Bristol, witnessed the charter of Archbishop John Cumin *c*.1192, in which the earliest allusion occurs to the *ordo Sancti Victoris* in relation to St Thomas's.[101] The registers of St Thomas's attest to continuing links with the Bristol community. A charter of Walter de Escotot *c*.1213, whose family had been enfeoffed by Hugh de Lacy in Meath, recorded that he was leasing his land and the vill of Donaghmore (Co. Meath) to the 'canons of St Thomas the martyr beside Dublin' for an annual render of five silver marks, which was to be paid to him each Michaelmas at Bristol in the church of St Augustine.[102] If the canons were prevented by adverse winds, or storms at sea, or the threat of pirates, or any danger affecting a sea journey, from delivering the payment, their delay would not be used as an occasion to bring legal action against them. These conditions had been sworn by Walter in the hundred court of Bristol. When this early absentee landlord made this arrangement he assumed that there would be regular ongoing contact between St Thomas's and St Augustine's.[103] A grant from Robert Poer 1186/7×1192 of the church of Dunshaughlin (Co. Meath) was witnessed by John, abbot of St Augustine's [Bristol], William, abbot of Keynsham, and Elias *famulus* of Keynsham.[104] Keynsham was a Victorine house, founded 1167×72, which was to acquire a series of advowsons in the diocese of Limerick through grants resulting from Hamo de Valognes's acquisitions.[105] A charter of Robert Artur *a*.1223 granting Shanbally beside Kill (Co. Kildare) to the canons of St Thomas was witnessed by John, *serviens* of the canons of St Augustine of Bristol.[106] A charter of Henry de Rochfort, 1194×1218, granting Kilmocar (Co. Kilkenny) to St Thomas's was witnessed by Robert, a canon of St Augustine.[107]

---

101 See above, pp 38–40.   **102** *RST*, pp 15–18.   **103** For the decision of the Escotot family to draw income from their Irish lands rather than carve out a personal role for themselves in Meath, see R. Bartlett, 'Colonial aristocracies of the high Middle Ages' in R. Bartlett and A. Mackay (eds), *Medieval frontier societies* (Oxford, 1989), pp 23–47 at pp 38–9. John, count of Mortain, issued a letter of protection, 1189×99, for the ships of St Augustine's Abbey, Bristol, in England, Wales, and Ireland: Walker, *Cartulary of St Augustine's Abbey*, pp 13–14, no. 21.   **104** *RST*, p. 27. William occurs as abbot of Keynsham, 1167×1172–1205: D. Knowles, C.N.L. Brooke and V.C.M. London (eds), *Heads of religious houses, 940–1216* (2nd ed., Cambridge, 2001), p. 168. John occurs as abbot of St Augustine's, Bristol, 1186/7–1216: ibid., p. 155. 'Brother Elias, canon of St Augustine of Bristol' (*RST*, p. 267), who witnessed a confirmation of Simon (de Rochfort), bishop of Meath, may possibly be the same individual as Elias, *famulus* of Keynsham. Cf. the arrangement reached in 1224 by Peter, abbot of Tewkesbury, with Henry, archbishop of Dublin, whereby the abbot would lease land in Lismore originally granted to them by John, count of Mortain (1189–99), for an annual payment of ten pounds of wax at Michaelmas to be remitted by the hand of the Benedictine prior of St James of Bristol: J.T. Gilbert (ed.), *Crede Mihi: the most ancient register book of the archbishops of Dublin before the Reformation* (Dublin, 1892), pp 59–60; CAAR, p. 45; cf. H.R. Luard (ed.), *Annales monastici*, 4 vols, Rolls Series (London, 1864–9), i, p. 67, where this agreement is dated to 1224.   **105** See J. MacCaffrey (ed.), *The black book of Limerick* (Dublin, 1907), pp 47–8, 83–5, 177. For lands in Waterford at the dissolution, see *EIMP*, pp 352–3. For its foundation history, see Vincent, 'Early years of Keynsham Abbey', 95–113. Hamo de Valognes, a tenant of Earl William of Gloucester, witnessed the latter's foundation charters for Keynsham: ibid., pp 106, 108.   **106** *RST*, p. 94.   **107** *RST*, p. 130. Robert, canon of St Augustine's, also witnessed a charter of Simon de Rochfort, bishop of Meath: E. St J. Brooks,

A late thirteenth-/early fourteenth-century manuscript roll of letters written by the abbot of St Augustine, Bristol, transcribed for use as a formulary, contains four letters written by David, abbot of St Augustine's (1216–34), to the abbot of St Thomas in Dublin.[108] They express gratitude for kindnesses received and the desire that the bonds of affection between the two communities would remain strong.[109] The abbot of Bristol was in Ireland in February 1218 when he sought to intervene in the dispute between William Marshal, lord of Leinster, and Albinus (Ailbe Ua Máel Muaid), bishop of Ferns, who had excommunicated the Marshal.[110] Travel to Ireland was also generated by the fact that St Augustine's, Bristol, acquired properties in Ireland that it still held at the dissolution.[111]

There is one piece of evidence that the canons of Saint-Victor in Paris were aware of the Dublin house, namely a commemoration of the *fratres* and benefactors of the monastery of St Thomas the martyr in Dublin in the necrology of Saint-Victor under 18 May.[112] As to why this entry is placed under that date, this was possibly regarded as the date of foundation, in line with the fact that Henry II issued his charter for St Thomas's at the council of Oxford in May 1177. The king certainly was at Oxford from around 8 May to 22 May, so it may be that St Thomas's celebrated their date of foundation from the granting of this charter,[113]

The Irish cartularies of Llanthony prima and secunda (IMC, Dublin, 1953), p. 35. **108** Sheehy, 'Diplomatica: unpublished medieval charters and letters relating to Ireland', *AH*, 25 (1962), 123–35 at 134–6; R. Hill, 'Letter-book of S. Augustine's, Bristol', 148, 155. Sheehy appears to have been unaware of Hill's article, nor did he publish the letters relating to the prior's intervention in Ireland on behalf of William Marshal. The letter-book contains fifty letters, some heavily abbreviated, of which four are addressed directly to canons of St Thomas's, Dublin. **109** Sheehy, 'Diplomatica', 134. **110** *Rotuli litterarum clausarum in turri Londinensi asservati*, ed. T.D. Hardy, 2 vols (London, 1833–44), i, p. 377; *Calendar of documents relating to Ireland, 1171–1252*, no. 818; Hill, 'Letter book', 144–5, 147, 153, no. 40; cf. p. 151, no. 26; R. Hill, 'Ecclesiastical letter books of the thirteenth century' (MLitt, Oxford, 1936), p. 232. David was one of the executors of the Marshal's will: Crouch, *William Marshal* (3rd ed., London, 2016), pp 174, 235–6, 247. **111** It included the church and vicarage of Ennereilly, Co. Wicklow: *CAAR*, p. 278. For its rectories in Co. Kilkenny, see *EIMP*, p. 208; G. Beechcroft and A. Sabin (eds), *Two computus rolls of St Augustine's Abbey, Bristol from 1491–2 and 1511–12*, Bristol Record Society, 9 (1938), pp 126–7, 268, 269, 284. The Irish possessions are not recorded in the abbey's cartulary, but possessions in the diocese of Ossory that were in dispute with the abbot of Jerpoint and Andrew Avenel are mentioned in a letter of 1218 from David, prior of St Augustine's, to his canons: Hill, 'Letter-book', 146, 153–4. Through the fourteenth and fifteenth centuries the abbots travelled regularly to Ireland to deal with their property there and sought royal licence to appoint deputies to act in their absence. See also B. Smith, 'Late medieval Ireland and the English connection: Waterford and Bristol, *c*.1360–1460', *Journal of British Studies*, 50 (2011), 546–65 at 550. **112** *Commemoratio sollempnis fratrum et benefactorum monasterii Sancti Thome Martyris Dublinie: Necrologium abbatiae Sancti Victoris Parisiensis*, p. 174.9 (as in note 58 above). = The Dublin entry is in the main hand. The necrology dates from the second half of the fourteenth century, though based on earlier material dating to the thirteenth century, with later additions. The necrology is also searchable online at http://www.sankt-georgen.de/hugo/forschung/prosopographie.php. I have not had access to A. Löffler and B. Gebert (eds), *Legitur in necrologio Victorino: Studien zum Nekrolog von Sankt Viktor*, Corpus Victorinum, Instrumenta, 3 (Münster, 2015). **113** R.W. Eyton, *Court, household and itinerary of King Henry II* (London, 1878), p. 214.

even though a foundation stone may have been laid earlier in March 1177, in the presence of the Cardinal legate, Vivianus. More likely, however, the consecration of the church of St Thomas, or its dedication as a Victorine community, may have been commemorated on 18 May. There is also a joint commemoration of a Hugh and Robert of Ireland, otherwise unknown, from whom Saint-Victor had received a gift of eleven pounds.[114]

Another tangential connection with Saint-Victor in Paris resulted from the fact that Lorcán Ua Tuathail, archbishop of Dublin, died in a Victorine community at Eu in Normandy on 14 November 1180. On 20 May 1191, Pope Celestine III wrote to the abbots of Saint-Victor and of St Mary of Eu informing them that the time was not opportune for the canonization of the archbishop, although the pope did not rule it out at a subsequent date. Following six further attempts, canonization was to be achieved in December 1225.[115] The community at Eu evidently had enlisted the support of the abbot of Saint-Victor in Paris to strengthen its first request. After his canonization Lorcán's remains were translated into a new resting place behind the high altar at Eu on 10 May 1226, when the archbishop of Rouen was assisted by the prior of Saint-Victor.[116] The death of Lorcán is recorded in the martryology of St Thomas in TCD MS 97, where he is described as *venerabilis pater noster*.[117] By reason of his death at Eu, Lorcán, who had been a promoter of the Arrouaisian observance and had lived according to its customs in Holy Trinity Cathedral in Dublin, was co-opted into the Victorine congregation. In any case, in March 1177, Lorcán had witnessed William fitz Aldelin's charter of foundation for St Thomas's alongside the papal legate, Cardinal Vivianus, and endorsed the establishment of this new religious house just outside the city walls.

THE PRIORY OF SAINTS PETER AND PAUL, NEWTOWN TRIM

After St Thomas's, the most influential Victorine house in Ireland was the priory of Saints Peter and Paul at Newtown Trim, which was founded in 1202 by Simon de Rochfort, first Anglo-Norman bishop of Meath, having secured permission, as he claimed, from the papal legate, John of Salerno, cardinal priest of the church of Santo Stefano on the Coelian Hill, during his mission to Ireland, to move the cathedral church of his diocese from Clonard to Trim.[118] It is possible that Simon

114 *Item obierunt Hugo et Robertus de Hybernia, de quorum beneficio habuimus xi libras* (under 23 July): *Necrologium abbatiae Sancti Victoris Parisiensis*, pp 216.2–3.   **115** Sheehy, *Pont. Hib.*, i, no. 24; cf. nos 170, 174.   **116** See C. Plummer, 'Vie et miracles de S. Laurent, archevêque de Dublin', *Analecta Bollandiana*, 33 (1914), 121–86 at 162. For the canonization process, see M.V. Ronan, 'St Laurentius, archbishop of Dublin: original testimonies for canonization', *Irish Ecclesiastical Record*, series 5, 27 (1926), 347–64; 28 (1926), 247–56, 467–80; idem, 'St Laurentius, archbishop of Dublin – lessons, hymns, litanies and prayers', *Irish Ecclesiastical Record*, series 5, 28 (1926), 596–612. See also M. Richter, 'Procedural aspects of the canonisation of Lorcán Ua Tuathail' in G. Klaniczay (ed.), *Procès de canonisation au moyen âge: aspects juridiques et religieux / Medieval canonization processes: legal and religious aspects*, Collection de l'école française de Rome, 340 (Rome, 2004), pp 53–65.   **117** Colker, *Trinity College Library, Dublin: descriptive catalogue*, p. 97.   **118** The dating for this

may have been a canon of St Thomas's; if so, his attainment of episcopal office would be in line with the high numbers of Victorine canons who were chosen as bishops in France at this time.[119] Certainly, Simon had strong links with St Thomas's Abbey, as attested in his charters. Not only did he issue a series of charters for St Thomas's relating to land and churches within his diocese of Meath, but more significantly he also occurred frequently as a witness to charters for St Thomas's concerning transactions that were not situated within his diocese. On the evidence of numerous charters issued by him, Simon de Rochfort was a very energetic churchman: a greater number of documents in his name has survived than arguably for any other bishop in medieval Ireland.[120] There are at least thirty-seven, eighteen of which are in favour of St Thomas's and he witnessed many more.[121] In the late thirteenth-century cartulary of St Thomas's he occurs as a witness to more than seventy-eight charters, and significantly not only for transactions within his own diocese of Meath, but also relating to ecclesiastical benefices or lands in Leinster and Munster, where his occurrence as a witness is more unusual and suggests his close ties with St Thomas's.[122] He was present in St Thomas's, for example, on the occasion of the burial of Thomas de Hereford, 1217×1221, when his widow, Beatrice Walter, confirmed grants made by her husband in Éle in north Munster out of her *maritagium*, Beatrice symbolically handing over a book *in manus domini Simonis Midensis episcopi* at the altar in the

---

move to John of Salerno's legation, that is, in 1202, derives from a papal mandate of Pope Boniface IX in 1397 addressed to the archbishop of Armagh, the bishop of Clunen (? Clonmacnois), and the abbot of St Thomas's ordering them to institute a commission of enquiry, following a request from King Richard II for a secular cathedral chapter to be established in the diocese of Meath. The circumstances whereby the cathedral church was located at an Augustinian priory in Newtown Trim had been rehearsed to the pope, namely that it had been moved from Clonard by Simon, bishop of Meath, with the assent of Cardinal John of Salerno as papal legate in Ireland, of Eugenius, archbishop of Armagh, and all the clergy of the diocese, with Simon instituting an Augustinian prior and canons at Newtown Trim. See *CPL*, 5, p. 75. This dates the shift to at or after John of Salerno's legation to the Irish church in 1202. It may be noted, however, that Simon's predecessor, Echtighern (Eugenius) Mac Máel Chiaráin, styled 'bishop of Clonard', recorded an adjudication *communi judicio capituli nostri tocius apud Atrum celebrati* that is, at Áth Truimm/Trim: *RST*, p. 256. In 1216 at a diocesan synod Simon justified the creation of rural deaneries on foot of a decree of Cardinal John Paparo at the synod of Kells, 1152. See below, note 125.   **119** Cf. William of Saltmarsh, bishop of Llandaff (1186–91), with no Welsh connections, who was previously a canon of St Augustine's, Bristol: D. Crouch (ed.), *Llandaff episcopal acta, 1140–1287* (Cardiff, 1988), pp xiv–xv.   **120** Simon was one of three candidates elected to the see of Armagh in 1204, though King John favoured the appointment of Ralph, archdeacon of Armagh: *Rotuli chartarum in turri Londinensi asservati, ad 1199–1216*, ed. T.D. Hardy (London, 1837), p. 133b; *Calendar of documents relating to Ireland, 1171–1251*, no. 200. The bishop *de Midia* was present at Lincoln on 21 November 1200 when William, king of Scots, did homage to King John for lands he held of him in England: Roger of Howden, *Chronica*, iv, p. 141. Simon witnessed ten charters at King John's court in November 1207 relating to land grants or confirmations in Ireland: *Rotuli chartarum*, pp 172–3.   **121** This compares with only one charter, for example, for St Thomas's, from John Cumin, archbishop of Dublin: above, p. 38.   **122** The high numbers relating to the ecclesiastical province of Dublin may, in part, have been determined by the exile from his archdiocese of Archbishop John Cumin between 1197 and 1206.

presence of many knights, citizens, clergy and laity.[123] Simon's involvement with St Thomas's is evident also in the dispute between the canons and the Cistercian monks of Bective Abbey over where the body of Hugh de Lacy, who had been killed at Durrow in 1186, should find its final resting place. This dispute had been referred for adjudication to Pope Innocent III and on 14 February 1205 Bishop Simon, as one of the judges delegate, decided in favour of St Thomas's.[124]

A distinctive feature of the witness lists to charters issued in the name of Simon de Rochfort is the very high number of clerics with the title of *magister*, indicating that those individuals had a *licentia docendi* acquired either from a university or cathedral school. Witnesses to episcopal *acta* reflect most frequently a bishop's *familia* and advisers, those in attendance in his entourage and episcopal court. Simon had around him a group of clerics with administrative training. No fewer than thirteen *magistri* occur in witness lists to his charters. They included Richard de Burford, Simon de Burford, who became archdeacon of Meath, Richard of Norwich, William Piro, William of Hereford, Osbert of Butterley, Gerard de Cusak, Walter de Grene, William de Sancto Dionisio, Simon of Athboy and Masters Raguel, Thurstin and Vivian. All of these persons, needless to say, were drawn from the colonial population and highlight the opportunities that were available to career clerics in Angevin Ireland in the early decades of the invasion. Since the priory church of Saints Peter and Paul at Trim served as Simon's cathedral church, at least some of these *magistri* can be assumed to have been canons at Newtown Trim. One may recall the close links between Saint-Victor and the university in Paris and the Victorine emphasis on education. Simon de Rochfort is also one of the relatively few bishops for whom decrees of a diocesan synod convened in his cathedral church at Newtown Trim (*De novo loco*) in 1216 survive.[125] It legislated for the organization of his diocese into five rural deaneries, claiming that the papal legate, John Paparo, at the synod of Kells in 1152 had decreed that smaller episcopal sees should be suppressed when their incumbents died and converted into churches for arch-presbyters, that is, archdeacons. Just as Simon had legalistically claimed Cardinal John of Salerno's authority for removing his episcopal see from Clonard to Trim in 1202, so for his re-organization of rural deaneries in 1216 he cited the authority of Cardinal John Paparo.

Links between St Thomas's and Newtown Trim are evidenced in a charter of Hugh de Ardiz granting all the ecclesiastical benefices of his land near Ratoath (Co. Meath) to the canons of St Thomas with the proviso that they make an annual

---

123 *RST*, pp 197–8.   **124** *RST*, pp 348–9. Pope Innocent's mandate is not extant. No doubt it was advantageous that the case was heard in the parochial church of Mullingar in the diocese of Meath, which by that date was impropriate to the canons of St Thomas's. In 1209, in consequence of loss of revenue that Bective Abbey may have incurred from the removal of Hugh de Lacy's body, the canons of St Thomas's agreed to compensate Bective with the land of 'Senrath' and contributed twenty marks towards their legal expenses: *RST,* pp 349–52.   **125** Text in G. Bray (ed.), *Records of convocation XVI: Ireland 1101–1690*, Church of England Record Society (Woodbridge, 2006), pp 111–12, reprinted from D. Wilkins, *Concilia Magnae Britanniae et Hiberniae*, 4 vols (London, 1737), i, p. 547, who acquired the text from John Stearne, bishop of Clogher.

payment of 20*s*. to the canons of St Peter's, Trim.[126] The prior of Newtown Trim also witnessed charters relating to St Thomas's Abbey.[127] Relations between the two communities were not without friction, however, as evidenced by a mandate of Pope Alexander IV in 1258 instructing the prior of Newtown Trim to restore property that he had illicitly taken from the abbot and community of St Thomas, Dublin.[128] There was a more dramatic instance in 1364, when King Edward III, on 1 April, ordered an inquisition into a complaint made by John Walsh, abbot of St Thomas's, that Thomas Scurlock, prior of Newtown Trim, and others had entered St Thomas's and carried away jewels and other goods.[129] This did not prevent Thomas Scurlock being elected abbot of St Thomas's in 1365.[130] Unfortunately, little documentary evidence survives for Newtown Trim, but the wealth of its endowment is evidenced by the scale and quality of the remains of its church, discussed below by Tadhg O'Keeffe. The building was begun by Simon de Rochfort and must have been one of the largest in Ireland. The extant remains may afford some indication of what the architecture of St Thomas's in Dublin may have been like, for which little evidence now remains.

THE PRIORY OF ST MARY, BRIDGETOWN

Another Victorine house with impressive extant physical remains is that of Bridgetown (Co. Cork). Bridgetown originated in an initial grant made before 1185 to St Thomas's in Dublin by the brothers, Alexander and Reimund fitz Hugh, of half the church of Kilcummer together with a carucate of land.[131] Kilcummer was subsequently confirmed by Alexander to the *monasterium Sanctae Mariae de Ponte in*

---

126 *RST*, pp 40, 265. Hugh's charter in favour of Newtown Trim, which he mentioned, does not survive. **127** *RST*, pp 44–5, 264, 317, 344. For the agreement in 1259 between the canons of St Thomas's and Hugh, bishop of Meath, with the consent of the prior of Newtown Trim, over the farm of the manor of Kilruddery (Co. Wicklow), formerly held from the canons by Ralph of Nottingham, see ibid., pp 178–9. **128** Sheehy, *Pont. Hib.*, ii, no. 460. **129** *Calendar of patent rolls, Edward III, 1361–1364*, p. 533. On 16 August 1363, an inquisition was ordered to investigate the removal of valuables and other goods from St Thomas's by John Walsh, described as canon of the abbey, though he had, in fact, been abbot since 1353, having been provided by the pope with the subsequent assent of the king: ibid., pp 421, 446. **130** Licence to elect an abbot of St Thomas's was sought on 12 May 1365 following the death of John Walsh before 2 April: https://chancery.tcd.ie/roll/39–Edward–III/patent, nos 6, 11; Gwynn, 'Early history', p. 34. **131** *RST*, pp 216–17. The other half of the church of Kilcummer was granted by Raymond le Gros to St Thomas's, who had been enfeoffed with lands in Cork by Robert fitz Stephen: Flanagan, '*Conquestus and adquisicio*', pp 140–2. Raymond fitz Hugh was killed in Ui Liatháin before 24 June 1185, while Robert son of Philip de Barri was killed at Lismore in the same year: *Expugnatio*, pp 234–5. For the place-name Cell Comair, see E. Hogan, *Onomasticon Goedelicum* (Dublin, 1910), p. 183; J.G. O'Keefe, 'The ancient territory of Fermoy', *Ériu*, 10 (1926), 179–89 at 177, 187, where Cell Comair is described as the burial ground of the two divisions of Uí Béce, and the Uí Chochláin are described as its clerics. In other words, it was the *tuath* church or proto-parochial church of Uí Béce by the early 1100s. For dispute between the bishops of Cloyne and Emly over the church of Kilcummer, which resulted from delineation of

Fermoy and canons under the Rule of St Augustine for the construction of a monastery there, that is, a separate foundation at Bridgetown ensued from an initial grant made to St Thomas's. Alexander's charter dates from *c.* 1202–7 and specifically granted free election of a prior drawn from a member of its community. However, if a suitable candidate could not be found within the house they were to elect one from the priory of Saints Peter and Paul 'of Mide', that is Newtown Trim, or from the house of St Thomas the martyr at Dublin, 'from which they had taken their beginning and the form of their *ordo*'. If no suitable candidate could be found in either of those houses, they were permitted to take one from another house of the same *ordo … vel alibi qui sit ejusdem substantiae ordinis si in praedictis ecclesiis sufficiens et idoneus non inveniatur.*[132] There is a clear echo here of the *Liber ordinis* of Saint-Victor which stated that, if no suitable candidate could be found within a community, a person should be chosen from among those who had left the house, or who observed the *ordo* of Saint-Victor.[133] There is therefore good evidence for links between the three Victorine communities at Dublin, Newtown Trim and Bridgetown in the early decades of the thirteenth century and this may be presumed to have led to exchanges in personnel.

THE PRIORY OF ST WOLSTAN, CELBRIDGE

Victorine houses in Ireland can also be shown to have shared the same lay patrons and benefactors. The foundation at Bridgetown by Alexander fitz Hugh in the first decade of the thirteenth century had been preceded by an earlier grant from Alexander before 1185 to St Thomas's of half the church of Kilcummer. A similar pattern is apparent in the case of the foundation of St Wolstan's Priory in Celbridge. It was founded by Adam de Hereford, the de Hereford family being among the earliest and most generous benefactors of St Thomas's.[134] The burial of

diocesan boundaries in the first half of the twelfth century, see P. MacCotter, *A history of the medieval diocese of Cloyne* (Dublin, 2013), pp 52, 56–7, 69–70, 182–3. **132** Charter in W. Dugdale and R. Dodsworth, *Monasticon Anglicanum*, new edition; ed. J. Caley, H. Ellis and B. Bandinel, 6 vols in 8 (London, 1817–30), vi, II, p. 1146, from an inspeximus of King Edward I, 11 February 1290; English translations in *Calendar of charter rolls, 1257–1300*, pp 341–2; *Calendar of documents relating to Ireland, 1285–1292*, no. 587. In December 1289 the prior and convent of Bridgetown had petitioned for confirmation of the charter of Alexander fitz Hugh and letters of protection: *Calendar of documents relating to Ireland, 1285–1292*, no. 558. Alexander's charter postdates the foundation of Saints Peter and Paul, Newtown Trim *c.* 1202 and predates 8 November 1207 by which date the witness, Philip de Barri, brother of Gerald de Barri, had died and his lands in Cork had been confirmed to his son, William, by King John: *Rotuli chartarum*, p. 172a; *Calendar of documents relating to Ireland, 1171–1252*, no. 340. **133** *Secundum consilium religiosorum alibi quaerenda est et eligenda, praecipue si fieri potest de his qui de domo nostro exierunt vel qui nostrum ordinem tenent:* Jocqué and Milis, *Liber ordinis*, p. 19, cap. 2, 31–2. At least a dozen French abbeys following their acceptance of Victorine customs received as abbot a canon of Saint-Victor, Paris: L. Jocqué, 'Les structures de la population claustrale dans l'ordre de Saint-Victor au xiie siècle: un essai d'analyse du *Liber ordinis*' in Longère, *L'abbaye Parisienne de Saint-Victor*, pp 53–95 a p. 62, note 21. **134** See *RST*, pp 75–91, 97–8, 121–4, 142–4, 157–9, 194–6, 298–300, 316, 328, 358–9, 362–7.

Thomas de Hereford there has already been noted.[135] Indeed, so important was the de Hereford family to St Thomas's that the canons uniquely inserted a memorandum into their register about the family's relationships and marriages.[136] Adam de Hereford's grant to Prior Richard, described as the founder of the said place, of lands by the Liffey, along with the pre-invasion churches of Donaghmore and Donaghcumper, is recorded in an unpublished charter witnessed by John Cumin, archbishop of Dublin, William Piro, bishop of Glendalough, and the ubiquitous Simon de Rochfort, bishop of Meath.[137] The charter may be presumed to be no earlier than 21 April 1203, when St Wulfstan was canonized by Pope Innocent III, and no later than the death of William Piro, bishop of Glendalough (before 30 July 1212). Although there is no specific allusion to St Wolstan's as Victorine – indeed the first such mention occurs in a papal letter as late as 1398 – the patronage of Adam de Hereford and the witnessing of his charter by Simon de Rochfort, bishop of Meath, leaves little doubt that it was Victorine from its foundation.[138]

THE PRIORY OF ST CATHERINE, LEIXLIP

The de Hereford family were also connected to the establishment of another priory near Dublin, that of St Catherine in Leixlip. In 1236 it was claimed that this was a dependency of St Thomas's in a papal mandate of Pope Gregory IX instructing the bishop of Meath, the abbot of St Mary's, Trim, and the prior of Newtown Trim to command the prior and convent of St Catherine to show obedience and reverence to St Thomas's, which *multis retro temporibus* had full correction of that convent in both spiritualities and temporalities.[139] The judges delegate, however, decided that St Catherine's should be free from obedience or correction, but should pay an annual render of twenty pounds of wax to the abbot of St Thomas's. Yet the abbot of St Thomas's had witnessed the two composite foundation charters of Warrisius Peche, suggesting at the very least that St Catherine's drew its canons from St Thomas's. Adam de Hereford, his son, Stephen, and Warisius Peche, who married a sister of Stephen de Hereford, were beneficiaries of St Catherine's.[140]

---

135 Above, p. 51.   **136** *RST*, pp 102–4.   **137** BL Add. MS 4787, f. 106 (manuscript of Sir James Ware); BL Lansdowne MS 418, f. 16 (manuscript of Sir James Ware); NLI MS 13, p. 231 (transcripts by Walter Harris). On 20 June 1626 Ware made extracts (BL Lansdowne MS 418, f. 16) from a register of St Wolstan's, the first entry being a summary of Adam de Hereford's charter taken from f. 1a of the original register which presumably was also the source for Ware's fuller transcript in BL Add. MS 4787.   **138** *CPL*, 5, p. 106.   **139** Sheehy, *Pont. Hib.*, ii, no. 229. For a papal letter of protection for St Catherine's, 27 July 1227, see ibid., no. 185, where reference is made to the Rule of St Augustine but not to subordination to St Thomas's. Sheehy published charters of Warrisius Peche and of Stephen de Hereford: ibid., pp 19–21. For Adam de Hereford as a benefactor of St Catherine's, see ibid., p. 67. There is a series of unpublished charters of Stephen de Hereford and his brother, Godfrey, for St Catherine's in Oxford, Bodl. MS Rawl. B. 499, ff 90r–93r.   **140** *RST*, p. 103, where Warisius is stated to have married a daughter of Stephen de Hereford. According to Brooks, *Knights' fees*, pp 207–8, this cannot be correct, and

Although Warisius Peche, as lord of Lucan, identified himself as the founder of St Catherine's and his was the most comprehensive charter and the one that the canons presented for confirmation to King Henry III,[141] it is apparent from unpublished charters that Adam, Stephen and Godfrey de Hereford gave earlier grants to St Catherine's, including the original site.

In 1314, it was claimed that the priory of St Catherine used to have eight canons celebrating divine service, but was now so impoverished and in debt that it could scarcely support two canons and that the prior had borrowed money under a contract of usury which was illegal.[142] Crucially, this impoverishment predates both the Bruce invasion, which began in May 1315, and the great European famine of 1315–17, which also affected Ireland. By 1323, the prior of St Catherine's, Richard Turnour, petitioned for its annexation to St Thomas's. It was stated that the number of canons was reduced to three, that they were often compelled to beg *more pauperum* for vital necessities, that the church and house and other buildings were in a state of collapse and there was insufficient means to repair the church. The annexation was completed with archiepiscopal and royal approval by 1327.[143] Thereafter, St Catherine's became an appropriated church served by a canon of St Thomas's and this accounts for the fact that its charters and documentation relating to its annexation were transcribed in the early sixteenth-century register of St Thomas's.[144]

THE PRIORY OF ST JOHN THE EVANGELIST, ENNISCORTHY

Another dependency of St Thomas's was located at Enniscorthy (Co. Wexford). A charter in the thirteenth-century register of St Thomas's records that Gerald de Prendergast granted the *domus Sancti Johannis* beside Enniscorthy to be a cell of the abbot and convent of St Thomas, Dublin, so that it should be under the Rule of St Augustine and the *consuetudines* of St Thomas's.[145] As Gerald stated in his charter, his father and mother were buried in the *domus* at Enniscorthy. There was a pre-invasion church site at Enniscorthy associated with St Senan of Scattery Island.[146] Gerald's father, Philip de Prendergast, had been a benefactor of St Thomas's Abbey. Not only had Philip witnessed a series of early Cork charters for St Thomas's[147]

it was rather that Warisius married Stephen's sister, Alda or Auda, as her second husband following the death of William Pippard in 1227.   **141** *Calendar of charter rolls, 1257–1300*, p. 93; Sheehy, *Pont. Hib.*, ii, pp 20–1. Warisius is also named as the founder in letters patent issued by Edward III authorizing the unification of St Catherine's with St Thomas's: *Calendar of patent rolls, Edward III, 1327–1330*, p. 187.   **142** Close roll 7 Edward II at http://chancery.tcd.ie/document/close/7edward–ii/12.   **143** *Calendar of patent rolls, Edward III, 1327–1330*, p. 187; *Calendar of patent rolls, Edward III, 1338–40*, p. 94.   **144** Oxford, Bodl. MS Rawl. B. 499, ff 85r–95v.   **145** *RST*, pp 186–8. At the dissolution the vicarage of St John was in the possession of St Thomas's: *EIMP*, p. 45.   **146** Ó Riain, *Dictionary of Irish saints*, p. 558, which details the occurrence of Enniscorthy in the hagiographical dossier of Senan.   **147** *RST*, pp 214 (*a.* 1185), 221 (*a.* 1199), 226; cf. pp 155, 157, 226, 338. He also witnessed Alexander fitz Hugh's charter for Bridgetown. See above, note 132.

but, along with Philip de Barri (d. 1207), he had granted two carucates of land at Shandon beside the bridge of Cork to the canons of St Thomas's,[148] which were subsequently exchanged with St Thomas's for two carucates beside the house of St John of Enniscorthy.[149] In 1226×7 Philip de Prendergast had reached an agreement with John de St John, bishop of Ferns, following a protracted dispute whereby he and his wife relinquished disputed lands in return for a grant from the bishop of the church of Enniscorthy, which was located near the de Prendergast castle there.[150] That agreement was confirmed 1230×31 by Philip's son and successor, Gerald, who had succeeded as Philip's heir by 1229, when he did homage for his father's lands.[151] Again, there is a discernible pattern of the same lay patrons being associated with more than one Victorine house. A confirmation issued by the bishop of Ferns stated that the canons of St Thomas's undertook to supply a prior and four canons for the church at Enniscorthy.[152] Conventual life at Enniscorthy was never developed on any scale (as was the case also at St Catherine's Leixlip) and at the dissolution the church of St John, Enniscorthy, was impropriate as a vicarage to St Thomas's Abbey.[153]

THE PRIORY OF ST CATHERINE, WATERFORD

Evidence for a priory dedicated to St Catherine at Waterford first occurs in 1207, when King John issued letters of protection for it.[154] A papal confirmation of Innocent III on 14 May 1210 took the prior and canons of St Catherine of Waterford under his protection, describing them as following the Rule of St Augustine and the *institutionem fratrum domus Sancti Victoris Parisiensis* and confirming their possession of eight pre-invasion churches.[155] Innocent also confirmed land

148 Philip was son and heir of Maurice de Prendergast, who arrived in Ireland with Robert fitz Stephen in 1169 and married Maud de Quency: Brooks, *Knights' fees*, pp 130–4. **149** *RST*, p. 186. The chapel of St Catherine, the tithes and one burgage in the tenement was excluded from the exchange. This affords early evidence for a dedication to St Catherine among the churches of St Thomas's. **150** Details were enrolled in 1595 by Sir Henry Wallop, who had secured a grant of Enniscorthy from Queen Elizabeth. For an English translation, see J.P. Prendergast, 'An ancient record relating to the families into which were married the co-heiresses of Thomas fitz Anthony, seneschal of Leinster', *Journal of the Kilkenny and South-East of Ireland Archaeological Society*, 5 (1864), 139–53 at 147–8; abstract in J. Morrin (ed.), *Calendar of patent and close rolls of chancery in Ireland, from the reigns of Henry VIII, Edward VI, Mary, and Elizabeth*, 3 vols (Dublin, 1861–3), ii, p. 329. **151** *Calendar of close rolls, 1227–1231* (London, 1902), p. 208. **152** *RST*, p. 190. It is noteworthy that no other charters relating to Enniscorthy were copied into the registers of St Thomas's. **153** *EIMP*, p. 45. **154** *Rotuli patentium*, p. 76b; *Calendar of documents relating to Ireland, 1171–1251*, no. 338. In a charter of liberties issued by King John to the city of Waterford on 3 July 1215, there is an allusion to the 'pool (*pulla*) of St Catherine': *Chartae, privilegia et immunitates*, pp 13–14 (from Rot. pat. 15 Jac. I, p. 5, m. 5); cf. Mac Niocaill, *Na Buirgéisi*, i, p. 277, § 54. The date given as 1205 is incorrect, as is plain from the place of issue and list of witnesses, and should be 1215. On the doubtful authenticity of parts of the charter, see G.H. Orpen, *Ireland under the Normans*, 4 vols (Oxford, 1911–20), iv, pp 313–14. **155** Sheehy, *Pont. Hib.*, i, no. 69. For identification of place-names, see K. Nicholls, 'Some place-names from

donated by Elias fitz Norman for the building of a grange. Elias was a benefactor also of St Thomas's in Dublin, to which he granted half of the *tuath* of Mathelcon/Maige Dá Conn in the diocese of Ferns.[156] He also witnessed five charters for St Thomas's Abbey.[157]

THE PRIORY OF ST MARY, MUCKAMORE

Muckamore (Co. Antrim) is assumed to have been a Victorine house, though the evidence that this early church site associated with St Colmán Elo[158] was Victorine is quite late. The assumption of a foundation date *c.*1183 is based in the first instance on a charter of John de Courcy, 1192×93, in favour of the church of St Patrick of Down which was witnessed by, among other ecclesiastics, G. of St Thomas, P. of Muckamore, and W. of Carrickfergus, priors.[159] The co-location of G. of St Thomas and P. of Muckamore has been interpreted as significant on the assumption that G. of St Thomas refers to St Thomas's in Dublin.[160] However, G. as prior of St Thomas's is otherwise unknown. Simon is named as prior in the 1187 letter of papal protection for St Thomas's and he is assumed to be the individual of the same name who occurs as abbot from 1192 until 1225. All the other witnesses to de Courcy's charter are drawn from Ulaid, so that a witness from Dublin would represent an anomaly. In fact, G., prior of St Thomas, should be identified as head of the Augustinian priory of St Thomas the martyr at Downpatrick, which was founded by John de Courcy as a dependency of St Mary's, Carlisle, and which came to be known as Toberglory.[161] The earliest reference to Muckamore as a Victorine house dates from 18 August 1474 in a papal mandate which refers to the 'prior of St Mary's Muckamore of the order of St Victor'.[162] The seventeenth-

---

Pontificia Hibernica', Dinnseanchas, 3:4 (1969), 85–98 at 88. **156** *RST*, pp 183–4. Maige Dá Conn is identified as Moyacomb alias Clonegall in bar. Scarawalsh, Co. Wexford, on the borders of Co. Carlow: Brooks, *Knights' fees*, pp 66–7; L. Price, *Place-names of Co. Wicklow*, 7 vols (Dublin, 1945–67), vi, pp 377–9. Elias belonged to the second generation of colonial settlers and was an associate of Theobald Walter (d. 1205) who arrived in Ireland in 1185. **157** See *RST*, pp 97, 105, 109, 367. **158** For this saint, see P. Ó Riain, *Dictionary of Irish saints*, pp 203–5. **159** *MRHI*, pp 188–9. For de Courcy's charter and its date, see G. Mac Niocaill, 'Cartae Dunenses: 12ú–13u céad', *Seanchas Ard Mhacha*, 5 (1970), 418–28 at 421. It should be stressed that the date 1183 does not derive from the charter evidence, but rather from the annals of Chester, which recorded that de Courcy made a grant of land to Chester Abbey in 1183 for the establishment of a Benedictine priory at Downpatrick: *Annales Cestrienses or chronicle of the abbey of St Werburg at Chester*; ed. R.C. Christie, Lancashire and Cheshire Record Society Publications, 14 (1886), pp 28–9. **160** As in L. McKeown, 'The abbey of Muckamore', *Down and Connor Historical Society's Journal*, 9 (1938), 63–70 at 64. **161** See *MRHI*, p. 170. The substance of de Courcy's charter is recited in an inspeximus of King Edward II enrolled on the patent rolls in 1318 and printed in Dugdale, *Monasticon Anglicanum*, vi, II, pp 1146–7; cf. *Calendar of patent rolls, Edward III, 1317–1321*, p. 224. On 28 January 1329, Gilbert de Morlound, a canon of St Mary's, Carlisle, whom the prior of St Mary's Carlisle was sending to Ireland, was granted safe conduct to his cell of St Thomas the martyr in Down to view the disposal of his goods there: ibid., p. 270. **162** *CPL*, 13, pp 370, 532–3. Cf. a mandate in 1487 in the register of Octavian de Palatio,

century antiquarian, Sir James Ware, who did so much to preserve sources relating to Irish ecclesiastical houses, did not list Muckamore as a Victorine house and this may be significant, given that he had access to a register that had been compiled in 1356 by Laurence, prior of Muckamore, from which Ware transcribed extracts on 25 February 1624.[163] However, as we have seen, specific allusions to the *ordo Sancti Victoris* are scarce in twelfth- and thirteenth-century sources. If Muckamore was indeed established as a Victorine house in the late twelfth century, its history was very different to the other houses, since it cannot be shown to have had links with those other Victorine houses that were located in areas that had come securely under English control and were staffed by canons of English descent. The case of Muckamore serves to highlight the paucity of evidence in relation to specifically Victorine observances.

CONCLUSION

There are serious shortcomings in the sources for Victorine houses in Ireland, which are very uneven, with far more evidence relating to the most important house of that *ordo*, St Thomas's Abbey, Dublin. Along with its three extant property registers, its location in close proximity to Dublin Castle meant that it figured in the records of English royal administration in Ireland more frequently than any other Victorine house. Charters constitute by far the most common type of record for all the Victorine houses: almost all the evidence for interaction between individual houses and their lay patrons is derived from charters. Unfortunately, the formulaic nature of charter diplomatic is not very informative about the reasons why in witness lists particular individuals occur at specific places at certain times. There were undoubtedly exchanges of personnel, yet the level of fraternity between houses should not be exaggerated, since there were also cases of inter-Victorine disputes, as is evident in the case of St Thomas's and Newtown Trim and St Catherine's, Leixlip.

To what extent was there a distinctive vocation and communal identity among Victorines in medieval Ireland as adherents of a particular *ordo* and how far would the laity have identified clear differences between Victorines and other Augustinian canons? Certainly, the Victorines shared with other Augustinian communities in Ireland the overriding importance of their possession and exploitation of parish churches, which was a key component of their income, and such churches were also the most frequent way in which they interacted with the laity. It is significant that among the first documents in the thirteenth-century register of St Thomas's is a blank pro-forma letter of presentation for a vicar by the canons to the relevant

archbishop of Armagh (1478–1513), referring to *Carolum Odurnyn, assertum priorem de Mucmor … ordinis Sancti Victoris sub regula Sancti Augustini*: M.A. Sughi (ed.), *Registrum Octavianai alias Liber Niger: the register of Octavian de Palatio, archbishop of Armagh (1478–1513)*, 2 vols (Dublin, 1998), ii, p. 505. **163** Reeves, *Ecclesiastical antiquities*, p. 98. English summaries of those abstracts are provided in McKeown, 'Abbey of Muckamore', pp 65–6.

diocesan bishop.[164] And on the evidence of the registers of St Thomas's, by far the most common property disputes were over advowsons of parochial churches.

Victorine houses in Ireland also share in common with other Augustinian communities in Ireland and elsewhere the chronology of their foundation, that is, largely confined to the late twelfth and early thirteenth centuries. The support of Irish bishops for the appropriation of parish churches was critical in the early decades. Place-names such as Donaghmore, Donaghcumper, Dunshaughlin, Kilcummer, indicate that many, if not most, were early church sites. That early episcopal support was perpetuated by the first Anglo-Norman appointees, of whom the most supportive was Simon de Rochfort, bishop of Meath, founder of Newtown Trim, and who emerges as a key figure for Victorine communities. Also important were William Piro, first Anglo-Norman appointee to the see of Glendalough, and John, bishop of Leighlin. Certainly in an Irish context, what was most distinctive about Victorine houses, by contrast, for example, with the Premonstratensians who secured both Gaelic and Anglo-Norman patrons, was that they were all founded by colonists and staffed by canons drawn from the Anglo-Norman community. This, in part, accounts for exchanges of personnel between Victorine communities, though it was also a feature attested among Victorines outside Ireland. Only one house, the royal foundation of St Thomas's, had abbatial status, and it alone also had a number of dependencies. Yet despite being a royal foundation, it can be argued that St Thomas's owed more to episcopal than to royal support, as is apparent from its registers. Compared with the close relations, for example, between the abbey of St Denis in Paris and the kings of France, or Westminster Abbey and the kings of England, St Thomas's did not derive comparable benefits from English royal patronage, though this was in part owing to its peripheral location far from the royal court. There is suggestive evidence that King John stayed in St Thomas's Abbey during his visit in 1210.[165] In 1227, Henry III was invited by the abbot to lay the foundation stone of a new church, though the king delegated this to his justiciar in Ireland.[166] In 1240, Henry ordered 800

---

164 *RST*, p. 4.   **165** This may be deduced from a reference in a charter of 1219 to the *aula domini regis apud Sanctum Thomam*: *RST*, p. 147. For the dating of this charter to 1219, see ibid., pp 145–6. This suggests that on his visit to Ireland in 1210 King John stayed at St Thomas's Abbey while at Dublin from 28 to 30 June and from 18 to 24 August. In 1488, there is mention of the great chamber, called 'the king's chamber', as the place where on 21 July Sir Richard Edgecomb received the homage and allegiance of the nobles who had declared for Lambert Simnel: Voyage of Sir Richard Edgecumbe at http://www.ucc.ie/celt/published/E480001-001/index.html. On 30 October 1540, when an extent was made at the time of the dissolution, St Thomas's was described as having 'a chamber and an upper room and other buildings, called the king's lodging, suitable for the king's deputy and the king's commissioners repairing to Ireland: *EIMP*, p. 26. Neither in 1219, nor 1488, nor 1540 was the king named, but remarkably in 1634 there is a reference to 'Kinge John's chamber' in a statement prepared for legal proceedings, on behalf of Lord Edward Brabazon, whose ancestor acquired a substantial portion of the property of St Thomas's at the dissolution and who took a case against the mayor and commonality of the city of Dublin in that year: H.F. Berry, 'Notes on a statement dated 1634, regarding St Thomas' Court and St Katherine's churchyard, Dublin', *JRSAI*, ser. 5, 37 (1907), 393–6 at 395.   **166** *Rotuli*

candles to be lit to celebrate the feast of St Thomas in the abbey church in Dublin.[167] He had hoped to rebuild St Thomas's on the scale of Westminster Abbey, though the plan never materialized.[168]

As for links of Victorine houses in Ireland with those abroad, there is some slight indication of contact between St Thomas's and Saint-Victor in Paris, with somewhat greater evidence for more sustained links between St Thomas's and the abbeys of St Augustine in Bristol and Keynsham. For the internal organization and regular life of the communities and numbers of canons within individual houses, evidence is more limited. The *Liber ordinis* of Saint-Victor mentions no fewer than twenty-three claustral office-bearers, but only the offices of abbot, prior, subprior, precentor and sacristan are mentioned in the charters of St Thomas's Abbey, to which can be added the *cellerarius*, who is addressed in a letter of David, abbot of St Augustine's, Bristol (1216–34).[169] Detailed analysis of the very valuable manuscript, TCD MS 97, which formerly belonged to St Thomas's Abbey, Dublin, and crucially contains a copy of the *Liber ordinis*, will doubtless shed more light on the interior life of at least the Dublin community, which was by far the most important of the Victorine houses in medieval Ireland.[170]

litterarum clausarum, ii, p. 199b; *Calendar of documents relating to Ireland, 1171–1251*, no. 1553. **167** *Close rolls of the reign of Henry III, 1237–1242* (London, 1911), p. 227; *Calendar of documents relating to Ireland, 1171–1251*, no. 2497. **168** A. Duggan, 'The cult of St Thomas Becket in the thirteenth century' in M. Jancey (ed.), *St Thomas Cantilupe, bishop of Hereford: essays in his honour* ([Hereford], 1982), pp 21–44 at p. 31, note 70. **169** Sheehy, 'Diplomatica', 135. For the duties of *cellerarius*, see *Liber ordinis*, pp 37–41. For mention of the precentor, equated with the *armarius*, see ibid., p. 129, l. 120. **170** See the contribution by C. Ó Clabaigh in this volume.

The monasteries of the canons of Prémontré, *c.*1180–*c.*1607

MIRIAM CLYNE

THE ORDER OF PRÉMONTRÉ AND SETTLEMENT IN IRELAND

The Premonstratensians became the largest order of medieval regular canons.[1] Norbert of Xanten's first community at Prémontré, in the diocese of Laon, took the vow of profession as Augustinian canons at Christmas 1121.[2] Further monasteries were founded in the vicinity, but on Norbert's election as archbishop of Magdeburg in Saxony (1126–34), the congregation of independent houses held together under his leadership was threatened with dissolution. It became of immediate concern to draw up constitutions to augment the basic Rule of St Augustine and to define the position of Prémontré in regard to the group of monasteries. These tasks were overseen by Hugh of Fosses, the first abbot of Prémontré (1128–61), who was, in effect, the founder of the order.[3] Under Hugh's direction, the communities took on a distinctly monastic character, based on the principles of the Cistercian *Carta caritatis* (the Charter of Love), but the Premonstratensians made their institution suitable for Augustinian canons who lived as monks. They were distinct from other religious orders in their liturgy, discipline and white clothing. Hugh put in place the central administration, the general chapter, held at Prémontré on the feast of St Denis (9 October). The

---

[1] Fr Norbert Backmund gives 578 foundations which he considered authentic. See N. Backmund, *Monasticon Praemonstratense, id est historia circariarum atque canoniarum candidi et canonici ordinis praemonstratensis*, 3 vols (Straubing, 1949–56). James Bond estimates that a total of 700 houses were occupied in the Middle Ages and, at any given time, there were approximately 500 in existence. See J. Bond, 'The Premonstratensian order: a preliminary survey of its growth and distribution in medieval Europe' in M. Carver (ed.), *In search of cult: archaeological investigations in honour of Philip Rahtz* (Woodbridge, 1993), pp 153–85, at pp 153, 159.　**2** The twelfth-century hagiographies on Norbert are: R. Wilmans (ed.), *Vita Norberti archiepiscopi Magdeburgensis* in G. Pertz and others (eds), *Monumenta Germaniae historica*, scriptores, 30 vols (Hanover, 1826–92), xii, 670–706 (*Vita A*); J.-P. Migne (ed.), *Vita Sancti Norberti in Patrologiae cursus completus*, series Latina, 221 vols (Paris, 1841–64), clxx, cols 1253–1350 (*Vita B*). *Vita A* and the addenda in *Vita B* are translated in T.J. Antry and C. Neel, *Norbert and early Norbertine spirituality* (Mahwah, 2007), pp 126–91.　**3** For debate on the formation of the institutional order, see, for example, S. Weinfurter, 'Norbert von Xanten und die Entstehung des Prämonstratenserordens' in K.-H. Ruess (ed.), *Barbarossa und die Prämonstratense*r, Schriften für staufischen Geschichte und Kunst, 10 (Göppingen, 1989), pp 67–100; G. Melville, 'Zur Semantik von ordo im Religiosentum der ersten Hälfte des 12. Jahrhunderts. Lucius II., seine Bulle vom 19. Mai 1144, und der „Orden" der Prämonstratenser' in I. Crusius and H. Flachenecker (eds), *Studien zum Prämonstratenserorden* (Göttingen, 2003), pp 201–24.

statutes enacted by the central authority regulated daily life at the monasteries.[4] All abbots were obliged to attend annually;[5] however, in practice those closer geographically to Prémontré were better represented than abbots from distant territories. The frequency with which Irish abbots participated in the general chapter is not known.

Monasteries were established in the two cultural traditions of Ireland.[6] Canons were sent *c.*1180 from the Scottish abbey of Dryburgh to St Mary's at Carrickfergus (Woodburn) and soon after to Dieux la Croisse (White Abbey) as part of John de Courcy's settlement of his newly conquered Anglo-Norman lordship of Ulster (Fig. 3.1).[7] Approximately twenty years later, Prémontré colonized Holy Trinity at Tuam in Connacht.[8] The introduction of the Premonstratensians to the Gaelic province was supported by Archbishop Felix Ua Ruanada (1202–35) and King Cathal Crobderg Ua Conchobair (1189–1224). Their arrival took place when the archbishop was initiating measures to dissolve the traditional church structure, and the white canons would bring monastic practices from mainstream Latin Christendom to his metropolitan area. Prémontré Abbey sent a second group of canons to the archdiocese in the 1220s to Holy Trinity on Lough Key, founded by the archdeacon of Elphin, Clarus Mac Mailin (Fig. 3.1; Plate 1).[9] The location of a third daughter of Prémontré, 'Ballinual' in the archdiocese of Armagh, has not been identified. Expansion was confined to Connacht and, in total, there were eight canonries (including 'Ballinual') where there was regular common life (Fig. 3.1). Canons went from Tuam to the abbey of St John the Baptist at the episcopal settlement of Annaghdown, probably introduced here by Bishop Muirchertach Ua Flaithbheartaigh (1201–41). A dependency – St Mary's Priory at Killamanagh – was established on the familial lands of the first abbot of Annaghdown, Tomás Ua Meallaigh. Holy Trinity Priory on Lough Oughter in Uí Briúin Bréifne, sponsored

---

4 The editions that applied when the Irish monasteries were founded were those of *c.*1155 and *c.*1175, P.F. Lefèvre and W.M. Grauwen (eds), *Les statuts de Prémontré au milieu du XIIe siècle*, Bibliotecheca Analectorum Praemonstratensium, 12 (Averbode, 1978); B. Krings (ed.), 'Das Ordenstrecht der Prämonstratenser vom späten 12. jahrhundert bis zum jahr 1227. Der Liber consuetudinum und die dekrete des Generalkapitels', *Analecta Praemonstratensia*, 69 (1993), 108–242. Significant amendments were made in the 1236–8 statutes and others in 1290, P.F. Lefèvre (ed.), *Les statuts de Prémontré réformés sur les ordres de Grégoire IX et d'Innocent IV au XIIIe siècle*, Bibliothèque de la Revue d'Histoire Ecclésiastique, 23 (Louvain, 1946).   **5** Lefèvre and Grauwen (eds), *Les statuts de Prémontré au milieu du XIIe siècle*, p. 45; Lefèvre (ed.), *Les statuts de Prémontré réformés*, p. 84.   **6** For detailed accounts of the circumstances surrounding the foundations see M. Clyne, 'The founders and patrons of Premonstratensian houses in Ireland' in Burton and Stöber, *Canons*, pp 145–72; M. Clyne, 'Premonstratensian settlement in the Czech Lands and Ireland, 1142–1250', *Journal of Medieval Monastic Studies*, 7 (2018), 127–52, at 137–8, 141–2, 144–7.   **7** Carrickfergus was established by 1183 when the prior witnessed de Courcy's charters to the Benedictines of Downpatrick. See R. Dodsworth and W. Dugdale (eds), *Monastican Anglicanum*, 3 vols (London, 1655–73), ii, p. 1021.   **8** The mother houses are known from the catalogues of the order. See Backmund, *Monasticon Praemonstratense*, iii, p. 433; J. Le Paige, *Bibliotheca Praemonstratensis ordinis*, Instrumenta Praemonstratensia, 3 (Averbode, 1998; facs. repr. of orig. publ. Paris, 1633), at p. 334.   **9** A.M. Freeman (ed.), 'The annals in Cotton MS Titus A. XXV', *Revue Celtique*, 41 (1924), 301–30; 42 (1925), 283–305; 43 (1926), 358–84; 44 (1927), 336–61, at 342,

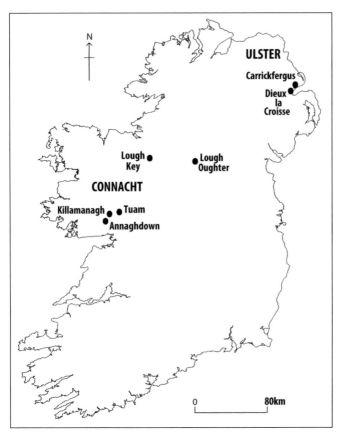

3.1 Map of Premonstratensian monasteries in Ireland.

by Cathal Ua Raghallaigh, was founded in 1237 by Archdeacon Clarus Mac Mailin and, at Christmas 1250, he brought the canons from Lough Key.[10] Irish abbeys did not have dependent priories for nuns.[11] Premonstratensian communities initially depended on the produce from their lands for their requirements in food and materials. Other income was generated by collecting tithes from rectories and vicarages. Of greater consequence, the canons, as ordained priests, could provide pastoral care and administer parishes, responsibilities that increased over time to become a characteristic of the order, including the Irish communities.[12]

The order of Prémontré followed the Cistercian practice of filiation. An obligation of father abbots was the annual visitation of daughter houses to maintain

304, no. 401; *ALC*, i, pp 95–7.   **10** Freeman (ed.), 'The annals in Cotton MS Titus A. XXV', 42, 303, no. 399; 43, 383, no. 399; *ALC*, i, pp 394–5.   **11** On the place of women in the order see B. Krings, 'Die Prämonstratenser und ihr weiblicher Zweig' in I. Crusius and H. Flachenecker (eds), *Studien zum Prämonstratenserorden* (Göttingen, 2003), pp 75–105; B. Krings, 'Les relations de l'abbé avec ses couvents de femmes' in D.-M. Dauzet and M. Plouvier (eds), *Abbatiat et abbés dans l'ordre de Prémontré*, Bibliotheca Victorina XVII (Turnhout, 2005), pp 129–44.   **12** For example, Holy Trinity Abbey, Lough Key, accumulated ten rectories and seven vicarages. See M. Clyne, 'The rental of Holy Trinity Abbey, Lough Cé' in Thomas Finan (ed.), *Medieval Loch Cé: history,*

standards of spiritual observance and discipline.[13] When it became impractical for abbots to fulfil this duty because of the many filiations in distant places, their visitation rights were taken away in the mid-twelfth century and control was assumed by the general chapter and the abbot of Prémontré as overall superior. The replacement system, a Premonstratensian innovation, grouped houses into geographical provinces, referred to as 'circaries' (*circariae*), where visitors (*circatores*) were appointed annually to correct irregularities and to report back to the general chapter the next year.[14] The Irish circary (*Circaria Hiberniae*), with Holy Trinity Tuam designated as the principal church, was formed by the fourteenth century when the annual payment for the support of the order (*tallia*) was estimated at three florins (*tres florenos Renenses*) for the six Irish abbeys, an amount considerably less than that for the houses in virtually all other circaries.[15] This is the single recorded tax assessment for Ireland.

This chapter will use the material sources of the monasteries as a guide, and the architecture, devotional imagery and archaeology complemented by the documentary sources, to illustrate the canons' daily life in the churches, cloisters and claustral buildings for over four hundred years from *c.*1180 to *c.*1607. The Irish experience will be brought into the wider European character of the order of Prémontré, and will also indicate the interaction between the communities and local lay society.

ON CONSTRUCTING AN ABBEY

The ordinance on constructing an abbey gives the directions that were considered necessary to maintain the vitality of the order.[16] Each community required a complement of at least twelve canons and their abbot to achieve the rank of an abbey. The buildings listed are the church, dormitory, refectory, room for guests and porter's lodge, so that the community could serve God and live by the Rule without delay. Such minimal legislation does not of course provide a model for the entire abbey, nor for the arrangement of buildings within the monastic precinct. Decisions based on the other accommodation for the anticipated number in the community could be left to the discretion of the founder, the patron, the colonizing canons, and the abbot of the mother house. The structural evidence suggests that the layout of Irish Premonstratensian houses was not uniform; however, scope for variation was acceptable so long as the canonries kept to the

archaeology and landscape (Dublin, 2010), pp 67–96, at pp 76–86. **13** R. Van Waefelghem (ed.), *Les premiers statuts de l'Ordre de Prémontré. Le Clm 17174(XIIᵉ)* (Louvain, 1913), p. 35. **14** Lefèvre and Grauwen (eds), *Les statuts de Prémontré au milieu du XIIᵉ siècle*, pp 47–8; Lefèvre (ed.), *Les statuts de Prémontré réformés*, pp 102–5. **15** Le Paige, *Bibliotheca*, pp 326–44, *Circaria Hiberniae* at p. 334. In 1633 Joannes le Paige published his lists compiled from fourteenth-century catalogues then preserved at Prémontré and other French abbeys; Backmund, *Monasticon Praemonstratense*, i, p. 17. **16** Lefèvre and Grauwen (eds), *Les statuts de Prémontré au milieu du XIIᵉ siècle*, pp 45–6; Krings (ed.), 'Das Ordensrecht der Prämonstratenser', 186.

3.2 St Mary's Abbey, Carrickfergus, denoted as 'Woodborne Abbaie' (extract from 'Map of Belfast Lough', by Robert Lythe, 1569, © National Archives, Kew, mpf 1/77.

basic framework of monastic planning and the arrangements contained the key buildings for communal life. Preservation of Irish monasteries varies. Holy Trinity on Lough Key is the most useful indicator for the activities undertaken by the canons in their daily routine because this abbey has the most complete structural remains – the church and the east range containing the chapter house, refectory, kitchen, and dormitory, which were built in the 1220s in the style of contemporary Gaelic architecture of Connacht (Plate 1) – and, moreover, the archaeological excavations uncovered information of significance to communal living.[17] The medieval ruins of Carrickfergus, Dieux la Croisse and Tuam have been casualties of urban development.[18] A map of Belfast Lough, drawn by Robert Lythe and dated 1569, indicates that the church, east range and two detached buildings, were standing at St Mary's Abbey, Carrickfergus (Fig. 3.2). Francis Grose's late eighteenth-century engraving of Tuam Abbey depicts the church and the west range – the east range had already collapsed (Fig. 3.3). The outline of the east and south ranges at Annaghdown can be traced on the ground, the wall bases for these ranges at Killamanagh still survive, but the medieval conventual accommodation

---

17 The excavations were carried out for and funded by the National Monuments Service, Dublin. This chapter interprets the excavation reports where descriptive details can be found, and all information in the text on the investigations is taken from M. Clyne, 'Archaeological excavations at Holy Trinity Abbey, Lough Key, Co. Roscommon', *PRIA*, 105C (2005), 23–98. References to the specialists' archival reports are noted below.   **18** For an eighteenth-century drawing of the ruined church of Dieux la Croisse, Benn, *The history of the town of Belfast*, p. 264.

at Lough Oughter Priory is no longer evident. The room for guests, or a guest house, has not survived in the architectural record at Irish canonries. The porter's lodge was usually at the main entrance, where the porter had charge of receiving guests and distributing alms to the poor. The importance of providing both services is emphasized in a letter of Bishop Reginald of Connor to King Henry III in 1224, when St Mary's at Carrickfergus was unable to deliver hospitality and charitable relief because the district was under military siege.[20]

The first requisite for new communities was to be supplied with the order's books to ensure liturgical uniformity in all churches when celebrating the Eucharist and Divine Office. The minimum specified was a missal, book of collects, gradual, antiphonary, hymnal, psalter, calendar of feast days, and the Rule.[21] A letter written *c.*1215 by Abbot Gervase of Prémontré (1209–20) to Abbot Walter of Vicoigne in Flanders (1211–29) discloses that three brothers from Holy Trinity, Tuam, had come to Prémontré the previous winter to get liturgical books.[22] Transcriptions of the customs too were brought back by the brothers that probably included the ordinal, the capitulary, the manner of reading chapters, and the music and common tones of the Divine Office.[23] The abbot general also reveals that the Connacht community was getting assistance with religious training at Prémontré. His letter concerns Isaac, the canon sent by his abbot to learn the discipline and severity of the order. He attributes the difficulties experienced by the first community at Tuam to the abbey's isolation, the small number of brethren and, in the mind of the abbot general, the cultural inferiority of the Gaelic race. Isaac and his brethren arrived at Prémontré each with a single tunic, age-worn and thin in texture. They had been wearing the same garments since leaving Tuam, a journey taking up to six weeks that covered approximately 750 kilometres overland across three territories and involving two sea crossings. Their abbey seemingly did not have the resources to supply the clothing stipulated by the central authority, which was at least two woollen tunics and a mantle, a scapular, and a cloak with a cowl.[24] Abbot Gervase writes that Prémontré is unable to cope with the needs of communities in distant territories, and, as his abbey could no longer alone support all who come, he sends Isaac to Vicoigne, entrusting Abbot Walter to supply the canon with enough garments and to comfort him while he endures the harshness of the routine.

The thirteenth-century copper alloy seal matrix of Holy Trinity, Tuam, used for authenticating the abbey's legal documents and transacting business, has three

---

20 W. Reeves, *Ecclesiastical antiquities of Down, Connor, and Dromore, consisting of a taxation of those dioceses, compiled in the year MCCCVI* (Dublin, 1847), pp 274–5.   21 Lefèvre and Grauwen (eds), *Les statuts de Prémontré au milieu du XIIᵉ siècle*, pp 45, 49; Krings (ed.), 'Das Ordenstrecht der Prämonstratenser', 186, 190.   22 C.L. Hugo (ed.), *Sacrae antiquitatis monumenta historica, dogmatica, diplomatica*, 2 vols (Stivagii (Étival), 1725–31), i, pp 67–8, no. lxxiii. The letter is assessed in relation to Abbot Gervase's correspondance on the abbeys in Bohemia and Moravia. See Clyne, 'Premonstratensian settlement in the Czech Lands and Ireland', pp 142–4.   23 These were the texts copied at Prémontré in 1214 by Abbot Emo of Witterwierum in Frisia that are noted by Gervase in another letter: Hugo (ed.), *Sacrae antiquitatis*, i, pp 120–1, no. cxxxvi.   24 Lefèvre and Grauwen (eds), *Les statuts de Prémontré au milieu du XIIᵉ siècle*, pp 50–1; Krings (ed.), 'Das

3.3 Holy Trinity Abbey, Tuam, showing the church and the west range in the background (from Francis Grose, *The antiquities of Ireland* (London, 1795), i, plate 37).

standing figures surrounded by the legend * SIGILLVM CONVENTVS [TRIT]ATIS DE TVAVM (Seal of the convent of the Trinity of Tuam) (Plate 2). The monogram of Jesus, 'IHC', on the centre figure identifies the depiction as the Trinity.[25] Their similarity in appearance and uniformity in size represents the consubstantiality and equality of the triune God. The Three Persons are tonsured and wear canons' habits – tunics secured with girdles at the waists.[26] Each figure is set in a niche with pillars supporting a pointed arch that may reflect the early Gothic abbey church, which was most likely built after four churches at Tuam were burned in 1244 (Fig. 3.3).[27]

THE CHURCH AND THE PERFORMANCE OF THE LITURGY

The vow of stability *(stabilitas loci)* taken by the Premonstratensian novice at profession permitted him to serve only at his abbey church, and, under normal

Ordenstrecht der Prämonstratenser', 192.   **25** H.M. Roe, 'Illustrations of the Holy Trinity in Ireland: 13th to 17th centuries', *JRSAI*, 109 (1979), 101–50, at 101–2, 141–2. My thanks to Professor Frank for his helpful comments on the iconography.   **26** I wish to thank Fr Anselm Gribbin OPraem., for identifying the clothing.   **27** *ALC*, i, pp 366–7.

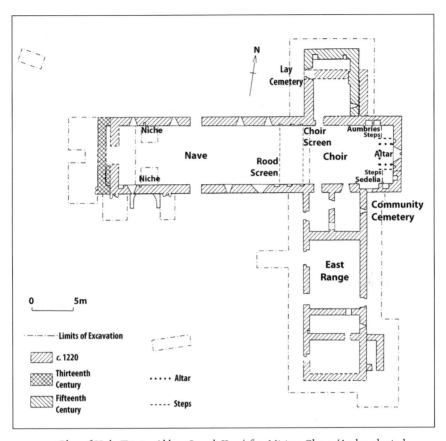

3.4 Plan of Holy Trinity Abbey, Lough Key (after Miriam Clyne, 'Archaeological excavations at Holy Trinity Abbey, Lough Key, Co. Roscommon', *PRIA*, 105C (2005), fig. 3, with permission Royal Irish Academy).

circumstances, he could not be translated to another house.[28] The church, the spiritual core of the monastery where the community spent the greater part of the day, was the most prominent building, symbolizing the dedication of the entire establishment to God's work (Plate 1). The highest place in the liturgy was the celebration of the Eucharist at the three daily Masses. Although the Premonstratensians shared much of their liturgy with other religious orders, they introduced further uses and rituals. Their Masses followed the early Roman Rite and their liturgical organization came from the leading French secular churches.[29] The edition of the ordinal brought to Tuam by the brothers was the *Ordinarius* of Prémontré, but the inclusion of further liturgical observances and extra feasts in the statutes of 1236–8 necessitated the compilation of a new customary,

28 The oath of profession is explained by Adam Scot, *De ordine* in J.-P. Migne (ed.), *Patrologiae cursus completus*, series Latina, 221 vols (Paris, 1841–64), cxcviii, cols 443–610, at col. 479.   **29** P.F. Lefèvre, *La liturgie de Prémontré: histoire, formulaire, chant et cérémonial* (Louvain, 1957), p. 57.

3.5 The aumbries in the presbytery of Holy Trinity Church, Lough Key.

Conseutudines ecclesie Premonstratensis, known as *Usus I*. Further changes in the ordinances of 1290 led to a much lengthier text, *Usus II*, in the early fourteenth century, which stayed as the prescribed ritual performance for the remainder of the medieval period.[30] Texts from continental abbeys and the Easby Ordinal from England show that though the Premonstratensian liturgy and customs were essentially observed, practices from local secular churches were adopted that were probably influenced by lay piety and the canons' duties in parishes.[31] Digressions were likely introduced into the liturgies at Irish canonries by these means, and possibly also from the cathedral churches, due to the location of the abbeys at Tuam and Annaghdown at episcopal seats.

The severity in the decoration of churches prevalent in the twelfth century was relaxed and the number of liturgical ornaments increased as the rituals became more complex. In the fifteenth and sixteenth centuries, the presbytery floor in the church at Lough Key Abbey had two steps at the sides of the stone high altar (Fig. 3.4). In respect to the number of lamps and candles, up to ten were permitted and a lamp was to permanently light the presbytery. The sacred ornaments prescribed for the celebration of Mass on the high altar were the chalice and paten and, on major feasts, a censer for burning incense, and *fistula argenta* (a silver tube

---

30 P.F. Lefèvre (ed.), *L'ordinaire de Prémontré, d'après des manuscrits du XIIᵉ et du XIIIᵉ siècle*, Bibliothèque de la Revue d'Histoire Ecclésiastique, 22 (Louvain, 1941); P.F. Lefèvre (ed.), *Coutumiers liturgiques de Prémontré du XIIIᵉ et du XIVᵉ siècle*, Bibliothèque de la Revue d'Histoire Ecclésiastique, 27 (Louvain, 1953). **31** Lefèvre, *La liturgie de Prémontré*, pp 18–20; J.A. Gribbin, *The Premonstratensian order in late medieval England* (Woodbridge, 2001), pp 114, 119, 128.

3.6 The sedilia in the presbytery of Holy Trinity Church, Lough Key.

or straw) so that the celebrant could share the consecrated wine from the chalice with the canons without spillage.[32] The reserved Host was placed in a *vasculum* (small vessel) and suspended above the altar. The splendour of the liturgical accessories was dependent on the wealth of the monastery or, more probably, on the generosity of donations. Fragments of the thirteenth-century chalice used in Lough Key Church indicate that it was made of expensive gilt copper alloy and silver, and 'bronze ornaments' from Dieux la Croisse Abbey were preserved until the nineteenth century.[33] Not all Irish houses were as prosperous. Killamanagh Priory was so impoverished in 1428 that the church did not have sufficient liturgical ornaments and books.[34] The pair of aumbries (cupboards) close to the altar in the

32 Lefèvre, *La liturgie de Prémontré*, pp 67, 69.　　**33** Reeves, *Ecclesiastical antiquities*, p. 277. **34** *CPL*, 8, p. 27.

north wall in Lough Key Church is embellished with human and animal heads, roll mouldings and engaged columns, and the stones projecting from the wall face at the sides imply that they once held carved woodwork (Figs 3.5, 3.6).[35] Both aumbries originally had (probably wooden) doors, and they were likely used for storing the sacred vessels and liturgical books.

The sedilia in the south wall of Lough Key Church had steps leading up to the bench that accommodated the three officiating clerics (Figs 3.4, 3.6). The twelfth-century canon put on a white linen alb to celebrate Mass. Vestments were to be of one colour and unadorned, but in 1228–36 a colour sequence was introduced, and, from the fourteenth century, vestments with silk embroidery and enriched with gems were worn by Premonstratensian celebrants.[36] The copper alloy seal matrix of the abbot of Holy Trinity Lough Key, inscribed ✱ S ABBATIS SCE TRITATIS DE LOCH QVU, has a standing figure holding a pastoral staff in his right hand (Fig. 3.7). He wears an alb beneath a chasuble, an apparelled amice, and a cope.[37] Of particular interest, the effigy is of a mitred abbot signifying the grant of pontificals (*pontificalia*, the insignia of a bishop) which was by papal indult. However, documentary evidence according the privilege to the abbot of Lough Key is not available. Episcopal insignia were forbidden in the constitutions; nonetheless, when the number of concessions was extended to the superiors of all monastic orders in the fifteenth and sixteenth centuries, many Premonstratensian abbots were wearing pontificals and ostentatious vestments.[38] The mitre and other insignia were worn by the abbot on solemn occasions, including feast days and processions, and beyond the abbey when he was on official business. The effigy of the abbot on his seal was his public image.[39] It was how he wished to impress all classes of society, his pontificals emphasizing his authority and dignity and his status as a prelate.

The community sat in stalls, usually of wood, placed along the walls of the choir to attend Mass, celebrate the Divine Office, or engage in private prayer (Fig. 4). The canons did not change from their ordinary habits except on special feasts, when all the community wore an alb to Mass.[40] The continuous daily round of Divine Office, consisting of the seven canonical hours, the Little Office of the Virgin Mary and the Office of the Dead, took longer than other parts of the

---

35 See R. Moss, 'Permanent expressions of piety: the secular and the sacred in later medieval stone sculpture' in R. Moss, C. Ó Clabaigh and S. Ryan (eds), *Art and devotion in late medieval Ireland* (Dublin, 2006), pp 72–97, at p. 72.   **36** Lefèvre (ed.), *L'ordinaire de Prémontré*, p. 6; Lefèvre, *La liturgie de Prémontré*, pp 67–8.   **37** The amice (a rectangle of white linen) with the apparel (a stiff, decorative band of fabric) attached to it gives the appearance of a collar on the chasuble. My thanks to Fr Anselm Gribbin OPraem., for discussing the vestments with me.   **38** Lefèvre (ed.), *Les statuts de Prémontré réformés*, p. 41. For grants of *pontificalia* to Premonstratensian abbots see A.A. King, *Liturgies of the religious orders* (London, New York and Toronto, 1955), pp 202–3. **39** For discussion on how abbatial seals projected the public image, M. Heale, 'Mitres and arms: aspects of self-representation of the monastic superior in late medieval England' in A. Müller and K. Stöber (eds), *Self-representation of medieval religious communities: the British Isles in context* (Münster, 2009), pp 99–123, at pp 105–7.

3.7 Seal matrix of the abbot of Holy Trinity, Lough Key
(© National Museum of Ireland).

liturgy. Access from the common dormitory on the upper floor of the east range at Lough Key was through a doorway to a wooden stairs in the choir that the community came down for the first office of the day, Matins, at midnight.

The joist sockets in the side walls of Lough Key Church are today the only evidence that choir and rood screens of wood separated the nave from the choir and presbytery, thereby marking out a distinct liturgical space for the community (Fig. 3.4). The screen facing the choir was known as the *pulpitum* and that facing the nave, the rood screen, with doors in both partitions leading through from the choir.[41] Above the rood loft (the upper storey gallery on the nave side), the main crucifix, the rood, was set up. A painted and gilded wooden crucifix was at the former priory on Lough Oughter when Monsignor Massari, dean of Fermo and secretary to the papal nuncio Rinuccini, visited the island in July 1646.[42] The crucifix found at Dieux la Croisse Abbey in the nineteenth century was of 'bronze', but this may refer to a processional cross rather than the rood, which was usually of wood.[43]

The nave in a Premonstratensian church, unless it was also the parish church as at Killamanagh, accommodated members of the laity and their families associated with the community, who might include benefactors, tenants, hired workers, and guests staying at the monastery. Lay people could attend Mass on Sundays and public holidays (Holy Days),[44] and Holy Communion was received at an altar beside the rood screen partition infrequently – the Fourth Lateran Council of 1215 making it obligatory at least once a year at Easter.[45] Premonstratensian spirituality

40 For the regulations on the choir habit, Lefèvre, *La liturgie de Prémontré*, pp 69–70.   **41** The development of choir and rood screens is discussed by E.C. Parker, 'Architecture as liturgical setting' in T.J. Heffernan and E.A. Matter (eds), *The liturgy of the medieval church* (Kalamazoo, MI, 2005), pp 245–93, at pp 270–4. For masonry examples of rood screens in friary churches, Colmán Ó Clabaigh, *The friars in Ireland, 1224–1540* (Dublin, 2012), pp 235–6.   **42** D. Massari, 'My Irish campaign', *The Catholic Bulletin*, 7 (1917), 247.   **43** Reeves, *Ecclesiastical antiquities*, p. 277. **44** Religious public holidays are listed by S. Borgehammer, 'A monastic conception of the liturgical year' in T.J. Heffernan and E.A. Matter (eds), *The liturgy of the medieval church* (Kalamazoo, MI, 2005), pp 13–40, at p. 17.   **45** N. Tanner (ed.), *Decrees of the Ecumenical councils,*

3.8 The Harrowing of Hell carving from Holy Trinity Church, Lough Key.

had many aspects in common with lay devotional practices in the liturgy, the celebration of feast days, and the iconography at their Irish churches.

Easter and its preceding *triduum sacrum* was the outstanding festival of the liturgical calendar. The stone image found in Lough Key Church associated with the Easter narrative portrays Christ wearing a loin cloth and holding the cross with his other arm outstretched, and behind him, one or possibly two people (Fig. 3.8). The scene depicts the Harrowing of Hell, relating to Christ's descent into hell in the period between his crucifixion and resurrection, when he defeated Satan and rescued the righteous souls.[46] The iconography illustrates an episode that was very popular with the laity, providing a presentation of salvation that they understood.[47]

---

2 vols (Washington and London, 1990), i, p. 245, no. 21. For the level of lay participation at Mass see M.R. Dudley, 'Sacramental liturgies in the Middle Ages' in T.J. Heffernan and E.A. Matter (eds), *The liturgy of the medieval church* (Kalamazoo, MI, 2005), pp 193–218, at pp 204–5; N. Tanner and S. Watson, 'Least of the laity: the minimum requirements for a medieval Christian', *Journal of Medieval History*, 34:4 (2006), 395–423, at 408–10.   **46** I wish to thank Fr Andrew Ciferni OPraem., for bringing my attention to this interpretation.   **47** The episode is retold in the widely circulated *Gospel of Nicodemus*, and was a common theme in contemporary literature, art and drama, as well as liturgical tracts, J.A. MacCulloch, *The Harrowing of Hell: a comparative study of an early Christian doctrine* (Edinburgh, 1930), pp 152–73, 199–281, 288–99; A.K. Turner, *The*

Besides the annual cycle of liturgical seasons commemorating the events of Christ's life, there were the saints' feasts celebrated throughout the Latin church. When the white canons arrived to Ireland in the late twelfth century, their high-ranking feasts numbered twenty-eight. This figure had risen to fifty-six by the time the final house was suppressed in the early seventeenth century. The Premonstratensian hierarchy of feasts had seven major groups, with the greatest being the category of *triplex festum*.[48] The anniversary of the consecration of the church, known as the 'Dedication of the Church', was a day with a greater degree of festivity, counting as one of the four most liturgically elaborate, when the canons dressed in albs for the procession before the conventual Mass.[49] The laity too celebrated, the feast was noted as an occasion when great numbers of people gathered at Killamanagh Priory in 1428.[50] The commemoration of St Martin of Tours (11 November), a universal holiday, was marked at Holy Trinity Abbey, Lough Key, in 1243.[51] Apostles' feasts too were public holidays, the feast of Ss Philip and James (1 May) was celebrated by the parishioners at Killamanagh in 1399.[52] Even amongst the order's houses in Ireland, the calendar of saints' feasts was far from homogeneous. Each monastery commemorated the saints who were revered in the region and the diocese and local saints' cults, the dates of the extra feasts were to be written into a supplement to the calendar.[53] St Finnian's day (12 December) is recorded at 1235 in the annals written by the community on Lough Key, Finnian being credited as the founder of many churches in the surrounding district of north Connacht.[54] Diocesan saints were commemorated at Tuam and Annaghdown. The feast of St Jarlath, bishop-patron of the archdiocese, was observed on 6 June at Tuam, where his relics were venerated at Templenascreen.[55] St Brendan's feast (16 May) was celebrated at Annaghdown, where the cathedral church dedicated to him was adjacent to the Premonstratensian abbey.[56]

Saints' images were a focus of attack by the iconoclasts at the suppression of the monasteries, and the empty niches in the nave at Lough Key are a reminder that they probably once displayed statues (Fig. 3.4). The cache of painted and gilded wooden statues lying 'exposed to the wind and rain' in a corner of the church at Lough Oughter Priory in 1646 included the universally popular St Catherine of

history of hell (London, 1995), pp 66–70. The Harrowing of Hell is in the collection of devotional texts in the *Leabhar Chlainne Suibhne*. See S. Ryan, 'Windows on late medieval devotional practice: Máire Ní Mháille's "Book of Piety" (1513) and the world behind the texts' in R. Moss, C. Ó Clabaigh and S. Ryan (eds), *Art and devotion in late medieval Ireland* (Dublin, 2006), pp 1–15, at p. 2. **48** King, *Liturgies*, pp 193–4. Lefèvre, *La liturgie de Prémontré*, pp 44–5, 93–4. **49** Lefèvre, *La liturgie de Prémontré*, pp 92–3; Lefèvre (ed.), *Coutumiers liturgiques de Prémontré*, pp 60–3. **50** *CPL*, viii, p. 27. **51** *ALC*, i, pp 360–1; *Ann. Conn.*, pp 78–9, no. 5. **52** *CPL*, 5, p. 268. **53** Lefèvre, *La liturgie de Prémontré*, pp 43–4. **54** Freeman (ed.), 'The Annals in Cotton MS Titus A. XXV', 42, 302, no. 397. On Finnian of Clonard see P. Ó Riain, *A dictionary of Irish saints* (Dublin, 2011), pp 319–21. **55** *CPL*, 17, part i, pp 103–4, no. 163. For the sources on Iarlaithe of Tuam see Ó Riain, *A dictionary of Irish saints*, pp 374–5. **56** St Brendan, best known from the medieval texts of the *Navigatio Brendani* (the 'Brendan Voyage'), reputedly founded the church at Annaghdown, where he died. For Bréanainn of Clonfert and his sister, Brígh of Annaghdown, see Ó Riain, *A dictionary of Irish saints*, pp 115–17, 119.

3.9 (*above left*) The carving of the Holy Trinity and the Virgin Mary at Holy Trinity Church, Lough Key, by Daniel Grose (detail from *The Irish Penny Magazine*, 9 November 1833). **3.10** The carving of the Holy Trinity and the Virgin Mary at Holy Trinity Church, Lough Key, by Robert Armstrong, 1842 (detail from PD 1956 TX [47], courtesy of the National Library of Ireland).

Alexandria and Mary Magdalene, both of whom were honoured by solemn feasts at Premonstratensian churches (25 November, 22 July respectively).[57] A statue of St Patrick was also at Lough Oughter Priory. His festival (17 March), celebrated throughout Ireland and in parts of Europe, was an occasion when large crowds attended Mass at Killamanagh Church in 1399.[58]

The feast of the patron saint of the monastery was a highpoint in the liturgical year. The (possibly wooden) image of the Trinity at Lough Key was burned in 1466.[59] The stone image carved in the fifteenth or early sixteenth century for this abbey, depicting the Trinity with the Virgin Mary, is now missing and the drawings are the only record (Figs 3.9, 3.10). The complex doctrine of the Trinity is captured by the sculptor in symbolic form, with the hand of God for the Father and the dove for the Holy Spirit in the top corners, and the Son seated on the Virgin Mary's knee. She is presented as the enthroned Madonna wearing a crown (Fig. 3.9), and holding a sceptre, denoting her as Queen of Heaven. The Child

57 Massari, 'My Irish campaign', p. 247. Lefèvre, *La liturgie de Prémontré*, p. 93.   **58** *CPL*, 5, p. 268. St Patrick's feast day occurs in the sixteenth-century calendar of the Premonstratensian abbey of West Dereham. See Gribbin, *The Premonstratensian order*, p. 123, note 10.   **59** *Ann.*

points to his mother (Fig. 3.9), or his hand is raised in blessing (Fig. 3.10), both gestures symbolizing the Virgin as the mother of the two natures of Christ, God and man.[60] She is the prominent figure, illustrating the intensity of devotion to the Virgin Mary, which was a fundamental element of the white canons' spirituality, one which they affirmed daily by singing her Mass and reciting her Office, and by observing her feasts with the triplex rank.[61] The laity too had a deep affection for the Virgin, their Books of Hours imitating monastic life were centred around her Office.[62] The statue of 'the Blessed Virgin and Child in her arms' at Lough Oughter Priory had stood on her altar, the focal point of her veneration.[63]

The excavations in Lough Key Church illustrate how the burial pattern of lay people expanded from the least liturgically important area, the west end of the nave, in the thirteenth and fourteenth centuries, to the most sacred, the presbytery, in the fifteenth and sixteenth centuries. A similar progression of burial from west to east occurred in the churches of religious orders in Europe.[64] The graves express the laity's desire for interment in sanctified ground and the aspiration for salvation through the commitment on the part of the canons to offer prayers for their souls. During the earlier period, thirty graves were uncovered in the nave floor of men, women and children who might have included benefactors of the monastery and their families and the documented distinguished laymen and churchmen, such as the 'archipresbyter' of Tibohine, Diarmait Mac Gilla Charruig (d. 1229), Tumna, Mael Ciaráin Ua Lenacháin (d. 1249), and Diarmait Ua Conchobair (d. 1294).[65] The cemetery for the less well-off people, probably the families of monastic tenants and hired workers, was outside the walls of Holy Trinity Church (Fig. 3.4). Graves were not inserted into the earlier floors in the presbytery and the choir, implying that these areas were reserved for the performance of the liturgy and worship by the religious community. There was one tomb in the presbytery beneath the bench of the sedilia that may have been purpose-built for the founder, Archdeacon Clarus Mac Mailin, who died at the abbey in 1251 (Figs 3.4, 3.6), rather than for the sponsors of the abbey, the Mac Diarmada of Mag Luirg, who were buried with the Cistercians at Boyle Abbey on the adjacent mainland.[66] But lay people were interred in the choir and presbytery floors as well as the in nave in the fifteenth and sixteenth centuries. Eighteen graves were beneath the altar and the stepped platform, which was believed to be of greatest benefit for the departed in pursuit

Conn., pp 534–5, no. 29.   **60** J. Bradley, 'The Ballyhale Madonna and its iconography' in E. Rynne (ed.), *Figures from the past: studies on figurative art in Christian Ireland* (Dun Laoghaire, 1987), pp 258–77, at pp 264–5.   **61** Lefèvre, *La liturgie de Prémontré*, pp 94–6; Lefèvre (ed.), *Coutumiers liturgiques de Prémontré*, pp 45–6, 49–50, 77–9, 80–1.   **62** R.S. Wieck, 'The Book of Hours' in T.J. Heffernan and E.A. Matter (eds), *The liturgy of the medieval church* (Kalamazoo, MI, 2005), pp 431–68, at pp 431–2.   **63** Massari, 'My Irish campaign', p. 247.   **64** For expansion of lay burials from west to east in Cistercian monasteries and the increase in the desire for monastic interment see E. Jamroziak, *The Cistercian order in medieval Europe, 1090–1500* (London and New York, 2013), pp 101–4.   **65** Freeman (ed.), 'The Annals in Cotton MS Titus A. XXV', 42, 297, no. 390; *ALC*, i, pp 390–3, 512–13.   **66** Freeman (ed.), 'The Annals in Cotton MS Titus A. XXV', 42, 304, no. 401; *ALC*, i, pp 306–7, 366–7, 396–7, 614–15, 644–5.

of salvation. The increase in requests for burial put extra demands on the canonical community to provide funeral services and to fulfil the obligations of commemoration and intercession, on top of their already considerable liturgical responsibilities.

THE CLOISTER AND CLAUSTRAL BUILDINGS

The timetable (*horarium*) for Premonstratensian communities was similar to that of other religious congregations, accounting for every minute of the day, the routine adjusting according to the liturgical calendar and to facilitate the hours of daylight between summer (Easter until the feast of the Holy Cross on 14 September) and winter (the intervening period until Easter).[67] Besides the liturgical obligations in the church, the rest of the canon's day at his monastery was filled through *lectio divina* (sacred reading), manual work, attendance at the chapter and meals. These activities were based in and around the cloister and the claustral buildings, the inner court being reserved for the community. White canons, like other cloistered religious, spent long hours in silence. Silence had to be strictly observed in the cloister, refectory and dormitory, as well as in the church, so that the canons could commune with God and lead a virtuous life. For everyday essential interaction a sign language was used.[68]

The cloister had two elements: the garth, usually an open quadrangle, and the covered galleries or walkways along the sides of the church and the claustral ranges. The galleries had seating for the brethren, where they engaged in *lectio divina* for two daily periods all year round – in the middle of the day and evening – with a third period allocated in the afternoon during winter. Sacred scripture was the principal reading material.[69] The cloister was available for the community to wash themselves, shave, and to wash and mend their garments. The shears found at Lough Key Abbey was suitable for cutting hair, thread and textile (Fig. 3.11). Shaving and maintaining the tonsure was regulated by the liturgical calendar and, in provinces with cold climates, communities could abstain from shaving between Christmas and the feast of the Purification (2 February).[70]

Manual work, undertaken for self-mortification as well as out of practical necessity, took place twice daily in winter, with a third period allotted in summer. This was essential for general well-being, creating a balance with the liturgical regime. The tasks assigned might be ordinary jobs that needed to be done, such as

---

67 Lefèvre (ed.), *Les statuts de Prémontré réformés*, pp 11–14.   **68** Ibid., pp 67–8. For the writings on silence and signs by Philip of Bonne Espérance (also known as Philip of Harvengt), *De institutione clericorum* in J.-P. Migne (ed.), *Patrologiae cursus completus*, series Latina, 221 vols (Paris, 1841–64), cciii, cols 943–6, 978–80, 1012–27, 1067.   **69** For Adam Scot and Philip of Bonne Espérance on the significance of *lectio divina*, Antry and Neel, *Norbert and early Norbertine spirituality*, pp 213–17; F. Petit, *Spirituality of the Premonstratensians: the twelfth and thirteenth centuries*, Premonstratensian Texts and Studies, 2 (Collegeville, MN, 2011), pp 280–95.   **70** Lefèvre (ed.), *Les statuts de Prémontré réformés*, pp 38–9.

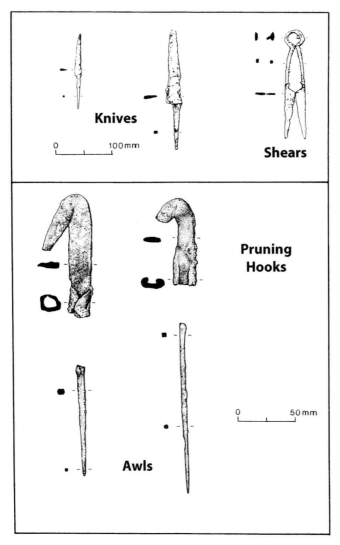

3.11 Iron objects from the excavations at Holy Trinity Abbey, Lough Key (after Miriam Clyne, 'Archaeological excavations at Holy Trinity Abbey, Lough Key, Co. Roscommon', *PRIA*, 105C (2005), fig. 22, with permission Royal Irish Academy).

the domestic chores of cleaning, carrying water and preparing food.[71] Brethren with special skills could be employed in transcribing liturgical texts or as craftsmen. Some of the iron tools recovered at Lough Key may have been used for manual labour; for example, the awls in leather working (Fig. 3.11). Canons were not exempt from physical labour in the gardens and on the monastic farms. The

---

71 Ibid., pp 14–16, 56.

pruning hooks could also function as weed hooks in the gardens on the island precinct on Lough Key (Fig. 3.11). When harvesting fuel for the kitchen fire from woodland and bog on the abbey's lands, the iron wedge was used in conjunction with an axe for felling trees and splitting logs, and the *sleán* for cutting turf (peat).

Every morning the community took their places in the chapter house in the east range, to discuss the day-to-day business of the monastery (Fig. 3.12). The abbot sat at the east side to represent Christ and the canons were seated along the other walls. The proceedings commenced with prayers blessing the work for the day, announcements of notices in the calendar, reading the anniversaries in the obit book and a chapter of the Rule of St Augustine, thus giving the name to the meeting.[72] A large part of the chapter was the confession of faults and corrections. Punishment was meted out depending on the severity of the fault, which ranged from reciting psalms, corporal punishment, being placed on a fast of bread and water, to expulsion from the order.[73] The admission of personal misdemeanours and the penalties inflicted were difficult to endure. Adam Scot, a canon of Dryburgh (later abbot) in the 1180s when a group of brethren was sent to colonize in Ulster, articulates with deep feeling and understanding the nature of communal living. In his spiritual dialogues on the burdens of monastic life, the question of how the chapter of faults is found to be troublesome is answered:

> Ut autem mihi videtur, nec illi nec iste sic umquam in me saevirent si me amarent. Cumque diebus singulis hoc modo me tractari video, mirum non est si magnam in me inquietudinem et impatientiam tolero. Unde etiam compellor sic diligere capitulum quasi profundum ergastulum vel etiam infernum.
>
> [It seems to me that neither those present nor he who presided should be so cruel if they loved me. And since I am treated this way every day, it is no wonder I am so upset and anxious. All this makes me love chapter as though it were a prison – or hell itself].[74]

Abbots were buried in the chapter house floor, their graves positioned around the presiding abbot's seat, thereby linking him with his predecessors and they, in turn, continued to have a presence amongst the living community.[75] Four abbots were interred in the chapter house floor at Lough Key during the thirteenth and fourteenth centuries (Fig. 3.12). Although the location of the four burials in the

---

72 Ibid., pp 9–11; Lefèvre, *La liturgie*, p. 53.   73 An entire section (of four) in the statutes deals with the faults and the appropriate punishments which are grouped from minor 'De levioribus culpis' to the most serious 'De gravissima culpis', Lefèvre (ed.), *Les statuts de Prémontré réformés*, pp 65–82. Expulsion was mitigated to incarceration in 1322, Le Paige, *Bibliotheca*, p. 833. For Victorine and Arrouaisian approaches to the chapter meeting see Ó Clabaigh below, pp 235–40. 74 Extract from Adam Scot, *De instructione animae* in J.-P. Migne (ed.), *Patrologiae cursus completus*, series Latina, 221 vols (Paris, 1841–64), cxcviii, cols 843–72, at col. 848. Translation in Petit, *Spirituality of the Premonstratensians*, p. 218.   75 Jamroziak, *The Cistercian order*, p. 167.

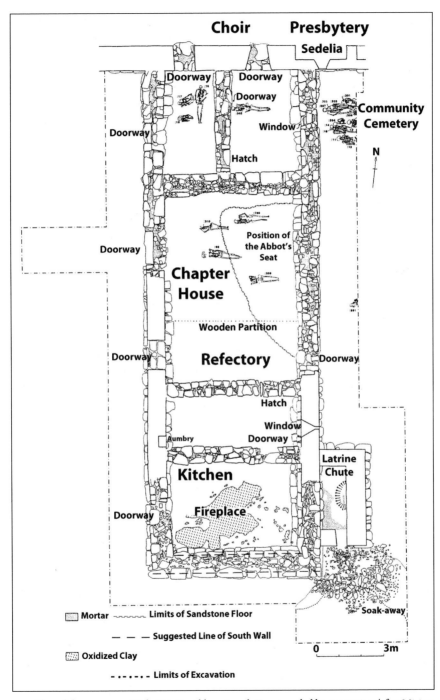

3.12 Plan of the east range, Holy Trinity Abbey, Lough Key, revealed by excavation (after Miriam Clyne, 'Archaeological excavations at Holy Trinity Abbey, Lough Key, Co. Roscommon', *PRIA*, 105C (2005), fig. 10, with permission Royal Irish Academy).

rooms between the chapter house and the choir make them less convincingly recognizable as former abbots, osteological analysis identified them as male adults, suggesting they too could be abbots. Documentation for this period records nine abbots who were drawn from royal and hereditary ecclesiastical families. Liathanach Ua Conchobair and his sons, Gilla Isú and Cathal, were abbots between *c.*1270 and 1343, but Gilla Isú, installed as bishop of Elphin (1284–96), was interred at the Cistercian abbey of Boyle.[76] Other abbots included the son of Mac Diarmada Ruadh, king of Tír Tuathail (d. 1381), and Edrúth Mac Craith of the distinguished ecclesiastical family (d. 1291).[77] The custom of burying abbots in the east range was not continued in the fifteenth and sixteenth centuries.

The community cemetery outside was adjacent to the east range and the presbytery, its proximity ensuring a continuing connection between the living and the dead communities (Fig. 3.12). The presence of a child of approximately eight years at death suggests the presentation of children, or oblates, by their parents, even though Premonstratensian legislation specifies that boys could not be received until they reached fifteen years.[78] The contemporary annals written at the abbey give eye-witness detail on the funeral of a canon. When Áed Ua Gibelláin died at Christmas 1236, his remains were waked in the choir overnight until Mass the next day and his honourable burial afterwards.[79] Further particulars on the ceremonies are supplied in the prescribed formula.[80] A single candle was lit at the head and feet of the corpse in the choir. Solemn requiem Mass was celebrated that day, if the hour permitted, or the next day, followed by the community singing psalms as the procession made its way to the cemetery, where the abbot, carrying the pastoral staff, presided. Burial in a coffin was not allowed.

The kitchen was at the far end of the east range at Lough Key Abbey, the room leading off it was most likely for storage and the preparation of food, and the meals were passed through the hatch in the wall to the refectory in the next room (Fig. 3.12). Household waste did not accumulate in the floors, indicating that the rooms were cleaned out regularly. Clean water for cooking and washing was probably fetched in vessels from the lake, the shore being only 20 metres from the kitchen door (Plate 1). Food was cooked in copper alloy cauldrons on or suspended over the open fireplace in the middle of the kitchen (Fig. 3.12). Two domestic hand-operated rotary querns for grinding corn to produce flour and meal were found in the room beside the kitchen, and at another Gaelic house, Killamanagh, grain too was processed by hand, work which was labour-intensive with low output.[81]

The community ate together in the refectory twice a day for the main meal (*prandium*) and supper (*cena*) in summer, except on days of fasting, and once a day

76 *ALC*, i, pp 466–7, 516–17, 644–5.   **77** *AFM*, iv, pp 674–5; *ALC*, i, pp 360–1.   **78** Lefèvre and Grauwen (eds), *Les statuts de Prémontré au milieu du XIIᵉ siècle*, p. 46.   **79** Freeman (ed.), 'Annals in Cotton MS Titus A. XXV', 42, 302–3, no. 398; 43, 382, no. 398.   **80** Lefèvre (ed.), *Coutumiers liturgiques de Prémontré*, pp 89–91; Lefèvre, *La liturgie de Prémontré*, pp 114–17.   **81** J. Higgins and A. McHugh, *The white Abbeytown, Cill-na-Manach 1260–1990: a history of the monastery of the white canons and other historical places in the district of Maigh Seola* (Galway, 1990), pp 47–9.

in winter, when there was continuous fasting.[82] The brethren sat at tables arranged along the walls facing the centre of the room. They ate in silence, except for the voice of the appointed canon delivering the reading that accompanied the meal. The canons used the iron knives carried on their girdles when eating (Fig. 3.11). Many of the items on the tables at Lough Key may have been of wood. While they did not survive in the archaeological record, their presence is suggested by identification of copper alloy rims from wooden drinking cups. Only one imported vessel was represented, a ceramic jug manufactured in Bristol that would have been highly prized. The lack of pottery vessels at this Gaelic house contrasts with the large quantities of both imported and Irish wares found at Anglo-Norman monasteries.[83] Ceramic tableware was surely used by the communities at Carrickfergus and Dieux la Croisse in the colony.

Initially the Premonstratensians subsisted on simple food and were vegetarian. Their frugal diet was combined with fasting regulations, imposed for reasons of self-denial, humility, and penance. The main meal was to consist of two dishes, and supplementary food was permitted at the abbot's discretion.[84] Ordinarily, the meals might consist of bread and cereals with seasonal vegetables and fruits. The daily amount of bread to be consumed by a white canon was according to the supplies of his convent.[85] Beer was the staple beverage in northern Europe and, in general, the allowance was a liberal one gallon a day or more for each canon or monk.[86] Eggs and dairy products were prohibited where a supply of fish could be had.[87] Freshwater and marine fish would have been important resources for Irish communities, though fisheries and fishing rights are not documented. Fish, including salmon, trout and eel, were readily obtainable at the monasteries on Lough Key and Lough Oughter, and at Annaghdown on the shore of Lough Corrib. Shellfish and species such as herring could be exploited at Carrickfergus and Dieux la Croisse on the Irish Sea. The canons at Lough Oughter Priory, according to local tradition, had a fishing station on a nearby island for a boat to land its catch and where there was possibly a building to store fish.[88]

The outright ban on the consumption of meat (the flesh of quadrupeds) except for brethren in the infirmary, prescribed in papal mandates for monasticism in general, was endorsed by the general chapter at Prémontré.[89] The regulation

82 Lefèvre (ed.), *Les statuts de Prémontré réformés*, pp 11–14, 17–19.   **83** See, for example, C. McCutcheon, 'The medieval pottery' in M. Clyne, *Kells Priory, Co. Kilkenny: archaeological excavations by T. Fanning and M. Clyne*, Archaeological Monograph Series: 3 (Dublin, 2007), pp 316–38; C. McCutcheon with C. Papazian, 'The medieval pottery' in A. Lynch, *Tintern Abbey, Co. Wexford: Cistercians and Colcloughs. Excavations 1982–2007*, Archaeological Monograph Series, 5 (Dublin, 2010), pp 148–58.   **84** Lefèvre (ed.), *Les statuts de Prémontré réformés*, p. 18.   **85** Ibid., pp 20–1.   **86** On monastic beer allowances see J. Bond, 'Production and consumption of food and drink in the medieval monastery' in G. Keevill, M. Aston and T. Hall (eds), *Monastic archaeology: papers on the study of medieval monasteries* (Oxford, 2001), pp 54–87, at pp 62–3.   **87** This regulation appears in the 1290 statutes, *Les statuts de Prémontré réformés*, ed. by Lefèvre, p. 20.   **88** P.F. O'Donovan, *Archaeological inventory of County Cavan* (Dublin, 1995), p. 187, no. 1576.   **89** Lefèvre (ed.), *Les statuts de Prémontré réformés*, pp 20–1, 32, 33.

seemingly was observed at Lough Key in the thirteenth century, when meat was not consumed in significant amounts.[90] Nonetheless, when meat-eating in the refectory was still forbidden in the fourteenth century, the refuse contained the highest proportion of meat bones. Beef was the most popular dish, with mutton and pork served less frequently. Charring on a cattle bone suggests that joints were spit roasted. By that time, meat was creeping into the diet at numerous Premonstratensian houses; however, perpetual abstinence was not mitigated until a papal dispensation in 1503 reduced the days to Wednesdays and Saturdays (abstinence on Fridays was understood), during Advent, and from Septuagesima to Easter.[91] The regulations on fasting followed a parallel path of mitigation, and the days were scaled down to much the same as those for abstinence. Such changes in communal living were part of the widespread expectations of an easier lifestyle prevalent among contemporary religious communities, the earlier austerity being less tolerated.[92]

The household waste disposed of in the latrines contained the remnants of the ultimate meals eaten at Holy Trinity Lough Key. Debris from the kitchen hearth included meat butchered from calves, lambs and piglets, as well as from mature animals. Domestic fowl, duck and goose, possibly reared on the island, were eaten. Cereals in the same deposits were wheat and oat, both of which were malted for brewing beer, with herbs added for flavour, clarification and preservation.[93] Wheat flour produced the best quality bread, and oat was used in the ordinary brown bread and as meal in dishes such as porridge and pottage (a soup or stew). Elderberries gathered in the wild were consumed.

CONCLUSION: THE FINAL STAGES OF COMMUNAL LIVING

Within 200 years of occupation, monastic buildings had fallen into disrepair, or were damaged during military conflict or by fire. Dieux la Croisse was already abandoned in the fourteenth century, the abbey possibly vacated in 1315–16 during the Bruce campaigns in the district, or when the neighbouring borough of Coole was destroyed by fire *c*.1333.[94] According to a papal mandate of 1474, St Mary's

90 All data on faunal remains are taken from M. McCarthy, 'Faunal report' in M. Clyne, 'Holy Trinity Abbey, Lough Key' (archival report, National Monuments Service, Dublin), pp 223–38. 91 Le Paige, *Bibliotheca*, p.730; J.B. Valvekens (ed.), 'Acta et decreta capitulorum generalium ordinis Preaemonstratensis', i, *Analecta Praemonstratensia*, 42 (Averbode, 1944), 139–40, 153, 192. On the changes in the legislation on abstinence and fasting see E. Delcambre, *Servais de Lairuelz et la réforme des Prémontrés*, Bibliotecheca Analectorum Praemonstratensium, 5 (Averbode, 1964), pp 4–10. 92 The revised statutes of 1505, though they followed the earlier legislation in the main, responded by acknowledging relaxations that had entered the order's houses, Le Paige, *Bibliotheca*, pp 841–58. For a useful account on the lead-up to and the contents of the 1505 statutes see B. Ardura, *The order of Prémontré: history and spirituality* (De Pere, Wisconsin, 1995), pp 157–62. 93 B. Collins, 'The plant remains' in M. Clyne, 'Holy Trinity Abbey, Lough Key' (archival report, National Monuments Service, Dublin), pp 219–22. 94 G.H. Orpen, 'The earldom of Ulster', *JRSAI*, 43 (1913), part i, 30–46, part ii, 133–43; 44 (1914), part iii, 51–66, at (1913), 135,

Abbey, Carrickfergus (Fig. 3.2), was rebuilt and renamed Holy Trinity. However, the architectural stone recovered belonged to the late twelfth-century Romanesque church, suggesting that it remained in use.[95] The standing buildings renovated or reconstructed impart information on the changing circumstances and fortunes of communities in the fifteenth and sixteenth centuries. Holy Trinity Priory on Lough Oughter was uninhabitable because its buildings were dilapidated, and when the monastery was again fit for habitation, a papal indulgence was issued in 1427 to encourage the laity to give alms to support the renovations of the church.[96] Today, the west end of the fifteenth-century church is preserved. Donations for the restoration of Killamanagh Church were sought from the parishioners in 1399 and 1428 in return for indulgences, because the priory was in ruins due to the area having suffered repeated catastrophes.[97] St Mary's was rebuilt as a parish church with a two-storey apartment in the west end for one canon to serve the pastoral needs. The monastery was no longer Conventual, as the thirteenth-century claustral ranges were not repaired. William de Burgo, the last documented abbot of St John's, Annaghdown, was appointed in 1497, the papal bull specifying that he was to administer both the spiritualities and the temporalities, and to receive obedience from the community; it further specified that liturgical activities should not be diminished because he was abbot *in commendam*.[98] Two years later, William was holding both monasteries at Annaghdown, having usurped the abbacy of St Mary's Augustinian house.[99] This monastery only is referred to at the dissolution, suggesting that the abbeys had been amalgamated.[100] The architectural evidence indicates the fate of St John's. The Premonstratensian church was rebuilt to its original plan with a nave and chancel, but as a parish church incorporating quarters for one cleric. Communal living had ceased, as the claustral buildings were not maintained.

The rental abstract of Holy Trinity, Lough Key, written by Abbot Cornelius McGyllohcran (Mac Giolla Chiaráin) in the late sixteenth century, refers to the four monasteries where common life existed at that time.[101] Because the abbot of Lough Key was the 'first or head of the order of Premonstratensians in Ireland' (*primum sive caput ordinis premonstratensis in Hibernia*), he had the right of obedience from the abbot or prior of Tuam, Lough Oughter and Carrickfergus, who were

---

137. The latest documentation on Dieux la Croisse are the catalogues of the order, Backmund, *Monasticon Praemonstratense*, p. 433; Le Paige, *Bibliotheca*, p. 334. **95** *CPL*, 13, part i, p. 419. Fragments of doorways and windows were brought to St Nicholas' Church in Carrickfergus, F.J. Bigger, 'The abbey of Holy Cross at Woodburn, near Carrig-Fergus', *UJA*, 13 (1907), 174–81, at 174–6. **96** *CPL*, 6, p. 231; 7, pp 505, 516. **97** *CPL*, 5, p. 268; 8, p. 27. The circumstances of the 'calamities' are not specified. However, this was a period of protracted warfare in Connacht between the Uí Conchobair and de Burgh and their allies. Clanricard territory where Killamanagh was located was invaded in 1419. See Art Cosgrove, 'Ireland beyond the Pale, 1399–1460' in A. Cosgrove (ed.), *A new history of Ireland: ii, medieval Ireland, 1169–1534* (Oxford, 2008), pp 569–590, at pp 576–9. **98** *CPL*, 16, part i, pp 461–2, no. 700. **99** *CPL*, 17, part i, pp 103–4, no. 163. **100** *Fiants Irel.*, ii, p. 130, no. 1567. **101** The rental abstract, Coolavin MS 142, preserved at Coolavin House, Co. Sligo, is published in M. Clyne, 'The rental of Holy Trinity Abbey', pp 86–8, 94–6.

obliged to report twice annually to the chapter, but details on the character of the assemblies are not provided. The summoning of provincial and general chapters in the circaries increased, especially from the late fifteenth century, as attendance at the general chapter at Prémontré declined.[102] Significantly, the rental of Lough Key Abbey informs on how communities in Ireland persisted, how their identity as white canons and loyalty to the order was sustained under adverse circumstances when the dissolution of monasteries was underway. After the English crown had officially suppressed the abbey, the community continued to live on Lough Key under the protection of Brian Mac Diarmada, *uachtarán* (head or superior) of Holy Trinity, who re-roofed the buildings in 1578.[103] Finally, the community was forced to leave when the new proprietor, Edward Crofton, took possession following the grant by James I in 1606/7.[104] The excavation evidence suggests that the monastery was made uninhabitable when the east range was set on fire, destroying the essential accommodation for communal living.

102 P.E. Valvekens, 'La situation financière du chapitre général Prémontré au début du seizième siècle', *Analecta Praemonstratensia*, 14 (1938), 137–88, at 139. For provincial and general chapters convened in England 1432–1504 see Gribbin, *The Premonstratensian Order*, pp 15–16, 234–44. **103** *ALC*, ii, pp 420–1, 422–3. The abbey was leased to John Crofton in 1570–1 and to Andrew Peppard in 1587, but neither lease came into effect, *Fiants Irel.*, ii, p. 231, no. 1742; iii, p. 32, no. 5070. **104** Margaret C. Griffith, *Irish patent rolls of James I; facsimile of the Irish Record Commission's calendar prepared prior to 1830* (IMC, Dublin, 1966), p. 70, no. XXIV.–47.

An archaeology of Augustinian nuns in later medieval Ireland

TRACY COLLINS

Female monasticism in medieval Ireland was particularly fluid and diverse, having elements in common with female monasticism in Britain and on continental Europe, but with features that appear distinct and peculiar to Ireland. A number of religious orders for women were established in later medieval Ireland; Benedictine, Cistercian and Franciscan female religious houses are recorded.[1] However, the most common by a considerable number, was the Augustinian order. This chapter outlines and discusses the archaeology relating to Augustinian nuns and also those of the Arrouaisian observance. First, however, it is necessary to briefly discuss terminology in relation to nuns of the Augustinian order, who are sometimes termed canonesses, and to elucidate Augustinians of the Arrouaisian observance.

The term canoness retains a broad meaning and its origin remains obscure.[2] It first appears in the West as early as about the eighth century, but it was already in use in the East since about the fourth century, specifically for women who had a special place in the church, most likely widows and virgins.[3] By the sixth to ninth centuries on the Continent, the term canoness referred to women who had adopted a religious way of life and lived in community, but – unlike nuns – made no permanent vows, so could leave whenever they wished and marry. Furthermore, these canonesses retained the right to own private property, they wore secular clothing, and they did not recognize claustration, as they performed various public duties. Canonesses formed strong family ties within imperial courts, particularly in Germany, where many noble women became canonesses.[4] The subtle differences between canonesses and professed nuns at this time makes it difficult to differentiate between the two groups of female religious, a situation that is further exacerbated in contemporary documentary sources which refer to both groups as 'sanctimoniales'.[5]

The church hierarchy made several attempts to control canonesses. For example, at the Council of Frankfurt in AD 794, a choice was offered to religious women; to follow a regular rule (the Benedictine Rule was preferred) or to continue in the

---

1 *MRHI*, pp 307–26.   2 E. Makowski, *'A pernicious sort of woman': quasi-religious women and canon lawyers in the later Middle Ages* (Washington, DC, 2005), pp 5–7, 14–22, 103–8; J. McNamara, *Sisters in arms: Catholic nuns through two millennia* (Harvard, 1996), pp 176–9, 191–2; S.F. Wemple, *Women in Frankish society: marriage and the cloister, 500–900* (Philadelphia, 1981), pp 168–74. For the early historical evidence for Irish female monasticism see Edel Bhreathnach's contribution to this volume, pp 20–6.   3 Makowski, *Quasi-religious women*, pp 4–5, 139–48.   4 McNamara, *Sisters in arms*, pp 181–96.   5 F. Griffiths, 'Canonesses' in M. Schaus (ed.), *Women and gender in medieval*

canonical life. At the Council of Aachen in AD 816, a rule for canonesses was created, which ultimately proved unsuccessful. By the twelfth century, secular canonesses were considered a degenerate form of religious life.[6] Many canonesses adopted the Augustinian Rule, becoming 'regular' canonesses, and it has been argued convincingly that these reformed female religious houses of 'regular' canonesses were increasingly similar to nuns.[7] Secular canonesses continued to exist in parallel to their cloistered counterparts but were generally held in contempt by the church hierarchy. For Ireland, as Edel Bhreathnach has demonstrated above, though there is currently little evidence for secular canonesses, it remains probable that women following that religious way of life did exist there. As the female religious discussed in this chapter were likely enclosed, it is preferred to term them Augustinian nuns rather than canonesses.

The Augustinian Rule was an amalgam of texts composed by Augustine of Hippo – including letters directed specifically to a female religious community. It emerged as a normative text in the eleventh century, with an early reference to it occurring at St Denis, Rheims, France in 1067.[8] Although evidence for its transmission to Ireland is obscure, it became increasingly influential in the course of the twelfth century.[9] Arrouaisian observance originated at the abbey of Arrouaise, now in northern France, where its first abbot, Gervaise, had established a segregated community of nuns and canons. Saint Malachy is credited with introducing the Arrouaisian observance to Ireland following his own visit to Arrouaise, with a number of brethren, probably in a similar way to his introduction of the Cistercian Rule.[10] Perhaps his influence is seen in the large numbers of Arrouaisian observance female religious houses established, although the relative autonomy of the Augustinian order in comparison to other orders may have made it a more attractive choice of patrons in Ireland.[11] The Arrouaisian way of life was primarily based on Augustine's Rule but was heavily influenced by the restraint and austerity of the Cistercian constitutions, and its mother house–daughter house arrangement (although this appears to have been resisted in the majority of Irish houses according to Dunning).[12] It has been noted that information on specific

Europe: an encyclopaedia (New York, 2006), pp 106–7; McNamara, *Sisters in arms*, pp 178–9.   **6** For example, at the Lateran Council of 1139 and Council of Rheims of 1148.   **7** Griffiths, 'canonesses', p. 107; Makowski, *Quasi-religious women*, pp 139–48.   **8** See the contributions to this volume by E. Bhreathnach and M.T. Flanagan. See also P.J. Dunning, 'The Arroasian order in medieval Ireland', *IHS*, 4 (1945), 297–315 at 309; N. Hadcock, 'The origin of the Augustinian order in Meath', *Ríocht na Midhe*, 3 (1964), 124–31 at 124.   **9** Dunning, 'The Arroasian order', 309; Hadcock, 'The origin', 124; *MRHI*, p. 146.   **10** Dunning, 'The Arroasian order'; M.T. Flanagan, 'St Mary's Abbey Louth and the introduction of the Arroasian observance into Ireland', *Clogher Record*, 10 (1980), 223–34. L. Milis (ed.), *Constitutiones canonicorum regularium ordinis Arroasiensis* (Turnhout, 1970). For background on Arrouaisian observance with references see B. Golding, *Gilbert of Sempringham and the Gilbertine order, c.1130–c.1300* (Oxford, 1995), pp 93–4. **11** D. Hall, *Women and the church in medieval Ireland, c.1140–1540* (Dublin, 2003), p. 67. **12** Dunning, 'The Arroasian order', 308. Arrouaisian nunneries were dependent on a mother house, although bishops maintained an important role, sometimes interfering, as recorded at Kilcreevanty, Co. Galway. See Hall, *Women and the church*, pp 161–3.

4.1 Distribution map of Augustinian and Arrouaisian nunneries in later medieval Ireland.
(Eight Augustinian houses denoted with wheel symbol.)

institutional arrangements, particularly of Arrouaisian female communities in Ireland, remains sparse and any conclusions must remain at the level of conjecture.[13]

AUGUSTINIAN NUNNERY NUMBERS AND DATES OF FOUNDATION

Nunneries of both Augustinian and Augustinian of Arrouaisian observance were by far the most popular for female religious communities in medieval Ireland (Fig. 4.1). Out of sixty-five nunneries known from medieval Ireland, fifty were Augustinian – almost 77 per cent of the total. Eight of these nunneries have been recorded in the historical sources as Augustinian, with the remaining forty-two recorded as being Augustinian of Arrouaisian observance.[14] Furthermore, the current archaeological evidence of nunneries in Ireland comprises entirely Augustinian nunneries, as there is currently no extant evidence from the nunneries of the other orders. Augustinian nunneries were founded throughout the medieval period from the twelfth century reforms to the eve of the dissolution, and the majority were dedicated to Mary.[15] Nunneries were established at pre-existing ecclesiastical sites and on virgin ground.[16] It is important to note that not all these nunneries were in use at the same time, and it can be estimated that no more than twenty-five of the total number may have operated contemporaneously.

In the cases of many nunneries, a precise foundation date cannot be attributed, although the century is known for all but one, Addrigoole, Co. Laois. The vast majority of Augustinian nunneries were founded during the course of the twelfth century, when thirty-two nunneries were founded before the arrival of the Anglo-Normans – illustrating the fervour of native Gaelic church reform. Twenty of these nunneries are thought to have been established in about 1144, that is, after Malachy's return to Ireland from the Continent in 1140 and before his death in 1148.[17] Twelve nunneries were founded in the thirteenth century and one in the fourteenth century, Molough, Co. Tipperary. Two nunneries were established late in the fifteenth century: Annagh, Co. Mayo, in 1440 and Ballymacdane, Co. Cork, in 1450. Two Augustinian nunneries were founded in the sixteenth century. Both these relatively late cases represent a move by nuns from another community: Termonfeckin nuns moving temporarily to Kellystown, both in Co. Louth, after 1507; and Grace Dieu nuns moving to their church at Portrane in 1539, both in Co. Dublin.

A most interesting phenomenon is that ten, or possibly eleven Augustinian nunneries were, for a time at least, co-located with Augustinian male religious houses. Flanagan has coined the term 'co-located' for houses of nuns and canons

---

13 Flanagan, *Transformation*, p. 152.   14 *MRHI*, pp 310–11. From now on for ease, all nunneries whether Augustinian or of Arrouaisian observance are termed Augustinian.   15 In fifteen of the fifty Augustinian nunneries, the dedication remains unknown.   16 Possibly eleven early medieval ecclesiastical sites subsequently became nunneries in the later period.   17 J.-M. Picard and Y. de Pontfarcy, *The Vision of Tnugdal* (Dublin, 1989), p. 155. The date of 1144 is important, as a papal letter of Celestine III dated 1195 confirmed thirteen places to the abbess at Clonard

living adjacent and perhaps sharing a church. This is a useful term as it first, immediately distinguishes them from mixed communities of the early medieval period in Ireland, and second, differentiates the Irish sites from the double houses of the later medieval period in England and France. Co-location would have made practical sense, not least as a nunnery required a priest to celebrate Mass. They have been characterized as 'monastic experiments' – perhaps representing pre-reform ecclesiastical groups of men and women, adopting the Augustinian Rule without making radical structural changes to their religious lives. These communities may well have been experimental, and a time-limited phenomenon, as several co-locations seem to have become single-sexed after a time, most becoming so by the end of the twelfth century.[18]

Termonfeckin, Co. Louth, became a female house, while Annaghdown, Co. Galway, exclusively male. It has been postulated that the Annaghdown nuns moved to Inishmaine, Co. Mayo, while nuns from Durrow, Co. Offaly, moved to the nunnery at Killeigh, also in Co. Offaly, although there was already an Augustinian (and later Franciscan) male religious house there. At Ardcarn, Co. Roscommon, the location of the nunnery there can be estimated, but the precise location of the male religious house remains unclear, though it was described in the sixteenth century as a church with two houses of stone, perhaps one each for canons and nuns. Co-location was not an exclusively Augustinian trait, as a number of Cistercian houses in Ireland,[19] England, and Normandy[20] also had nuns and monks in close proximity. Considering the number of co-located sites identified in Ireland, is it intriguing what little trace has been recognized in the archaeological record, and currently there is no evidence to elucidate how they might have functioned.

FOUNDERS

Augustinian nunneries were founded by bishops, such as John Cumin of Dublin;[21] Gaelic kings such as Diarmait Mac Murchada[22] (who might be considered a relatively prolific founder of religious houses), the O'Connors in Connacht[23] and the Mac Carthys in Munster;[24] and prominent wealthy families, in the main Anglo-Normans, for example, the Fitzmaurices;[25] religious personages such as St

(which at that time was the mother house for all nunneries of Arrouaisian observance). J. Brady, 'The nunnery at Clonard' *Ríocht na Midhe*, 2 (1960), 4–7.   **18** Flanagan, *Transformation*, p. 150.   **19** R. Stalley, *The Cistercian monasteries of Ireland: an account of the history, art and architecture of the white monks in Ireland from 1142 to 1540* (New Haven, 1987), p. 6.   **20** For example, M. Carter, 'Silk purse or sow's ear? The art and architecture of the Cistercian nunnery of Swine, Yorkshire' in J. Burton and K. Stöber (eds), *Women in the medieval monastic world* (Turnhout, 2015), pp 253–78 at pp 257–8. For Bec, Normandy, France, see L.V. Hicks, *Religious life in Normandy, 1050–1300: space, gender and social pressure* (Woodbridge, 2007), pp 19–20, 136–9.   **21** M. Murphy, 'Cumin, John' in S. Duffy (ed.), *Medieval Ireland: an encyclopedia* (New York, 2005), pp 118–20.   **22** P. Crooks, 'Mac Murchada, Diarmait' in ibid., pp 299–302.   **23** F. Verstraten, 'Ua Conchobair' in ibid., pp 464–6.   **24** H.A. Jefferies, 'Mac Carthaig (Mac Carthy)' in ibid., pp 289–90.   **25** G. O'Carroll, *The earls of Desmond: the rise and fall of a Munster lordship* (Limerick, 2013).

Malachy;[26] or other religious houses. In thirteen cases, the original founder of the nunnery remains unknown.

It is a persistent perception that women were particularly involved in the establishment of nunneries. However, in only three cases are named women associated with the foundation of a nunnery: Derbforgaill (daughter of king of Meath), and her 'completion' of the Nuns' Church at Clonmacnoise, Co. Offaly in 1167; Lismullin, Co. Meath, founded in 1240 by the bishop of Meath at the request of his sister Alice de la Corner; and the establishment of the nunnery at Cork in 1297 at the instigation of a recluse, Agnes de Hareford. It is highly likely that many more women instigated the founding of nunneries in medieval Ireland, but their agency has now been masked by the documented actions of fathers, brothers, husbands, and sons.[27]

Today it is difficult to pinpoint precisely *why* the Augustinian Rule was favoured by patrons and nunnery communities, in preference to other affiliations, such as Benedictine or Cistercian, which were far more common for nunneries in Britain for example, or the Franciscan (or Poor Clare) Rule, or the Dominican Rule, which were popular on the Continent.[28] It can be postulated that the Augustinian Rule was considered relatively flexible (in that, for example, a minimum number for a community was not prescribed), and that Augustinian nunneries had an independence and autonomy that other orders did not offer.[29] These characteristics were likely attractive to members of the religious communities and to the founders – who were in many cases related.[30] The ethos of an order may also have been considered, although there is no firm evidence to show that it was in the past. It can also be suggested that the Augustinian Rule permitted a certain flexibility in function – where a nunnery might also be a school, a community burial place, or a shared parish church, fulfilling all the parochial functions for its local community. Furthermore, the impact of influential individuals in the choice of the Augustinian Rule should not be overlooked. A charismatic and well-connected person, the most well-known being Malachy, or Gille of Limerick, may have exerted their considerable influence on wealthy founders and newly established religious communities during church reforms.[31]

---

26 M. Holland, 'Malachy (Máel Máedóic)' in Duffy (ed.), *Medieval Ireland*, pp 312–14. 27 Flanagan, *Transformation*, p. 200; Hall, *Women and the church*, pp 45–59; S. Thompson, *Women religious: the founding of English nunneries after the Norman conquest* (Oxford, 1991), p. 177. 28 R. Gilchrist, *Gender and material culture: the archaeology of religious women* (London, 1994). C. Bruzelius, 'The architecture of the mendicant orders in the Middle Ages: an overview of recent literature', *Perspective*, 2 (2012), 365–86, at 368. 29 D. Robinson, *The geography of Augustinian settlement*, 2 parts (Oxford, 1980), pp 5–11; Dunning, 'The Arroasian order', 308, 315; K. Nicholls, 'Medieval Irish cathedral chapters', *AH*, 31 (1973), 102–11; T. O'Keeffe, *An Anglo-Norman monastery: Bridgetown Priory and the architecture of the Augustinian canons regular in Ireland* (Cork, 1999), p. 17; L.B. Green, 'Unveiling the cloisters: Augustinian nunneries in twelfth-century Ireland', *History Studies*, 2 (2000), 37–49; Hall, *Women and the church*, p. 67. 30 Hall, *Women and the church*, pp 176–85. 31 Flanagan, *Transformation*, pp 54–91, 118–68; J. Fleming, *Gille of Limerick, c.1070–1145: architect of a medieval church* (Dublin, 2001).

PRECINCT ENCLOSURE AND FEATURES

The extant archaeological remains of Augustinian nunneries in Ireland show that in most cases their enclosure was not a hard line in the landscape, and their enclosure may not always have been given material expression. This is because no extant later medieval nunnery in Ireland now possesses any trace of surrounding precinct walls in stone. It is certainly possible that some razed nunneries did have precinct walls, particularly those in more urban environments.[32] Notwithstanding these, the absence of substantial stone enclosures at extant nunneries is a pattern which cannot be easily dismissed.[33] One likely possibility is that less permanent or natural forms of enclosure, such as hedgerows, may have been employed, as Gerald of Wales described in *Speculum ecclesiae*, regarding a nunnery identified as Termonfeckin, Co. Louth: '... the monasteries were customarily enclosed, not with a wall or a ditch but only with hedges made of sharpened stakes and blackthorn, in which there are many openings not made by chance but deliberately'.[34] Therefore, while none of these nunnery sites have extant enclosing stone walls, it is possible that their topography and vegetation may have been considered by the communities of nuns to provide a symbolic enclosure. This phenomenon is not unique to the Irish context: 'it is clear that women's monastic communities did not always have protective physical walls; their walls were often notional and sprang from understandings of nunnery space'.[35] This symbolic enclosure was dependent on the social relationships between those inside and outside the nunnery, 'upon mutual respect between those who lived inside as well as outside the convent walls'.[36] This mutual respect was part of the codified behaviour and social order of the medieval period, notwithstanding the violent encounters of that age.[37]

The re-use of many Augustinian nunneries since their dissolution has resulted in their archaeology being severely compromised. However, there is some extant evidence at thirty sites. While there is little if any extant trace of precinct boundaries, there is archaeological evidence of some of their precinct features. For example, there are just two extant nunnery gateways in Ireland – at Inishmaine, Co. Mayo, and St Catherine's, Co. Limerick. Inishmaine's gatehouse is a substantial

---

32 For example, at St Peter's Cell, Limerick.   **33** A number of nunneries in Ireland have walls around their perimeters, but these are later additions usually for the purpose of surrounding a modern graveyard, and as such do not represent precinct walls, e.g., Aghade, Annaghdown, Ballynagallagh, Derrane, Kilcreevanty, Killaraght, Killevy, Killone, Molough, the Nuns' Church, Clonmacnoise, Portrane and Tisrara. The wall at St Catherine's is also of later date and is related to Old Abbey House.   **34** I am grateful to Brian Golding for supplying this translation: B. Golding, *Speculum ecclesie* (forthcoming). Flanagan, *Transformation*, pp 153–4. I am also grateful to Marie Therese Flanagan for drawing attention to a manuscript illustration of Kildare in Gerald of Wales' *Topography of Ireland*, which shows the nunnery surrounded by a hedge rather than a wall. NLI MS 700 f. 31r.   **35** J. Smith, *Ordering women's lives: penitentials and nunnery rules in the early medieval west* (Aldershot, 2001), p. 179.   **36** E. De Paermentier, 'Experiencing space through women's convent rules: the Rich Clares in medieval Ghent (thirteenth to fourteenth centuries)', *Medieval Feminist Forum*, 44:1 (2008), 53–68 at 57.   **37** Gilchrist, *Gender and material culture*, p. 152.

4.2 The fifteenth-century gateway into the nunnery at Inishmaine, Co. Mayo.

4.3 Remains of the columbarium or dovecote at St Catherine's nunnery, Co. Limerick.

two-storey structure dating to the fifteenth century (Fig. 4.2). St Catherine's gateway, unlike that at Inishmaine, was for vehicles, such as carts, destined for the agricultural area of the nunnery. To the east is a sunken way, leading to a causeway – the likely pedestrian entrance to the nunnery. This is not an unusual arrangement and in Britain many gateways contained separate formal entrances for carts and pedestrians.[38]

The precinct area would have contained the necessary features and structures for the nunnery's home farm, such as barns, small enclosures used as haggards or paddocks, orchards, dovecotes, fishponds, brew and bake houses, and mills. There is archaeological evidence for some of these features at Augustinian nunneries. For example, the only extant columbarium or dovecote at a nunnery is at St Catherine's, Co. Limerick (Fig. 4.3). Rules governed the provision of dovecotes and it was important that the owners of the pigeons maintained enough arable land under corn from which the birds could feed.[39] Therefore, the presence of a dovecote at St Catherine's shows that it was at the centre of a productive estate and suggests grain was grown or received by the nunnery. While there is no extant evidence for a mill at St Catherine's, it is highly likely that one existed along one of the fast-flowing streams which run adjacent to the nunnery.

Written sources highlight other nunnery precinct features.[40] For example, Grace Dieu, Co. Dublin, had two dovecotes, along with a bread house, two granaries, a barn, a kiln, two stables, a cow house, a sheep house, two pig sties and other buildings, two haggards, a garden, two orchards, and six acres of pasture.[41] Timolin, Co. Kildare, and Lismullin, Co. Meath, also owned watermills.[42] In addition, Grace Dieu operated a horse-powered mill. From this meagre evidence it can be inferred that many nunneries probably once had mills of various types, though in most cases mill type or function is not specified.

There is no historical evidence for fishponds at nunneries in Ireland. Archaeological extant evidence proves there was a fishpond at St Catherine's.[43] This long rectangular pond is water-fed through a culvert at its eastern end from a stream and is emptied through a second culvert at its western end, which re-joins the stream.[44] A fishpond could be used as both a store for live fish and also a

---

38 Gilchrist, *Gender and material culture*, p. 73; R. Morant, *The Monastic gatehouse* (Lewes, 1995), pp 61–5. The Franciscan Friary at Adare, Co. Limerick, although a later foundation (1464) than St Catherine's, has both a wide and narrow entrance feature extant in its precinct wall, confirming the existence of such an arrangement in Ireland.   **39** Dovecotes had to be sited in the centre of the demesne land, so that the pigeons would eat only the owner's grain and not the neighbours. C. Ó Clabaigh, *The friars in Ireland, 1224–1540* (Dublin, 2012), pp 132–3.   **40** The majority of this information derives from post-dissolution surveys. N.B. White, *Extents of Irish monastic possessions, 1540–41* (Dublin, 1943).   **41** In some cases, mill-races were constructed to power the mill and this occurred at Grace Dieu. See M. MacCurtain, 'Late medieval nunneries of the Irish Pale' in H.B. Clarke, J. Prunty and M. Hennessy (eds), *Surveying Ireland's past: multidisciplinary essays in honour of Anngret Simms* (Dublin, 2004), pp 129–44 at p. 139.   **42** *EIMP*, pp 171, 255–6. **43** It is shown on the first edition six-inch ordnance survey map as an ornamental pond in the garden of Old Abbey House but is accepted as being of probable medieval date.   **44** Its modern dimensions are 5m in width (north–south) by *c.*20m in length. It is about 1m in depth.

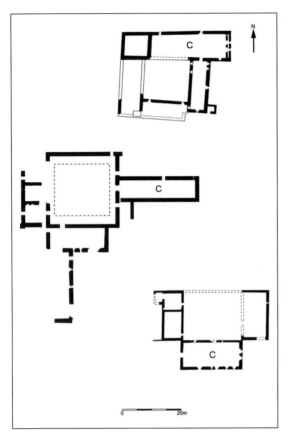

4.4 Claustral ground plans of Killone, Co. Clare, St Catherine's, Co. Limerick, and Molough, Co. Tipperary. C denotes church in each case.

breeding place, where stocks could be increased.[45] At St Catherine's therefore, the nuns maintained two obvious secure food sources, the pond and the dovecote.[46] Other water-derived food sources can be deduced from the historical sources of nunneries and their locations. For example, Molough, Co. Tipperary, possessed an eel weir, presumably on the adjacent River Suir.[47] There is no extant evidence in the outer courts of nunneries in Ireland for gardens, barns, granaries or other outbuildings, as can be still seen in Britain.[48] It is possible that structures were made of timber and consequently have not survived.

45 Currie has argued that religious houses' fishponds were unlikely to have been commercial enterprises. Fresh fish was probably only eaten on special feast days or served to visitors, and everyday fish fare was dried and salted sea species. C. Currie, 'The role of fishponds in the monastic economy' in R. Gilchrist and H. Mytum (eds), *The archaeology of rural monasteries* (Oxford, 1989), pp 147–72, at pp 152, 154–6, 159–60. **46** A second nunnery fishpond is tentatively identified from nineteenth-century mapping at Kellystown, Co. Louth. **47** *EIMP*, p. 336. **48** E.g., Bradford-on-Avon, Wiltshire, J. Bond, 'Medieval nunneries in England and Wales: buildings, precincts and estates' in D. Wood (ed.), *Women and religion in medieval England* (Oxford, 2003), pp 46–90 at pp 72, 84–5.

4.5 Kilcreevanty, Co. Galway. Ruins of nunnery walls extant in graveyard, with structure platforms just visible in foreground.

NUNNERY LAYOUT

It is recognized that male Augustinian architecture does not conform to the perceived standard male monastic claustral plan.[49] This is also the case for Augustinian nunneries, and indeed nunneries of other religious orders. It is estimated that in Ireland only eleven or so larger nunneries ever developed a fully-formed claustral plan,[50] and there are now just three where a claustral layout can be clearly demonstrated: Killone, Co. Clare, St Catherine's, Co. Limerick, and Molough, Co. Tipperary (Fig. 4.4). They date to the twelfth, thirteenth and fourteenth centuries respectively, and all have evidence for subsequent remodelling. Despite having a shared claustral plan, they greatly differ in layout, illustrating O'Keeffe's view of Augustinian male architecture: 'There is, then, no such thing as a typical Augustinian monastery, within Ireland or without, and so a study of

---

49 T. O'Keeffe, *An Anglo-Norman monastery*, pp 112–13; T. O'Keeffe, *Medieval Irish buildings, 1100–1600* (Dublin, 2015), pp 103–4. **50** This estimation is based on available archaeological remains, historical descriptions and dissolution surveys.

Augustinian monastic architecture in Ireland would thus be nothing less than a study of the entire spectrum of architectural forms and sculptural motifs used in the ecclesiastical environment of medieval Ireland.'[51]

To illustrate this point, the important nunnery of Kilcreevanty, Co. Galway, which became the mother house of Augustinian of Arrouaisian observance nunneries in Connacht after 1223, has the remains of a large church, possibly with a transept and little extant evidence of a cloister, which cannot now be identified on the ground. There are several low rectangular platforms to the west and southwest of the church, footings of large free-standing structures associated with the nunnery, showing that it may have had a more fluid layout (Fig. 4.5). Another example is Bartlett's seventeenth-century depiction of Armagh, showing the nunnery of St Brigid to the south-east of the city, within a circular enclosure.[52] One explanation is that this nunnery is thought to have originated in the early medieval period and so it is possible that its earlier morphology was maintained. Caltragh, Collinstown, Co. Westmeath, is today manifested as an irregular-shaped earthen enclosure on the edge of Lough Lene without any indication of a cloister complex, despite its identification as a likely nunnery.[53]

Somewhat surprisingly, it remains unknown what accommodation the Augustinian nuns at Kildare used. From historical evidence it had a 'fortilage' or castle within its precincts, while Timolin nunnery was described as 'a castle and other houses, dwelling-places of the nuns'.[54] For smaller communities, accommodation attached to the church was used as at Inishmaine, Co. Mayo, Drumalgagh, Co. Roscommon, and Annaghdown, Co. Galway, for example. The existence of these alternative layouts to the cloister is supported by a note in Archbishop Alen's Register (dated to *c.*1172–1534) regarding the nuns of Timolin, Co. Kildare, and Grace Dieu, Co. Dublin. An entry dated 14 March 1326 states that they were 'originally cloistral without a cloister and regulars without a rule.'[55] Alternative layouts of nunneries have been identified elsewhere, particularly in Germany, where they are termed 'open systems'. Moreover, they have been identified in all of the nunnery orders established in medieval Germany.[56]

NUNNERY CHURCHES

There is extant evidence of portions of twenty nunnery churches, sixteen of which have meaningful ground plans. They are aisleless parallelograms, without transepts or the use of meaningful architectural proportions, but were usually long and

51 T. O'Keeffe, *An Anglo-Norman monastery*, p. 12.   **52** C. McCullough and W.H. Crawford, *Irish historic towns atlas no. 18: Armagh* (Dublin, 2007), p. 2, map 4.   **53** R. Masterson, *Medieval Fore, County Westmeath* (Dublin, 2014), p. 11.   **54** *EIMP*, pp 163, 171.   **55** C. McNeill (ed.), *Calendar of Archbishop Alen's register, c.1172–1534* (Dublin, 1950), p. 180.   **56** C. Mohn, *Mittelalterliche Klosteranlagen der Zisterzienserinnen: Architektur der Frauenkloster im mitteldeutschen Raum. Berliner Beitrage zu Bauforschung und Denkmalpflege 4* (Petersberg, 2006).

4.6 Piscina and tomb niche in church of St Catherine's, Co. Limerick.

narrow. There is no archaeological evidence for structural internal differentiation in any of the churches, but it is likely that the space was divided by timber or textile screens. The use of internal space within nunnery churches in Ireland closely follows arrangements found in England and on the Continent and evidence suggests that nuns used both the east and west ends of their churches in different periods, sharing the sacred space with clergy, and when parochial, also with the laity.

The use of west end galleries in nunnery churches is a feature common in nunnery churches in Germany for example and was, somewhat unusually, used in the nunnery on Iona, Scotland, but no such evidence was found in any of the churches in Ireland. Rather, where the west end was utilized by the nuns, the ground floor seems to have been used, as seen in some nunnery churches in France. Other church features extant include many variants of windows and doors, piscinas (at Ballymacdane, Co. Cork and St Catherine's, Co. Limerick), bellcotes (at Molough, Co. Tipperary and Killone, Co. Clare), and some decorative features, such as stone heads (Killone) (Fig. 4.6). No altars are currently known. These features are similar to those in male foundations, sharing the same 'vocabulary' of religious house architecture. On the basis of the extant evidence of nunnery churches in Ireland it is concluded that they had more in common with the architectural traditions of medieval parish churches than of male monastic churches.[57] This may be because nunneries were firmly embedded within their

---

57 For overviews of parish churches see: O'Keeffe, *Irish buildings*, pp 127–39; E. FitzPatrick and R. Gillespie (eds), *The parish in medieval and early modern Ireland: community, territory and building* (Dublin, 2006).

4.7 Possible anchorhold attached to northern side of church of Templenagalliaghdoo, Errew,
Co. Mayo.

regional and local religious contexts, and further from the national and
international male monastic sphere.

Of interest in relation to nunnery churches is the possibility of previously
undocumented anchorholds at two churches: St Catherine's, Co. Limerick, and at
the small church of Templenagallighdoo, adjacent to the Augustinian male
religious house at Errew, Co. Mayo, which, based on the place-name, is likely to
have been a female foundation, or perhaps housed a female anchorite (Fig. 4.7).
While anchorites are known from historical evidence in Ireland, their archaeology
and architecture remain elusive. Indeed, it is possible that anchorites at nunneries
may have been female or male, as the documented female anchorite at the male
Premonstratensian house on Trinity Island, Lough Key, Co. Roscommon attests.[58]

CONCLUSIONS

Diversity, or 'multiformity', is key to understanding the archaeology and
architecture of Augustinian nunneries in medieval Ireland.[59] Variation in nunneries
in England has been considered a defining feature of later female monasticism there

---

58 C. Ó Clabaigh, 'Anchorites in late medieval Ireland' in L. Herbert McAvoy (ed.), *Anchoritic
traditions of medieval Europe* (Woodbridge, 2010), pp 153–77; M. Clyne, 'Archaeological excavations
at Holy Trinity Abbey, Lough Key, Co. Roscommon', *PRIA*, 105C, 2 (2005), 23–98.   **59** As
elsewhere in the medieval world, see C. Bruzelius and C. Berman, 'Introduction', *Gesta: monastic*

since the 1920s;[60] however, this variation usually occurred within the context of the claustral plan, as eventually most nunneries there did develop a cloister. In medieval Ireland, notwithstanding the lack of above-ground remains, claustrally arranged nunneries were not the norm and a range of layouts was adopted. It would appear from the archaeological evidence that only some nunneries utilized the claustral plan, which was similar but not the same as that of male religious houses and was used in distinctly more flexible ways. Others did not choose a claustral plan at all. This suggests that Augustinian female religious were not constrained by a claustral layout because it was not deemed necessary for them to fulfil their roles as brides of Christ.

Augustinian architecture, whether male or female, has always been seen as fluid, being previously (though unfairly) considered as deviant from the typical monastic standard, resulting in its scholarly neglect.[61] The flexibility of the Augustinian Rule would appear to offer a convenient explanation as to why nunnery layouts in later medieval Ireland were so diverse and did not correspond to their own standardized form. However, this conclusion is problematic. The Augustinian Rule cannot be considered to be the primary reason for nunnery diversity in Ireland, as nunneries of other orders in different regions also show diversity in plan: for example, Benedictine nunneries in England, and perhaps most starkly, Cistercian nunneries in Germany.[62] So, the preference of the Augustinian Rule and Arrouaisian Observance in later medieval Ireland can be considered as a contributing factor to the variety of nunnery layout and architecture, but cannot be considered the primary reason for it. Other distinctly regional elements – for example, the re-use of or continuity of use at some earlier sites in the twelfth century by Gaelic patrons – may have led to non-claustral forms being perpetuated, especially at co-located religious houses.

It can be concluded that multiformity, both between orders and within the same order, is not unusual in a female monastic context in any part of the medieval monastic world. Because of this variation, it is very difficult to generalize about

architecture for women, 31:2 (1992), 73–5; J. Burton and K. Stöber (eds), *Women in the medieval monastic world* (Turnhout, 2015); S. Vanderputten, *Dark Age nunneries: the ambiguous identity of female monasticism, 800–1050* (Ithaca, 2018). **60** A. Clapham, 'The priory and manor house of Dartford', *Archaeological Journal*, 83 (1926), 67–85 at 78, fn 1; J. Bond, 'Medieval nunneries in England', p. 86; J. Burton, *Monastic and religious orders in Britain, 1000–1300* (Cambridge, 1994), p. 106. **61** For discussion see for Ireland: O'Keeffe, *An Anglo-Norman monastery*; T. O'Keeffe, 'Augustinian regular canons in twelfth- and thirteenth-century Ireland: history, architecture and identity' in Burton and Stöber, *Canons*, pp 469–84. For Britain: Robinson, *Augustinian settlement*, pp 22–73; D. Robinson, 'The Augustinian canons in England and Wales: architecture, archaeology and liturgy 1100–1540', *Monastic Research Bulletin*, 18, 2–29 at 11–25; G. Coppack, 'Thornholme Priory: the development of a monastic outer court' in R. Gilchrist and H. Mytum (eds), *The archaeology of rural monasteries* (Oxford, 1989), pp 185–222; G. Coppack, *Abbeys and priories* (Stroud, 2006), p. 12; K. Stöber, 'The regular canons in Wales' in Burton and Stöber, *Canons*, pp 87–113; K. Stöber and D. Austin, 'Culdees to canons: the Augustinian houses of north Wales' in J. Burton and K. Stöber (eds), *Monastic Wales, new approaches* (Cardiff, 2013), pp 41–54 at pp 41–6. **62** Golding, *Gilbert of Sempringham*, pp 71–101; Burton, *Monastic and religious orders*, pp 100–8;

monastic architecture and archaeology of female religious. The identification of a fluidity of form in the physical layout of nunneries has certainly placed a greater emphasis on the nature of the ritual and performance of the liturgy and the rhythm of the divine office: space as practiced place.[63] A claustral plan was clearly not essential in the creation of this rhythm. Any place where the Divine Office was celebrated could become, through repetition and performance, imbued with a sacred quality, which could accommodate and facilitate the nuns' vocations as brides of Christ. The role of women themselves in the designing and determining of space within female religious communities requires further consideration, sources permitting, but it can be concluded that the typical monastic standard claustral plan was not considered appropriate or necessary for all female communities, and certainly was not a prerequisite for Augustinian nuns in medieval Ireland.

Gilchrist, *Gender and material culture*, pp 39–41, 61; Bond, 'Medieval nunneries in England', p. 86; Mohn, *Mittelalterliche Klosteranlagen*. **63** A. Müller, 'Presenting identity in the cloister, remarks on Benedictine and mendicant concepts of space' in A. Müller and K. Stöber (eds), *Self-representation of medieval religious communities: the British Isles in context* (Berlin, 2009), pp 167–87, at p. 169; M. De Certeau, *The practice of everyday life* (Berkeley, 1984).

The canons and canonesses of St Augustine at Clonfert

CHRISTY CUNNIFFE

INTRODUCTION

The regular canons of St Augustine and the Arrouaisian canonesses were introduced to Clonfert, Co. Galway in the mid-twelfth century. Unfortunately, neither house survives to any great extent today. Both establishments continued in operation until the sixteenth-century dissolution of the Irish monasteries. It is argued that they initially functioned as a double or co-located monastery, but by the thirteenth century the two were independent entities. Their introduction to Clonfert heralded a number of important changes. In the first instance, the establishment of the Augustinians at Clonfert indicates significant physical expansion and development of the settlement. Their foundation is also linked to the wider twelfth-century reform movement active throughout the country and was also clearly an act of royal patronage, showing secular interest in the growing settlement.

DISCUSSION

Without adequate records or material evidence from excavation, it is impossible to know how the regular canons related in a social or commercial sense with the wider population within the settlement at Clonfert beyond their role of providing pastoral care. The layout of the churches and domestic buildings used by the canons and nuns was very practical and functional, to meet the requirements of worship and the everyday needs of the community. They were well located, taking into consideration such practical things as proximity to a supply of fresh water for domestic use and to a stream of running water for the convenient disposal of effluent.[1] It must also be noted that religious houses were not only places of worship, but also functioned as centres of learning and provided 'relief to the poorer sections of society' and 'nursing care for the elderly and the sick among the population'.[2] The scant remnants of the two religious houses at Clonfert still act as physical reminders of their former presence and prominence.

---

1 B. Little, *Abbeys and priories in England and Wales* (London, 1979), p. 10; T. O'Keeffe, *Medieval Ireland: an archaeology* (Stroud, 2001), p. 139.   2 T.B. Barry, *The archaeology of medieval Ireland* (London & New York, 1987), p. 162. See the contribution below by Hogan pp 151–2 on the charitable activities of the canons of Llanthony in Drogheda.

Clonfert was within the territorial limits of the provincial overlords – the Uí Chonchobhair dynasty, and at some time in the period *c.*1140–48 Toirdealbhach Ó Conchobhair patronized a monastery for regular canons of St Augustine at Clonfert, though the Uí Mhadáin and Uí Chormacáin families managed to take control of the abbacy on a regular basis during its lifetime.[3] Watt refers to Ó Conchobhair as 'perhaps the most assiduous promoter of all of the Augustinian canons'.[4] He cites the foundation of houses at Annaghdown, Clonfert, Roscommon, Cong, Tuam, Clonmacnoise and Cloontuskert (Co. Roscommon) as products of Ó Conchobhair patronage. A total of four houses for regular canons was erected in the diocese of Clonfert; St Mary *De Portu Puro* in Clonfert, St Mary *De Patrum* in Clontuskert, St Mary *De Via Nova* in Abbeygormican and St Catherine in Aughrim (Fig. 5.2). The site of the Abbey of St Mary *de Portu Puro* is some 500m south-east of the cathedral, outside of the enclosing *vallum* of the early medieval foundation.

The Augustinians had a preference for dedicating their houses to the Virgin Mary or other saints of international origin, as distinct from more traditional local saints. This even occurred where 'their foundations were superimposed on older monastic sites with prominent native patrons', such as at Clonfert.[5] Blake suggests that the name *de Portu Puro*, 'of the Clear Harbour', refers to the presence of a harbour on the Shannon at Clonfert.[6] Little by way of historical information is available regarding the earlier life of the foundation, but records are somewhat better for the late medieval and early modern period.[7] The abbey was in need of repair in the earlier part of the fifteenth century. In 1414, Pope John XXIII granted indulgences for the repair of the cathedral and of the abbey church.[8] The abbey was stated to be very poor and it was difficult to support the abbot and eight canons.[9] By the end of the fifteenth century it had fallen into the hands of laymen and was in decay again.[10] The various letters that issued between the papal chancery and the diocese are important sources of information, helping to identity some of the regular canons at Clonfert. Several entries concern complaints made by third parties to the papacy concerning appointments of which they disapproved and other such matters. For example, in 1441 and again in 1447, the abbot William Ó Mhadáin (O'Madden) was accused by his namesake Roderick Ó Mhadáin, a canon, and in 1486–7, John Obroym, a canon of illegitimate birth and a native of the city (*et nativium civitatis*), was granted a dispensation to become the sacrist of the abbey.[11] In 1488 it appears that the pope was falsely informed by William Obrogay, a canon of the monastery, that the abbot also named William (probably Ó Mhadáin):

---

3 *MRHI*, p. 164.   **4** J. Watt, *The church in medieval Ireland* (Dublin, 1972), p. 46.   **5** M. Mac Mahon, 'The charter of Clare Abbey', *The Other Clare*, 17 (1993), p. 26.   **6** J. Blake, 'A note on Roland de Burgo alias Burke, bishop of Clonfert; and the monastery "De Portu Puro" at Clonfert', *JGAHS*, 4 (1905–6), p. 230.   **7** P. Larkin, *A calendar of papal registers relating to Clonfert diocese* (2016). This very useful publication contains all of the references relating to Clonfert in the medieval papal registers.   **8** *CPL*, 6, p. 411.   **9** *MRHI*, p. 65.   **10** P.K. Egan, *Parish of Ballinasloe* (Galway, 1994), p. 44.   **11** *CPL*, 11, p. 142.

had perpetrated diverse excesses and crimes, impetrated certain letters surreptitiously extorted from the present pope to certain judges in those parts, which judges, wrongfully proceeding, promulgated an unjust definitive sentence in favour of the said William Obrogay, and against the said abbot William, from which the latter has appealed to the apostolic see, in the matter of which appeal he has impetrated other papal letters, perhaps not yet presented, to certain judges in those parts, proposes after the said sentence has been annulled, to cede the rule and administration of the said monastery.[12]

It seems from a petition made in 1488 by Bishop Matthew Macraith and the same abbot William, that the fruits of the church of Clonfert had become so much reduced in value that they were 'insufficient for the support of the pontifical dignity', that its removable goods were 'wrongfully occupied by divers laymen', and that the bishop was not strong enough to recover them due to 'the power of the occupiers'.[13] The document also outlines that the 'observance of the regular discipline and divine worship are so much neglected, and the care of its buildings so much wanting, that the buildings of the house thereof are falling to ruin'. The bishop and abbot concluded that there was no hope of observance being restored or the building being repaired if the monastery were to be governed by an abbot:

> as hitherto, inasmuch as the canons, disregarding the obedience and authority of the abbot for the time being, or rather despising the same, share amongst themselves and occupy the greater part of the monastery's goods, and connive at their being occupied by others, to the great hurt of the said monastery and the evil example and scandal of very many persons, especially of the vulgar sort, who ought to receive an exemplary life from the said canons.[14]

The document also notes that:

> the bishop has no suitable habitation in that city, and that if the abbatial dignity were suppressed, and the said monastery united and appropriated in perpetuity to the episcopal *mensa*, and the perpetual vicarage of the parish church of Lochryach in the diocese of Clonfert, were united and appropriated anew (*de novo*) to the said monastery, (its former union thereto having been dissolved by authority of the ordinary), the said Matthew and the bishop for the time being would cause the said buildings to be repaired, and would keep such canons in the said monastery that by their exemplary and laudable life divine worship would be increased therein and regular discipline observed, and the said Matthew and the bishop for the time being could more easily see the recovery and restoration of the goods and of the

12 *CPL*, 14, p. 241. 13 Ibid., p. 242. 14 Ibid., p. 242.

monastery and church, making a fitting habitation for themselves in the houses of the said monastery, and more becomingly keep up their state as the pontifical dignity demands.[15]

It is obvious that the bishop was successful in this because the abbey continued in use until well after the Reformation. It is interesting to find that he planned to reside in the abbey. Whether this actually occurred is unclear, but it appears likely that it did. The ruined bishop's palace at Clonfert dates from the sixteenth century. Macraith would not have felt the least bit out of place living within the precincts of the monastic house, as prior to his elevation to the bishopric of Clonfert he was the abbot of the Augustinian house of Clare Abbey in Co. Clare. The pope was notified on 19 October 1499, by Malachy Omaytina (Ó Mhadáin), a scholar in the diocese of Clonfert, that Thady Machagan (Mac Aodhagáin), canon of Clonfert, who held:

> *in commendam* the monastery of Blessed Mary, *de Portu Puro, Clonfer(ten)*, by apostolic concession and dispensation, has dared to assemble together on a certain day a certain body of men and with it to insult and attack an adversary or several adversaries of his, in which insult deaths followed on both sides, contracting irregularity; to burn or cause to be burned several buildings of private men; to leave undone religion and the conventual way of life in the said monastery and Divine Office therein; and also to appropriate the portion of several canons of his monastery and deny those portions to them, and to come and go contrary to his own oath.[16]

This entry highlights the way in which powerful native families embedded themselves in the church at that time. Apart from highlighting how Mac Aodhagáin usurped church revenues it also notes the burning of private buildings by him – an important point, as it hints at the presence of a wider lay community within the settlement. It is apparent that Malachy had a more personal request to make of the pope, as it can be seen from the same notice that he sought the pontiff's approval to become a cleric.[17]

In 1543, Bishop Roland de Burgo secured a royal grant uniting the monastery of regular canons *de Portu Puro* with the bishopric of Clonfert.[18] In actual fact, the monastery was already united to the bishopric by papal authority since 1488.[19] The canons remained undisturbed and the abbot, Henry Ó Cormacáin, retained the temporalities till his death about 1561. They were then in dispute between the bishop and others until 1567, when William Ó Cormacáin was placed in the abbacy by the pope. He and de Burgo agreed to divide the spiritualities and temporalities

---

15 Ibid., p. 242.   16 *CPL*, 21, p. 145.   17 Ibid., p. 145.   18 Monasterium de Portu Puro Civitatis Clonfertensis unitum perpetuo episcopatui Clonfertensis cui unitesunt infrascripte vicaries per patentes litteras Regine: K.W. Nicholls, 'Visitations of the dioceses of Clonfert, Tuam and Kilmacduagh, *c*.1565–1567', *Anal. Hib.*, 26 (1970), 148.   19 Egan, *Parish of Ballinasloe*, p. 51.

between them and, on Ó Cormacáin's death, the bishop enjoyed all the revenues until his death in 1580.

Martin Blake draws attention to an exchequer inquisition during the reign of James I that provides an insight on the later ownership of the building and its lands.

> Inquisition taken at Galway the 7th August 1607, before a Jury, who find: That the Monastery of Clonfert formerly called Monastery *'De Portu Puro'* was never surrendered to the King: That said monastery was granted by fiant of King Henry VIII to Roland Burke late Bishop of Clonfert in which fiant it is recited that the Abbey was annexed to the See of Clonfert: That Henry O'Cormacan was Abbot and died seized of the lands and the temporalities and spiritualities of said Abbey: That after the death of said Henry O'Cormacan, Bishop Burke and others were in dispute about the profits of the Abbey for five or six years: That William O'Cormacan (1567) then betook himself to Rome and obtained the Abbey from the Pope: That an agreement was then come to between said William and Bishop Burke that the temporalities and spiritualities should be divided between them: that on the death of said William O'Cormacan in 1571, Bishop Burke received the whole until his death: That (Stephen) Kirwan was appointed Bishop of Clonfert after the death of Roland Burke, and came to an agreement with Redmond Burke *son* of Roland and gave to him moiety of the profits: That after the death of said Redmond Burke, said Bishop Kirwan took the whole of the mesne profits: That the total quantity of land amounts to 6 quarters, and the annual rent of the quarter of Down McMearan: That after the death of said Bishop Kirwan, the mesne profits came to the hands of the Bishop of Clonfert that is now (Roland Lynch).[20]

In 1607, Sir John King of Dublin, an Englishman and a member of the government of Connacht, was granted, among other church lands, 'the site, etc., of the late monastery of *Portu Puro* of Royal Canons of St Augustines order, in the city or town of Clonfert, with the church steeple, and dormitory thereof, and all its hereditments; for rent of 3*l*.'[21] This throws light on the condition of the abbey at that time and also alludes to Clonfert as a 'city' or 'town'. The term city (*civitas*) in this context probably indicates an episcopal city or simply 'bishop's seat', but the reference to the 'town' in this document presumably indicates a complex cathedral-based settlement with at least some urban characteristics. It is apparent that the abbey church had a tower or 'steeple', as it is referred to in the document, which is helpful in understanding the various architectural components of the building. The reference to a dormitory is also important but is hardly surprising as the

---

20 Blake, 'A note on Roland de Burgo alias Burke', pp 230–2.   **21** M.C. Griffith, *Irish patent rolls Ireland James I: facsimile of the Irish record commissioners' calendar prepared prior to 1830* with foreword prepared by M.C. Griffith, vol. 4 (IMC, Dublin, 1966), p. 97.

archaeological evidence shows that an extensive monastic footprint survives on the ground. It appears from this that the abbey buildings still survived, though no longer functioned as a religious house.

Robert Dawson, the former dean of Downpatrick, Co. Down, succeeded to the bishopric in 1627. The king's letter of August 1626 promoting him to Clonfert ordered that he be assisted in restoring the abstracted revenues of the see, but he had achieved no success by 1630.[22] However, with Wentworth's help, he managed to recover the abbey in 1634, it being granted to him and his successors in pure alms by king's letter, 'in as full a manner as Sir Henry Lynch bart now holds it'.[23]

ARCHAEOLOGY OF ST MARY DE PORTU PURO

The remains of the Augustinian abbey had all but disappeared by 1838 when it was visited during the progress of the Ordnance Survey. Patrick O'Keeffe then recorded that it had 'all disappeared excepting a small fragment of one wall twelve feet high, seven broad and three feet thick'.[24] That section of wall is still visible, though it has decreased considerably in height (Fig. 5.1). A large rectangular earthen platform survives, within which a series of raised earth-covered wall-footings, of a quadrangular structure, are discernible. This section of the building represents the claustral range; the large rectangular area correlates to the outline of the cloister garth. The surviving portion of wall is the inner claustral wall of the east range of the conventual buildings. A short, well-defined section of wall extends to the east at the south-east corner of this wall, indicating the position of a probable cross wall. Also evident is a linear bank of earth covering a stone core, which runs parallel to the line of this wall at roughly 8.5m from it. This feature is located at a point where one might expect to find the east wall of the east range containing individual claustral buildings, such as the sacristy, chapter house and parlour. It is interesting to speculate about the size of the building. The presence of what is likely to be a crossing-tower raises the possibility that this was a well-developed and formidable building in its day.

Evidence for burial occurs in the general precincts of the abbey; human bone is revealed whenever farm animals break the surface. It is certain that there would once have been a graveyard here for the canons. However, it is uncertain whether the graveyard also accommodated members of the lay population living outside of the abbey walls, which would have been normal practice.

The surviving raised platform is cut by the line of the public road. This is a relatively late intrusion in the landscape, probably constructed in the mid-to-late eighteenth century. The road-take splits the site, destroying most of the evidence

22 R.P. Mahaffy, *Calendar of state papers relating to Ireland preserved in the Public Records Office, 1647–1660* (Her Majesty's Stationery Office, London, 1903), p. 77.   23 Egan, *The parish of Ballinasloe*, p. 76.   24 O'Flanagan, *Letters containing information relative to the antiquities of County Galway collected during the progress of the Ordnance Survey in 1839* [typescript in 2 vols] (Bray, 1928), p. 37.

5.1 Wall footing of the Augustinan abbey, Clonfert, viewed from the west.

for structures that may have existed to the north of the quadrangle. Fortunately, a short section of wall survives in the roadside hedge. This appears to be part of the south wall of the nave of the abbey church. Nothing else survives above ground level.

A quantity of reused carved blocks of dressed ashlar likely to have originated from the Augustinian abbey survives in the window embrasures and chimneys of the *c.*1640 addition to the bishop's palace, situated about 500m north-west of the abbey. Indeed, the whole later phase of the palace building could have been constructed with stone quarried from the abbey.

Augustinian houses generally follow a claustral plan, where all the buildings of the monastery, including the church, are conjoined and look inwards onto a central courtyard or cloister.[25] This layout had developed from complex sources before the early ninth century, when it appears fully formed, based on the so-called Plan of St Gall, a manuscript ground plan of a conjectural Carolingian monastery.[26] It became the dominant plan type used throughout medieval Europe, being used first by communities following the Rule of St Benedict and, from the end of the eleventh century, by those following the Rule of St Augustine. In late medieval Augustinian houses the church normally occupies the north side of the cloister square with the domestic buildings arranged around the other three sides. Tadhg

---

25 T. O'Keeffe, *An Anglo-Norman monastery: Bridgetown Priory and the architecture of the Augustinian canons regular in Ireland* (1999), p. 50. See also T. O'Keeffe, 'Augustinian regular canons in twefth- and thirteenth-century Ireland: history, architecture and identity' in Burton and Stöber, *Canons*, pp 469–84. **26** W. Horn and E. Born, *The plan of St Gall* (Berkeley, 1979).

O'Keeffe argues that this saved time while moving between different parts of the monastery; for example, the dormitory was always east of the cloister adjacent to the church at upper-storey level, thus 'shortening the trip from the bed to the choir'.[27] However, there is no evidence for the use of the claustral plan in Augustinian houses of the pre-1170 period in Ireland.[28] This architectural scheme consisting of an enclosed cloister garth, surrounded on each side by covered walks, was one of the most attractive and enduring forms devised in European architecture. As the Latin word *claustrum* implies, here was a secluded inner sanctum, a peaceful courtyard, which served as the hub of monastic life. The covered ambulatories provided an excellent circulation system, giving easy access both to the church and to the major rooms of the monastery'.[29] As Stalley also notes, the square form of the cloister plan held an important symbolic meaning for the medieval mind. The existence of four separate passages was appropriate for those religious disposed to think in allegorical terms, the number four provoked thought of the evangelists, the cardinal virtues, the rivers of Paradise, the seasons of the year and so forth. Therefore, whether viewed in utilitarian, aesthetic or symbolic terms, the cloister was eminently suited to monastic life.[30]

At Clontuskert, *c.*7km to the north-west of Clonfert, a well-preserved example of an Augustinian priory survives. By examining the structure there it is possible to visualize how the destroyed buildings at Clonfert may have appeared. Harold Leask noted that the plan of an Augustinian priory 'was not invariable', as was the case with Cistercians, where a standard plan was usually followed.[31] Nevertheless, in the layout of the claustral buildings the regular canons generally followed the Cistercian plan, except for minor details. The east range contained the most important apartments such as the sacristy, which was next to the church choir and presbytery, as well as the chapter house, parlour, scriptorium and calefactory, (warming room) all on the ground level. The dormitory was on the floor above, while the 'latrines (the *domus necessarium*) were normally placed at the south end of this range projecting eastwards from it'.[32] Wherever it was possible, monastic complexes incorporated a watermill in which grain for consumption by the community was ground.[33] Mills also provided a valuable source of income to a monastery as it could use the mill 'for its own purposes; on the other hand, it might also exercise the right of multure, that is, charge villagers to have their corn ground there'.[34]

The documentary sources testify that there was a mill attached to the abbey at Clonfert. It is uncertain when this mill was constructed, the only record available relates that following the abbot's death in 1571 the possessions, then including *c.*220

---

27 O'Keeffe, *An Anglo-Norman monastery*, p. 50.   **28** T. O'Keeffe, *Medieval Ireland*, p. 139.
29 R. Stalley, *The Cistercian monasteries of Ireland* (London, 1987), p. 51.   **30** Ibid., p. 51.
31 Leask, *Irish churches and monastic buildings II, Gothic architecture to AD 1400* (first published 1960) (Dundalk, 1966), pp 20–1.   **32** D. Doggett, 'The medieval monasteries of the Augustinian canons regular', *Archaeology Ireland*, 10:2 (1996), 32.   **33** J.P. Greene, *Medieval monasteries* (London & New York, 1995), p. 126.   **34** J. Burton, *Monastic and religious houses in Britain 1000–1300* (Cambridge, 1994), p. 241.

5.2 Distribution map of Augustinian monasteries and nunneries in Clonfert diocese (drawing: D. Boland).

acres of land and a watermill valued at £6, went to the bishop.[35] The mill is no longer evident, and the mill-race has been the target of several schemes of drainage. Importantly, the field within which the mill originally stood is still known as the Mill Park, an English and thus later fieldname, but nevertheless a useful indicator of the presence of a mill. The mill stream forms the eastern boundary of the abbey precincts and, at its northern end, appears to divide into a series of leats or streams running in various directions. A short section of the tail-race is revetted by a pair of parallel dry-stone walls.

On the north-western edge of the abbey site a penannular mound of earth-covered masonry survives. This appears to be the remains of a medieval dovecote

35 *MRHI*, p. 165.

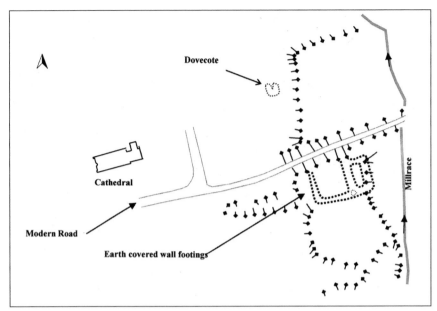

5.3 Relationship between the Augustinian abbey and the cathedral.

5.4 Clonfert Abbey well.

originally associated with the abbey. A dovecote or *columbarium* was a common feature of both male and female monastic establishments. The field within which it is found is known as the Pigeon Park, confirming the former presence of a pigeon house. It comprises of a circular stone-built structure measuring *c*.4.70m in diameter internally, with walls *c*.1.10m thick. The general form and size of the

5.5 Surviving fragment of a Romanesque shrine in Clonfert.

structure fits closely with that of a dovecote at the Augustinian nunnery at Old Abbey, Co. Limerick, discussed above by Tracy Collins (Fig. 5.3).

About 200m south of the abbey, a fresh-water well known as the Abbey Well occurs (Fig. 5.4). It survives as a shallow spring enclosed by a circular stone well, with three steps leading down to the water level. West of the well the faint outlines of earthworks consisting of low banks and shallow depressions survive.

A significant entry in the annals for 1162 records that the: 'clergy of Brendan removed from the soil the bones of Moineann and Cummian Fada and placed them in a shrine'.[36] As Loiuse Nugent demonstates below, the regular canons were active promoters of pilgrimage and it is probable that they were the clergy responsible for commissioning the shrine. A fragment of a Romanesque shrine survives at Clonfert and it is possible that this is the structure referred to in the annals (Fig. 5.5).

THE CANONS' ESTATE

Despite the lack of extents or estate maps to identify the properties owned by the abbey, it is still possible from topographical evidence to pinpoint the abbey estate. Indeed, quite a large monastic estate comprising three townlands can be identified in the landscape. The townland where the actual monastic complex was located is known as Abbeyland Little. This townland contains 231 acres, 1 rood and 37 perches. A sizeable section of Abbeyland Little comprises of bog, possibly indicating that the community might have actively managed some of this property

---

36 *AFM*: 1162; J. O'Donovan, *Annals of the kingdom of Ireland by the Four Masters, from the earliest period to the year 1616* (Dublin, 1854).

as turbary. It would have provided an easily accessible source of fuel. However, the type of evidence required to support this argument is not available – the bogs themselves have been worked over for such a long period of time that any evidence that may have been available has been lost. Turf was cut in Ireland during the medieval period.[37] Turf was also cut by the canons at Norton Priory in Yorkshire, as we find that in 1376 the prior of Norton was paid twelve pence for a cart load of turf sent from the priory to Halton Castle.[38] It is known that in some English monastic houses coal was mined, not necessarily by the canons themselves but by their estate workers.[39]

The second townland that constituted the larger part of the estate is Abbeyland Great. It lies some 4km south-west of the abbey site and consists of 811 acres, 1 rood and 1 perch. Although it has not been studied in any great detail, it contains a number of extant ring-forts, while others were removed in the second quarter of the twentieth century during a phase of field clearance and enlargement. Abbeyland Great may have constituted an out farm to the abbey and possibly functioned in the manner of a grange to the monastery. Added to this is the townland of Cloncondra, comprising of 233 acres and 19 perches, which also formed part of the Butson estate. These three parcels of land combined add up to a sizable landholding, comprising of nearly 1,300 acres in today's reckoning. As Christopher Butson was the last Protestant bishop to live in Clonfert, all three townlands were acquired by him at the time of the amalgamation of the dioceses of Clonfert and Killaloe in 1834.

HISTORICAL BACKGROUND TO THE NUNNERY OF ST MARY,
CLONFERT

Diane Hall's pioneering work on women and the church in medieval Ireland provides a good understanding of the workings of medieval religious houses for women.[40] It gives an insight on the various reasons why women chose to enter religious communities in the first place and shows how they were perceived by the broader lay community. As well as the large monasteries for men that dotted the landscape of medieval Ireland, there were also, as Edel Bhreathnach and Tracy Collins have demonstrated above, communities of women who devoted their lives to doing the work of God and to prayer. Those who chose to become nuns were identifiable by their withdrawal from families and their communal life under religious vows. Like their counterparts throughout medieval Europe, Irishwomen entered religious life for various reason, 'some through intense personal religious feeling', others due to 'family pressures or lack of alternatives'.[41]

37 J. Feehan and G. O'Donovan, *The bogs of Ireland: an introduction to the natural, cultural and environmental heritage of Irish peatland* (Dublin, 1996), p. 5.   38 J.P. Greene, 'Methods of interpretation of monastic sites' in R. Gilchrist and H. Mythum (eds), *The archaeology of rural monasteries*, BAR British Series 203 (Oxford, 1989), p. 57.   39 Greene, *Medieval monasteries*, p. 57.   40 D. Hall, *Women and the church in medieval Ireland* (Dublin, 2003), p. 63.   41 Ibid.

Life as a medieval nun began with a ceremony whereby the novice 'committed her celibacy to the church as a bride of Christ'.[42] She was often expected to make a donation to the order. This could be a monetary arrangement or could consist of items such 'veils, cloaks and other garments which comprised a nun's habit' and might also include whatever bedding she needed.[43] Likewise, her family often gave a donation to the house. While this was not mandatory, it ensured that the new member would not be a financial burden on the community. It also guaranteed that the novice's family would be remembered in the community's prayers.[44] There appears to have been a willingness among Irish women to enter the orders, as Hall points out they appear to have entered the newly established nunneries eagerly in the 'heady years of reform'.[45] A reference to a synod held in Clonfert in 1179 indicates there were women who were defying family opposition by joining nunneries. The reference 'noe portion canons should be sought of women theire husbands still liveing' has been interpreted by Gwynn to mean that no woman could be admitted as a canoness while her husband was still living.[46] This implies that during the height of the twelfth-century reform women were joining religious institutions without the approval of their families.[47]

Patrick Egan states that the regular canonesses had three nunneries within the diocese of Clonfert: St Mary's in Clonfert; St Mary's, Kileen in Creagh and St Mary's, Clonoghil in Taughmaconnell.[48] However, he does not record the nunnery at Ohilbeg in the parish of Clonfert. It must have operated at all times as a dependency of St Mary's, Clonfert. The remains at Clonoghil consist of a simple rectangular structure with evidence of an annexe to its western end. Its main entrance was in the south wall, with the base blocks of another doorway in the southern side of the west gable wall, giving access to the western chamber. An extensive series of earthen and stone enclosures survive, indicating an active medieval landscape. Kileen, on the other hand, retains part of the western gable wall only, but equally it has a very active landscape, comprising earthen and stone banks and enclosures.

Gwynn and Hadcock suggest that the house of Arroasian canonesses at Clonfert initially operated as part of a double foundation with the Augustinian abbey, but by the late thirteenth century the nunnery occupied a site of its own. The original foundation may have been one of those that St Malachy established in 1144.[49] This new house for the canonesses was erected some 500m south of the cathedral and at a similar distance from the house of canons. The documentary sources are quite scant in relation to St Mary's Nunnery. The archaeological evidence, while also

42 R. Gilchrist, 'Unsexing the body: the interior sexuality of medieval religious women' in R.A Schmidt and B.L. Voss (eds), *Archaeologies of sexuality* (London & New York, 2000), p. 91. **43** E.E. Power, *Medieval English nunneries c.1275–1535* (Cambridge, 1922), pp 19–20. **44** S.K. Elkins, *Holy women of twelfth-century England* (Carolina, 1988), p. 98. **45** Hall, *Women and the church*, p. 68. **46** *Ann. Clon.* 1170. This date has been rectified to 1179 by A. Gwynn SJ, *The Irish church in the eleventh and twelfth centuries*, ed. Gerard O'Brien (Dublin, 1992), p. 137. **47** Hall, *Women and the church*, p. 68; Gwynn, *The Irish church in the eleventh and twelfth centuries*, p. 138. **48** Egan, *Parish of Ballinasloe*, p. 23. **49** *MRHI*, p. 307.

scant, provides some useful clues that help to fill this lacuna. The two sources combined provide some idea of what was happening there during the medieval period.

As Edel Bhreathnach has shown above, contemporary records for female religious houses in Ireland are usually much more meagre than for male foundations and sometimes non-existent for several centuries before the dissolution.[50] A similar point is made by Burton about women and the religious life in Britain. She concluded that, 'the study of religious women and their communities' in the medieval period poses a number of problems. She states that one of the major reasons for their neglect in the past 'is the scarcity of source material, specifically a lack of records produced within the communities themselves'.[51] This has certainly been the case for Clonfert, where the extant sources are of limited use; nevertheless they provide some insight into the workings of the foundation.

The church of St Mary, Clonfert [Cluain Feartabrenynd], with appurtenances, was confirmed to Kilcreevanty *c.*1223, when the latter was made the mother house of the Arrouaisian canonesses in Connacht.[52] As noted, the nunnery of St Mary *de Portu Puro* appears to have moved to its new site by the thirteenth century, possibly at the time of, or before, its confirmation to Kilcreevanty. The papal taxation of 1302–7 records a valuation of forty shillings as the 'rent and revenue of the Abbess Monygayun.'[53] In a petition made to Pope Bonifice IX *c.*1399 concerning the nunnery at Kilcreevanty, a large number of the nunneries and associated properties subject to it were listed. In the diocese of Clonfert these included the nunneries of 'St Mary Cluaynochkyl, St Mary *Cluayn Feartabrenynd* [Clonfert] and St Mary Kyllin with houses and other appurtenances'. The same document includes a reference to the tithes of the lands of 'Ochyllbeg'. While not evidence in itself that Ohilbeg functioned as a nunnery at that time, it does show that it was the property of nuns. The next reference to the nunnery of St Mary at Clonfert occurs in 1562, when it was transferred to the earl of Clanrickard along with the other nunneries under the jurisdiction of Kilcreevanty.[54]

THE ARCHAEOLOGY OF THE NUNNERY

When Patrick O'Keeffe surveyed the site in 1838, during the progress of the Ordnance Survey, he recorded that there were at that time three houses, a ruined nunnery, the ruins of a Roman Catholic chapel and a limestone quarry in the townland. This indicates that the ruins of the nunnery were still intact then. A rectangular structure set back from the line of the other buildings, as shown on the first edition map, appears to represent this building. The position of the feature on the site conforms to the general catchment of the graveyard. It consists of a

---

50 Ibid., p. 307.   51 Burton, *Monastic and religious houses*, p. 85.   52 *CPL*, 4, p. 335; *MRHI*, p. 315.   53 H.S. Sweetman, *Calendar of documents relating to Ireland 1302–1307*, vol. 5 (1881), p. 221. 54 H.T. Knox, *Notes on the early history of the diocese of Tuam, Killala and Achonry* (Dublin, 1904).

5.6 Transitional tapered grave-slab (drawing: R. Cunniffe).

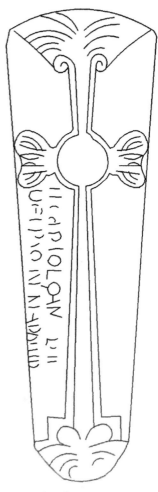

rectangular unicameral structure laid out on an east–
west axis. An ornate transitional style tapered grave-slab
was removed from the site in the late 1890s and erected
on the north wall of the cathedral vestibule. It is a
significant element that hints at high status burial there.
In his discussion O'Keeffe said it was a 'very curious
tombstone where it is said to have stood, somewhat in
the shape of a coffin, ornamented with a cross and
exhibiting an inscription which is certainly ancient but
so effaced that I could not decipher it'.[55] He further
noted that 'Petrie has seen this tombstone?'[56] It is
apparent that George Petrie did see the stone, as in his
correspondence with O'Donovan, he comments that
'the inscription at the Nunnery excited me much and I
spent two hours in a fruitless attempt to copy it, but the
day was unfavourable and there was no sunshine'.[57]

This grave-slab that O'Keeffe noted in 1838 is
ornately decorated with a cross, with terminals finished
in stiff-leaf foliage, and a stepped base possibly meant
to represent a debased form of Mount Calvary. The
slab is executed in a late Romanesque style of *c.*1200
(Fig. 5.6). The survival of Romanesque grave-slabs is
quite a rare occurrence. The inscription is incised in
black lettering arranged along both sides of the cross
shaft. The script is recorded as being in Latin by
Macalister, but is more probably in Old Irish, as one
part of the inscription appears to read as *Or Do* (a prayer
for).[58] The quality of the slab and the use of a very elaborate style of inscription
suggests that it was in all probability erected for someone of high status, possibly
an abbess of the nunnery and perhaps even for Abbess Monygayun herself.
However, Diane Hall is of the opinion that the presence of 'gravestones at the sites
of medieval nunneries demonstrates that the grounds were used for lay burial and
that wealthy patrons would expect burial within the church itself'.[59] The ruling of
Pope Honorius III decreed that in the nunneries transferred to Kilcreevanty 'burial
in their place shall be free to all, except to the excommunicated and interdicted'.[60]

55 M. O'Flanagan, *Letters containing information relative to the antiquities of the County of Galway collected during the progress of the Ordnance Survey in 1839* (Bray, 1928), p. 37.　56 Ibid., p. 37.　57 Ibid., p. 39.
58 R.A.S. Macalister, *Corpus inscriptionum insularum Celticarium*, vol. 11 (1949), ed. D. McManus
(Dublin, 1996), p. 4.　59 Hall, *Women and the church*, p. 172.　60 CPL, 4, p. 335.　61 O'Keeffe,

A community graveyard is one of the main elements that one expects to find associated with an abbey or nunnery. The enclosed area outside of churches was used for community burial. The cemeteries of the medieval period tended to be smaller and more crowded, as there was less concern about undercutting of graves.[61] The medieval nuns' graveyard of St Mary's, though apparently out of use for a very long time, has, over the years, revealed itself. While it is not specifically identified as a nuns' graveyard on the first edition or on subsequent Ordnance Survey maps, what is recorded is 'Tomb' and beside it, 'Site of Nunnery'. This reference to a tomb, which is probably the grave-slab discussed above, is enough to illustrate that burial occurred here in the past. No actual upstanding remains of the graveyard survive. What is known is that in the western section of the site, where a modern farmhouse and some associated farm buildings are situated, evidence of burial occurs; human bones are exposed when the soil is disturbed. A noticeable kick in the townland boundary separating Nuns' Acre from Clonfert South acknowledges this outline, which seems to determine the presence of the graveyard itself. Further evidence of the graveyard came to light when mechanical excavation of a large foundation pit to accommodate the construction of a storage tank was carried out in December 2006. The digger-bucket sliced through a number of skeletons, exposing the broken lower limb bones of those interred. Despite the poor condition of the exposed burials it was possible to ascertain from the position of the skeletal evidence that burial was aligned in an east–west orientation. Following close examination of the section-face of the burial site, no traces of wood or wood staining indicative of coffins was distinguished. It was deduced that coffins were not used and that the corpses were probably interred in shrouds. With the exception of a very small fragment of clear medieval window glass, no artefacts were recovered (Fig. 5.7).

The townland of Nuns' Acre has an unusual profile, having a narrow finger-like strip projecting at its south-western corner. This narrow strip of land is noted on the first edition map as containing the 'site of' an 'R.C. Chapel'. The use of the term 'site of' indicates that by 1838, when the survey was undertaken, the chapel was already ruined. However, an outline of a rectangular building is shown, suggesting that the wall-footings must have still been evident. The orientation is wrong for a medieval church, as it is aligned along a general north–south axis. This suggests that it is a later building or a conventual building adapted for use as a Catholic chapel. Nuns' Acre is recorded as formerly being in the possession of the earl of Clanrickarde. The entry in *Griffiths' Valuation* for 1855 shows him as the lessor of the property. The Clanrickardes acquired much of the properties and lands attached to Kilcreevanty in 1562.[62] The property was thus under Clanrickarde control and was not diocesan land. The Protestant bishop, even if he wished to, would have been unable to stop its construction.

While quite a large number of the names of the canons can be identified from the chronicles, nothing survives to identify the names or private lives of the women

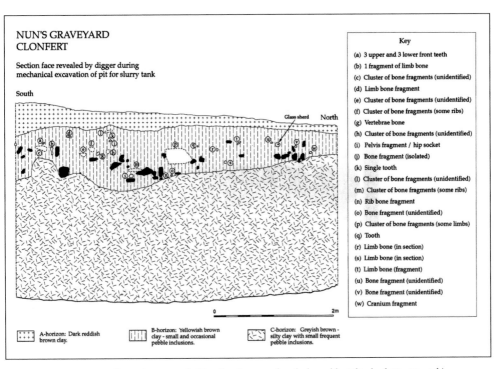

**NUN'S GRAVEYARD
CLONFERT**

Section face revealed by digger during
mechanical excavation of pit for slurry tank

South

Glass sherd · North

Key

(a) 3 upper and 3 lower front teeth
(b) 1 fragment of limb bone
(c) Cluster of bone fragments (unidentified)
(d) Limb bone fragment
(e) Cluster of bone fragments (unidentified)
(f) Cluster of bone fragments (some ribs)
(g) Vertebrae bone
(h) Cluster of bone fragments (unidentified)
(i) Pelvis fragment / hip socket
(j) Bone fragment (isolated)
(k) Single tooth
(l) Cluster of bone fragments (unidentified)
(m) Cluster of bone fragments (some ribs)
(n) Rib bone fragment
(o) Bone fragment (unidentified)
(p) Cluster of bone fragments (some limbs)
(q) Tooth
(r) Limb bone (in section)
(s) Limb bone (in section)
(t) Limb bone (fragment)
(u) Bone fragment (unidentified)
(v) Bone fragment (unidentified)
(w) Cranium fragment

0   2m

A-horizon: Dark reddish brown clay.

B-horizon: Yellowish brown clay - small and occasional pebble inclusions.

C-horizon: Greyish brown - silty clay with small frequent pebble inclusions.

5.7 Section of nuns' graveyard, Clonfert (surveyed and plotted by Elizabeth FitzPatrick)
(drawing: A. Gallagher).

who resided in the nunnery at Clonfert. As noted above, the documentary sources record the identity of only one nun, that of the Abbess Monygayun in the papal taxation of 1302–7.[63] While this is an important reference, it reveals nothing about her as a person, or of her social and family background. It is obvious that as abbess, she was an important person within the community and that she was responsible for its management. The abbess or prioress managed the estates themselves, but they employed bailiffs and stewards, as well as labourers, to undertake the manual work.[64] Hall remarks that in Gaelic Ireland, the women who became the superiors of large nunneries, were generally the daughters of local ruling families.[65] Although we have very little knowledge of the educational attainments of these women, they were obviously sufficiently competent to manage their convents, estates and employees.

The survival of a rare medieval wooden Madonna and Child adds a further piece to the story of the canonesses (Fig. 5.8). Housed today in the nearby Catholic parish church, it consists of a small polychrome statue carved from a single block of oak. Knowledge of its origin derives mainly from folklore, which states that is was hidden in a tree during the Penal era to protect it from destruction and was

63 Sweetman, *Calendar of documents*, pp 221–3.   **64** B.L. Venarde, *Women's monasticism and medieval society: nunneries in France and England, 890–1215* (London, 1997), p. 166; Hall, *Women and the church*, p. 133.

supposedly discovered by a man when felling the tree. Tradition claims that he was alerted to its presence when he saw blood issue from the saw-cut. An alternative account observes that:

> in the Catholic Church of Clonfert a statue of the Virgin and Child cut or carved out of solid Bog oak … Some say it was found in a drain, others that it was embedded in a tree. An old woman Mrs Murphy, Abbeyland, – 76 years says it was formerly in the old Catholic Church, Ballinakill, as the present church was built over one hundred years ago. The statue referred to above must have been found in the eighteenth century.[66]

While both the nunnery and the abbey were dedicated to St Mary, it seems more probable that it originated in the nunnery. The presence of a Catholic chapel in Nuns' Acre suggests that mass was celebrated there at least until the end of the eighteenth century. It seems to have fallen out of use and a replacement chapel was built at Ballinakill, where the informant states the Madonna was kept. It makes sense that the Madonna was taken there from Nuns' Acre. As Hall shows, a feature of nunneries established during the thirteenth century was their conscious break with the older 'Celtic' monasticism, and the way they embraced new reforms was through their dedications to St Mary.[67] O'Dwyer makes the point that 'it was most probably the Augustinian canons and nuns who popularized dedication to Our Lady'.[68]

5.8 The Clonfert Madonna.

THE NUNS' ESTATE

Monastic estates generally came about as gifts from benevolent donors, often the founder. Sometimes the founder might be a male family member of one of the nuns, perhaps setting up an establishment for a sister or daughter. As Edel Bhreathnach has shown above, women too could be significant benefactors of

65 Ibid., p. 134. **66** The Schools Collection, Clonfert, Teacher: C. Ó Ríoghbhardáin, Informant: Mrs Murphy, vol. 0055, p. 69. **67** Hall, *Women and the church*, p. 73; P. O'Dwyer,

religious communities, though their benefactions more often took the form of gifts in kind. Depending on the donor's resources, estates could vary in size but regardless of their extent, they represented a mutual conviction on the part of the donors and the religious communities as to the value of the religious life.[69] In return for material support, benefactors expected to benefit from the prayers of the community, in life and more importantly after death. Major benefactors would also have expected that the communities they endowed would provide a worthy burial place and memorial for them in due course.

While the site of the nunnery at Clonfert is easily identifiable, it has proven much more difficult to identify the extent of the nuns' estate. This is not unique to Clonfert, as Hall notes that a lack of 'source materials hampers the recreation of the estates of nunneries of medieval Ireland'.[70] Although the place-name 'Nuns' Acre' is significant, the area of land it contains was certainly too small to constitute a working estate. In reality its size suggests that it could only have contained the nunnery precinct proper with its various buildings, along with its graveyard, and perhaps a garden and an orchard. There may have been other property close by that was worked by them, but this is not apparent today. So, was there a larger estate connected to the nunnery and if so can this be identified? While no records or extents survive to help with identifying the estate lands, a tract of land in Ohilbeg townland is recorded as being associated with the nunnery of St Mary at Clonfert. Ohilbeg is situated on the western edge of the parish of Clonfert. A small foundation or daughter house was erected here, which probably functioned as an out-farm to the convent of St Mary located in the settlement at Clonfert. In the 1302–7 papal taxation list Ohill townland appears as the 'prebend of the canon of Ochkill' and is valued as 5s. 8d., while the tithe payable is valued at 6d.[71] Knox draws attention to the 'Chapel in Ohilbeg'.[72] Egan refers to the surviving ruins of the medieval nunnery of St Mary, at Ohilbeg, which he says may have been in existence in the early Christian period.[73] He argues that it continued until the Reformation, when Kilcreevanty and its possessions were surrendered to the crown, and subsequently granted to the earl of Clanrickarde in 1562. There is a local account of Ohilbeg convent which relates that:

> Ochill monastery was a branch house of the Clonfert monastery. There is a chalice in Laurencetown church now, which belonged to that old monastery of Ochill. This chalice is three hundred years old. The traditional name of the Ochill church is Kilcraobton … After the destruction of the church mass was said in what is known as Mullin's field, Ochill. Convenient to the old monastery in Connor's field there must have been a graveyard – human bones and broken tombstones have been found there … Near the

Mary: a history of devotion in Ireland (Dublin, 1988), p. 73.   **68** Ibid.   **69** Hall, *Women and the church*, p. 123.   **70** Ibid.   **71** Sweetman, *Calendar of documents*, vol. v, p. 231.   **72** Knox, *Early history of Tuam, Killala and Achonry*, p. 281.   **73** P.K. Egan, 'The convent of St Mary's Oghill', *Past and present, Lawrencetown community hall* (1995), p. 61.

monastery was a Blessed Well … it is said that a fair was held … about 150 years ago.[74]

It is interesting to note that the church was referred to as Kilcraobton, an obvious corruption of Kilcreevanty. It seems therefore that the property at Ohilbeg constituted the extent of the nuns' estate and that a small nunnery was erected there to manage the estate. The mother house was in Clonfert until both houses were confirmed to their new mother house at Kilcreevanty, Co. Galway, in 1223. Like the other houses of canonesses in the diocese, Ohilbeg was confirmed to Kilcreevanty in 1223, and is recorded as one of the many monastic properties in Connacht later conferred on Richard Burke, earl of Clanrickarde, by Henry VIII during the dissolution of monasteries in Connacht. It comprised of a 'messuage and 1 quarter of land, containing 30 acres arable, and 24 acres pasture in Oghilebege in Shillannighy' (Silanmchada).[75] It is also noted that Ohilbeg held the right to hold a twice-weekly market on Wednesday and Saturday, and an annual fair on 25 March, the feast of the Annunciation, one of the major Marian feast days in the liturgical calendar.[76] It was still in the hands of Clanrickarde in the mid-nineteenth century, as is evident from *Griffiths' Valuation*.

The scant remains survive as a series of wall footings and earth-covered foundations, representing the lower course of the north and south side walls of the nave and the rectangular earth-covered outline of other walls at the west end. The rectangular remains are aligned east–west, with a feature attached to the west end that extends past both north and south walls. A sub-circular enclosure encompassing the site is an indicator that this was an earlier site, as noted by Patrick Egan – perhaps marking the presence of an earlier monastery of nuns that adapted the Arrouaisian Rule in the twelfth century.[77] A destroyed children's burial ground located to the east of the site may be the location of the community's graveyard. Ohilbeg is recorded as containing a chapel until as late as the nineteenth century.

The building at Ohilbeg may have been modified for other use, as it is also recorded as Ohil Castle. A conjectural drawing of the ground plan based on a survey of the partially visible wall-footings of the nave and an interpretation of the grassed-over remains of the west end suggests that it had a residential tower at its west end. The presence of this tower may have led to the structure being described as a castle later in its history. If this interpretation is correct, then it may have been roughly similar in plan and elevation to the fortified church of Taghmon in Co. Westmeath. It can be seen from Taghmon that these towers were defensive in their outward appearance. In her study of priests' residences in late medieval Ireland, Helen Bermingham identifies four different types prevalent in Ireland, including residential towers at the west end of the church.[78] Egan describes a similar

---

74 Egan, 'The convent of St Mary's Oghill', p. 61.   75 Griffith, *Irish patent rolls*, pp 179–80.
76 Ibid.   77 Egan, 'The convent of St Marys Oghill', p. 61.   78 H. Bermingham, 'Priests' residences in later medieval Ireland' in E. FitzPatrick and R. Gillespie (eds), *The parish in medieval and early modern Ireland* (Dublin, 2006), p. 169.

arrangement at Bealaneny in the parish of Taughmaconnell, Co. Roscommon, where the ruined remains of the Carmelite foundation contained what he described as a small church with a 'semi-fortified house at its western end'.[79]

CONCLUSION

The limited extent of upstanding remains of both the abbey, and the nunnery, makes it hard to interpret exactly how these houses looked. However, judicious use of the various published documents, place-name evidence and the rather sparse archaeology allow us to piece together a useful account of both buildings and their associated history. Initially, the abbey of St Mary *de Portu Puro* was founded as a house for canons and canonesses; however, by the thirteenth century the convent had relocated to a new site. Despite attempts by Bishop Roland de Burgo to take control of the Augustinian Abbey as conferred by papal permission to his predecessor in 1488, the O'Cormacans managed to hold on to it until *c*.1567. An equally difficult dispute took place between Robert Dawson, the Protestant bishop, who on appointment to Clonfert in 1627 found that much of the episcopal properties had been alienated. The quarrying of material from the abbey for the enlarging and rebuilding of the bishop's palace *c*.1640 likely saw the final destruction of the abbey. The convent and its daughter house at Ohilbeg fared much better under the protection of the earls of Clanrickarde, as both became sites of Catholic chapels. The Clonfert chapel remained in use until the eighteenth century and its ruins were still extant in 1838. The memory of the Ohilbeg chapel survives in the form of an inscribed chalice bearing its name.

79 P.K. Egan, 'The Carmelite cell of Bealaneny', *JGAHS*, 26 (1956), 25.

The role of the regular canons of
St Augustine in the formation of the
parochial network in Ireland

ADRIAN EMPEY

The regular canons of St Augustine in their several manifestations were the most numerous and widespread order in Ireland. They also came close to monopolizing parochial tithes in Anglo-Norman dioceses. In Ossory they possessed seventy-three out of ninety-two appropriated churches, while in the diocese of Meath they were reckoned to hold three-quarters of its constituent parishes.[1] Only the Knights of St John of Jerusalem, together with their preceptories, offered serious competition: they held seventy-five rectories at the dissolution.[2] Indeed the knights themselves possessed an Augustinian rule: like the canons, their priory in Kilmainham doubled as the parish church.

Since the introduction of the canons was closely associated with the twelfth-century reform programme, this aspect of their presence in Ireland begs a number of questions, not least because the effective implementation of reforms rested in the final analysis on the structures that empowered them. In this regard it is important to acknowledge what we do not know, otherwise assumptions will silently occupy the vacuum. It was one thing to create a territorial diocesan system; it was quite another to build a parochial network upon which diocesan administration rested. In short, a diocese without parishes may be likened to a pub with no beer. There is no doubt that the pattern of Anglo-Norman parochial endowment was intimately linked to the structures of lordship. What implications had this for the organization of pastoral care? To what extent were the canons involved in the governance of their appropriated parishes? Further, how seamless was the transition from the pre- to the post-Anglo-Norman period? Were the levels of parochial engagement constant, or were there important differences?

Regrettably, such questions cannot be resolved by resorting to the Augustinian Rule, due not only to the multiplicity of its forms, but also to its application in diverse contexts. Such chameleon-like diversity arose partly from unresolved tensions about opting for monastic or clerical models of organization; and partly because many Augustinian houses were frequently reformed versions of older

---

1 S. Preston, 'The canons regular of St Augustine: the twelfth-century reform in action' in S. Kinsella (ed.), *Augustinians at Christ Church: the canons regular of the cathedral priory of Holy Trinity, Dublin* (Dublin, 2000), pp 23–40 at p. 35; L. Milis, *L'ordre des chanoines reguliers d'Arrouaise: son histoire et son organizaton de la fondation de l'abbaye-mère (vers 1090) à la fin des chapitres annuels (1471)* (Brugge, 1969), p. 375. 2 *MRHI*, p. 335.

A regular Canon   *of St Augustine.*

6.1 An Augustinian regular canon, Mervyn Archdall, *Monasticon Hibernicum* (Dublin, 1786).

foundations that brought with them clusters of impropriated parishes binding them
to a flawed institutional church, as well as importing deeply rooted traditions not
necessarily imbued with the spirit of Gregorian reform. Thus, for example,
Cunibert, bishop of Turin, committed the care of some forty parishes to the canons
of St Jean d'Oulx. Innocent II, a keen upholder of the order, confirmed the
possession of some thirty parishes both to Saint Martin de Nevers and Saint Jean
des Vignes at Soissons. The Augustinian Hospice of Great St Bernard was
supported by about eighty benefices, mostly parish churches.[3] While many
Augustinian houses remained aloof from involvement in pastoral care, opting
instead for the contemplative life, others took it to heart. Nor should we overlook
the impact of a long, heart-searching debate in the twelfth century, principally
among Cistercians and Augustinians, about the morality of accepting tithes.[4] Hard
choices had to be made. Among those who favoured gifts of dependent parishes
was the abbey of St Victor, Paris, which took pastoral responsibility seriously,
systematically designating obedientiaries to its dependent cells.[5] Faced by such
diversity of practice, the guiding principle may be summed up in the words of
Charles Giroud: *'tout d'abord, les circonstances de lieu y sont pour beaucoup'*, which may
be rendered in the phrase coined by real estate agents: 'location, location, location.'[6]
Put another way, context is everything, so it is to context that we must now turn.

The emergence of the new regular orders was not just one aspect of the great
reforming monastic impulses of the late eleventh and early twelfth centuries
(Fig. 6.1). It was closely associated with both the growing pastoral needs of a
society undergoing significant demographic change, and the drive by churchmen,
led by the reforming popes and enforced by reforming bishops, to recover control
of the church's institutions where it had been lost or diminished over the course
of centuries.[7] Twelfth-century popes lavished privileges on Italian Augustinian
houses as a means of effecting pastoral reform, for example San Frediano of Lucca,
which also exercised jurisdiction over San Andrea in Carrara. As Karl Bosl has
pointed out, we must not forget that the Lateran Palace was situated beside the
Congregation of the Regular Canons of St John Lateran itself. Other influential
Augustinian centres included Santa Maria in Reno in Bologna, close to the
epicentre of the emerging study of canon law.[8] Both St Frediano and Santa Maria
in Reno held important titular churches in Rome: respectively, Santa Croce in
Gerusalemme, Santa Pudenziana and Santa Prassede. Not only did the canons
prosper in expanding urban centres; they were also strategically located along
pilgrim routes. It is not by accident that they formed the chapter both in Santiago
de Compostela and in Jerusalem, where they were in possession of the Holy
Sepulchre. They were also active in numerous towns in Germany and were

3 See C. Giroud, *l'Ordre des chanoines réguliers de Saint-Augustin et ses diverses forms de régime interne*
(Martigny, 1961), p. 75; also H. Feiss, 'Pastoral ministry: preaching and confession' in Feiss and
Mosseau, *Saint Victor* pp 147–86.   **4** See G. Constable, *Monastic tithes from their origins to the twelfth
century* (Cambridge, 1964), pp 137–65.   **5** Giroud, *Ordre des chanoines*, pp 75–6.   **6** Ibid., p. 75.
7 See K. Bosl, *Regularkanoniker (Augustinerchorherren) und Seelsorge in Kirche und Gesellschaft der
europäischen 12. Jahrhunderts* (Munich, 1979), pp 17–21.   **8** Bosl, *Regularkanoniker*, pp 35–40.

prominent as missionaries in Pomerania, East Saxony, Silesia, and to a lesser degree in Livonia. Examples of this vibrant missionary activity include Vizelin, who was commissioned by the archbishop of Hamburg to convert the Slavs in 1134, and who founded Augustinian houses at Neumünster and Segeberg, which were to play a prominent role in the Baltic missions; while further east Meinhard, a canon of Segeberg, played a pioneering role in the evangelization of Livonia in the 1180s.[9] In Ireland, Anglo-Norman Augustinian foundations were likewise associated with the new towns. In this they anticipated the mendicant orders. It is partly for this reason that Bosl argues that the regular movement was more in keeping with the spirit of this new mobility – in contrast to the backward-looking Bernard of Clairvaux – and better equipped to meet its demands.[10] He attributes this venturesome *esprit de corps* to the Augustinian theological emphasis on *caritas*, with its insistence on social involvement. In contrast to the older monastic emphasis on withdrawal and sanctification (*Isolation und Selbstheiligung*), *caritas* found its fullest expression (*Hauptberuf*) in caring for one's fellow men, which is the essence of the cure of souls (*cura animarum*).[11]

While the connection between reforming popes in the second quarter of the twelfth century and the canons, who stood firmly by the papacy in conflicts with the empire, has been well understood, the role of the canons in pursuit of reform in the new territories and in the administration of new dioceses offers illuminating parallels with Ireland, both before and after the Anglo-Norman conquest, not least in the dioceses of Prague and Olmütz in Bohemia. As in the case of Malachy, the reform movement was initially driven by native reformers, in particular Henry Sdik, bishop of Olmütz (1126–50), and his nephew Daniel, provost of Prague Cathedral, 1140 (?) and bishop of Prague, 1148–67. Both bishops were regular canons: Henry, as a consequence of a pilgrimage to the Holy Sepulchre, while Daniel studied under Hugh of St Victor in Paris. Daniel was well-connected politically, widely travelled and corresponded with Hildegard of Bingen among others. Like his contemporary Malachy, he had no shortage of friends in high places. The situation in Prague was the occasion of several papal legations concerned with promoting reform between 1143 and 1146 that included two distinguished canons, Gerhoh von Reichersberg and Arnold of Brescia. Thanks in part to papal interventions, Daniel was elected provost of Prague Cathedral, becoming Henry's right-hand man in charge of diplomatic relations, both with Rome and with Vladislav, duke and subsequently king of Bohemia. The upshot of all this artful manoeuvring was the rapid progress of reform after 1140. As in Ireland, it was spearheaded by the introduction of the new orders: Strahov, Doxan (for nuns), and Leitomischl (Premonstratensian); and Sedletz, Plass, Nepomuk and Münchengratz (Cistercian), which were largely colonized from Germany. Daniel

9 Bosl, *Regularkanoniker*, p. 33. For Vizelin and Meinhard see H. Helbig and L. Weinrich (eds), *Urkunden und erzählende Quellen zur deutschen Ostsiedlung im Mittelalter* (Darmstadt, 1975), pp 104–5; J.A. Brundlage (ed.), *The chronicle of Henry of Livonia* (New York, 2003), pp 4–6, 25–30.   **10** Bosl, *Regularkanoniker*, pp 23–7.   **11** Bosl, *Regularkanoniker*, pp 25–6.

was elected bishop of Prague in 1148, where he and Henry's successor in Olmütz pursued a policy of converting existing Benedictine houses into Premonstratensian foundations (notably Hradisch). While this achievement owed much to the zeal of the two episcopal reformers, its success depended on close collaboration with Rome and the secular authorities, combined with the introduction of new reforming orders, and in particular the pastoral investment of the Premonstratensians.

However, the Augustinian input into the transformation of the church in Bohemia was not just the product of evangelical zeal, although that should not be lightly discounted. Both of Henry's successors in the see of Olmütz were regular canons, 'graduates' of recently founded Bohemian Premonstratensian houses, powerhouses of ongoing reform.[12] It was, however, one thing to reform the episcopal sees; it was quite another to create enduring structures in the regions upon which the successful implementation of reform ultimately rested. On his return from Italy in 1160 Daniel set about the task of creating archdeaconries, besides ten administrative centres (*Seelsorgskontrollsprengel*) located mainly in episcopal estates belonging to Prague. He placed chapter canons from Prague Cathedral (*mit Kanonikern des Prager Domkapitels*) in charge of these.[13] Not content with that, he went on to create a network of rural deaneries. The effect of these changes not only extended his pastoral grip on his diocese, but also strengthened the position of the church in the regions subject to the duke of Bohemia, who was raised to the rank of king by the emperor in 1158.[14] Such involvement by the regular canons in the upper echelons of diocesan administration was by no means peculiar to the dioceses of Prague and Olmütz. In Halberstadt, Bishop Reinhard assigned most of the archdeaconries to Augustinians as a means of modernizing the parochial structures deriving from the tenth century. Similar arrangements obtained in the dioceses of Salzburg and Magdeburg.[15]

What might all this have to do with Ireland? First, it seems that in Bohemia, as in Ireland, the introduction of reform was effected in two stages. The first step – laying the foundations – was characterized by the introduction of the new orders in the 1140s, chiefly Augustinians and Cistercians, which in turn became the jumping-off points for a new generation of reforming bishops. The parallels with Malachy, credited with introducing fifty-four houses of monks, canons and nuns, seem obvious.[16] Second, reforming intentions were all well and good, but if they were to be extended and deepened their success rested on the creation of diocesan and parochial structures where they were either absent or deficient. Such structures were essential for mediating canon law and the will of the bishop. This occurred

12 Bishop John from Strahov and another John from Leitomischl (Bosl, *Regularkanoniker*, p. 36). **13** The chapter canons were not, however, Augustinian.   **14** Bosl, *Regularkanoniker*, p. 36. **15** Bosl, *Regularkanoniker*, p. 48; see also C. Morris, *The papal monarchy: the Western church from 1050 to 1250* (Oxford, 1991), pp 247–8.   **16** See M. Clyne, 'The founders and patrons of Premonstratensian houses in Ireland' in Burton and Stöber, *Canons*, pp 145–76 at p. 146. The basis for this number seems to be the *Visio Tnugdali*, composed around 1149 (see D. Ó Corráin, *The Irish church, its reform and the English invasion* (Dublin, 2017), p. 86. While its reliability seems questionable, it is not fantastic).

in Bohemia after 1160, anticipating similar changes wrought in Ireland by the Anglo-Norman church by a decade or two. Moreover, the roles of Augustinians and Cistercians in the new territories contrasted with the older ecclesiastical heartlands, where diocesan and parochial structures – the product of centuries of evolution – were under more restrictive episcopal control. This naturally restricted the pastoral role played by the new orders.[17] While it is true that Ireland was not a new mission field, its diocesan structures were very recent, lacking organizational depth. Ireland was not Livonia, but neither was it France.

What exactly did the Augustinians accomplish before the Anglo-Norman intervention? How did they fit into the wider European framework that we have just discussed? And how did that initial input dovetail with that of the post-conquest houses? Given that an estimated forty-five Augustinian houses were introduced before 1169, such issues seem unavoidable, not least because the context was different. If some of these houses were intended to fulfil the role of cathedral chapters, as they did in Italy, France, the Iberian Peninsula, and Germany, then clearly they were unsuccessful.[18] Only Christ Church Cathedral chapter – which in many ways ticks all boxes of comparable chapters on the Continent – survived this transition. It looks as if St Mary's Abbey served for a time as the chapter of the diocese of Clogher (Airgialla), at least until Louth was absorbed into the diocese of Armagh.[19] Others, such as Leighlin, may have had a transitory existence. There is no good reason to doubt Gaultier of Arrouaise's claim that Malachy copied the Rule of Arrouaise with the intention of providing 'almost all clergy in episcopal sees' (*fere omnes clericos in episcopalibus sedibus*) with it.[20] Whether he meant the adoption of the rule by all cathedral chapters, or the creation of Arrouaisian communities in the proximity of cathedrals – perhaps with a view to their eventual adoption as cathedral chapters – the fact remains that they failed the test of time comprehensively. Certainly there were a number of Augustinian houses founded close to episcopal seats, but they were separate from cathedral chapters, Armagh being a prime example.[21] It looks as if the tidal forces of conservatism were too great for such an innovation to survive and thrive.

What role then did the regular canons play in the emerging territorial dioceses? Whatever rudimentary diocesan structures may have existed before 1169, they likely did not include archdeaconries or rural deaneries, since their existence in turn hinges on the emergence of a close-knit network of parochial churches. Were the canons instrumental in creating and administering parishes? As we shall see,

---

17 'Si les Clunisiens font peu, Bénédictins, Cisterciens, Prémontrés administrant de nombreuses paroisses. Cette participation se fait plus intense à partir de xiie siècle, surtout dans les pays germaniques; en France, en Italie ou en Espagne, l'épiscopat se montre reticent' (see F. Lot and R. Fawtier (eds), *Histoire des institutions françaises au moyen age: tome III, institutions ecclésiastiques* (Paris, 1962), pp 214–19 at p. 216).   **18** See K. Nicholls, 'Medieval Irish cathedral chapters', *Archivium Hibernicum*, 31 (1973), 101–11.   **19** See M.T. Flanagan, 'St Mary's Abbey, Louth, and the introduction of the Arrouaisian observance into Ireland', *Clogher Record*, 10:2 (1980), 223–34 at p. 226.   **20** See P.T. Dunning, 'The Arroasian order in medieval Ireland', *Irish Historical Studies*, 4:16 (1945), 297–315 at 299–300.   **21** Ó Corráin, *Irish church*, pp 86–7.

Augustinian houses were notably dependant on parochial income, as has been demonstrated statistically in a recent study of English houses.[22] The Augustinian priory of Louth is a possible candidate. It appears to have adopted the rule sometime in the 1140s. When it was dissolved, the priory church was declared to be the immemorial parish church. Moreover, the priory enjoyed a significant income from thirty-six churches, very much along the lines of the post-conquest foundations, as we shall see.[23] What we do not know is when these dependent parishes were granted to the priory. They may well have been granted in the 1180s by the new lords of Louth. It should be noted that John, lord of Ireland, was careful to retain the cantred in which Louth was situated in his demesne, taking care to build a castle there.[24] In general, however, we do not find these earlier houses holding large territorial blocks of tithes of the sort attached to Anglo-Norman foundations, a contrast that must raise doubts about the association of pre-conquest houses with the emerging parochial network.[25]

In one important respect, however, the Irish houses followed the European pattern in that many of them were re-foundations of ancient monastic communities. This meant that they carried over a lot of baggage from the remote past that was not part of the Augustinian package. Ó Corráin has pointed out that in practice 'many of the "new" Augustinians were traditional Irish clergy of the old order in a new and trendy black habit'.[26] At several of these houses coarbs and erenaghs continued to make their appearance in the annals. In short, there is a strong element of *plus ça change plus c'est la même chose*. If this is generally true, it may help to explain why their imprint on the Irish church is not as dramatically evident as in other places. Given the uncertainty of the role of the regular canons in cathedral administration, their seeming lack of engagement in parochial structures, besides not having a missionary role, it is difficult to pinpoint the precise nature of their contribution to reform by comparison with other parts of Europe. Moreover, some recent scholarship has cautioned against the spontaneous attribution of change to the direct influence of Gregorian reform in twelfth-century Ireland.[27] That is not to say that fidelity of the canons to the ideal of the *vita apostolica* failed to make an enduring impression on the clergy of Ireland. Indeed, we know that many of the next generation of reform-minded Irish bishops were schooled either in Augustinian or Cistercian houses. If comparisons are to be sought, I would suggest that the first stage of reform in Bohemia in the age of Henry Sdik and Daniel – if not exactly analogous – is at least illuminating.

22 See N. Nichols, 'The Augustinian canons and their parish churches: a key to their identity' in Burton and Stöber, *Canons*, pp 313–37. 23 *EIMP*, pp 228–34; *MRHI*, pp 185–6. 24 See G.H. Orpen, *Ireland under the Normans*, 4 vols (Oxford, 1911), ii, pp 124, 250. He may well have retained Louth because of its ecclesiastical importance as almost certainly the headquarters of the Arrouaisian filiation in Ireland. As a rule, John retained religious houses founded by Irish kings. 25 It does not appear from M. Clyne's study that Premonstratensian houses in Gaelic Ireland had a significant parochial connection ('Founders and patrons of Premonstratensian houses,' passim). 26 Ó Corráin, *Irish church*, p. 86. 27 See D. Bracken and D. Ó Riain-Raedel (eds), *Ireland and Europe in the twelfth century* (Dublin, 2006), in particular M. Holland's chapter on

Given these uncertainties, how seamlessly did the second wave of Augustinian foundations that followed in the wake of the Anglo-Norman settlement connect with the earlier movement? Was it more of the same, or something of a different order? In fact, several connected factors contributed to a profoundly altered context. In the first place, the nature of patronage was markedly different. Second, the new foundations were built into the fabric of the emerging parochial system, a process that was decisively influenced by a third development, what might be described as 'the great European gold rush.' Across Europe, the acquisition of tithes by monasteries increased sharply in the twelfth century. F.L. Ganshof observed that 'from about 1150 to 1250 [tithes] were the principal source of wealth of many a religious house.'[28] With regard to England, Ulrich Rasche places the beginning of this tsunami of monastic impropriations at around 1180, resulting in the transfer of one-third or more of all parishes in England to monastic patronage.[29] Nichols has shown on the basis of his analysis on the *Valor ecclesiasticus* (1535) that 78 per cent of thirty-seven Augustinian houses with an income of more than £200 derived more than a quarter of their income from spiritualities; 58 per cent with an income of less than £200 drew more than 25 per cent of their income from this source; while 25 per cent of those above or below the £200 income level derived in excess of 50 per cent of their income from spiritualities.[30] While no such analysis exists for Irish houses, other than the figures I quoted for Meath and Ossory at the outset, the proportion of income from spiritualities for Augustinian foundations in colonial Ireland was probably on average comfortably in excess of 50 per cent. Thus the post-conquest Augustinian foundations present us with a stunning example of this process of lay off-loading of tithes. These new houses guzzled tithes with the zeal of mackerel in pursuit of hapless sprats. The inevitable consequence of this situation was that the Augustinians were firmly anchored in the institutional church at parochial level.

This is not the place to recite the reasons why there were so many free-floating tithes available in Ireland for investment in colonial foundations, other than to say I have discussed them at some length elsewhere.[31] Some observations, nevertheless, need to be made. To begin with, something needs to be said about the composition of Anglo-Norman patrons. As we might expect, the great lords – with the exception of Strongbow – are well represented: the abbey of St Thomas the Martyr, Dublin, was founded by Henry II (1177); Hugh de Lacy greatly enriched the de Lacy foundation of Llanthony Prima and Secunda with tithes from his lordship of Meath; de Courcy founded houses at Carrickfergus (Woodburn), Downpatrick, and probably White Abbey;[32] William de Burgh founded Athassel; and William Marshal

the question of lay control (pp 128–42) and R. Stalley's chapter on Cormac's Chapel (pp 162–75). **28** See Constable, *Monastic tithes*, p. 107.   **29** See U. Rasche, 'The early phase of appropriation of parish churches in medieval England', *Journal of Medieval History*, 26 (2000), 213–37. **30** Nichols, 'The Augustinian canons and their parish churches,' pp 317–18.   **31** See A. Empey, 'The origins of the medieval parish revisited' in H.B. Clarke and J.R.S. Phillips (eds), *Ireland, England and the Continent in the Middle Ages and beyond: essays in memory of a turbulent friar, F.X. Martin, OSA* (Dublin, 2006), pp 29–50.   **32** See Clyne, 'Founders and patrons of Premonstratensian

founded St John's Priory, Kilkenny. However, a large number of houses were patronized by their vassals. For such men, anxious about their celestial prospects, the Augustinians were made to measure, not merely because these vassals lacked the territorial resources necessary to found a Cistercian abbey, but because unlike the Cistercians, the canons had no qualms about pocketing multiples of surplus tithes in lieu of land. Furthermore, Augustinian priories, being much smaller, were more cost effective. Dickinson could not have put it better: 'No other order offered the founder of a religious house such a choice of spiritual prospects.'[33]

A marked feature of tithing allocation in Anglo-Norman dioceses consists in the granting of substantial blocks of contiguous parishes to monastic corporations, to the extent that the territorial parameters of lordships can be reconstructed in detail on that basis alone. The lordship of William de Burgh in Munster, whose priory of Athassel held the tithes of more than forty parishes, is a case in point.[34] Similarly the lands held by Meiler Fitzhenry may be identified from the rectories held by the Augustinian abbey of Greatconnell.[35] Other examples include Geoffrey fitzRobert's priory of Kells in Ossory;[36] Selsker Priory, Wexford, the rectories of which not only correspond to the cantred and deanery of Fernegenel, but also to the Roche lordship;[37] the Augustinian convent of Graney, founded by Walter de Riddlesford, corresponding to the cantred of Omurthy;[38] and Inistioge priory, corresponding to the cantred of Ogenty, together with outlying fiefs belonging to its founder, Thomas fitzAnthony.[39] Even in the highly subinfeudated deanery of Skreen, Co. Meath, where six feudal tenants granted tithes to six monastic foundations, it is possible to identify blocks of contiguous fiefs according to the pattern of grants.[40] It is clear, therefore, that new foundations were funded either by the wholesale gift of parishes within the borders of a lordship, or from a combination of lordships, often explicable by marriage alliances. By such means the tithes of entire cantreds and lordships were appropriated wholesale by favoured foundations.

houses', pp 148–55.　**33** J.C. Dickinson, *The origin of the Austin canons and their introduction into England* (London, 1950), p. 137.　**34** See A. Empey, 'The settlement of the kingdom of Limerick' in J. Lydon (ed.), *England and Ireland in the later Middle Ages* (Dublin, 1981), pp 1–25 at p. 6. **35** P. MacCotter, *Medieval Ireland: territorial, political and economic divisions* (Dublin, 2008), pp 33–5. While MacCotter uses the Greatconnell tithes to reconstruct the cantred of Leys, he does not do the same for the cantred of Offelan, although the Fitzhenry lands can be traced in detail across the southern parishes of the cantred (see *EIMP*, pp 157–64; A. Hogan (ed.), *The priory of Llanthony Prima and Secunda in Ireland, 1172–1541: lands, patronage and politics* (Dublin, 2008), pp 64–5, 239–40). **36** See A. Empey, 'The sacred and the secular: the Augustinian priory of Kells in Ossory 1193– 1541', *IHS*, 24 (1984), 131–51 at 141–2; *EIMP*, pp 188–93.　**37** *EIMP*, pp 367–71; B. Colfer, *Arrogant trespass: Anglo-Norman Wexford 1169–1400* (Enniscorthy, 2002), pp 104–6. It is clear from the tithe endowment that the cantred included the adjoining parish of Killurin; see also E. St John Brooks, *Knights' fees in counties Wexford, Carlow and Kilkenny* (IMC, Dublin, 1950), p. 145. **38** *EIMP*, pp 123–5; see also MacCotter, *Medieval Ireland*, pp 177–8.　**39** *EIMP*, pp 184–8; see also Empey, 'Inistioge in the Middle Ages' in J. Kirwan (ed.), *Kilkenny: studies in honour of Margaret M. Phelan* (Kilkenny, 1997), pp 9–15.　**40** A.J. Otway-Ruthven, 'Parochial development in the rural deanery of Skreen', *JRSAI*, 94, Part 2 (1964), 111–22.

A further observation concerns the fragmentation of tithes as they evolved over centuries, whereby tithing gifts became increasingly complicated by prior claims upon them. Thus, for example, William of London gave the monks of Hurley his tithe at Egareston: 'that is, a third of the tithe of my demesne grain, two parts of the tithe of money, and the entire tithe of cheese, except for three cheeses, and of wool, linen, apples, horses, calves, pannage, and pennies, and two parts of the piglets'.[41]

About 1080, a knight, whose brother was a monk at St Cyprien in Poitiers, gave the abbey all the tithes from his own demesne and from the monks' land in the parish, along with half the other tithes, retaining the other half on account of the service due to other lords.[42] Such complexities, so typical of England or France, seldom if ever arose in Ireland in the early decades of the Anglo-Norman period because the clock had only started. No one, it seems, had prior claims on tithes or fractions of them. The absence of such claims explains why Ireland did not have a repetition of the endless lawsuits about tithes and advowsons granted before the conquest that occurred in England after 1066. In Ireland, a standard grant of *omnes decimae* meant *omnes* down to the last *decima*: indeed, to the last piglet.

Such considerations raise a further issue: to what extent were the canons directly involved in pastoral care? After all, the proximity of parishes to priories presented opportunities for such involvement in a context where parochial clergy may have been in short supply: if regular clergy – as we shall see – may have been reluctant to come to Ireland, why would secular clergy be more adventurous? A feature of Anglo-Norman priories in Ireland is that their community churches almost invariably doubled as the parish church. This situation owed nothing to chance: had there been parishes in existence at the time the priories were founded, it would not have been possible to confer parochial status on them without trespassing on prior rights. Even after their dissolution, priory churches continued in use as parish churches. In England, on the other hand, impropriated churches were not in territorial concentrations as in Ireland. Of the ten churches attached to the priory of St Peter, Thurgarton, diocese of York, only one was easily accessible, and even that was located at some distance across the Trent.[43] What, one wonders, were the founder's intentions? Unfortunately, foundation charters do not specify pastoral services, although in Ireland this may have been expected because the population of the parish and the manor were one and the same.

A memorandum in the register of the priory of Kells in Ossory states that Geoffrey fitzRobert, lord of Kells (*c.*1192–1211), invited four regular canons from England to celebrate the liturgy in the church on the site of his new priory. In time he recruited four more canons from the priory of Bodmin, whom he personally accompanied back to Ireland. In the interval, the first group lived in cabins

---

41 Constable, *Monastic tithes*, p. 100. It is not apparent why he withheld portions of the tithe. Presumably they had prior claims upon them. **42** Constable, *Monastic tithes*, p. 100. **43** Dickinson, *The origins of the Austin canons*, p. 230; H.M. Colvin, *The white canons in England* (Oxford, 1951), p. 284.

(*habitacula*) beside the church. The fact that canons in this period were required by the rule to be assisted by three or four others when serving in a parish – a rule later relaxed in practice – lends credence to this account. Since the priory church was the parish church of the seignorial manor, it looks as if their patron intended them to serve both the religious community and the population of the manor.[44] Furthermore, since they held the rectorial tithes of every parish in his lordship, the canons were obliged at a minimum to present suitable vicars in their place. In St Peter's Church, Drogheda, archbishops of Armagh in the early thirteenth century required the canons of Llanthony Prima to reside there, serving the church in person (*per se*) together with their chaplains.[45] This requirement was relaxed by Archbishop Abraham O Conallain sometime between 1257 and 1260. Instead, the priory had to pay fifteen marks a year to a vicar, while the priory's proctor was obliged to attend St Peter's at major festivals.[46] Some canons continued to serve dependent churches well into the thirteenth century, and even later.

In 1247, the bishop of Ardagh licensed the prior of Tristernagh, by reason of poverty, to provide for their dependent church of Rathaspick either through the agency of a canon or a chaplain.[47] In 1381, a memorandum relating to Llanthony Secunda recorded that the parish church of St Kenan (St Cianán), Duleek, had been in possession of the priory time out of mind. It was served by one or two canons, two parish chaplains and four clerks (*clerici*), who celebrated the liturgy there daily.[48] But there were limitations to parochial involvement. Most Anglo-Norman houses were numerically small, even at the height of their prosperity in the thirteenth century. Kells Priory had only a prior and two canons at the time of dissolution. Its mother house, St Petroc's, Bodmin, had only eleven canons in 1381.[49] Clearly there was no way such communities could satisfy the pastoral demands of multiple parishes, notwithstanding the relaxation of the quorum requirement.

The responsibilities of pastoral oversight did not end with the institution of a vicar. In 1264 the bishop of Meath ordained that the vicar of St Mary's, Drogheda:

> should receive all the tithes and incomes of the same church … [and] should pay each year twenty-four marks to the said prior and convent [Llanthony

---

44 *EIMP*, pp 311–12. The memorandum is marred by mistakes. William the Marshal was not called Strongbow, while the title 'baron of Kells' is not attested before the fifteenth century. Nor does the foundation charter refer to a church dedicated to St Kevanus (St Kieran?). A marginal note states that the memorandum was written *manu recentiori*. A possible explanation for these errors is that they may be the product of a careless fifteenth-century summary of a chronicle (since lost) mentioned in the text. In spite of its inaccuracies, the substance of the memorandum is consistent with what we know from Geoffrey's foundation charter (see E. Curtis (ed.), *Calendar of Ormond deeds, 1172–1350* (IMC, 6 vols, Dublin, 1932), i, pp 14–16).   **45** E. St John Brooks (ed.), *The Irish cartularies of Llanthony Prima & Secunda* (IMC, Dublin, 1953), nos. xi and xiii.   **46** Brooks, *Cartularies of Llanthony Prima & Secunda*, no. xxi.   **47** M.V. Clarke, *Register of the priory of the Blessed Virgin Mary at Tristernagh* (Dublin, 1941), no. xlviii.   **48** Brooks, *Cartularies of Llanthony Prima & Secunda*, no. 98 at p. 289. Note the relaxation of the requirement to have three or four canons in Duleek.   **49** D. Knowles and R.N. Hadcock, *Medieval religious houses: England and Wales* (London, 1953), p. 148.

Secunda] … at two terms a year … [And] the same vicar should fully sustain all ordinary burdens to the said church and he will answer for one third share of extraordinary burdens, the rest of the said incomes to be converted to their own use. It is our wish also, that the said prior and convent … should find for him a place within or without the land pertaining to the said church that is suitable to construct buildings for the said vicar. And as is fitting, they should help the said vicar to create buildings there. And the stone buildings with a garden and rabbit warren shall remain in possession of the aforesaid prior and convent for their use and in their possession and lordship.[50]

The consequence of these obligations is that large swathes of Anglo-Norman dioceses lay in the pastoral control of Augustinian houses. For example, most parishes in southern Ossory fell within the remit of three houses: Kells, Inistioge and the convent of Kilcullaheen. In theory at least, if not always in practice, monastic corporations were better placed than lay lords to act as 'promoters of holy vocations'[51] in finding suitable candidates for presentation to parishes – a key objective of the reformers. For sure, such pious ambitions did not inhibit the more humdrum pursuit of corporate advantage when it came to protecting their prerogatives. In 1206, the foundation of the hospital of St Mary outside the eastern gate of Drogheda by a wealthy burgess gave rise to concerns for the rights of St Peter's Church. This resulted in a formal agreement (*forma pacis perpetue*) between the rector, prior of Llanthony Prima, and the hospital. At issue were rights of burial in the hospital cemetery, conditional rights to confession, viaticum, extreme unction, the hospital chantry, and restrictions placed on the offering of oblations by parishioners. The hospital was denied liturgical privileges in respect of baptism, marriage, and the churching of women. Moreover, all hospital chaplains were required thereafter to take an oath to observe the agreement.[52] The canons of Llanthony and Tristernagh were no less exacting when it came to licensing chapels. Typical of such arrangements is an agreement *c*.1202 between Sampson de Trombe regarding his private chapel in the parish of Colpe, diocese of Meath, which was impropriate to Llanthony Prima. It is clear that Sampson was renewing an earlier arrangement made with the previous tenant, Richard Chamberlain, probably in the late twelfth century. Sampson undertook to provide a chaplain at his own expense, pay two shillings at two terms to the mother church of Colpe, pay tithes and obventions owed to Colpe without deceit on the oath of the chaplain. Sampson was to swear that he would not overlook any parochial dues. No Mass was to be

50 Hogan, *The priory of Llanthony*, pp 319–20.   **51** The phrase 'promoter of holy vocations' was applied to Thurstan, the reforming archbishop of York, who was an ardent supporter of the canons in his archdiocese as a means of promoting reform and affirming his own authority (see Janet Burton, 'The regular canons and diocesan reform in northern England,' in Burton and Stöber, *Canons*, at p.1 and passim.)   **52** Brooks, *Cartularies of Llanthony Prima & Secunda*, no. lv; cf. nos xcviii, xcix.

celebrated in the chapel on festive days, when his chaplain may celebrate it in the parish church, except of course at specified high feasts, when that privilege was reserved to the parochial chaplain. Finally, the right to maintain a chapel was subject to termination if Sampson failed to observe the terms.[53] Such watertight arrangements leave us in no doubt that the Augustinians took oversight of their dependent parishes very seriously indeed, applying the full rigour of canon law in defence of their parochial rights.

What of the Augustinian guiding principle, *caritas*? Agreements of the kind we have discussed tell us something about the business methods employed by the canons in respect of their parochial oversight. Much the same could be said about their administrative abilities revealed in the account rolls of the priory of the Holy Trinity, Dublin, in the middle of the fourteenth century.[54] Such material, however, tells us little about their spiritual *esprit de corps*. A close reading of the memorandum in the register of Kells offers some insight into the character of the community that Geofrey fitzRobert founded around 1193. The mother house, the priory of St Mary and St Petroc, was founded by Algar *c.*1120, who took over an older monastery. In due course it was colonized by canons from Merton.[55] Its founder went on to become bishop of Coutances in 1132, which suggests that the reformed house had a high reputation. Indeed, its readiness to send four canons to Ireland in the 1190s indicates that its zeal was in no way diminished by the passage of seventy years. The fact that Geoffrey had to accompany the four canons to Kells may indicate some hesitation, but come they did, unlike the less courageous Cistercians of Buildas who declined an invitation to colonize Dunbrody on foot of a fearsome report by a lay brother about the hazards of the wild Irish frontier. It did not take long for the canons of Kells to make their mark. Hugh de Rous – possibly one of the four who accompanied Geoffrey to Ireland – went on to be the first Anglo-Norman bishop of Ossory (1202–18). He is generally credited with initiating the building of St Canice's Cathedral. About the same time Thomas fitzAnthony, lord of Thomastown and Inistioge, invited two of the brethren, Algar and Alured, to take his new priory of Inistioge in hand *ad reformandos et instruendos ceteros canonicos*, a form of words that suggests they were commissioned to sort out a troublesome community. Alured became prior of Inistioge, while Algar – whose name recalls the founder of Bodmin – was sent to Rome to secure privileges both for Kells and Inistioge (*utriusque domus*). He was to spend a long time in the papal curia and was eventually appointed by a pope to a see in northern Italy.[56] All of this would indicate a vigorous band of brothers intent on reshaping the church.

---

53 Brooks, *Cartularies of Llanthony Prima & Secunda*, nos xliv, xlv; Clarke, *Register of Tristernagh*, pp 97–8 (Litera xxi), pp 101–2 (Litera xxvii). Regarding licences for chapels see Hogan, *Priory of Llanthony Prima and Secunda in Ireland*, pp 127–9.   **54** See J. Mills (ed.), *Account roll of the priory of the Holy Trinity, Dublin, 1337–1346*, with an introduction by J. Lydon and A.J. Fletcher (Dublin, 1996).   **55** Dickinson, *The origins of the Austin canons*, pp 118–19.   **56** *EIMP*, pp 311–12. Algar's appointment to a north Italian see is interesting, given the importance of the role played by the canons in Italy and their close association with, and commitment to, papal reform.

The contribution of the regular canons in promoting reform in Ireland would be hard to overstate, if at times it is hard to see them in sharp focus. However, it is undeniable that they played a key role in the formation of a parochial system that was inextricably bound up with these Anglo-Norman houses. Whether that largely took the form of hands-on pastoral oversight – at least initially – or the secondary provision of suitable clergy to benefices is impossible to say. Either way much of the parochial network was in their charge. The vision and inspiration of Malachy was – rightly – sung by Bernard of Clairvaux. The more prosaic work of parish building and parochial oversight, on the other hand, failed to inspire a singer worthy of the song. The only effective means of earthing reform lay in the creation of a parochial system that would enable a bishop to exert control throughout his diocese. Much of that heavy lifting was done by the regular canons. From a wider perspective, it is important to visualize the Augustinian contribution in Ireland against the backdrop of their achievements in Europe as a whole. I have proposed that their role in Bohemia in particular offers interesting comparisons, and hopefully some illumination.

The settlement of the Augustinian canons of Llanthony Prima and Secunda in Ireland, 1172–1541

ARLENE HOGAN

Llanthony, a tranquil area situated in the isolated valley of Ewyas, surrounded by the Hatterel hills in Monmouthshire, gave its name to an enduring house of regular canons. While many houses of canons, established in Wales with the aim of providing spiritual benefit for the founder in perpetuity, remained small, Llanthony, by comparison, grew to become one of the most powerful Augustinian houses of the medieval period.[1] Engendered by faith and the need for solitude, the initial foundation was established c.1103, by William, a knight of Hugh de Lacy (d. c.1115), who had been granted these lands in Wales by Henry I.[2] Llanthony was derived from the Welsh Llanhonddu, Llan meaning a place dedicated to religion, Honddu being the river beside which the original church was constructed.[3] In c.1108, Anselm, archbishop of Canterbury since 1093, insisted that the metropolitan authority of his church extended over the whole of Wales,[4] and instituted Llanthony as a priory of Augustinian regular canons,[5] bringing the first clergy to serve at Llanthony from the church of St Botolph's (1105), the first Augustinian house in England. St Botolph's was founded for the Arrouaisians at Mont St Eloi and St Quentin de Beauvais and Llanthony therefore became affiliated to the congregation of regular canons of Arrouaise. The new foundation was dedicated to St John the Baptist and housed in 'the humble chapel of St David the Archbishop'.[6] However, in 1136, following the death of Henry I in December 1135,

---

1 K. Stöber, 'The regular canons in Wales' in Burton and Stöber, *Canons*, pp 97–113 at p. 102. **2** J.N. Langston, 'Priors of Llanthony by Gloucester', *Transactions of the Bristol and Gloucestershire Archaeological Society*, 63 (1942), 1–143. **3** Giraldus, *The journey through Wales, and description of Wales*, ed. & trans. Lewis Thorpe (London, 1978), p. 97. **4** M. Chibnall, *The Normans* (Oxford, 2000), p. 68. **5** Anselm had consecrated the first bishop of Waterford in 1096, providing continuing contacts between the sees of Canterbury and Dublin: M.T. Flanagan, 'High-kings with opposition, 1072–1166', *NHI*, i, pp 899–933 at p. 911. The authority of Canterbury was an important fact in the lives of the Llanthony canons when they arrived in Ireland in the wake of the Anglo-Norman incursion. **6** Giraldus states that it was 'adorned with woodland moss and wreathed about with ivy' and situated in 'the deep vale of Ewyas, shut in on all sides by a circle of lofty mountains and which is no more than three arrow shots in width' and goes on to say that 'it rains a lot there because of the mountains, the winds blow strong, and in winter it is always capped with clouds'. He further adds, 'The climate is temperate and healthy, the air soothing and clement, if somewhat heavy, and illness is rare', and that the new church was 'roofed in with sheets of lead and built of squared stones': Giraldus, *Journey through Wales*, p. 97.

the majority of Llanthony canons found it necessary to take refuge in nearby Hereford due to unrest.[7] From Hereford, the canons moved to Gloucester where a new foundation was established in 1137, under the auspices of Milo fitzWalter, earl of Hereford,[8] known to modern historians as Llanthony Secunda.[9]

The Augustinian canons of Llanthony Prima and Secunda were subsequently introduced into Ireland by Hugh de Lacy I (d.1186),[10] and were active in Ireland from c.1174 to 1541. Hugh, a loyal supporter of Henry II, was on the king's service on the Irish campaign in 1171, and was granted the whole of the then kingdom of Meath in 1172, for his loyalty and service to the king. He was, by the introduction of the Augustinian canons of Llanthony into Ireland, establishing a necessary component in the domination of a newly acquired territory.[11] The canons understood the customs of the English church, sang familiar forms of the liturgy, and could provide chaplains to the newly landed knights.[12] Settlers would now come who would consolidate the process of the conquest. Those who came were awarded land as part of the subinfuedation process and subsequently granted the tithes of their newly acquired land to Llanthony, suggesting that the establishment of the Llanthony farming granges in Ireland at Colpe and Duleek was coterminous with the colonization of Meath.

Our information in relation the settlement of the Llanthony canons in Ireland comes almost solely from the Llanthony Prima and Secunda cartularies now housed in The National Archive, Public Record Office at Kew. The cartularies were combined into one work and edited, in 1953 in a Latin edition, by Eric St John Brooks.[13] The purpose of the cartularies was to record the legal agreements previously made with the Llanthony canons concerning the grants of tithes and church benefices in the form of charters into one transportable manuscript, during

---

7 *Historia et cartularium Monasterii Sancti Petri Gloucestriae*, ed. W.H. Hart (London, 1863), i, p. xxix. 8 Giraldus, *Journey through Wales*, p. 100. 9 The term 'daughter house' is first used in the cartularies in 1204, in the first ratification charter relating to the separation of the houses: 'from the foundation of the daughter house, the canons of that same daughter house successively made profession to the priors of the mother church'. Arlene Hogan, *The priory of Llanthony Prima and Secunda in Ireland, 1172–1541: lands patrons and politics* (Dublin, 2008), charter, 9a p. 254 (hereafter, Hogan, *Priory of Llanthony*). 10 '1186, Hugh de Lacy was killed', B. Williams (ed.), *The annals of Ireland by friar John Clyn* (Dublin, 2007), p. 136 (hereafter, *Clyn*). There were three men with the name of Hugh de Lacy who were instrumental in the affairs of Llanthony. Hugh, the founder for the Augustinian canons at Llanthony, 1103; Hugh I, the knight on the king's service in 1171, the donor of lands in Ireland to Llanthony; and Hugh II, earl of Ulster, son of the donor. 11 The granting of the land of Meath to Hugh de Lacy I in 1172, by Henry II, for the service of fifty knights, has been taken as the starting date for this chapter even though the charters begin c.1174: 'King Henry the brave, landed at Waterford with five hundred knights and among other things gave Meath to Hugh de Lacy', J.T. Gilbert (ed.), *The chartularies of St Mary's Abbey, Dublin; with the register of its house at Dunbrody and the Annals of Ireland* (2 vols, London 1884–6), ii, p. 273. 12 M. Chibnall, 'Aspects of knighthood: knights and monks' in Susan Ripyard (ed.), *Chivalry, knighthood, and war in the Middle Ages* (Cambridge, 1999), p. 33. 13 *Irish cartularies of Llanthony Prima and Secunda*, ed. Eric St John Brooks (IMC, Dublin, 1953).

a particularly litigious time, when evidence of ownership in the courts was vital.[14] Also recorded in the cartularies are confirmations by bishops, archbishops and papal legates, together with papal bulls, royal letters, inspections of charters, records of lawsuits and ecclesiastical tax estimates, together with litigation regarding tithes. As the manorial system established by the Anglo-Normans included the duty of all free-tenants to pay suit of court at the manor-court every three weeks, which is recorded several times in the charters, we can conclude that it was at these occasions that the charters may have been presented and witnessed. By combining the 168 charters in the Prima cartulary and 107 charters in the Secunda volume, and translating them in chronological sequence, the role that the canons played in the history of Ireland becomes clear, not only in the early period of colonization in the areas in which they were active, but also, up to and including late medieval Ireland, before the dissolution ended their involvement, both temporal and spiritual, in the country in which they had become an integral part for a period of 367 years. Within the confines of a single chapter only the briefest overview of the Llanthony canons in Ireland is possible. I have therefore decided to focus primarily on the canons' involvement with Drogheda.

INITIAL SETTLEMENT

After their separation in 1136, both houses of Llanthony, Prima and Secunda, were governed by a joint prior resident in Wales. Peaceful during the initial period, the establishment of a second house for the canons inevitably led to conflict when the daughter house became more powerful than the mother house. After years of discord, when all valuables (even the bells) were removed from Llanthony in Wales to the Gloucester house, a final split, begun 1204, between the two houses became inevitable.[15] The subsequent legal case was heard in Rome by Pope Innocent III, who deemed that the possessions hitherto belonging to one house of Llanthony, should be divided into two and that each house should have its own prior and convent.[16] Constant disagreements in relation to their Irish benefices led to a decision in 1211–13 by Irish arbitrators Simon, bishop of Meath, Ralph, archdeacon of Meath, and Gerard Cusack, that 'lots would be drawn' and the divided churches

---

14 The first time Llanthony Prima is mentioned in the Prima cartulary is *c*.1177–91, in charter lxxxiii, of Reginald de Turburville, concerning tithes in his vill of Trubley, County Meath. Hogan, *Priory of Llanthony*, p. 235. **15** Giraldus describes Llanthony at this time as 'formerly a happy delightful spot, most suited to the life of contemplation, a place from its first founding fruitful and to itself sufficient … it has since been reduced to servitude through the boundless extravagance of the English … the neglect of its prelates and patrons … far worse, the daughter has been odiously supplanted by the mother', Giraldus, *Journey through Wales*, p. 98. **16** Hogan, *Llanthony*, charter 9a, p. 254. **17** Ibid., charter xlviii, p. 270. Duleek was established as a monastic site as early as the fifth century and the abbots of Duleek (coarbs of St Cianán) are recorded in *AU* and *AFM* from 783 to 1098. Duleek was chosen as one of two bishoprics at the synod of Ráith Bressail, 1111, but dropped in the same year in favour of Clonard: *MRHI*, p. 75; see also, J. Bradley, 'St Patrick's Church, Duleek', *Riocht na Midhe*, 7:4 (1980–1).

1 Aerial view from the south-east of the Premonstratensian abbey of the Holy Trinity on Trinity Island, Lough Key. © Photographic Unit, National Monuments Service, Department of Culture, Heritage and the Gaeltacht.

2 Seal matrix of the Premonstratensian abbey of the Holy Trinity, Tuam.
© National Museum of Ireland.

3 (*opposite*) St Kevin's Cave, Glendalough, Co. Wicklow.
Photo © Christiaan Corlett, courtesy of Culture Stock.

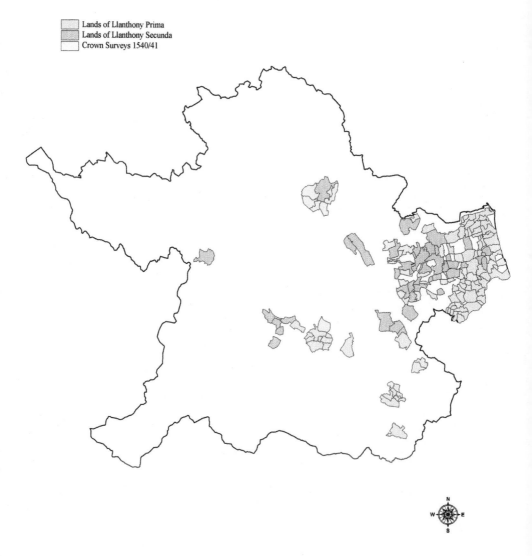

4 Llanthony lands in Co. Meath.

Lands of Llanthony Prima
Lands of Llanthony Secunda
Crown Surveys 1540/41

5 Llanthony lands in Co. Westmeath.

6 Llanthony lands in Co. Dublin.

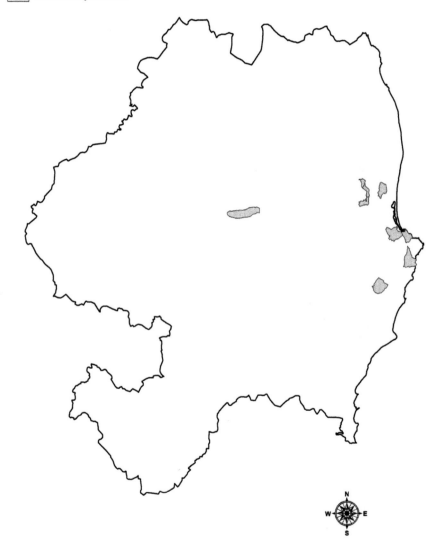

7 Llanthony lands in Co. Wicklow.

Legend:
Lands of Llanthony Prima
Lands of Llanthony Secunda
Crown Surveys 1540/41

8 Llanthony lands in Co. Louth.

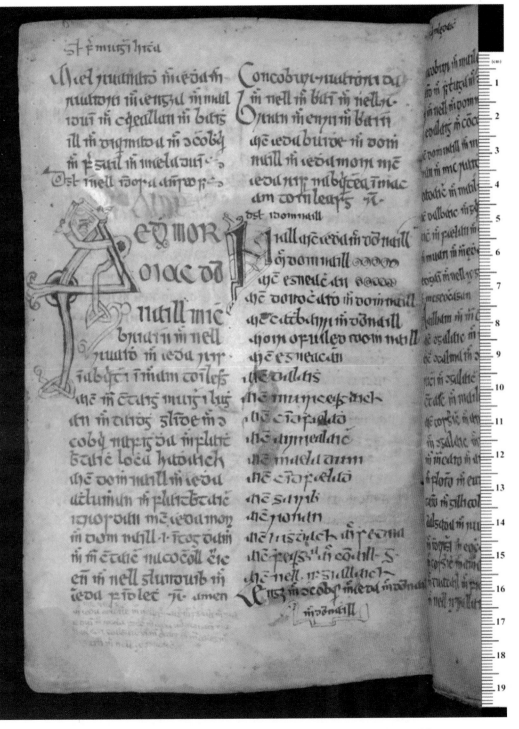

9 Ádam Ó Cianáin miscellany, NLI MS G 2, fol. 9v, incorporating an initial created from intertwined animals and blocks of colour similar to those of the twelfth century. Courtesy of the National Library of Ireland.

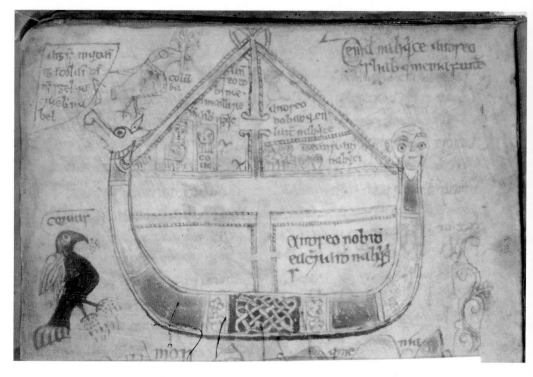

10 Ádam Ó Cianáin miscellany, NLI MS G 3, fol. 16v, detail of an illustration of Noah's Ark. Courtesy of the National Library of Ireland.

11 (*opposite*) Augustinian canons playing musical instruments: Psalter of Stephen de Derby, Oxford, Bodleian MS Rawl. G 185, fol. 68. © The Bodleian Libraries, The University of Oxford.

et super filium hominis quem confirmasti tibi·

Incensa igni et suffossa: ab increpatione vultus tui

Fiat manus tua super virum dextere tue ¶ Speabunt·

e·: et super filium hominis quem confirmasti tibi·

Et non discedimus a te et vivificabis nos: et no

men tuum invocabimus·

Domine deus virtutum converte nos·: et ostende

faciem tuam et salvi erimus

propicius esto peccatis nostris dne· dne· Exultate. Exultac

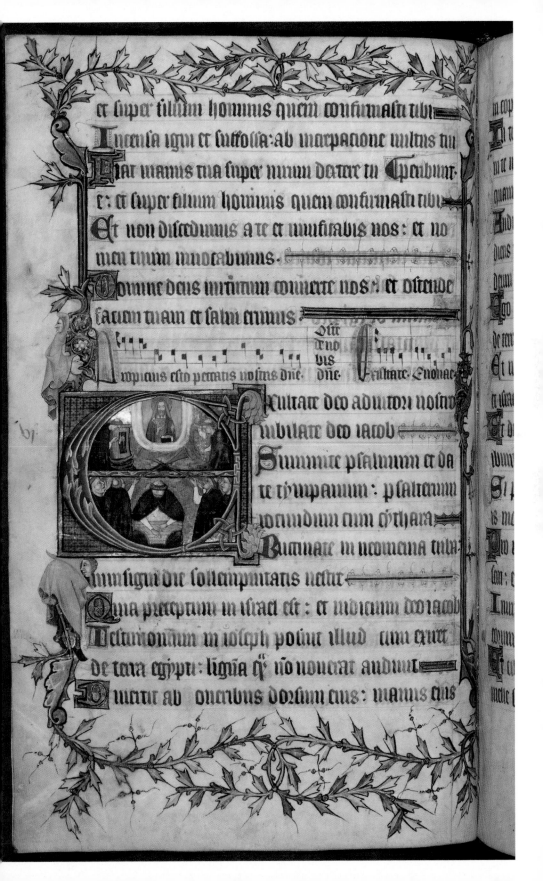

Exultate deo adiutori nostro

Iubilate deo iacob

Sumite psalmum et da

te tympanum·: psalterium

iocundum cum cythara

Bucinate in neomenia tuba

in insigni die sollempnitatis vestre

Quia preceptum in israel est·: et iudicium deo iacob

Testimonium in ioseph posuit illud cum exiret

de terra egypti: linguam quam non noverat audivit

Divertit ab oneribus dorsum eius: manus eius

Et exultauerunt filie iude : propter iudicia tua domine

Quoniam tu dominus altissimus super omnem terram : nimis exaltatus es sup omnes deos

Qui diligitis dominum odite malum custodit dominus animas sanctorum suorum : de manu peccatoris liberabit eos

Lux orta est iusto : et rectis corde letitia.

Letamini iusti in domino : et confitemini memorie sanctificationis eius. antiphona

Cantate domino et benedicite nomini eius. Psalmus. Ps. Cantate domino canticum nouum : quia mirabilia fecit. Saluauit sibi dextera eius. Et brachium sanctum eius. Notum fecit dominus salutare suum : in conspectu gentium reuelauit iustitiam suam.

Recordatus est misericordie sue : et ueritatis sue domui israel. Viderunt omnes termini t

13 The Domnach Airgid shrine. © National Museum of Ireland.

KL Iulius

Prima dies mensis et septima truncat ut ensis

vii G ... Oct. sci iohis bap. iiii le. ...
viii A vi ... Octo. petri et pauli aplor ...
    B v
xvi c iiii Translatio sci martini iiii le.
    d iii
    e ii Oct. aplor. petri et pauli iiii le.
xiii f ... Translatio sci thome ...
    g vii id'
    A vii id'
    B vi id' Septem fratrum ...
    c v id'
viii d iiii id'
vii e iii id'
    f ii id' Oct. sci thome mr. ... dies caniculares incipiunt. Principium canicule.
xv g id'
iii A xvii kl Augustus.
    B xvi kl Sci kenelmi reg. et mr. iii le. Sol in Leone.
    c xv kl
xii d xiiii kl Orate pro ...
    e xiii kl Sce margarete v. iiii le. ...
ix f xii kl Sci victoris ... Sce praxedis v. ...
    g xi kl Sce marie magd.
xvii A x kl Sci apollinaris ...
    B viiii kl
xvii c viii kl Sci iacobi iiii le. Christofori et cucuphati ...
viii d vii kl
    e vi kl
    f v kl
ii g iiii kl Septem dormientium. Simplicii faustini ...
iiii A iii kl Oct. abdon et sennis ...
    B ii kl Sci germani epi iiii le.

In principio. Simon ... Petrus ... Travisc ... Adonay. Ad aperiat. Videdum. Aspiciens.
... kl ang. ... septembr. ... kl octobr. ... kl nouembr. ... decc.

Regula ad inueniend hystorias epe cantare post hystoria. Deus omnium. usq ad natale domini.

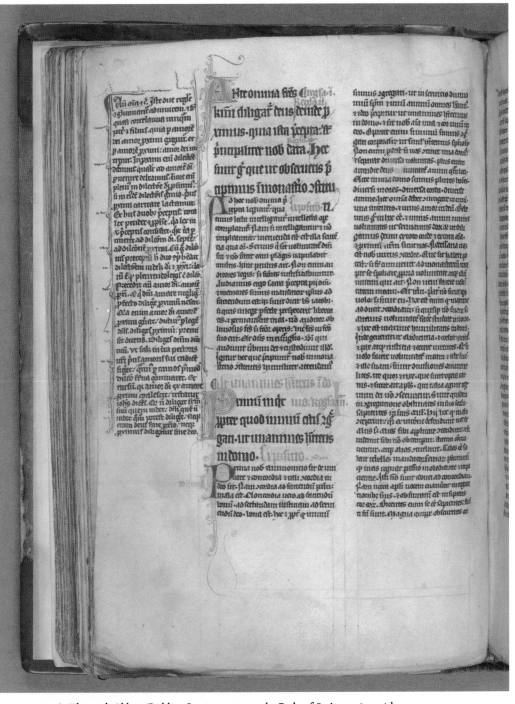

15 St Thomas's Abbey, Dublin. Commentary on the Rule of St Augustine with commentary attributed to Hugh of St Victor: TCD MS 97, fol. 73. Reproduced with the permission of the Board of Trinity College, Dublin.

14 (*opposite*) St Thomas's Abbey, Dublin. Calendar showing entries for July: TCD MS 97, fol. 4r. Reproduced with the permission of the Board of Trinity College, Dublin.

S·MALACHIAS·EX·CAN·REG·DUNENSIS·IN·HYBERNIÁ·ARC=HEPISCOPV·SOROREM·SVAM·E
PVRGATORIO·LIBERAVIT·AC·FCEMINAM·ABS·LINCTIONIS·EXTREMÆ·SACTO·MORTVÃ·EXCT·

16 Seventeenth-century depiction of St Malachy in the habit of a regular canon from St Dorothea's Abbey, Vienna. Now in Stift Klosterneuburg. Photo by Sarah Deichstetter.

would be won 'by the gift of fate'.[17] Following this crucial decision it is reasonable to assume that it was at this time that the Secunda canons settled permanently at Duleek, to serve their vocation from the church of St Michael, and the Prima canons moved to their manor-farm nearby at Colpe, to serve their vocation from the parish church of St Columba. The ultimate agreement was not reached until 1217, by which time the inevitable separation of the two houses was at last completed and reflected in Ireland.[18]

It is evident from the grants of tithes and church benefices to Prima and Secunda that are recorded in the cartularies for Dublin, Meath, Westmeath, Louth and Wicklow, the five principal areas in which benefices were awarded, that they are in areas where the land is fertile undulating lowland, perfect for the mixed farming and arable cultivation economy that dominated throughout the period in which Llanthony held an interest in the lands of Ireland. It can also be seen that, for the most part, the areas are adjoining and that the tithes from these large consolidated blocs of land cover several parishes. As each parish consisted of several townlands and each parish held within it the mother-church and usually several dependent chapels, all of which owed tithes and usually altarage and burial rights to Llanthony, the result was a formidable infrastructure requiring tight organization by the Llanthony proctors working on behalf of their mother houses from their cells at Colpe and Duleek, adjacent to both Drogheda and the Boyne estuary.[19]

18 During the initial phase of separation Prima in Wales was granted the priory of Connell in Kildare in 1202, by Meiler fitzHenry when he was justiciar. However, it is important to note that this foundation, unlike the cells at Colpe and Duleek, was an independent Augustinian foundation which King John confirmed in 1205. While Connell was the medieval name given to the priory in the cartulary of Llanthony Prima, the modern name given is Greatconnell. Meiler, in granting the priory of Connell to the canons of Llanthony Prima, may have been courting the favour of Walter and Hugh de Lacy II, as he had been instructed by King John in 1205, as his justiciar, 'to place undoubted reliance on Hugh de Lacy, earl of Ulster'; further, the king ordered that 'the justiciar shall wage no war against the marchers unless by the advice of Walter de Lacy, and the same Hugh his brother': *CDI*, 268, p. 40. Hugh de Lacy had been created earl of Ulster in May 1205.   **19** Within Co. Meath the area that Llanthony held an interest in in terms of tithes covered many of the townlands in the parishes of Colpe, Julianstown, Moorechurch, Stamullin, Clonalvy, Ardcath, Kilsharvan, Donore, Dowth, Duleek, Dunboyne, Girley, Rathbeggan, Rathfeigh, Rathkenny, Timoole, Trubley, Skreen, Cookstown, Ratoath, Killeen, Kilmessan and Knockmark, which for the most part but not all covered the prime area along the east coast, including large stretches south of the River Boyne to an area along the border of south Meath; adjoining and crossing over the boundary of north Co. Dublin. In Co. Dublin the parishes in which Llanthony held an interest were mainly on the northern boundary of the county and lay together in one bloc. They included the parish of Balrothery, Naul, Hollywood, Garristown and Palmerstown. Nearer Dublin, tithes were also held in the parishes of Swords, Coolock and Donnybrook. In Dublin city the canons were awarded Buttevant Tower and land outside the Newgate near Kilmainham. In Westmeath, it can be seen that the parishes from which Llanthony held tithes are also largely grouped together and form one bloc close to the eastern border of Meath and then spread westwards across the middle of the county. The parishes included Killua, Killucan, Killulagh, Delvin, Mullingar, Kilbixy, Drumraney and Kilkenny West. In Co. Louth the canons had fewer tithes and they were mainly held in the parishes of St Peter's and St Mary's in Drogheda. However, further north in Louth, close to the

SEPARATE ADMINISTRATION

The location of the parish of Colpe and the Prima church of St Columba lies today approximately two kilometres from the sea and, as in the medieval period, stretches northward to the south bank of the Boyne River. At this point today, several causeways traverse the river to a point midway, where the river deepens to provide a channel for large shipping vessels. During the medieval period a causeway provided a short crossing to the northern banks of the Boyne and would have placed the town of Drogheda and its eastern gate of St Laurence only a short journey away. A charter of Ralph Whiterell in *c*.1206, granting extra land to enlarge the cemetery at the dedication of the new church of St Columba, Colpe, gives a useful description of the position of the land in relation to the Boyne: '... of which three acres lie towards the west between the causeway ... and one acre towards the south lying between the house of the prior and the cemetery of St Columba'.[20] Mention of a causeway suggests access across a river and verse eighteen of the contemporary poem 'In Praise of Ragnall King of Man' would seem to confirm this: 'Thou wilt restrain a man and plunder, thou wilt burn a house and destroy; was red hot metal placed on thy forge? Thou wilt dry up the strait of Colpa on its bed'.[21]

The 'strait of Colpa', in the context of the poem, is in fact the mouth of the Boyne River and a well known and important landing place, vital for transport and the shipping of supplies.[22] Significantly, the River Boyne provided one of the three major trading routes of the Irish Sea province, linking the River Dee and the north Welsh coast and the Isle of Man with the Boyne and the Liffey, thereby connecting with the important ports of Chester, Holyhead and Dublin.[23] Trading through Chester, on the western seaboard of England, was of particular importance in relation to Drogheda.[24] These sea routes were busy, notwithstanding high winds,

---

sea, tithes were held in Parsontown and Dunany. In Wicklow benefices were held in the parishes of Castlemacadam, Newcastle, Kilpoole and Rathnew. Inland in Wicklow, Llanthony held the churches of Glendalough. In February 1216, the dioceses of Dublin and Glendalough were amalgamated, and confirmed by Honorious III later that year. **20** Hogan, *Llanthony*, charter cxix, p. 262. **21** Coiscfi fher agus airgfea, loiscfi tegh agus tolefa, nar ladh caer ar do heardcha?, sergfa ar a lar cael Colptha: *In Praise of Ragnall King of Man*, ed. B. Ó Cuív, *Eigse*, 8 (1956–7), 283–301, verse 18. **22** According to ancient legend when the Milesian brothers invaded Ireland, one of them, Colpa, the brother of Heremon the Milesian chief, was drowned at the mouth of the Boyne; hence it was called Inbher-Colptha. A. Cogan, *The diocese of Meath, ancient and modern* (Dublin, 1862), p. 177; see also, P.W. Joyce, *Irish place names* (Belfast, 1984). **23** B. Hudson, 'The changing economy of the Irish Sea province: AD 900–1300' in B. Smith (ed.), *Britain and Ireland, 900–1300* (Cambridge, 1999), pp 39–66 at p. 40. The first link was across St Georges' Channel, which linked the Bristol Channel, the Severn and south Wales with south-east Ireland, in particular with the rivers Nore, Suir and Barrow. The other route was a north–south passage extending southwards to the Bay of Biscay and Galicia, while the northernmost extension carried along the western coast of Scotland to Iceland, due north then turning east past the Orkneys and Shetlands to Norway and the Baltic. **24** W.R. Childs and T. O'Neill, 'Overseas trade' in *NHI*, ii, pp 492–532 at p. 495.

storms and the constant worry of piracy,[25] the perils of which, many years later in 1446, the canons of Llanthony were to discover when two of their number were captured at sea and forced to pay ransom.[26]

In relation to the Secunda canons, proximity to Drogheda was equally vital. As late as 1381, in the *Memorandum in Hibernia*,[27] there is a valuable description of their cell of St Michael which not only gives their location but information in relation to a medieval farming grange. It tells us that the house lay between the King's Highway and the Nanny River, both of which would have provided access to Drogheda, with the chapel of the Secunda canons, located on the eastern side of the court within their grange and, 'if all the land of Ireland were to be under interdict, it was possible for the priest to celebrate the sacraments there'. The *Memorandum* continues with a description of the east range where there was a hall, a straw-thatched kitchen, a dairy and a small connecting stable roofed with stone tiles,[28] together with a long room and connecting wardrobe and lastly 'the knight's room'. Below the east range was a cellar serving as a pantry for bread and ale and a larder. There was also a small stable for the proctor's horses. Aligned along the south range was a bakery and malt-house also roofed with stone tiles. Within these buildings were two furnaces, one a kiln and the other an oven for two-and-a-half crannocks,[29] and an upper room for malt to be stored which led to a kitchen, as well as a granary for threshing corn and a trough for pouring malt. There was also a bake-house and a pigsty with a thatched roof. On the west range there was a two-storey stone gate with a thatched roof which led into the haggard, where there was a tiled granary and a small pigsty for piglets and sows and a long cattle-shed for oxen and cows. The north range accommodated a sheepfold with a long stable all roofed with thatch, and a slated stone gate, which had a guest room above the doorkeepers room. It goes on to describe two thatched dovecotes in the meadows above the Nanny River and a watermill, near where the proctors kept their ground corn and malt. As payment for grinding corn, the miller took half the flour.[30] Today, while nothing is visible above ground of the Secunda house at Duleek except a section of the later medieval church of St Michael, it is still possible to descend into the cellar of the later Georgian house at the site and find masonry remains of the grange.

It should be noted perhaps at this point that out of the sizeable catalogue of books that were in the Llanthony library at Gloucester, compiled in the early fourteenth century, it is interesting that there are none of the customary didactic treatises relating to estate management; *Rules, Seneschaucy and Walter*, nor the farming treatise of the audit known as *Husbandry*,[31] that might have been expected given the enormity of the the Llanthony benefices. This leads to the conclusion

---

25 R. Bartlett, 'Colonial aristocracies of the high Middle Ages' in R. Bartlett and A. Mackey (eds), *Medieval frontier societies* (Oxford, 1989), pp 23–47 at p. 39.   **26** T. O'Neill, *Merchants and mariners in medieval Ireland* (Dublin, 1987), p. 123.   **27** Hogan, *Llanthony*, charter 98, pp 347–60. **28** 'Petris tegulis': probably a type of slate.   **29** A crannock is a measure of corn; or a basket. C. Trice Martin, *The record interpreter* (Guilford, 1982), p. 224.   **30** Hogan, *Llanthony*, charter 98, pp 347–60 at p. 347.   **31** D. Oshchinsky, *Walter of Henley* (Oxford, 1971), pp 3–8.

that where farming was concerned, the canons were mainly involved with the collection, storage, sale and shipment of tithes from the sizeable acreage from which they had been granted the tithes. Although the Extent of Llanthony Prima, 1408, does refer to three-crop rotation and the value of arable compared to meadow land.[32]

Notwithstanding the upheavals caused by the separation of their mother houses, the Llanthony canons continued to manage their benefices in Ireland. However, by 1217, when the final settlement took place, the political landscape of Ireland had completely changed. Gone were the knights of Hugh de Lacy I, men with a tangible feeling of power, acquisition and subjugation who arrived in Ireland in his wake after 1171. Gone were the original settlers who were granted land and benefices as part of the subinfuedation process. What remained was a tightly-knit Anglo-Norman community of descendant families who became entrenched as they settled, intermarried and supported one another and grew to become an integral part of Irish life. To this day, many of the names of the original settlers can be seen on the map of the areas in which they settled and their descendants carry names such as Cusack, Lacy, Bruton, Petit, Messet, Talbot, Tyrell, Dullard, de Craville, Hussey, Capella, and Nugent. Most settlers recorded in the charters were either Anglo- or Cambro-Norman and all granted the tithes and benefices of their newly gained Irish lands and churches to Llanthony. Others, such as Richard Fleming, may have come from Roche, an area in Pembrokeshire at the southern tip of Wales, where a small group of people of Flemish origin had settled and who had come to the aid of Diarmait Mac Murchada in 1167.[33] However, it could also be said that some came directly from Normandy. Hugh de Lacy I had granted the churches of Fore in Meath to the abbey of St Taurin at Evreux *c.*1185. It was at this abbey at Evreux that the sons of Hugh de Lacy I, Walter and Hugh, had taken refuge in 1210, when King John banished them from Ireland, having seized the castles of Walter de Lacy and confiscated the earldom of Ulster from Hugh de Lacy II for their support of William de Braose.[34] Evreux is situated no more than a day's ride from the small townlands of Mandeville, La Haye, Criquetot, Bray, Normanville and Turberville, all names of men found in the Llanthony cartularies and who also granted benefices to Llanthony.[35]

---

32 Hogan, *Llanthony*, charter clxv, pp 380–9 at p. 386.   33 Seán Duffy, *Ireland in the Middle Ages* (Dublin, 1997), pp 62–3.   34 William Petit, Richard Tuite, Richard de Feypo, Richard de la Capella and Hugh Hussey went to King John in Dublin, 28 June 1210, as messengers on behalf of Walter de Lacy, praying that the king should 'relax his ire', and that Walter 'will not plead, but places all his castles and lands in the hand of his lord, to retain or restore as he pleases'. *CDI*, 402, p. 60; 'William [de Braose] fled with his wife to Ireland and was harboured by Walter and Hugh de Lacy', ibid., 408, pp 65–6; William was father-in-law to Walter. In 1213, King John recalled Walter de Lacy from exile in France and restored his lands in England and the March but without Ludlow Castle. By 1215 Walter was restored to his Irish lands and also regained Ludlow Castle.   35 Today a large medieval timber sculpture of the Irish St Fechin stands to the left of the chancel of the church at Evreux, linking the church to its foundation and to earlier Irish history. Hogan, *Llanthony*, p. 66.

DROGHEDA

The town defences of Drogheda enclosed an area of 113 acres and had a circumference of 2.35 kilometres, making Drogheda one of the largest defended Irish towns in the country in the early thirteenth century.[36] Therefore, one of the most important grants to Llanthony Prima was the church of St Peter, *c.*1186, on the Louth [Uriel] side of Drogheda, as the confirmation charter of John, lord of Ireland, testifies.[37] They were received into this benefice by Malachy at the presentation of Hugh de Lacy I, in the presence of John, archbishop of Dublin.[38] This charter also provides the first reference to Drogheda, of which there are forty-eight mentions between both cartularies. Drogheda was to play an enormous part in the management of the Llanthony farming granges and the history of the Llanthony canons in Ireland, and judging by the line of the early town defences, it could be argued, given the scale of endowments for Llanthony at Drogheda, that the canons had an exceptional level of control in the embryonic town.[39] The Prima canons held many of the benefices within the town north of the Boyne, while the Secunda canons held many of the benefices within the town south of the Boyne, on the side of Meath and where they had possession of the church of St Mary. In relation to the Secunda church of St Mary, there is no record of the initial grant in the cartularies. The first mention of the church is in 1211, which together with the chapel of St Nicholas was part of the settlement between the two mother-houses.[40] As the Secunda church of St Mary was situated south of St Mary's bridge, but within the town walls of Drogheda, and as the bridge bore the name of St Mary, it is probable that their lands stretched as far as the banks of the River Boyne from which they could receive and ship produce.

As the town of Drogheda developed, there does not appear to be evidence of a *locator* who recruited colonists on behalf of a lord or principal tenant.[41] However, the strict assignment of burgage plots mentioned in the charters indicates that the colonizing of Drogheda was not arbitrary but structured, and that the people who came to live there during the late twelfth and early thirteenth centuries, in spite of the freedoms granted by Walter de Lacy, were not free to choose where in the

---

36 Drogheda was not unknown before this period however, and it is recorded as a place-name before the advent of the Anglo-Normans. Unlike many Irish towns Drogheda did not develop around an older core, but was established by Hugh de Lacy I, *c.*1182, and grew on either side of the banks of the Boyne as a double borough until 1412, when the two were united.   **37** Hogan, *Llanthony*, charter lxi, p. 239.   **38** St Bernard in his *Life of St Malachy* stated that when Malachy became bishop of Down in 1137, he formed 'de filiis suis conventum regularum clericorum'. *MRHI*, p. 146; C. Ó Clabaigh, 'The Benedictines in medieval and early modern Ireland' in M. Browne and C. Ó Clabaigh, *The Irish Benedictines: a history* (Dublin, 2005), pp 79–121. **39** Allocating appropriate land for the benefit of any religious foundation was essential for its survival. Equally important were three other elements; the requirement for arable land from which tithes could be rendered; access to water and river transport in order to ship produce; access to a stone quarry in order to construct buildings.   **40** Hogan, *Llanthony*, charter 28, p. 266. **41** M. Hennessy, 'Manorial organizaton in early thirteenth-century Tipperary', *Irish Geography*, 29 (1996), 124, for a discussion of locators.

town they could live.[42] For example, as part of the settlement of possessions between the two Llanthony houses in 1211–17, Secunda was awarded 'all revenues and payments from parishioners who dwell in the eastern part of Drogheda above the Boyne and of all others who had refused to settle in the burgages assigned to them'.[43] Notwithstanding strict laws of settlement, the building of the new bridge implied the need for skilled craftsmen, labourers and tradesmen who depended on services to buy their food, some of which could have been supplied by the Llanthony canons from their stall under the Thostal.[44] In 1203, Nicholas de Verdun had been given custody of the new bridge in place of his father Bertram,[45] and Walter de Lacy erected a mill at the bridge in 1207, presumably on the Meath side as his lands in Meath were returned to him by the king earlier that year.[46]

The charters also reveal that the canons had their own quay-side area in Drogheda, mentioned for the first time in the settlement grant made to Llanthony Prima in 1217, concerning their chapel of St Saviour, which gave its name to the quay. The grant was given by the then justiciar of Ireland, Geoffrey de Marisco, when he granted six feet of land at the eastern entrance of the chapel of St Saviour, next to the bridge at Drogheda, outside the quay of the canons, in order to create stairs up to the eastern entrance, so that 'the clerics and other faithful of holy church may have a suitable and more appropriate entrance for the purpose of celebrating divine service'.[47] Moreover, immediately to the west of the quay, recessed steps were discovered in 1981, which would have provided access to the quayside. This western stairway would also have given an entrance to those arriving with goods to be loaded on or off waiting ships. The southern end of a thirteenth-century burgage plot was also revealed during excavations on the site of St Saviour's, due west of the chapel, defined by a series of wattle walls with a metalled path 3.4m wide and lined by wattle fences.[48] The extension of the quay in 1217 gave easier access to nearby Bothe Street, which, as its name suggests, was an area where merchants could sell their wares.[49] Dyer Street, lying at right angles to Bothe Street, also reflects the trade after which the street was named, indicating a tightly organized and developing mercantile town.

42 Walter de Lacy, eldest son of Hugh de Lacy I, had conferred all of his burgesses at Drogheda with the law of Breteuil as early as 1194; the rights included freedom from toll, use of wood, pasture, and water passage, and a grant of three acres of arable with each burgage at a fixed annual rent of 12 pence. MacNiocaill, *Na Buirgéisí* (2 vols, Dublin, 1964), i, pp 172–3.   **43** Hogan, *Llanthony*, charter xlvii p. 272.   **44** The repair of roads and bridges was considered one of the *trinoda necessitates*, together with the maintenance of castles and the military forces for which every Norman lord was taxed. Under John, the burden imposed by the construction and repair of stone bridges became such that it was one of the causes of the 1215 rebellion against him. P. O'Keeffe and T. Simington, *Irish stone bridges* (Dublin, 1991), p. 27.   **45** *CDI, 1171–1251*, 185, p. 29.   **46** Ibid., 384 and 382, p. 57.   **47** Hogan, *Llanthony*, charter c, p. 277. In the following year on 16 September 1219, Geoffrey de Marisco was informed by the king that Luke de Netterville had been appointed archbishop of Armagh: *CDI*, 894, p. 133.   **48** ACS-Projects http://www.acsltd.ie/project6.html p. 1.   **49** ACS-Projects http://www.acsltd.ie/project6.html p. 1. Bothe Street is now called Shop Street, and runs from the river up to Peter's Street, where the medieval church of St Peter once stood and where today the eighteenth-century Church of

Further excavations in 2000, in the area of St Saviour's quay, revealed a harbour, which from its position strongly suggests that it was the private harbour of the Llanthony canons.[50] Among the finds were metal objects, such as the type of nails found in ship building. Also exposed was a section of revetment next to the south-west corner of St Saviour's that braced a large rectangular masonry structure dated to the thirteenth century and which appeared to be the remains of a crane base.[51] A great crane would have been necessary to bear the weight of, for example, a millstone. Milling grain was an essential part of life, and the location of the new mill at the bridge in Drogheda, constructed by Walter de Lacy in 1207, is testament to the practical nature of the harbour area. As grain prices doubled in England between 1160 and 1210,[52] the Llanthony canons could only benefit from a harbour so close to their farming granges in order to ship grain out of Ireland. While Llanthony Secunda did not appear to have a harbour at Gloucester, they did have their own quay-side, situated south of the castle weir and mill and adjacent to their priory, making shipping between their cell in Ireland and their mother house at Gloucester very expedient.[53] Even today, the 'Llanthony quay' at Gloucester, together with the sparse, beautifully constructed remains at the nearby almost vacant site of Secunda, stand testament to the once powerful priory.

Interestingly, dendrochronological evidence taken in 2006 from the timber wreck of the *c.*1525 sailing vessel found sunken at the mouth of the Boyne, confirms that the boat was constructed using oak grown in eastern County Antrim, and as the repairs were also found to be of the same local timber, it suggests that the vessel was built nearby. The planks were fastened with iron clench nails, similar to the nails found in the excavated Llanthony harbour. The boat was fully laden with a cargo identified as salted herring.[54] Notwithstanding the later date, the Llanthony canons were active in Drogheda until the dissolution and would have been familiar with the loading of their own cargo, and may have utilized a similar fully sea-going clinker boat to ship their produce out to their mother houses or possibly for sale to a merchant in England.

Ireland church of St Peter stands.   **50** Included in the harbour infill were artefacts that included pottery, wooden objects, English and French glazed ware and metal objects such as nails. The harbour, enclosed by masonry, appears to have been constructed during the mid-thirteenth century. ACS-Projects http://www.acsltd.ie/project6.html.   **51** The excavation, which was carried out by Malachy Conway in 2000, revealed a crane base that was an un-mortared limestone structure which survived, 8.0m west–east by 10.3m north–south and standing 3.1m high. Internally, the south and west walls were stepped in profile and externally the south face was battered above the line of revetment. ACS-Projects http://www.acsltd.ie/ project6.html. **52** O'Neill, *Merchants*, p. 56.   **53** J. Rhodes, 'Llanthony Priory', *Glevensis*, 23 (1989) 16–30: 25. In 1277, Queen Eleanor, living in Gloucester Castle as a widow [of Henry III], sought and gained permission from the prior of Llanthony to use the bridge that separated the castle from the canons' garden so that she and her household might walk in the garden. Idem, p. 27. The canons were known to have 'private parties' in their house by the same weir but they were eventually prohibited. J. Moorman, *Church life in England in the thirteenth century* (Cambridge, 1945), p. 339. **54** Holger Schweitzer, 'Drogheda boat: a story to tell', *Proceedings from the twelfth symposium on boat and ship archaeology*, ed. Nergis Gunsenin (Istanbul, 2009), pp 225–31.

Shipping of grain back to their mother houses, as already stated, was an essential part of the canons' administration in Ireland, for which the Prima canons had one storage cellar beside the quay of St Saviour on the Louth side of Drogheda granted by a burgess, Alan Prodfot, c.1230, together with the land on which the chapel was constructed, which suggests that apart from a chantry, the chapel also served a more practical purpose.[55] Not surprisingly, the practice of shipping Irish produce out of Ireland angered the bishop of Meath, Richard le Corner, who, in 1231–3, in an attempt to prevent Llanthony Prima and Secunda from removing goods from Ireland, brought a case against them, heard in the church of Saint Peter. However, a judicial sentence was handed down in a lengthy judgement in favour of Llanthony.[56] Consequently, licence was once again granted to the prior of Llanthony Secunda in 1238 'to convey into England his corn in Ireland, for three years from Easter, derived from his tithes and demesne lands'.[57] Several years later, Raymond de Domina, c.1250, awarded the gift of two of his three cellars, together with his houses and court, 'in the vill of the bridge at Drogheda', to the Secunda canons, suggesting the need for further storage before shipping.[58] As late as 1327, John, bishop of Meath, threatened the canons by saying that he would not allow the prior of Llanthony Secunda to have the profits accruing from their Irish holdings unless the canons paid him forty marks yearly out of the church of Duleek.[59] In 1387, the prior of Duleek, underlined the point and not for the first time, when he stated; 'that the house of Duleek ... is not a priory or the cell of a priory, but merely a grange or house for receiving possessions, goods, fruits and the income of the said religious men, for their own use and advantage and the use of their house, to live and be stored there'. The description of the Secunda house (above) would seem to verify this; although mention of the 'knights room' suggests that hospitality of the most basic kind was offered but not the kind of hospitality that a 'visitation' by an archbishop would demand.

The possessions referred to by the prior could include commodities such as poultry, dairy produce, fish, meal, vegetables, fruit, firewood, straw, bread and ale and even tithes of the gorse, heather and hay for sale by the canons. The canons also had an orchard and garden next to Cowgate in the parish of St Peter, as well as at Duleek, from which they could sell and profit in terms of vegetables and fruit. However, their sale of grain was more likely to have been on a much larger scale, and probably involved a personal arrangement between buyer and seller, involving grain stored either in their tithe-barns for local sale and consumption or stored in their cellars at Drogheda for export, and include a seller of tithes, rather than the more improvised nature of selling from their stall under the Thostal. Altar dues, apart from tithes, were also a large part of the canons' income as evidenced, for example, by the dues from the church of St Cianán at Duleek, which raised the substantial income of £13 6s. 8d. from the offerings of wax (implying beehives),

---

55 Hogan, *Llanthony*, charter cii, p. 329.   56 Ibid., charter 91, pp 293–6.   57 *CDI*, 2439, p. 365.
58 Hogan, *Llanthony*, charter 57, p. 311.   59 Philomena Connolly, 'Irish material in the class of ancient petitions', *Anal. Hib.*, 34 (1987), 1–106:29.

wool, lambs, geese, pigs, garlic, onions, flax, hemp, canvas and dairy produce, according to the Secunda extent of 1381.[60] Significantly, Ireland, and particularly the church of St Cianán, was to play no small part in terms of finance in relation to the building of the great new church at Llanthony in Wales begun *c.*1185, as it was decided as part of the initial settlement dividing the two houses of Llanthony in 1205, that the total income from the church of St Cianán must go towards construction of the new church for twelve years.[61] Some years later, the tithes of Platin, near Duleek, were also earmarked for this purpose.[62]

The increase of licensed markets and fairs at Drogheda during the early thirteenth century also reflects urban growth and its consequential mercantile expansion.[63] The eight-day fair that took place at Drogheda following a royal grant in 1222[64] would have served to reduce transportation costs for Llanthony, as the larger fairs were visited by many international traders, meaning the cash raised by the canons by the sale of goods in Ireland could be sent directly to their mother houses rather than transporting goods. The volume of shipping indicated by the harbour, together with the extended quay beside the bridge of St Mary, suggests heavy traffic which would have necessitated a strengthening of the bridge – which seems to have taken place in 1228, when the burgesses of Drogheda were allowed to charge customs on certain goods for one year to aid in the construction.[65] For example, for one sack of wool, the custom charged was 1*d.*, hides 4*d.*, hogshead of wine 1*d.*, a cart for conveyance, ½*d.*, and for every ox or cow ¼*d.*[66] Such sums put into perspective the fact that Llanthony Secunda could send £81 5*s.* 7*d.* cash to England, which was the income for one year after expenses, during the time of Prior Walter (1283–1300). Notwithstanding the later date, it is a sizable sum. It is also indicative, not only of the buoyant economy at that time, but also of the size and wealth of the Llanthony holdings in Ireland.[67]

However, apart from grain and other produce mentioned above that could be marketed at a fair or shipped out by Llanthony, fish were very important, and numerous references mentioned in the Llanthony charters indicate that fish provided significant revenue. Tithes could be collected from the many fish-ponds under the control of the canons as, for example, the tithes of fish at Mornington, on the banks of the Boyne, close to Colpe.[68] In practical terms, it would have taken relatively little time to sail up river from Colpe with a catch of fish which could be delivered directly into their harbour at Drogheda, either for sale or for preservation in salt, which was another vital commodity that was delivered into Drogheda, as evidenced from the salted herring cargo of the later clinker boat

---

60 Hogan, *Llanthony*, charter 98, pp 347–60.   61 Ibid., charter 11a, pp 256–7.   62 Ibid., charter xlvii, pp 272–3.   63 R. Britnell, 'The proliferation of markets in England, 1200–1349', *EHR*, 34:1 (1998), 209–21 at 211.   64 *CDI, 1171–1251*, 1010, p. 155.   65 *CDI, 1293–1301*, 251, p. 106; 311, p. 145.   66 C. Buldorini, 'Drogheda as a case study of Anglo-Norman town foundation in Ireland, 1194–1412' (PhD, TCD, 2009), p. 127.   67 Customs were also charged for seven years when a grant of murage was given to the burgesses of Drogheda on both sides of the Boyne; Uriel in 1295 and Meath in 1296. *CDI, 1293–1301*, 251, p. 106; 311, p. 145.   68 Hogan, *Llanthony*, charter 98, pp 347–60.

(above), sunk at the mouth of the Boyne. Salt was also needed for the preservation of butter and cheese.[69] The 1381 Secunda Memorandum reveals that the canons held a large benefice from Theobald de Verdun at Lougher, where there was a west-facing manor house in the form of a semi-moated castle,[70] and where the canons could fish freely up to a point half-way across the River Boyne.[71] At Dowth, while the weir was the property of the lord of Dowth, the canons nevertheless took the tithe. In 1386, Richard, proctor for Llanthony Secunda at Duleek, had permission to export two pipes of cod, two pipes of salmon and two pipes of herring,[72] and in the same year licence was granted to Richard Chiriton, prior of Llanthony Secunda at Gloucester, to ship two pipes of white fish and two pipes of salmon from Ireland to England, suggesting that Llanthony profited greatly from their tithes of fish alone.[73] Fishing rights often caused contenious issues however, witnessed by the case that arose between the abbot of Mellifont and the crown in 1380, when the abbot raised the height of his salmon-weir on the Boyne to the point that it obstructed the passage of large, fully laden boats between Drogheda and Trim. He appeared before chancery and argued successfully that as he had freehold of the weir it was his right.[74] In fact, the trade in fish was important enough to provoke a major row in Drogheda in 1430, between Llanthony and other clergy which was eventually settled by the archbishop of Armagh.[75]

As well as collecting tithes of grain and the sale of fish, tithes raised from the hunting of deer, and other wild game, would have produced food as well as fur,[76] and 'revenue from animals' is a common phrase in the charters. Obviously, this referred to tithes raised mainly by cattle and rabbits but it is not unreasonable to suggest that the canons also had revenue from the sale of pelts and hides from animals as well as wool. There is evidence that the Gloucester house had considerable income from wool in England,[77] and the Llanthony charters in relation to Ireland mention the tithes of wool as early as *c.*1188, in two charters of William

---

69 O'Neill, *Merchants*, p. 90. In 1402–3, certain burgesses at Drogheda, when sailing to Ulster, brought one-and-a-half weys of salt for the purpose of preserving meat, ibid., p. 88; see also W. Childs and T. O'Neill, 'Overseas trade' in *NHI*, ii, pp 492–532.   **70** The simple depiction of the semi-moated castle given by the scribe helps to augment the image of the kind of manor-house an Anglo-Norman knight, with the status of de Verdun, might have inhabited in Ireland. **71** Hogan, *Llanthony*, charter 98, pp 347–60.   **72** *Rot. pat. Hib.*, 63, p. 130. The contracted Latin text cites 'millwell' [milwellus] for the first fish listed which is a type of fish, mostly cod. *Revised medieval Latin word list*, ed. R.E. Latham (Oxford, 1999), p. 306. For further reading, see, C. Currie, 'The role of fishponds in the monastic economy' in R. Gilchrist and H. Mytum (eds), *The archaeology of rural monasteries*, BAR Series 203 (Oxford, 1989).   **73** *Rot. pat. Hib.*, 180, p. 135b. **74** Close roll 4 Richard II (14 Nov. 1380, Dublin). The case against the abbot was brought to chancery, and claimed that he had blocked the king's *watershard*, which was a 24ft-wide stream of water which ran through the centre of rivers in order that large, fully loaded vessels might sail unhindered, and which must not be blocked.   **75** *Rot. pat. Hib.*, p. 147. See also A.E. Went, 'Fisheries on the River Liffey' in Clarke, *Dublin*, pp 132–91.   **76** K. Nicholls, 'Gaelic society and economy in the high Middle Ages' in Cosgrove (ed.), *Med. Ir.*, pp 399–438: 416.   **77** As, for example, when in 1318 a burgess from Cirencester arranged to buy wool from Llanthony Secunda for that year for 100 marks: *VCH Glouc.*, p. 89.

Messet at Kilmessan,[78] in Meath, and also in *c.*1202 in a charter of William Petit concerning the churches at Rathkenny and Mullingar.[79] The bitter row between the parishioners of Colpe and the canons of Llanthony Prima concerning the tithes of lambs in 1380, also underlines the value of this product.[80] Indeed it could be said that the canons were obdurate in their pursuit of any parishioner who omitted to pay tithes of any kind, as Thomas Begg had learnt one year earlier in 1379, when the very serious penalty of excommunication for non payment of tithes of ale was imposed on him by the Prima canons.[81]

HOSPICE CARE DROGHEDA

While the management of their benefices to support their mother houses was of primary purpose for the Llanthony canons in Ireland, the establishment of medical institutions to care for the sick, children, guests and the poor, the four categories distinquished for special care,[82] was of major importance. Leprosy in Ireland had been prevalent from the fifth century,[83] and archaeological excavations in 1994 revealed the remains of a Magdalen chapel associated with a leper hospital located outside the walls to the north of Drogheda.[84] The Llanthony canons were already associated with the leper hospital at Duleek,[85] and according to the Llanthony charters, there was also a Magdalen hospital for lepers, beside the bridge of St Mary which was moved in 1206 to a new location outside the eastern gate of St Laurence to which Llanthony granted free chantry services and a cemetery,[86] indicating that there were at least two leper hospitals in the early thirteenth century just outside the walls of Drogheda to the north and to the east. As well as care for the lepers, two significant charters of 1214 confirm the committment of the Llanthony canons in relation to care of the sick by their involvement in the foundation of another hospital, the hospice of St Mary d'Urso. Ursus de Swemele, from whom the hospice took its name, was a wealthy burgess who established the infirmary,[87] which was situated outside the medieval west gate of the town on the Louth side. The remains of the hospice can be seen clearly on the skyline today, located inside the line of the later medieval town walls, and the architectural remains suggest that it may have been typical of a monastic or semi-monastic hospital in that it probably had an open-ward infirmary which would have necessitated the large numbers of staff implied by the charter. The Prima canons granted the hospice free burial rights with confession and the last sacrament for the brothers and sisters who worked in the infirmary and also for all of the servants who worked for the foundation. They also granted a chantry in the hospice on condition that the income from their

78 Hogan, *Llanthony*, charters lxxiv, p. 241 and xxiii, p. 242.   **79** Ibid., charter 12, p. 252.   **80** Ibid., charter clxiii, p. 347.   **81** Ibid., charter clx, p. 345.   **82** L. Milis, *Angelic monks and earthly men, monasticism and its meaning to medieval society* (Woodbridge, 1992), p. 53.   **83** G. Lee, *Leper hospitals in medieval Ireland* (Dublin, 1996), p. 15.   **84** D. Murphy, 'Recent archaeological discoveries in Drogheda', *Old Drogheda Society Journal*, 11 (1998), 6–17: 7.   **85** Hogan, *Llanthony*, charter 6, p. 251.   **86** Hogan, *Llanthony*, charter l, p. 260.   **87** Hogan, *Llanthony*, charters lv, pp 274–5 and lvi, p. 274. Further grants of Ursus can be found in Dugdale, *Monasticon Anglicanum*, 6, 1139; Brooks, *Cartularies of Llanthony Prima and Secunda*, p. 68.

parishioners on the four main festivals of Christmas, the purification of St Mary, Easter and the passion of the apostles Peter and Paul would go to the mother church of St Peter, indicating that their involvement with the local community at Drogheda encompassed all levels, ecclesiastical and mercantile as well as care for the sick and the poor.

Although the majority of grants in Ireland had been received by the canons by the second half of the twelfth century, they were continuing to receive small but important grants in Drogheda following the settlement between their mother houses in 1217. Included were fourteen acres of land at Parsonstown, north of Drogheda, c.1220,[88] the tithes of the church of Dowth,[89] and all of the land and garden between the east side of St Peter's and the town walls of Drogheda, c.1230.[90] At the same time, a pond with land that lay between the western side of the canons' house and the town walls of Drogheda was granted to them,[91] together with all of the land with buildings opposite the bakehouse, and a half burgage plot outside the east gate.[92] Roger Chester, the steward of Drogheda,[93] a wealthy landowning burgess, with his wife Petronella, gave the Prima canons the gift of rents that were owed to him by various people c.1247–56, to maintain 'the light of one candle' day and night before the high altar of the church of St Peter. Land was also gifted, which lay between the west gate and Roger Chester's grange, together with land in the same area at the corner of the road leading towards the land of the Friars Preachers.[94] Prima, c.1290, also paid for the remission of rights in a lane in Drogheda between the cemetery of St Peter up to the land of the prior.[95] Interestingly, earlier, c.1230, the cartulary of the Augustinian house of Tristernagh in the territory of Kilbixy in what is now Westmeath records that a Henry Chester of Drogheda, possibly father of the steward, Roger, quit-claimed land that lay between the land of the monastery of Holmcultram,[96] and land of Richard Camie, to the House of St John of Drogheda which seems to indicate that at this period of time, when in terms of settlement, expansion and trade in Drogheda, there were parcels of yet undeveloped land being moved around between the families of wealthy settlers and the religious orders. Apart from Drogheda, the canons received, c.1275, the important new grant of Buttevant Tower in Dublin, together with all of the adjacent land towards the church of St Olave.[97]

88 Hogan, *Llanthony*, charter cxii, p. 278. This charter was witnessed by Henry de Audley, from a Staffordshire family who also had lands in nearby Dunleer, granted to him by Hugh de Lacy II. Frame, *Ire. and Britain*, p. 44. **89** Hogan, *Llanthony*, charter cxvi, p. 279. The first mention of this church was in 1202x24, in a confirmation charter of the chapter of Clonard: ibid., charter 85, p. 253. The benefice was still held by Llanthony in 1381, and listed in the Secunda extent, ibid., charter 98, pp 347–60, and at the dissolution in 1541. *Crown surveys of lands, 1540–41, with the Kildare rental. Begun in 1518*, ed. Gearóid MacNiocaill (IMC, Dublin, 1992). **90** Hogan, *Llanthony*, charter ciii, p. 285. **91** Ibid., charter civ, p. 285. **92** Ibid., charter cv, p. 286. **93** Ibid., charter civ, p. 285. Roger Chester is a witness as steward of Drogheda. **94** Ibid. charter cvii, p. 310. **95** Ibid., charter cviii, p. 328. **96** Hugh de Lacy was a benefactor to the abbey of Holmcultram in Cumberland, although no extant charter granting Irish land to the abbey exists. Cf. *Holm Cultram Register*, ed. F. Grainger and W.G. Collingwood (Kendal, 1929), p. 97, no. 269, confirmation by Pope Alexander III of 'in Ireland whatever Earl Rycard and Hugh de Lacy have given'. *Tristernagh cartulary*, charter xxvi, fn. p. 25. **97** Hogan, *Llanthony*, charter 66,

What becomes clear is that Llanthony farmed out many of their benefices, evidenced, for example, by the arrangement the Augustinian house of Tristernagh had with the Secunda canons, to whom they paid a substantial annual pension of £3 14s. 4d., for the churches of Shanonagh and Laragh in Westmeath that were granted to Thomas de Craville by Hugh de Lacy I.[98] We know that Thomas gave the tithes of this land to Llanthony from the evidence found in the 1211 settlement charters.[99] However, if the canons at Tristernagh were more than fifteen days late, a large fine of £1 was imposed by Llanthony.[100] While Thomas had gifted benefices to Secunda, he also rented from them the churches, chapels and tithes in Wicklow in 1232, for fifty years under the obligation: '… to pay one hundred shillings each year … to the prior and convent or their assignees … to be made at St Thomas's, Dublin, through the hand of the prior… and undertake to pay a fine of 40s., for late payment',[101] which also indicates that Llanthony interacted with other houses that acted as recipients for monies and documents, and their clergy as bankers, until the absentee proctors returned to Ireland.[102] Interaction with other Augustinian houses is again demonstrated when in 1256, William de Culna, a Prima canon, is recorded as being chancellor of St Patrick's Cathederal.[103] That the proctor of a Llanthony Prima cell in Ireland could attain such high office in another foundation demonstrates that within the Augustinian network, appointments could be made wherever needed. It also shows how politically mobile and adept the Llanthony canons were in the thirteenth century in Ireland.

Ominous clouds were on the horizon however, and the vicissitudes of the fourteenth century, such as the famine of 1315–17, war at the hands of Edward and Robert Bruce, the regular warfare between English settlers and the indigenous Irish population, and the outbreaks of the Bubonic Plague which first arrived in Drogheda in 1349, and which saw flagellants process through the streets in the aftermath of the first outbreak,[104] saw Ireland sink into deep recession. All of which mitigated against the preservation of the Irish muniments concerning the

p. 322. See also, L. Simpson, *Excavations at Isolde's tower* (Dublin, 1994); and idem, 'Forty years a-digging: a preliminary synthesis of archaeological investigations in medieval Dublin' in S. Duffy (ed.), *Medieval Dublin I* (Dublin, 2000), pp 11–68 at p. 53. The grant of these premises by the mayor and commonality of Dublin, to their clerk William Picot, is among the entries in the *Calendar of ancient records of Dublin*, ed. J.T. Gilbert (18 vols, Dublin, 1889–1944), i, p. 95, for the years 1261–3. Brooks, *Cartularies of Llanthony Prima and Secunda*, note: p. 252. Buttevant Tower was demolished in 1675 in order to erect a new gate, Essex Gate, on the site. P. Healy, 'The town walls of Dublin' in Clarke, *Dublin*, pp 183–201. **98** '…to one Thomas de Craville he gave in heritage … Laraghcalyn likewise and Shanonagh, according to the people, gave Hugh de Lacy …' G.H. Orpen (ed.), *The song of Dermot and the earl* (Oxford, 1892), ll 3166–70, p. 231; also E. Mullally (ed.), *The deeds of the Normans in Ireland* (Dublin, 2002), ll 3167–71, p. 134. **99** Hogan, *Llanthony*, charter 65, p. 309. Thomas de Craville is referred to as chancellor of St Patrick's, by 1243. **100** Ibid., charter 98, pp 347–60. **101** Ibid., charter 73, p. 299. **102** Ibid., charter lix, pp 264–6, at p. 265. **103** Ibid., charter 22, p. 314. **104** B. Smith, 'Disaster and opportunity: 1320–1450' in Smith (ed.), *The Cambridge history of Ireland* (Cambridge, 2018), vol. i, p. 246; *Clyn*, pp 174, 180, 214. As late as 1534, a synod of the clergy met at the church of St Peter and, after chanting the *Veni creator spiritus*, Archbishop Cromer dissolved the synod due to the 'plague raging in the town'. *Archbishop Cromer's register*, L.P. Murray and A. Gwynn (eds), *Louth*

Llanthony holdings, leading to an ignorance of tenure in relation to certain assets when the scribes compiled the extents of possessions. This affected all religious houses as well as Llanthony and is reflected in the fact that only one charter breaks the silence of a 52-year lacuna between 1326 and 1378 in the combined cartularies of Prima and Secunda.[105] If poverty had been suggested by the break in the charters, the evidence of destitution found by Richard Chiriton in 1381, following his appointment in 1377 as proctor of Secunda at Duleek, is unmistakable as he made his way around their benefices in order to compile the Memorandum.[106]

In Drogheda, the situation was reflected by the suspension of the stall at the Thostal, implying that marketing was at a standstill, and the cellars under the chapel of St Nicholas were worthless because the canons didn't know by what title they held them; they also had several tenements but didn't know where they were. They were to hold an enquiry to sort out the problem. At Platin, the tithes of which, in the early thirteenth century, had contributed to the construction of the new church of Llanthony in Wales, had only a derelict chapel. At Tristernagh, the pension paid to the canons for the churches of Laragh and Shanonagh had already been suspended for nine years by the prior because the churches were now deemed to be worthless, suggesting that up to 1372 the churches were profitable. However, the arrival of proctor Chiriton marked a turning point and he aided, during his twenty-four year rule, to restore the house to profit again. Twenty-seven years later, William Temset, the scribe of the Prima extent of possessions, would meet a similar picture as he travelled across Ireland in an attempt to locate all of the possessions held by the house. His account is less descriptive but more informative in relation to the crops to be sown and the acres under cultivation, which had been drastically reduced.[107] In relation to Drogheda, Prima received 15s. for two tenements in the same street as the Tholsel, but no longer received anything for their two cellars under the chapel of St Saviour.

In 1421, Anne, countess of Stafford, who had inherited the patronage of Llanthony Secunda, agreed that it be passed to the crown.[108] Llanthony Prima in Wales followed in 1461.[109] Twenty years later, on 10 May 1481, the priory of Prima was sold to Secunda by permission of Edward IV for the sum of 300 marks.[110] Only five canons remained in Wales.[111] The two houses were finally reunited on 8 February 1482. As both of the cartularies MS C.115/75 and MS 115/80 eventually

Archaelogical Society Journal, 10 (1929–44), 126.   **105** Evidence of a break in the records occurs in several other manuscripts. In the *AI*, a break occurs in the Munster section in 1326 and resumes in 1390 with only one entry for 1359, p. 435–6. From 1315 to the next century, no further annal survives in the *ALC*; the rest is taken from the *AC*. M. Lyons, 'Manorial administration and the manorial economy in Ireland, *c.*1200–*c.*1377' (PhD, TCD, 1984), p. 2. The records of chapter meetings of the Dominican friars were also broken between 1315 at Trim, and 1340 at Kilmallock. A. Hogan, *Kilmallock Dominican Priory* (Limerick, 1991), p. 54.   **106** Hogan, *Llanthony*, charter 98, pp 380–9.   **107** Ibid., charter clxv, pp 178–93.   **108** Dugdale, *Monasticon Anglicanum*, 6, 139.   **109** When the earl of March came to the throne as Edward IV.   **110** Langston, 'Priors', p. 125. Dugdale, *Monasticon Anglicanum*, 6, 139.   **111** John Adonis, a canon at Llanthony in 1482, applied for 'Dispensation to receive and retain for life any benefice with or without cure', etc.: *CPL*, 13, p. 746.

became part of the Scudmore inherited cartularies collection,[112] it suggests that once the houses were reunited, the Prima cartulary, together with other related muniments, were transferred to the library at the Gloucester priory, and eventually to the The National Archive, Public Record Office at Kew, where they are today. Thereafter, all benefices accrued in Ireland for Llanthony at both Colpe and Duleek would have been returned to the Gloucester house of St Mary, until the dissolution, which in Drogheda was 12 May 1541. The crown surveys at this time indicate that the Llanthony holdings at Drogheda comprised of three cellars which were rented by merchants for 18s. 8d., an orchard and garden rented for 14s., and a tenement near the Tholstal rented for 19s. Tithes brought in a further £50.

The crown surveys indicate that the tracts of land from which Llanthony held the tithes at the dissolution in 1541, awarded to the Augustinian canons of Llanthony in the twelfth century by Hugh de Lacy I, his family and knights, had, with very little variation, remained in their possession. The churches and chapels granted during the initial phase of their advent into Ireland, c.1174, also continued under their authority until the sixteenth century. The enabling grants of tithes and benefices granted to the canons permitted them to reap the benefits of the fertile undulating lowland of the four main counties in the northern hinterland of Dublin, for the benefit of their mother houses in Wales and England.

What has been revealed by the Llanthony charters resembles a contemporary microcosm of the wider social and political situation existing in Ireland from the twelfth century, and also highlights the many instances where the complex prosopographical web of the interweaving associations of descendant settler families becomes evident in the confirmations of advowsons and tithes of land. The loyalty that bound together many families meant that the majority of lands from which Llanthony held the benefices often changed hands through intermarriage, but were never alienated. The charters have also shown that in the nascent town of Drogheda, the support of Hugh de Lacy I was as pivotal to the lives of the canons as the canons were crucial to the early development of the town. Local gentry and the merchants of Drogheda worked side by side with the canons in the running of their harbour, which provided the link between the Llanthony estates and their mother houses abroad until the dissolution of the monasteries ended forever their involvement with the land of Ireland. The original Hugh de Lacy, by endowing the nascent church of Llanthony with gifts of land in 1103, was fulfilling the role of a newly established land baron. It was also a means of consolidating temporal and spiritual possessions, for, while gaining land on earth he might also, through the perpetual prayer of dependant canons, gain a place in heaven. It could also be argued that the introduction of the Llanthony canons into Ireland by his descendant, Hugh de Lacy I, in c.1174 was as much a part of the colonization of Ireland as the settlement of the canons onto de Lacy lands at Ewyas in c.1103 had been part of the colonization of Wales.

---

112 Master Harvey's exhibits, duchess of Norfolk deeds: Scudmore inherited cartularies; now housed at the Public Record Office, Kew.

Transeptal churches of the regular canons in Ireland

TADHG O'KEEFFE

Augustinian regular canons and Cistercian monks were the principal recipients of the acts of monastic patronage by secular lords between the middle decades of the twelfth century and the second quarter of the thirteenth. The number of new foundations for these canons and monks was already in a steep decline in both Gaelic and Anglo-Norman districts when the first mendicant communities arrived in the 1220s and attracted a new wave of patronage. One casualty of this fall-off in the rate of foundation of abbeys and priories was the transeptal monastic church.

A transeptal church is basically a cross-shaped church defined by a continuous transeptal arm running north–south across its long axis, close to its east end. The arm is typically bisected by the crossing, the place where the two axes of the church intersect, and the transepts to the north and south of the crossing are typically of similar size, with the features of one often mirrored in the other. The plan type has a pedigree that can be traced back more than seventeen centuries to the earliest Christian era, and the essence of its form has remained relatively stable through that period, but the role of the transeptal space in the liturgical life of its host building has changed since it first appeared in fourth-century churches. In the early Middle Ages the spaces within transepts were generally spaces of sanctity, extensions of the presbyteries, with arcuated walls providing visual barriers, and screens providing physical barriers, on their western sides. From at least the eighth century in parts of northern Europe, as churches began to be planned using repeated geometric modules (normally squares), the transeptal space was reimagined as an intermediate, even liminal, space between the congregation and the sanctuary. The crossing, a space formalized in modular church architecture, remained exclusive to the church's consecrated community and was screened off accordingly, but the transepts to the north and south were often made accessible to both worshippers (approaching from the west) and clergy (approaching through the screens from the crossing). Ambulatories sometimes allowed worshippers move eastwards beyond the transepts, but only for the purpose of venerating relics.

The last transeptal church to have been built for a monastic community in medieval Ireland was that attached to Hore Abbey, Co. Tipperary, founded for Cistercians in 1272, and even it is a chronological outlier, separated by many decades from earlier examples. The friars did not give the type a new lease of life. They continued the centuries-old practice of living in a cloistered setting, and so adopted the type of monastic plan used by canons and monks, but had no use themselves in their churches for the additional space provided by transepts. They

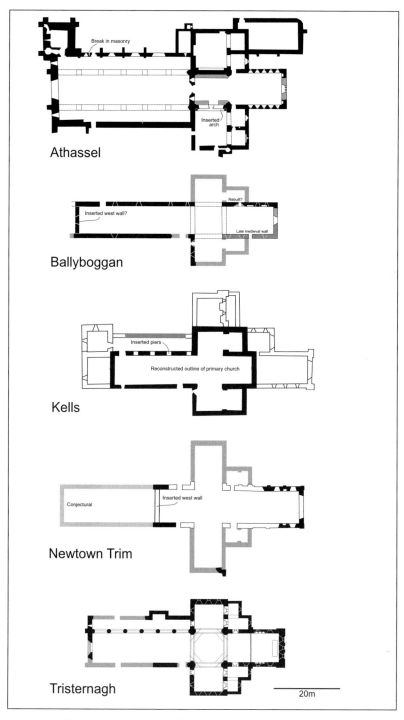

8.1 Plans of Augustinian transeptal churches built by Anglo-Normans; Holy Trinity cathedral church is not included as its plan reflects its pre-invasion predecessor.

sometimes allowed benefactors to build chapels which modern scholars tend to describe (somewhat misleadingly) as transepts, but these were 'single-arm' additions in the sense that they projected to one side only, and friars generally only permitted them to be attached to the naves of their churches.

How long was the history of the building (as distinct from the use) of the transeptal monastic church in Ireland before it went out of fashion? It appears from the archaeological record to have been relatively short. No conventionally transeptal churches, monastic or otherwise, are known for certain to have been built in Ireland before the introduction of reformed monastic observances of continental origin. The first one to have been built was probably the original cathedral church in Dublin, with its Benedictine chapter (discussed below). The type only became common once the first Cistercians arrived in the 1140s. All of the known Augustinian examples – six surviving and two destroyed – post-date the invasion of 1169, including the one example known to have been built under native Irish patronage. The period of their construction was very short indeed: the first was started in 1177 or 1192, and all but one of the rest were started by 1210, the exception being the Gaelic-Irish example. Of the eight, two were Victorine.

My aim in this chapter is to present an account of each of the Anglo-Norman churches and its architecture (Fig. 8.1), elaborating on earlier accounts or presenting new interpretations as necessary; a contextual analysis of the one Irish example, Ballintubber, Co. Mayo, would draw us into the problematic 'Transitional' architectural tradition of the so-called 'School of the West', and more space would be needed than is available here in order to do it justice.[1] The seven Anglo-Norman churches are discussed in alphabetical order. Most space is devoted to Athassel priory church, a building of immense historical and archaeological interest around which architectural historians have tended to skirt, and Ballyboggan priory church, a little-known monument.

ATHASSEL PRIORY, CO. TIPPERARY

The earliest surviving record of the foundation of this priory comes from a 1377 compilation of tales of miracles attributed to St Edmund, the martyred ninth-century Anglo-Saxon king, preserved in MS Bodley 240 (Oxford): *Circa annum Domini 1182, dominus Willemus de Burgo filius comitis Canciae, fundavit monasterium canonicum nigrorum in territorio de Atheschille in Hibernia, in honore Sancta Marie et Sancti Edmundi regis et martiris.*[2] The date of 1182 is too early for William de Burgh; he came to Ireland in John's entourage in 1185. Other written records indicate that St Edmund was the sole dedicatee,[3] but the Blessed Virgin Mary is depicted on the

1 See, for example, B. Kalkreuter, *Boyle Abbey and the School of the West* (Bray, 2001). 2 T. Arnold (ed.), *Memorials of St Edmund's Abbey* 3 (London, 1900), p. 347. 3 See, for example, Chancery: Inquisitions Ad Quod Damnum, Henry III to Richard III, s.a. 1329 (National Archives, Kew, C 143/202/21), and *CPL*, 12, p. 245, s.a. 1465.

mid-1330s seal of the prior.[4] It might be relevant to note that the Augustinian priory of Walsingham in Norfolk, where William de Burgh's mother was buried (his father's burial place is not known), was dedicated to the Blessed Virgin Mary.[5] James Ware, who also identified William as the founder but understood Athassel to be dedicated to Edmund alone, dated the foundation to 'about the year 1200' and added that King John confirmed its possessions on 20 April 1205.[6] We can probably trust Ware on the date: his record that Walter and Richard de Burgh, successive earls of Ulster, were buried in the priory in 1271 and 1326 respectively can be verified from other sources.[7]

The de Burghs were Athassel's principal benefactors for more than a century after its foundation, and senior members of the family were present there in life as in death.[8] Familial devotion to St Edmund probably explains in large part the priory's dedication, but there must have been other factors as well. Edmund had not been venerated in Ireland before the invasion, and monasteries dedicated to him were actually very rare in England.[9] The first act in the (ultimately unsuccessful) promotion of a cult in Ireland was in Dublin immediately after the invasion when, during the episcopate of Lorcán Ua Tuathail, two chapels were built at the east end of the metropolitan church and were dedicated to *Sancti Edmundi regis et martiris et Marie que dicitur alba et sancti laudi* (St Edmund, king and martyr, St Mary called Alba, and St Laud).[10] It is reasonable to speculate that William de Burgh decided on Athassel's dedication knowing that it would attract attention within the settler community, regardless of how the saint was being venerated in Dublin. The early success of the abbey of St Thomas the Martyr in securing temporalities and spiritualities across the English lordship in Ireland might have persuaded him that the veneration of a different martyr-saint would help to

4 National Archives, Kew, DL 25/535/453 (dated 1335) and DL 25/284/230 (dated 1336). My thanks to Dr Francis Young for first drawing my attention to these seals.   **5** C. Ellis, *Hubert de Burgh: a study in constancy* (London, 1952), p. 191.   **6** J. Ware, *The antiquities and history of Ireland* (Dublin, 1705), p.104; other possessions, acquired by the priory after William's death, required confirmation in 1206 (see *CDI, 1171–1251*, no. 294, pp 44–5).   **7** For Walter see S. Mac Airt (ed.), *The annals of Inisfallen: MS Rawlinson B. 503* (Dublin, 1951), p. 371, s.a. 1272; for Richard see R. Butler (ed.), *Jacobi Grace Kilkenniensis Annales Hiberniae* (Dublin, 1842), pp 103, 161. The tomb from Athassel which is now displayed in Cashel may have been carved for one of these two men: see C. Manning, 'The Athassel tomb', *Irish Arts Review*, 22:4 (2005), 132–5.   **8** For example, a letter from Richard de Burgh, earl of Ulster, to the bishop of Worcester in 1310, was sent from Athassel (National Archives, Kew, SC 1/35/91). The register of Athenry Dominican friary describes Athassel as the customary burial place for the de Burghs (A. Coleman, 'Regestum Monasterii Fratrum Praedicatorum de Athenry', *AH*, 1 (1912), 201–21, at 212).   **9** A.M. Binns, *Dedications of monastic houses in England and Wales, 1066–1216* (Woodbridge, 1989), pp 65–6.   **10** H.J. Lawlor, 'A calendar of the *Liber Niger* and *Liber Albus* of Christ Church, Dublin', *PRIA*, 27C (1908–9), 1–93, at 69; A. Gwynn, 'Some unpublished texts from the Black Book of Christ Church', *Anal. Hib.*, 16 (1946), 281, 283–337, at 309. The cathedral priory of Holy Trinity had a community of Augustinian canons of the Arrouaisian observance; Edmund's veneration by the Benedictines of Bury St Edmunds leads one to wonder whether the new chapel of the late twelfth century at Holy Trinity saw the transfer of a dedication from an altar or chapel in that cathedral when it had a Benedictine community.

enrich his foundation. It is conceivable that Athassel's architecture, being relatively early in the history of Gothic in Ireland, was even modelled to some degree on St Thomas's,[11] possibly to reinforce an association between the two 'martyr churches' in the consciousness of the settler community. Athassel's proximity to Cashel, an episcopal seat then under Gaelic-Irish authority and a place where royal sanctity was a familiar and politically potent concept, was possibly also a factor in the choice of an English king-saint as its (joint) dedicatee. Whatever its explanation, the dedication of Athassel to St Edmund manifested itself in the priory's iconography and material culture, including in the seal of at least one of its priors (see below), and it is possible that some relic of the saint was brought to Tipperary for the church's consecration.[12] The later fourteenth-century record in MS Bodley 240 informs us that the priory had near its high altar an image of St Edmund holding his lance aloft and that from this image he miraculously hurled the lance to the floor of the church as a sign whenever the founder's descendant, the head of the de Burgh family line, was *in proximo morituri*, approaching death.[13]

For a monastery of its physical size, Athassel's profile in historical sources is relatively low, reflecting to a degree the fact that its affairs were mainly regional (specifically the Cashel–Limerick diocesan region) rather than national. Still, within its region it was a very prominent place, familiar by name if not by sight to people of power and influence.[14] Although the MS Bodley 240 reference suggests that Edmund was still miraculously flinging his lance in Athassel late in the fourteenth century, the priory may have entered the phase of terminal decline earlier in that century. Following the grant of a yearly fair in 1224,[15] a borough had been established at Athassel, possibly even within the precinct walls.[16] It was attacked in the early fourteenth century,[17] and it is likely that the priory community suffered from the ordeal, if only mentally. After Richard de Burgh's death and burial in Athassel in 1326, the priory drifts off the radar. In 1484, it was noted that the canons of the priory 'live in private habitations, and not in the monastery, and that divine worship is almost extinct in the church of the monastery, the buildings of which are in need of no little repair'.[18] Two years later, 'threatened with the ruin of its buildings, and … in great need of repair', Athassel had a lay administrator appointed.[19]

11 Michael O'Neill has pointed to stylistic parallels between Dublin's Holy Trinity Cathedral and Athassel ('Christ Church Cathedral as a blueprint for other Augustinian buildings in Ireland' in J. Bradley, A.J. Fletcher and A. Simms (eds), *Dublin in the medieval world* (Dublin, 2009), pp 168–87). By rethinking the accepted chronology of both buildings, as I do in this paper, a case could be made in principle for an architectural link between St Thomas's and Athassel. On the early history of St Thomas's Abbey see Marie Therese Flanagan's contribution to this volume. **12** None is recorded, but there were relics in eleven ecclesiastical institutions in England, although only one Augustinian house – Waltham Abbey, Essex – had one (Andrew Gourlay, 'Things left behind: matter, narrative and the cult of St Edmund of East Anglia' (PhD, University of Glasgow, 2017), pp 118–21). **13** Arnold, *Memorials* 3, p. 347. **14** See, for example, *CDI, 1171–1251*, no. 175, p. 75. **15** *CDI, 1171–1251*, no. 1221, p. 186. **16** A record of the town's destruction at the hands of the Fitzgeralds in 1581 suggests that the monastery and town were identified as one (*AFM* 5, p. 1755), suggesting that the wall around the former embraced the latter. **17** Butler, *Annales Hiberniae*, p. 97. **18** *CPL*, 13:1, p. 193. **19** *CPL*, 14, p. 28.

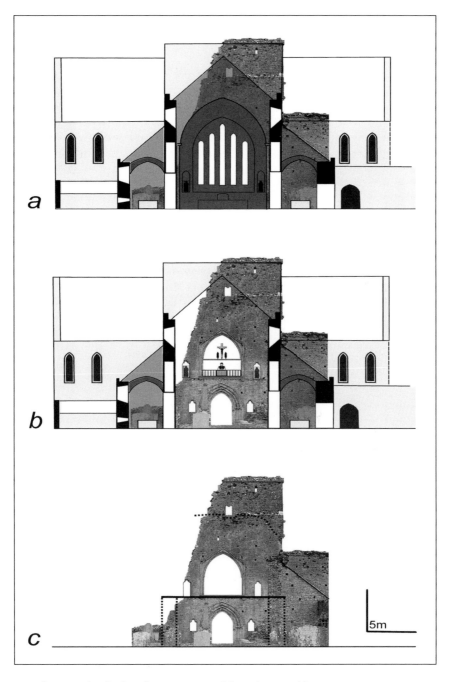

8.2 The west side of Athassel's crossing viewed from the west: (a) reconstruction cross-section of the second quarter of the thirteenth century; (b) reconstruction of the screen wall, *c.*1300; (c) the level and width of the gallery floor behind the rood, and the line dividing the fabric of screen wall from that of the inserted domestic tower.

8.3 View of Athassel's presbytery looking eastwards.

The priory church was one of the finest Gothic buildings in Ireland. It had a two-aisled nave, the outer walls of which survive, and there are some substantial remains of rectangular transepts with pairs of conjoined east-facing chapels, a square crossing with a tower above it, and a rectangular choir. There was a large tower attached to the external north-west corner of the nave and a rectangular mortuary chapel attached to the external north-east corner of the north transept; both are now heavily ruined. Most of the fabric of the church and claustral complex dates from the thirteenth century, but not from one phase within that century, while some alterations were made between *c.*1300 and the dissolution. The structural history of the church has been discussed by a number of writers,[20] but discrepancies and disagreements between the accounts necessitate the detailed discussion which follows here.

Building work on the church would have begun at its east end, starting with the choir. A grant and confirmation to the prior and canons in 1206 of lands and possessions[21] indicates clearly that the process of endowing the priory was underway when William de Burgh died in 1204, so it is likely that work on the east end of the church started during William's lifetime and that by about 1210, or 1215 at the latest, the choir had been built and work on the transepts was in progress. The choir that we see today clearly has original early thirteenth-century walling on all sides, and original fenestration in its side walls, but there is infill and a late medieval traceried window where originally there would have been five graded lancets (Fig. 8.2). A fortuitous survival is the pair of niches that flanked the outer lancets (Fig. 8.3). These niches were especially well-suited to the display of statues, but could also have been used to frame painted panels (with space left for candles in front of them). We do not know the medium in which that image of St Edmund recorded in the fourteenth century was rendered, but his possession of a lance in that image would lead one to think that it was not a stone sculpture. It may have been a wooden statue (to which was affixed an iron lance) or a painting. Whatever it was, the likelihood is that it was made for, or was imported into Ireland for use in, the niche on the north side of the altar, with the other niche displaying an image in the same medium of the Blessed Virgin Mary.

The flat east end of the choir is matched by the east ends of the transeptal chapels in an arrangement reminiscent of Cistercian design (Fig. 8.4), and the debt to Cistercian architecture is also evident in the manner in which those chapels had continuous lean-to roofs (rather than pitched roofs with small gables, as had the transeptal chapels built later in the thirteenth century at nearby Cashel Cathedral). In an apparent deviation from the Cistercian template, however, there was access

---

20 For example, R. Cochrane, 'Notes on the Augustinian priory of Athassel, Co. Tipperary', *JRSAI*, 39 (1909), 279–89; H.G. Leask, *Irish churches and monastic buildings*, II (Dundalk, 1960), pp 94–9; R. Stalley, *Architecture and sculpture in Ireland, 1150–1350* (Dublin, 1971), pp 125–30; idem, 'Athassel (Tipperary), Augustinian Priory', *Archaeological Journal*, 153 (1996), 315–20; M. Quinlan Architects, *Conservation plan: Athassel Augustinian Priory, County Tipperary* (Dublin, 2009), pp 8–49; O'Neill, 'Christ Church Cathedral as a blueprint'; R. Moss, 'Athassel, Augustinian Priory', Co. Tipperary' in R. Moss (ed.), *Art and architecture in Ireland: medieval, c.400–c.1600* (Dublin, 2014), pp 193–4. **21** *CDI, 1171–1251*, no. 294, pp 44–5.

8.4 The south transeptal chapels at Athassel.

from the choir to the adjacent transeptal chapel on each side; the only door which survives has a *pointed* segmental arch, for which one could allow an early thirteenth-century date. Another un-Cistercian feature (and a curious feature by any measure) was the apparent lack of original access from the aisles of the nave into the transepts. There is a small blocked doorway in the west wall of the south transept but it does not appear to be original (unlike the original doorway into the south transept from the north cloister alley, it had no relieving arch) and it was too modest in scale anyway for an opening in such a position.

Few items of medieval monastic architecture in Ireland are as head-scratchingly inscrutable as Athassel's crossing. There are three specific problems of interpretation. First, the two eastern piers survive, though neither is complete, and there is also a fragment of the north-west pier, while the south-west pier is no longer visible thanks to a thick wall inserted into the crossing to carry the weight of a later tower (Fig. 8.5). Curiously, the eastern piers not only have different cross-sections and base-profiles but they rise from different levels on the floor, that on the north being higher than that on the south, and each has a vertical joint on its

8.5 View of Athassel's crossing from the presbytery.

east side. One can only assume that what we see is what was intended; to suggest that several phases of work are represented in the piers would be to argue for an abnormally complex sequence, probably involving changes of mind. The crossing arches associated with these piers are gone, but springers on the south-east pier reveal their level (Figs 8.2a, 8.6).

Second, a (later blocked) crossing arch survives at a high level at the junction of the crossing and south transept (Fig. 8.7), and one can see that it, and a now-lost partner arch on the other side of the crossing, were alterations because the moulded responds were supported by inserted pedestals (Fig. 8.8). There were solid walls originally between and below these arches, and these predate the arches; the evidence of the south transept tells us that these walls were almost entirely broken through at some stage, but that the entire space was 'refilled' causing the blocking that one sees today.

Third, the west side of the crossing has Athassel's well-known screen wall, its lower level penetrated by a doorway and its upper level having a blocked rood-gallery opening (Figs 8.2b, 8.9). This wall requires stone-by-stone recording because

Level of springing of original crossing arch into south transept

8.6 Athassel's crossing from the north transept.

it has patches of masonry of different character, which suggests different phases. In its entirety, though, it is clearly not original: it stands very slightly proud of the line of the west wall of the transepts. Some of its elements appear to have originated elsewhere too. For example, the doorway looks to have been reassembled, suggesting that it might originally have been the west doorway of the nave. Also, the capitals on the string-course below the blocked gallery seem to be *spolia*. The screen wall rises as a tower, its fenestration asymmetrical above the blocked gallery. The absence of scarring from a lost nave roof has led to the belief that the nave was in ruins when the crossing tower was built.[22] There is some

---

22 Stalley, *Architecture and sculpture*, pp 128–9; idem, 'Athassel (Tipperary)', p. 317; O'Neill, 'Christ Church Cathedral as a blueprint', p. 170.

8.7 The inserted crossing arch at Athassel viewed from the south transept.

confusion in the literature about the relative chronology of the tower, and I will attempt below to resolve the sequence.

The screen wall provided an unusual monumental setting for the display of the rood, the great crucifix. This was in the canopied opening directly above the doorway, so one looked up at it from the nave. Roods varied in size, from the modestly small (which could be supported on a horizontal beam) to the very large

8.8 The pedestal on the west side of the crossing at the south transept at Athassel.

(which required suspension from chains). It is not clear how the rood was displayed at Athassel because the blocking of the opening has disguised the evidence, but the opening is large enough to accommodate a *pulpitum* with a rood beam above it (Fig. 8.2b). The prior's seal of the mid-1330s possibly even records the arrangement (Fig. 8.10). The pointed oval seal has, from top to bottom, a crucifixion scene set on a horizontal base; the Virgin and child to the right of a nimbed figure who can

8.9 Athassel's screen wall viewed from the nave.

8.10 The seal of Prior Peter of Athassel, attached to a letter of 1335 (National Archives, Kew, DL 25/535/453; reproduced with permission).

be identified as St Edmund,[23] again set on a horizontal base; and the top half of a suppliant figure in profile, probably the priory's founder, within a round arch. All three elements are contained within an architectural frame. Are we looking at a representation of Athassel's rood, with the Virgin and child, accompanied by St Edmund, depicted on the front panel of the *pulpitum* below it, and the doorway into the crossing below that again? Today the doorway in the screen wall opens into the roofless crossing, but originally the whole space of the crossing was roofed over to provide a platform behind the rood gallery above (Fig. 8.2c). In other words, the doorway did not open directly into a space that stretched as far as the end wall of the choir but, rather, into the space under the gallery.

The nave, finally, was one of the more advanced essays in Gothic architecture in Ireland. It has two parts: one is the west façade and the westernmost bay, and the other is the five-bay unit between there and the crossing. These belong to different phases of construction: the façade is not quite perpendicular to the axis of the nave nor is it perfectly parallel with the axis of the transepts, and there is also a vertical break in the masonry immediately west of the north wall doorway. Michael O'Neill has suggested that the façade and adjacent bay are later than the rest of the nave.[24] I would suggest the opposite: the west front of the nave was built first, so that the church had a near-complete face to the world before work on the rest of the nave was started, and its slight misalignment relative to the rest of the church is an original error of surveying.

Unfortunately, the internal aisle walls of the nave are gone, taking with them key evidence, including about its elevations (Fig. 8.11). The inner, or church-side, face of the south wall of the nave is so damaged and patched-up that it holds few clues that are not available elsewhere in the building. Fortunately, the church's

---

23 At Lakenheath, Suffolk, a mural shows St Edmund standing to the right of a Virgin and child, his left-hand raised in salutation. It is dated to *c.*1330 (R. Pinner, *The cult of St Edmund in medieval East Anglia* (Woodbridge, 2015), p. 216), which makes it roughly contemporary with the Athassel seal.   **24** O'Neill, 'Christ Church Cathedral as a blueprint', p. 172.

8.11 The interior of the façade of the nave of Athassel.

north wall is fairly intact. It preserves some engaged colonettes and wall scars, and these indicate that the north aisle had six rib-vaulted bays. A single, much damaged, colonette on the south wall confirms the same scheme in the south aisle. There is no scarring from a rib-vault on the west wall of the transept where it faces into the south aisle, and there was probably no scarring on the corresponding wall on the other side of the church either. Although unusual, it would support the thesis that the nave was built from west to east and that work on the transeptal arm was finished before the nave-builders reached it.

All that remains from the two rows of piers down the centre of the nave are the lower parts of half-responds in the west wall of the crossing. They reveal that the piers of each aisle wall were not of the same plan at the time that the church fell into ruin: the north half-respond was half-octagonal with filleted shafts facing north, west and south, whereas that on the south is a half-quatrefoil with no fillets or additional embellishments. These responds indicate that the two aisle walls had piers of different plan, those on the north side having a version of the octagonal form that one sees in the east end of St Patrick's Cathedral, Dublin, and those on the south resembling the slender quatrefoil piers of the nave of St Canice's Cathedral, Kilkenny.

It has been assumed by all who have commented on the church that the two rows of arcades were made at the same time, and I will follow that assumption here. One cannot tell from their shapes whether the piers on both sides of the church supported vault ribs over the central aisle of the nave. Filleted shafts facing into the body of the church from the north aisle wall raise the possibility that the clerestory wall was also articulated internally, and, further, that vault ribs sprung from those shafts at a level halfway up the clerestory windows to support a stone canopy. However, the quatrefoil piers of the south aisle wall do not point to an articulated clerestory level on that side of the church. The size of all of these piers, combined with the width of the central aisle, would suggest strongly that the long spine of the church actually had a timber roof. That is probably the most reasonable interpretation of the evidence that is visible without excavation.

I want to suggest gingerly an alternative that has not been suggested before. Excavation would be needed to test it. External buttresses on the north wall of the nave and the greater thickness of its external south wall would be consistent with multi-bay, quadripartite rib-vaulting over the nave's central aisle. It is also worth noting that the side aisles in Athassel were not provided to aid circulation – they did not connect with the transepts – but terminated at altars. If these non-circulatory spaces were regarded as worthy of vaulting, one would think that the central vessel would be vaulted also. Michael O'Neill did speculate that the collapse of a main vault could explain why the interior of the church is now an empty shell,[25] but he assumed, as have all commentators, that the two arcaded walls that carried the original nave roof are represented by the responds in the west wall of the transept arm and that they were built contemporaneously. Is it possible that the nave was indeed vaulted, that the design of the north-side piers – a design consistent with the springing of vault ribs – was originally replicated on the south side, with the vaults carried therefore on two identical arcuated walls, and that a catastrophic collapse of the south side of the church led to the building of a replacement arcuated wall with quatrefoil piers? This is a complex scenario but it does not require special pleading. The quatrefoil piers of the south aisle wall match the piers of the surviving transeptal arch which we know to have been an insertion. Also, insofar as one can determine it by observation rather than by exact measurement, the inserted arch in the south transept seems to be slightly more aligned with the south aisle wall in the nave than is the case on the north side of the church. Such a scenario actually offers a context for a rebuilding of the west wall of the south transept, and permits speculation that there was originally access to the transept from the nave aisle.

So, what is the sequence and chronology of phases in Athassel priory church? I suggest that the evidence that can be observed today supports the following mix of hypotheses and conclusions:

---

25 Ibid., p. 172.

1. The choir and transepts were planned and started as one, and there is no reason to query a date of 1200–10 for the earliest phase of that work. After all, the priory had endowments in 1206 and was in the process of acquiring more (under the headship of a prior who was actually named Edmund). The nature of the crossing of *c*.1210 is uncertain. First, there may have been relatively plain arches rising not from projecting responds but from the flush wall surfaces, possibly with soffit arches on corbels (as at many Cistercian sites, and at Tristernagh). Second, there may have been a low crossing tower simply to take the four roof-ends created by the transeptal plan; the tower attached to the church's west façade housed the priory's bell or bells. There is a possibility that there was no tower originally and that the four roofs simply converged on a single point,[26] but a simple tower would have spared the builders the challenge of complex carpentry. One cannot rule out the possibility that the church originally followed the early Cistercian scheme in which differential relative heights of the four roofs allowed builders to eschew towers in transeptal churches.

2. The four complex piers with their crossing arches might represent an early alteration to the plan; the evidence that they were inserted is ambiguous, but to modern eyes they do not look well integrated aesthetically with the architecture of the choir. Assuming the suggestion that there were simple crossing arches originally to be correct, the height of the crossing arches was probably not changed in this phase. I think it likely that the transepts were not left fully open to the crossing when these piers were built but were blocked from the outset with the perpyn walls of which very slight traces can be discerned in the later blocking of the south transept. This would make sense because the length of the church's presbytery would have pushed the choir stalls westwards under the crossing. I think that this was also the arrangement at Newtown Trim.[27]

3. The crossing piers are probably roughly contemporary with the building of the west end of the nave, and together they suggest a confluence of ambition and enrichment in the Athassel community. If the choir was finished by *c*.1210 and the transepts finished in the following decade, work on the nave is likely to have been underway by 1230 at the very latest (unless, as seems unlikely, the community was happy to leave Athassel without a nave). I would suggest that the crossing piers and west façade were built in the 1220s, and that the nave was completed in the 1230s.[28] The probability is that the nave was timber-roofed but there could have been a vault supported by two arcuated aisle walls of the type

26 Quinlan Architects, *Conservation plan*, p. 32. **27** T. O'Keeffe, 'The design of the early thirteenth-century cathedral church of Newtown Trim, Co. Meath', *Ríocht na Midhe*, 29 (2018), 14–26. **28** This chronology differs from that of other writers. Among modern writers, Stalley dated the nave to the period *c*.1260–*c*.1320 ('Athassel (Tipperary)', p. 319), and Moss has concurred ('Athassel, Augustinian Priory', p. 193). These dates are too late; the church could not have been left without a nave for decades. Based on his revised chronology for the nave of Holy Trinity Cathedral Church, O'Neill has dated the Athassel nave to 'perhaps the latter half of the 1230s or a little later' ('Christ Church Cathedral as a blueprint', p. 171).

attested to on the north side of the church. It might be noted that there was a quarter-century-long dispute between Athassel and the diocese of Limerick when Hubert de Burgh, its one-time prior who was elevated to the see of Limerick in 1223–4, appears to have transferred benefices to Athassel without permission from his chapter. Is this what funded the building of the new crossing piers and the nave?[29]

4. The date at which the screen wall was assembled is difficult to establish; wicker centring behind the blocked opening to the south of the blocked rood gallery would suggest a fifteenth-century date, but that seems too late otherwise. However slapdash some of the masonry might now appear (thanks to the loss of plaster) on its west side, the screen wall's face towards the choir was very ordered indeed. This was a fully-functioning piece of liturgical architecture rather than a wall cobbled together using disarticulated older forms for some sort of aesthetic effect. It is probable that a collapse of the original crossing tower (perhaps caused by fire, of which there is some evidence) provided the opportunity for this new composition; after all, there was no need for the crossing arch facing the nave to have been taken down in order to facilitate the insertion of a screen wall, and indeed the composition would have been enhanced visually had the arch been part of it. The crossing arches into the transepts also came down at this time. Although the original piers seem to have been retained, new transeptal arches with half-respond piers were built on inserted pedestals, thus widening slightly the crossing on its north–south axis and allowing the floor of the rood gallery to be supported on the low screen walls below these arches.

There is a possibility that the south aisle wall of the nave also needed replacement at this time and for the same reason, and that an original vaulted roof collapsed, to be replaced with a timber roof. It is entirely possible that images of Edmund and the Blessed Virgin Mary were moved from the east wall of the choir to the rood screen when this screen wall was built – the king-saint appears in the decorative scheme of East Anglian rood screens[30] – but it is more likely that the images were moved into the niches on either side of the rood opening. The gabled frame over the rood resembles closely the small gables over statue niches in the transepts of Cashel Cathedral, dated approximately by Stalley to the period between 1260 and 1290.[31] The Athassel gabled frame was made specifically for the display of the rood cross and its flanking figures (the Virgin and St John at very least), so a date in the second half of the thirteenth century is probable for the entire wall. Screens were funded by patrons anxious

29 J. McCaffrey (ed.), *The black book of Limerick* (Dublin, 1907), p. cxv. The first Anglo-Norman bishop of Ossory, Hugh de Rous, was accused of something similar in respect of Kells Priory, Co. Kilkenny (M. Clyne, *Kells Priory, Co. Kilkenny: archaeological excavations by T. Fanning & M. Clyne* (Dublin, 2007), p. 4).   **30** Pinner, *The cult of St Edmund*, pp 210–11.   **31** R. Stalley, 'The construction of Cashel Cathedral' in R. Stalley (ed.), *Irish Gothic architecture: construction, decay and reinvention* (Dublin, 2012), 55–98, at p. 83.

that they should be identified as such,[32] and an entire screen wall, as at Athassel, would have been especially expensive, even without the cost of painted timberwork. One of the two successive de Burgh earls of Ulster, William (d. 1271) or Richard (d. 1326), built the Athassel wall. Richard is the more likely.

5. The nave was certainly not in ruins when the screen wall was built but it was effectively gone by the time the vault was inserted into the crossing tower to support domestic accommodation. The cusped ogee twin-light high on the west (nave-facing) side of the crossing marks very clearly the level of this later phase (see Fig. 8.2c); one can see the same level in the breaking of the roof line of the south transept (see Fig. 8.7). All traces of the nave-roof abutment were lost when the tower was raised to its final height. Stalley dates that late domestic phase to the second half of the sixteenth century,[33] which I think is too late for its architectural features. It is possibly the work of the lay administrator appointed to the priory in 1486.

BALLYBOGGAN PRIORY, CO. MEATH

Ware identified 'the Blessed Trinity' as the dedication of this priory but stated that he could find no evidence of its antiquity except that its founder was reputedly one Jordan Comin.[34] This is probably the Jordan Comyn who, around 1206, witnessed an agreement between Elias Comyn (his brother?) and Holy Trinity Cathedral (where John Comyn, presumably his uncle, was archbishop) pertaining to lands in north Dublin.[35] Ballyboggan's Holy Trinity dedication would tend to support this identification of Jordan, as might the priory's possession of lands in the Cabra area of Dublin in the early fifteenth century.[36] Anthony Cogan documented the resolution in 1399 of a claim that the priory was actually dedicated to the Blessed Virgin Mary, a claim that had not been killed off entirely half a century later.[37] From at least the fifteenth century, though, the priory was known as Holy Trinity *de lauda Dei*, with the Latin phrase (the praise of God) used as an alias for the place-name.[38] The moniker recalls the names given in the twelfth century to Cistercian houses, such as Abbeyleix, Co. Laois (*de lege Dei*), Kilbeggan, Co. Westmeath (*de flumine Dei*) and Fermoy, Co. Cork (*de castro Dei*),[39] and it appears to have no parallel among Augustinian houses in Ireland. More interesting than its

---

32 R. Marx, 'Framing the rood in medieval England and Wales' in S. Buckelow, R. Marks and L. Wrapson (eds), *The art and science of the church screen in medieval Europe: making, meaning, preserving* (Woodbridge, 2017), pp 7–29, at pp 27–9. **33** 'Athassel (Tipperary)', p. 317. **34** Ware, *Antiquities and history of Ireland*, p. 86. Castlejordan, several kilometres to the south-west, was a possession of the priory at its dissolution (*EIMP*, pp 311–12). **35** E. St John Brooks, 'The early Irish Comyns', *JRSAI*, 86 (1956), 170–86, at 180–1. **36** RCH 179/22, s.a. 1405; RCH 191/110, s.a. 1408. **37** A. Cogan, *The diocese of Meath, ancient and modern*, vol. 1 (Dublin, 1862), p. 169; *CPL*, 10, p. 420, s.a. 1448. **38** *CPL*, 7, p. 484, s.a. 1426; *CPL*, 9, pp 222–3, s.a. 1441; *CPL*, 15, pp 201–2, s.a. 1487. It was called *Landadey* when its alleged dedication to St Mary was last noted (*CPL*, 10, p. 420, s.a. 1448). **39** J.T. Gilbert, *Chartularies of St Mary's Abbey* 2 (London, 1884),

alleged dedication to the Blessed Virgin Mary is the fact that Ballyboggan was not dedicated to the Holy Cross. The priory possessed a 'holy cross' until it, along with other venerated objects in Meath and beyond, was burned in 1538 during the systematic destruction of Christian relics and shrines.[40] Cogan noted that it was a 'great crucifix'.[41] It attracted pilgrims, which is how it came to the attention of the Reformation authorities, so it was presumably a reliquary for a fragment of the True Cross rather than a rood cross, as Cogan's description might suggest. Had there been such a relic in Ballyboggan at its foundation the priory might have been named after it; one supposes, then, that it was a later acquisition. Oddly, the priory appears not to have prospered greatly from possession of it: Ballyboggan was fairly ruined when suppressed in 1537, and the sale of its goods and chattels raised a meagre 26s.[42]

We have no dates for Jordan Comyn, so his identification allows no more than a very approximate foundation date to be stated for the priory, although various sources give the date as late twelfth century.[43] There is a case for dating the foundation to the first decade of the thirteenth century. I have speculated elsewhere that, *pace* Gwynn and Hadcock,[44] Anglo-Norman canons of the Augustinian abbey of Ss Peter and John at Clonard did not relocate to Newtown Trim after Clonard was attacked by the Irish in 1200 but, rather, that some of them moved to new priories at Ballyboggan and Tristernagh, both in the same English lordship.[45] Plans for a priory at Tristernagh were being made in the few years immediately before Clonard was attacked, but building work started very shortly after the attack, suggesting that its patron saw opportunity in an exodus of canons from the older site. There is no evidence that similar plans were being made for a priory at Ballyboggan in the late twelfth century, but the approximate date of its architecture would support the thesis that Clonard's misfortune provided the opening for a patron to set up a new house in the area. Ballyboggan had a direct link with Clonard late in the Middle Ages,[46] although that might be a factor of their proximity – they are less than ten kilometres apart – rather than a specific reflection of a more ancient affiliation.

Although its ruins are quite substantial, the priory church (Fig. 8.12) has generally escaped the attention of architectural historians.[47] It was an unaisled nave-

pp 217–18.   **40** *AU* 1538, p. 625. For the role of the Augustinian canons in promoting pilgrimage see the chapter by Louise Nugent below.   **41** *Diocese of Meath*, 1, pp 169–70.   **42** C. McNeill, 'Accounts of sums realized by sales of chattels of some suppressed Irish monasteries', *JRSAI*, 12 (1922), 11–37, at 15; B. Scott, 'The dissolution of the religious houses in the Tudor diocese of Meath', *AH*, 59 (2005), 260–76, at 261–2. See also his contribution to this present volume, pp 252–65. If Helen Roe's dating of it is correct, a tomb panel from Ballyboggan, originally part of a Throne of Grace composition and now in Ballynabracky R.C. church, was carved within a generation of the priory's dissolution (Helen M. Roe, 'Illustrations of the Holy Trinity in Ireland: 13th to 17th centuries', *JRSAI*, 109 (1979), 101–50, at 107, 129).   **43** The earliest such assertion seems to be L.-A. Alemand, *Monasticon Hibernicum: or, the monastical history of Ireland* (London, 1722), p. 36.   **44** *MRHI*, p. 163.   **45** T. O'Keeffe, *Tristernagh Priory, Co. Westmeath: colonial monasticism in medieval Ireland* (Dublin, 2018).   **46** *CPL*, 9, pp 222–3, s.a. 1441, and especially *CPL*, 15, pp 201–2, s.a. 1487.   **47** An exception is C. Casey and A. Rowan, *The*

8.12 Ballyboggan Priory church from the north-west.

and-chancel church with transepts. The nave and chancel survive, although there are gaps in the fabric and some later alterations. The nave was long at almost 35m internally, although it was not as long as Athassel, but the stub of a west-running wall continuous with its south wall suggests that it was longer originally, with the present west wall built to shorten it slightly at some stage of the thirteenth century (Fig. 8.13). One struggles to explain why a rural and rather isolated priory, distant from any borough, had so long a nave. It was also a dark space, its few windows tucked under the roof where they denied sight lines between the inside and the outside. This sparse fenestration gave the nave an acute, almost military, austerity which might have appealed to canons who were a little uncertain about their safety on the southern boundary of the lordship of Meath.[48]

The chancel had a brighter and more elegant simplicity than the nave. Unfortunately, later rebuilding on its east and south sides has done it an aesthetic disservice. The two long windows in the north wall close to the altar were presumably matched on the opposite wall, and the outer windows in the five- or seven-lancet east wall were of the same height (Fig. 8.14). Individually these

buildings of Ireland: north Leinster (London, 1993), pp 209–10. **48** T. O'Keeffe, *Medieval Irish buildings, 1100–1600* (Dublin, 2015), p. 159.

8.13 The west wall of Ballyboggan nave looking eastwards towards the presbytery.

windows allowed in little light, but cumulatively, and thanks to their concentration and gradation, they would have made the altar area very bright. The composition may have been simple, and the dressing of the stones comparably unfussy, but this was very effective architecture indeed, enhanced by the raising of the chancel's floor level well above that of the nave. The only puzzle is that one of the two wall-tombs in the north wall, later thirteenth century in date, was allowed to block part of one

8.14 The north-east corner of Ballyboggan presbytery showing the original side-wall lancets, part of the original east window, and the two inserted wall-tombs.

of the windows. One assumes that there was no space further to the west because of choir stalls. There was a window above the suggested position of the stalls: its wide opening remains on the inside of the chancel and part of its outer stonework is visible on the outside, above a string-course (Fig. 8.15). There was presumably a corresponding window on the opposite wall. Both Newtown Trim and Tristernagh churches had short windows in the same position relative to the crossing.

8.15 The external north wall of Ballyboggan's presbytery.

The transepts are gone, apart from the west wall of the south transept. This is sufficient to give us the north–south length of each transept, and to show us, first, that two windows illuminated the transept from the west, and second, that there was a doorway (as expected) into the transept from the north walkway of the cloister. Also, sufficient survives of the original fabric around the crossing for one to be fairly confident that the crossing arches sprang directly from the wall surfaces, possibly with soffit arches springing from projecting corbels, but that they did not have piers to support them. The walls themselves are too thin to have supported a tower of any height or mass, so the crossing was probably marked externally by a tower just about high enough to clear the roofs. The rubble from the collapsed tower is grassed over on the floor of the church.

A break in the masonry in the external north wall of the chancel (Fig. 8.15) is the most difficult feature to explain in Ballyboggan. The lower part of the break has the 'ghost' of a wall best interpreted as the east wall of a transeptal chapel, and some angled stones might mark its sloping roof, although there is no actual scar. The upper part of the break, above the 'ghost' wall, is more difficult to explain. Stone-by-stone measurement (and excavation) might resolve its history. It is probable that this break is evidence of redesign or rebuilding in the thirteenth century (the approximate date of the window above the string-course), and that it is contemporary with the inserted west wall of the nave. But it might also be a result of *how* the chancel was built: inadequate bonding between two separately-built vertical sections might manifest itself over time in a split. The 'doorway' into the space where the north chapel would have been is a much later feature; it seems that there was no access in the thirteenth century between the chancel and any chapel. In this regard, Ballyboggan differed from Athassel and from its neighbours in the lordship, Newtown Trim and Tristernagh.

Nonetheless, Ballyboggan's closest cousin from an architectural perspective is undoubtedly the church of Newtown Trim Priory, discussed below. It is a simpler, less sophisticated, version of Newtown Trim, but it should not be regarded as a cheaper copy of it. For all its simplicity, it was a 'knowing' work of architecture, a structure designed and built by masons who understood the aesthetic of Gothic sufficiently to strip away ornament without loss of effect. From the outside, its plain walls might have reminded the natives living around Ballyboggan of the unadorned walls of their own pre-invasion churches, and to that extent it lacked the exotic quality of the diocesan mother church, but on the inside the view up the nave towards the chancel was different from anything they would have known in the native tradition. Cistercian churches offered a not dissimilar experience, and they too were colonial.

Ballyboggan's canons may have colonized the site from Clonard, but the church's builders did not come from there. There could not have been any Gothic architecture in Clonard before the attack of 1200; it is too early in the history of the style in Ireland. In the absence of documentary evidence to the contrary, the most likely scenario is that Ballyboggan was built by masons employed at Newtown Trim. The earliest date at which masons could have been spared duties at the mother church and allowed work *full-time* on another project is 1216; a synod was held in Newtown Trim in that year, which suggests that the initial phase of construction work there must have been finished by then.[49] However, if canons from Clonard did indeed move to Ballyboggan, building work must have started earlier. The technical challenge posed by the design chosen for *de lauda Dei* was not such that work needed to be delayed until a large work gang arrived from Newtown Trim. There is no reason, in other words, to think that there was a long interval between the commencement of the two projects. The identification of Jordan Comyn as Ballyboggan's founder would also suggest that work was well underway on it, if not largely finished, by 1216. Is it far-fetched to suggest that practical, workshop, support for a new priory in the Clonard vicinity was a condition of Simon de Rochfort's permission to move the mother church for Meath from Clonard to Newtown Trim?

---

49 R. Carey Bates and T. O'Keeffe, 'Colonial monasticism, the politics of patronage, and the beginnings of Gothic in Ireland: the Victorine cathedral priory of Newtown Trim, Co. Meath', *Journal of Medieval Monastic Studies*, 6 (2017), 51–76.

DUBLIN, HOLY TRINITY CATHEDRAL PRIORY

The literature on the transeptal church of Holy Trinity Cathedral Priory is substantial,[50] but the chronology of its crypt relative to its superstructure remains a subject of dispute, as does the date of the Gothic nave. There is insufficient space here to review the various arguments, so I will summarize my own views on these matters, expressed most recently in a short paper in 2017.[51]

The crypt, which has the same transeptal plan as the present church above it, was laid out in the eleventh century and served an aisled, transeptal, church to which a cloister was attached from the outset. I think it can be assigned to the episcopate of Dúnán and dated to the second quarter of the century. Aspects of its design point to influence from Germany. Dúnán was probably trained as a Benedictine in Cologne. The transepts and the first two (western) bays of the presbytery in the present cathedral are Romanesque in style and can be attributed confidently to the first half of the archiepiscopate of John Comyn (1182–1212). The eleventh-century nave, associated with the crypt, was retained while Comyn replaced the east end of the church. There was a delay before the new nave was built, and when it did appear it was in the Gothic style. Its date of construction is disputed, but I favour a start-date early in the episcopate of Henry of London (1212–28). Whatever its duration, there is a plausible explanation for the interval between the completion of the east end of the cathedral and the start of work on a new nave: Gothic alterations were made to St Thomas's after it was elevated to the status of an abbey in 1192 (see below), and John Comyn, having more or less completed the east end of Holy Trinity in the mid-1190s, might have suspended the Romanesque rebuilding of its nave once he saw a radically different style of architecture start to appear in the royal church a short distance away. In summary, then, Dublin has had a monastic cathedral church of transeptal plan since the eleventh century.

DUBLIN, ST THOMAS'S PRIORY/ABBEY

The wealthiest of all Augustinian houses in Ireland, this royal foundation, dedicated to St Thomas the Martyr, began life in 1177 as a priory and was elevated to the status of an abbey of the Victorine observance in 1192.[52] Unfortunately, its church

---

50 See, for example, R. Stalley, 'The medieval sculpture of Christ Church Cathedral, Dublin', *Archaeologia*, 106 (1979), 107–22; idem, 'The construction of the medieval cathedral, *c.*1030–1250' in Milne, *CCCD*, pp 53–74; T. O'Keeffe, 'Architecture and regular life in Holy Trinity Cathedral, 1150–1350' in S. Kinsella (ed.), *Augustinians at Christ Church: the canons regular of the cathedral priory of Holy Trinity, Dublin* (Dublin, 2000), pp 23–40; S. Kinsella, 'Mapping Christ Church Cathedral, Dublin, *c.*1028–1608: an examination of the western cloister' in Bradley, Simms and Fletcher (eds), *Dublin in the medieval world*, pp 143–6; O'Neill, 'Christ Church Cathedral as a blueprint'. **51** T. O'Keeffe, 'A cryptic puzzle from medieval Dublin', *Archaeology Ireland*, 31:2 (2017), 39–43. **52** A. Gwynn, 'The early history of St Thomas's Abbey, Dublin',

was a casualty of both Henrician destruction and post-medieval urban growth. Archaeological excavations have revealed some *in situ* walling, apparently from the south side of the church, and assorted pieces of medieval (including thirteenth-century) carved stone from doorways and windows, as well as part of a possible shrine for a corporeal relic of St Thomas Becket.[53] There is insufficient evidence from the site itself to attempt a reconstruction of the church's plan that is not overly conjectural, but there is indirect evidence that one can draw on to visualize its basic character.[54]

The clues are at Newtown Trim, Co. Meath, discussed below. This cathedral priory was colonized by Victorine canons from St Thomas's Abbey after 1202. Although very ruined, it is the earliest work of cathedral architecture in the Gothic style in Ireland, and is probably also the earliest surviving substantial work of non-Cistercian Gothic in Ireland. Its ground plan, which includes a transeptal arm with two transeptal chapels *en échelon*, is not strikingly unusual and could conceivably reflect influence from any number of contexts, even Cistercian, but its unusual – and, in the Irish context, exceptionally early – Gothic elevations and vaulting must reflect the influence from a single source, most likely in a place with direct links with England. That would point to Dublin, and to the mother house, St Thomas's Abbey.

The original priory church of the royal monastery could not have been a Gothic building, as the new style only appeared in England itself in the 1170s. Nonetheless, it was almost certainly a transeptal church: it is barely conceivable that a royal foundation saddled with a considerable political burden – reparation for a scandalous murder – would be a plain rectangle with a simple chancel. Moreover, by the 1170s English Augustinian churches were invariably transeptal,[55] so there was a template of sorts to be followed. The likelihood is that the change in status of St Thomas's in 1192 was accompanied by new building work, and that Gothic was introduced into Dublin, if not Ireland, for the very first time in that context. Newtown Trim's architecture is the circumstantial evidence that St Thomas's had a Gothic phase in the 1190s. Excavation might one day reveal whether the transeptal 1177 church was simply modified (through the introduction of vaulting, for example), or was substantially rebuilt. But in the meantime, looking towards Dublin from Newtown Trim, we can be satisfied that St Thomas's was transeptal from 1192, and probably from 1177.

JRSAI, 84, 1 (1954), 1–35; Virginia Davis, 'Relations between the abbey of St Thomas the Martyr and the municipality of Dublin, *c.*1176–1527', *Dublin Historical Record*, 40:2 (1987), 57–65; Áine Foley, *The abbey of St Thomas the Martyr, Dublin* (Dublin, 2017). See also the contribution to this volume by M.T. Flanagan.   **53** C. Walsh, 'Archaeological excavations at the abbey of St Thomas the Martyr', *Medieval Dublin I* (Dublin, 2000), pp 185–201; P. Duffy and T. O'Keeffe, 'A stone shrine for a relic of Thomas Becket in Dublin?', *Archaeology Ireland*, 31:4 (2017), 18–23.   **54** R. Carey Bates and Tadhg O'Keeffe, 'Colonial monasticism, the politics of patronage, and the beginnings of Gothic in Ireland: the Victorine cathedral priory of Newtown Trim, Co. Meath', *Journal of Medieval Monastic Studies*, 6 (2017), 51–76; O'Keeffe, 'A cryptic puzzle from medieval Dublin', p. 43.   **55** J.A. Franklin, 'Augustinian and other canons' churches in Romanesque

8.16 St Catherine's Priory, Waterford, *c.*1590, redrawn from TCD MS 4877 (2).

The other major urban house of the Victorines, St Catherine's Priory in Waterford, founded in the first decade of the thirteenth century,[56] might also have been transeptal. It does not survive, but a map of the city's walls at the end of the sixteenth century shows an unaisled church with a tower, and a wide arched entrance into the north wall of the tower *might* be a transeptal arch rather than a doorway (Fig. 8.16).[57] Not all Victorine houses in Ireland were transeptal, however. Bridgetown Priory, Co. Cork, colonized from St Thomas's and Newtown Trim, has the most extensive remains of any house of that observance in Ireland. Its church is not transeptal but is, rather, a long nave-and-chancel building.[58]

Europe: the significance of the aisleless cruciform plan' in J.A. Franklin, T.A. Heslop and C. Stevenson (eds), *Architecture and interpretation: essays for Eric Fernie* (Woodbridge, 2012), pp 8–98. **56** *MRHI*, p. 197.   **57** TCD MS 4877 (2). My thanks to Eamonn McEneaney, Waterford Museum of Treasures, for drawing my attention to this.   **58** T. O'Keeffe, *An Anglo-Norman*

KELLS PRIORY, CO. KILKENNY

The history and archaeology of this priory have been published,[59] so a summary will suffice here. Geoffrey FitzRobert founded the priory in 1193 but encountered difficulty attracting canons to it. Eventually four canons arrived from Bodmin Priory. Adrian Empey has suggested that building work on the priory did not begin until after *c.*1202, but there was a church at the time of the foundation charter, dated 1204–6.[60] The original church was cruciform with a short chancel, a square crossing, narrow transepts and with single transeptal chapels of, unusually, the exact same width as the transepts, and an unaisled nave a little more than twice as long as the chancel. The crossing arches, among the earliest examples of non-Cistercian Gothic stonework in Ireland, were fairly low. The church was enlarged later in the thirteenth century, its east limb lengthened considerably and a north aisle added.

NEWTOWN TRIM CATHEDRAL PRIORY, CO. MEATH

An attack on Clonard by the native Irish in 1200 was the pretext for the move of the diocesan centre for Meath from the site of St Finian's old monastery to a new, apparently green-field, location outside the town of Trim. Simon de Rochfort, bishop of the diocese since 1192, agitated for the move and used his network of contacts – the de Lacy family circle; the canons of St Thomas's in Dublin – to ensure that the new cathedral church would be a showpiece building served by a monastic chapter. He styled himself bishop of Meath, rather than of Clonard, after the move. Colonization of the new monastic cathedral from St Thomas's Abbey implies that it had a Victorine chapter. It was not unique in Europe in that regard, but Victorines, being scholastic, contemplative and silent, were not well suited to the task of running diocesan mother churches and therefore were rarely charged with the task. Moreover, the Victorines of Newtown Trim had no local connections but were entirely outsiders, a kind of spiritual elite parachuted from Dublin into the rural diocese, and it is hard to believe that they had much interest in its parish clergy or had any desire to recruit and train Meathmen for their community. For these reasons, the choice of Victorines might have contributed to the early failure of Newtown Trim to achieve uncontested recognition as the cathedral for Meath, a failure indicated at first by the silence of the sources and then, in 1255, by the licence given by Alexander IV to Hugh of Taghmon, bishop-elect of Meath, for the building of a new cathedral because the diocese did not have a 'fixed' cathedral.

---

monastery: Bridgetown Priory and the architecture of the Augustinian canons regular in Ireland (Kinsale, 1999). **59** Clyne, *Kells Priory*. **60** A. Empey, 'The Augustinian priory of Kells: an historical introduction' in Clyne, *Kells Priory*, 1–11, at p. 4. See also his contribution to this volume.

8.17 The east end and crossing of Newtown Trim cathedral church viewed from the site of the south transept; the side walls of the presbytery are on the right-hand side.

The project of making Newtown Trim the diocesan centre for Meath was headed for success while Simon was alive and while the de Lacy family was fully engaged in the affairs of Trim and its district. Work on the priory had progressed enough for a synod to be hosted in 1216. However, by the time Simon died in 1224, the de Lacys were distracted by the internecine turmoil that wrecked their final years as key players in the Anglo-Norman polity. His death spelled disaster for Newtown Trim. Its canons never appear in the records during episcopal appointments elsewhere in Ireland, and, other than Simon, only one medieval bishop – William Sherwood (d. 1482) – was buried in the church.[61]

The architecture of the church has been discussed elsewhere recently,[62] so I will offer only some summary comments, with additional glosses, here. The cathedral

61 R. Carey Bates and T. O'Keeffe, 'Colonial monasticism, the politics of patronage, and the beginnings of Gothic in Ireland: the Victorine cathedral priory of Newtown Trim, Co. Meath', *Journal of Medieval Monastic Studies* 6 (2017), 51–76; T. O'Keeffe, 'Trim before 1224: new thoughts on the caput of the de Lacy lordship in Ireland' in P. Duffy, T. O'Keeffe and J.-M. Picard (eds), *From Carrickfergus to Carcassonne: the epic deeds of Hugh de Lacy during the Albigensian Crusade* (Turnhout, 2017), pp 31–56.   62 Carey Bates and O'Keeffe, 'The Victorine cathedral priory of Newtown Trim'; O'Keeffe, 'The design of the early thirteenth-century cathedral church'.

church was a long, unaisled, cruciform building. Parts of the north and south walls of the presbytery survive but the crossing and transeptal arm has been reduced to foundation level (Fig. 8.17). Each transept originally had a single chapel projecting eastwards, giving the church a stepped elevation as it was viewed from the east. The very fragmentary remains of the chapel on the north side reveal a plan that is unparalleled to my knowledge in a transeptal chapel. The chapel was divided longitudinally in two by an arch springing from responds, meaning that it was rather like a small nave-and-chancel structure in its own right. The interior is most easily visualized as vaulted in the manner of a Cistercian transeptal chapel, but with a transverse arch halfway along its length.

The presbytery was lit by three tall lancets on each side, separated externally by pilasters. There was vaulting over the entire east limb of the church as far as the crossing; one can see the outlines of the arches. The nature and chronology of this vaulting is problematic. The grooves which show us the curvature of the vaults have the appearance of inserts. Also, these grooves are more consistent with wooden vaults than stone vaults. However, there are four factors to be addressed as to why one should hesitate before drawing that conclusion. First, would the choir have external pilasters between the windows if no vaulting was intended? Second, an inserted vault implies that the original early thirteenth-century choir was simply timber-roofed, and yet the original and near-contemporary nave was vaulted. Third, the history of the cathedral makes it difficult to think of a period when a vault *could* have been inserted. If no vault was intended in 1205, would the builders have had a change of mind as early as the eve of the 1216 synod? Finally, the architecture of Newtown Trim is likely to reflect the post-1192 design of the Abbey of St Thomas the Martyr, and it is most likely that it was vaulted.

The crossing had a square tower, into which the roofs of the choir, nave and transepts all ran at the same height. Inside the tower, plain arches of equal height would have looked into all the arms of the church. Doorways led off the transeptal chapels into the choir, a feature also encountered at Athassel and Tristernagh.

The nave was unaisled, but it was rib-vaulted, which was quite unusual for an unaisled church, and it was also penetrated by wall passages, which was even more unusual in an unaisled church (Fig. 8.18). Close study of the masonry high on the nave wall raises the possibility that the nave of Newtown Trim was originally roofed in timber, a suggestion that would lead one to speculate that the choir was indeed also originally roofed in timber. However, the arrangement of nave windows, with one per bay at each level, suggests that there were vertical dividers for vaulting from the outset. And, given the short history of the church, when could such an alteration have been made?

As was noted above, Newtown Trim's architecture is likely to reflect that of the royal church of St Thomas the Martyr. The 1177 church would have provided a clear model for its transeptal plan, just as earlier English Augustinian churches would have provided the model for St Thomas's. Newtown Trim's unusual transeptal chapels are likely to imitate chapels in the 1177 building, and the same may be true also of the two levels of wall passages. The specifically Gothic feature

8.18 The east end of the south wall of the nave at Newtown Trim.

of Newtown Trim is its rib-vaulting and this must reflect a redesigning of the St Thomas's Church after 1192. The execution of Gothic features in the Meath cathedral church appears idiosyncratic, as if the masons were experimenting with the structural and spatial possibilities of the newly introduced Gothic style. Future discoveries at the St Thomas site might help us to understand Newtown Trim's oddities.

TRISTERNAGH PRIORY, CO. WESTMEATH

The Priory of the Blessed Virgin Mary in Tristernagh has recently been the subject of research, so my comments here are brief.[63] Work on its transeptal church began shortly after 1202 under the patronage of Geoffrey de Costentin. He was making plans for the foundation from the very end of the twelfth century, so it is possible that he accelerated the process of foundation once Simon de Rochfort moved the diocesan centre from Clonard to Newtown Trim, giving canons of the older monastery a chance to relocate. Gabriel Beranger and Maria Angelo Bigari visited Tristernagh and made a record of its architecture in 1779, four years before the church was almost completely demolished by the landlord whose family inherited the property in the mid-sixteenth century. Bigari's two drawings of the church are an especially valuable record. The church had a six-bay nave, aisled on its north side, transepts with pairs of conjoined east-facing chapels arranged *en échelon* north and south of a square crossing, and a rectangular choir. The Tristernagh aisle was original (unlike at Kells). The crossing was surmounted at the outset by an octagonal lantern tower carried on pointed arches supported by corbels. The historical evidence suggests that the church was built at the start of the thirteenth century, and English parallels for its single-aisled nave would support that.[64] Tristernagh was a more sophisticated work of architecture than its near-contemporary, Ballyboggan, and while it has similarities with Newtown Trim, such as doorways into the transeptal chapels from the choir, it is the work of a different master mason.

CONCLUSION AND REFLECTION

The sequence of foundation and construction of the transeptal Augustinian churches can be worked out with reasonable precision. The transeptal plan of Holy Trinity Augustinian Cathedral Priory reflects an inheritance from its Benedictine past. St Thomas's Church in Dublin was certainly the first in the sequence of transeptal churches founded as Augustinian *ab initio*. It was probably transeptal when founded as a priory church in 1177 and, if not, would certainly have been made so once elevated to the status of an abbey church in 1192. Masons from there must have been responsible for Newtown Trim's church. Ballyboggan's church is at least one step removed again, but is in the lineage. The third Meath church of the start of the thirteenth century, Tristernagh, lacked Newtown Trim's idiosyncratic sophistication and was more elaborate than Ballyboggan. It was probably not the work of the builders of the other two churches, even if the circumstances that led to its colonization – the attack on Clonard in 1200 – were,

63 O'Keeffe, *Tristernagh Priory*.   64 Franklin, 'Augustinian and other canons' churches'; H. Summerson and S. Harrison, *Lanercost Priory, Cumbria: a survey and documentary history* (Kendal, 2000).

as I suggest, the same. Its architecture, particularly the use of a north aisle, was more conventionally English than that of its two contemporaries. We might understand it better had more survived of its neighbouring Cistercian houses at Abbeylara and Abbeyshrule, both founded around the same time. St Thomas's influence possibly reached Athassel too in the early thirteenth century but other influences and impulses, including Cistercian, shaped Athassel's architecture. Kells was founded around the same time, *c.*1200, and in its earliest phase it resembled Ballyboggan but on a smaller scale. The native Ballintubber Abbey, founded in 1216,[65] is relatively late in the sequence.

This survey suggests that for a brief period of time, starting no earlier than the mid-1170s and ending no later than the mid-1210s, the island's English communities of Augustinian regular canons had an architectural identity only slightly less coherent than that of the Cistercians. The churches described above constitute a first generation of colonial Augustinian foundations in Ireland – priories like Bridgetown and Ballybeg, Co. Cork, belong to a later generation – so it can be no surprise to find that they followed the English plan-template for churches of regular canons. These early Augustinian communities also played a role, independent of contemporary English Cistercians in Ireland, in introducing Gothic forms into the repertoire of Irish architecture and its ornamental sculpture.

The identification of the transeptal church as the manifestation of a 'big bang' of Augustinian monastic culture after the invasion must have implications for how we understand the observance of the Rule and the nature of the Augustinian regular community before the invasion. It is commonplace to regard Augustinian abbey and priory architecture in twelfth- and thirteenth-century Ireland as heterogeneous,[66] but the archaeologist who makes that judgement does so by leaning on Gwynn and Hadcock's list of Augustinian foundations and their chronology.[67] He or she has no means of evaluating whether they correctly enumerated pre-invasion examples of reformed monasteries which adopted the Rule. There were certainly native-born canons of the Arrouaisian observance before the invasion (and some of the earliest communities of that observance in the English lordship in Ireland must have included such natives[68]), but how many communities of Augustinian regular canons were there otherwise, and why did they not embrace the claustral architecture that suited regular life in England and beyond? Viewed through the lens of the early Anglo-Norman foundations, the archaeologist is led to wonder, and to ask of the historian, whether monasteries like Ballysadare, Co. Sligo, and Monaincha, Co. Tipperary, to name but two identified as Augustinian by Gwynn and Hadcock,[69] had regular communities that differed only from those of the invaders in their ethnic constitution.

---

65 *MRHI*, pp 158–9. **66** For example, T. O'Keeffe, 'Augustinian canons regular in twelfth- and thirteenth-century Ireland: history, architecture and identity' in Burton and Stöber, *canons*, pp 463–78. **67** *MRHI*, pp 146–200. **68** O'Keeffe, *Tristernagh Priory*, p. xx. **69** *MRHI*, pp 160–1, 187–8.

The material culture of the canonical movement in medieval Ireland

RACHEL MOSS

Growth in the popularity of the Augustinian canons across Ireland during the twelfth and thirteenth centuries can be credited, in part at least, to their flexibility. By the end of the twelfth century their influence could be seen in the administration of cathedrals, the promotion of familial interests and management of pilgrimage. Over the course of the later medieval period, their roles shifted and adapted, not least in the face of competition from the popular mendicant orders. Just as the wide variety of architectural forms found in the standing remains of the canons' houses in Ireland reflect this broad remit, so too their original moveable possessions and artistic adornment of buildings would most likely have differed from house to house.[1] It is at best challenging to make general statements about 'canonical' art in later medieval Ireland. However, there are certain characteristics, maintained throughout the Middle Ages, that appear to be particularly associated with the order.

Prominent among these is an apparent keenness to use visual means to convey a sense of antiquity, continuity and by association, authority – a characteristic also identified in the material culture of the canons in England and Wales.[2] However, while in England and Wales this inclination is focused in particular on the maintenance of the memory of secular founders and patrons, in Ireland it appears to have had a broader range of manifestations.

MATERIAL CULTURE AND THE PROMOTION OF PILGRIMAGE

In the early years of the order's establishment it was common practice to locate canons' houses close to earlier ecclesiastical sites. In these circumstances, it was perhaps inevitable that certain traditional modes of worship were adopted, and indeed propagated by the canons, thus facilitating a more gradual transformation of liturgical and administrative practice. One key aspect of this was an interest in and promotion of Irish saints' cults. Pádraig Ó Riain has demonstrated that this was manifest in the twelfth century in the compilation of martyrologies and *Lives* of saints, and the active promotion of pilgrimage to sites administered by the

---

1 For an overview of the architecture of the canons in Ireland see T. O'Keeffe, 'Augustinian regular canons in twelfth- and thirteenth-century Ireland: history, architecture and identity' in Burton and Stöber, *Canons*, pp 460–74.   2 J. Luxford, 'The idol of origins: retrospection in Augustinian art during the later Middle Ages' in Burton and Stöber, *Canons*, pp 417–42.

canons, such as St Patrick's Purgatory and Monaincha, can also be traced to this period.[3]

Central to the cult of any saint was his or her relics and the reliquaries that contained them. By the twelfth century, devotional images, whether in paint, timber or stone, were also becoming a common feature across Western Europe, a means of creating a more direct, tangible saintly presence.[4] Material evidence for a flourishing in the manufacture or refurbishment of such objects to parallel the production of related literary material is, unsurprisingly, scant. However, examination of individual sites, and fragmentary survivals, whether in physical form, or in the historic record, can serve as a useful starting point to assess the influence of the canons' on the production of this type of art.

The Augustinian priory of St Saviour's at Glendalough was established by Laurence O'Toole, abbot of Glendalough between 1153 and 1162.[5] Glendalough was a site of some significance, and already a place of pilgrimage, if not perhaps in the form that we interpret the term today.[6] It had been elevated to the status of episcopal see in the 1111 synod of Rathbresail, with the city of Dublin encompassed in the diocese. However, in 1152, shortly before the arrival of Lawrence, its fortunes were reversed, with Dublin securing archiepiscopal status at the synod of Kells, and thus reducing Glendalough to a suffragan bishopric.

It was in this climate of uncertainty that the canons were introduced to Glendalough. While the church there could not hope to compete with the large and eclectic collection of relics held by the rival Dublin diocese at Christ Church Cathedral, and the growing fame of its miraculous crucifix, this did not discourage the canons from garnering the support of saints to secure the status of the site.[7]

The commissioning of two texts has been attributed to the Glendalough canons within the first few decades of their establishment. The so-called Drummond missal and martyrology (New York, Pierpont Morgan Library MS M 627) was most likely commissioned from the canons at Armagh, while Ó Riain has argued that evidence in the 'original' Latin *Life* of St Kevin strongly suggests its composition following the arrival of the Anglo-Normans, most likely at the hand of the canons at Glendalough.[8] As with most hagiographies, reference to specific

---

3 P. Ó Riain, *Four Irish martyrologies: Drummond, Turin, Cashel, York*. Henry Bradshaw Society, 115 (London, 2002); J.-M. Picard and Y. de Pontfarcy, *Saint Patrick's Purgatory: a twelfth-century tale of a journey to the other world* (Dublin, 1985); Gerald of Wales, *The history and topography of Ireland*, ed. and trans. by J. O'Meara (London, 1982), p. 60.   **4** R. Marks, *Image and devotion in late medieval England* (Stroud, 2004); R. Moss, 'Devotional images' in R. Moss (ed.), *Art and architecture of Ireland, volume 1, medieval c.400–c.1600* (London, 2014), pp 280–2.   **5** C. Plummer, 'Vie et miracles de St Laurent', *Analecta Bollandiana*, 33 (1914), 121–86 at 135.   **6** The deaths of individuals at Glendalough while on 'pilgrimage' are recorded in *AFM*, s.a. 951, 1030 and 1122.   **7** R. Ó Floinn, 'The late-medieval relics of Holy Trinity Church, Dublin' in A. Simms, A.J. Fletcher and J. Bradley (eds), *Dublin and the medieval world: studies in honour of Howard B. Clarke* (Dublin, 2009), pp 369–89; M.T. Flanagan, 'Devotional images and their uses in the twelfth-century Irish church: the crucifix of Holy Trinity Dublin and archbishop John Cumin' in H.B. Clarke and J.R.S. Philips (eds), *Ireland, England and the Continent in the Middle Ages and beyond: essays in memory of a turbulent friar, F.X. Martin OSA* (Dublin, 2006), pp 67–87.   **8** P. Ó Riain, 'The Lives of Kevin

9.1 Cró Coemgán or St Kevin's House, Glendalough, Co. Wicklow. Photo: Rachel Moss.

relics or reliquaries presumably in existence at the time of composition was an important means of verifying links between the saint and the place with which he was most closely associated.

Collectively, between the 'original' Latin version, and slightly later vernacular *Lives*, Glendalough was framed as a popular burial place for local nobility who wished to be buried close to the relics of the apostles in Cró Coemgán.[9] One such relic was his bell, known as the *bo-bán*, mentioned in the Annals of the Four

(Caoimhghin) of Glendalough' in C. Doherty, L. Doran and M. Kelly (eds), *Glendalough: city of God* (Dublin, 2011), pp 137–44 at p. 143. It should be noted that this is at odds with the opinion of A. MacShamhráin, who placed the composition of the Latin *Life* in the eighth or ninth century. A. MacShamhráin, *Church and polity in pre-Norman Ireland: the case of Glendalough* (Maynooth, 1996), pp 9–10. **9** The vernacular *Lives* have been dated to the late twelfth, or more probably thirteenth century. MacShamhráin, *Church and polity*, p. 128; Christina Harrington, *Women in a Celtic church: Ireland* (Oxford, 2002), p. 198; Ó Riain, 'The Lives of Kevin', p. 144.

9.2 St Mochta's House, Louth, Co. Louth. Photo: Rachel Moss.

Masters in 1144 as being used for swearing oaths.[10] In the cemetery, soil brought by Kevin himself from Rome meant that 'for obtaining the remission of sins from God it is the same for anyone to visit Rome and to visit the relics and bed of Coemgán'.[11]

The bed of Coemgán was located in a relatively inaccessible cliff overlooking the upper lake at Glendalough. An adjacent church, Temple-na-Skellig, is twelfth century in date, and was certainly in existence by 1198 when it was mentioned in a charter.[12] This, together with Kevin's relics, was a 'must visit' for pilgrims, and certainly by the early 1260s it was under the control of the canons, when a 'prior Donochu' was described as 'prior *de rupe* [cliff] juxta Glendalache'.[13]

Tomás Ó Carragáin has convincingly identified the building referred to as Cró Coemgán with the church now commonly known as St Kevin's House or Kitchen (Fig. 9.1).[14] Although earlier in date than the arrival of the canons, it seems likely that they would have taken on the management and maintenance of the building as the administrative structures of the site changed.[15] The steep-pitched stone roof of St Kevin's is a feature found at a number of churches that apparently fulfilled a similar reliquary function.[16] Given the continued occupation of Glendalough as a

10 *AFM*, s.a. 1144.   11 *BNÉ*, ii, p. 121.   12 *Calendar of Archbishop Alen's register*, ed. C. McNeill (Dublin, 1950), pp 83–4.   13 *Calendar of Archbishop Alen's register*, p. 101.   14 T. Ó Carragáin, *Churches in early medieval Ireland* (London, 2010), pp 268–78; ibid., 'Recluses, relics and corpses: interpreting St Kevin's House' in Doherty, Doran and Kelly, *Glendalough*, pp 64–79.   15 *Calendar of Archbishop Alen's register*, p. 8.   16 Ó Carragáin, *Churches*, pp 255–91.

9.3 Teach Molaisse or St Molaisse's House, Inishmurray, Co. Sligo. Photo: Rachel Moss.

place of pilgrimage up until the nineteenth century, it is noteworthy how apparently unaltered this building has remained.

The canons' desire for an appropriately 'ancient' setting for the display of relics is further suggested by St Mochta's House at Louth (Fig. 9.2), built adjacent to the canons' priory there in the thirteenth century, in a similar, and by that time very antiquated, form.[17] At Inishmurray, in Co. Sligo, a much smaller stone-roofed structure, Teach Molaisse, yielded a radiocarbon date for the mortar in the earliest part of the structure of the eighth century (Fig. 9.3). However, it shows evidence of significant 'restoration' at the end of the medieval period, most likely by the canons at Aughris, who were managing pilgrimage to the island at that time, again demonstrating a desire to maintain a strong visual link with what was most likely believed to be the actual church built by the saint.[18]

---

17 Ó Carragáin, *Churches*, pp 280–2.   **18** R. Berger, 'Radiocarbon dating of early medieval Irish monuments', *PRIA*, 95C (1995), 159–74 at 172; J. O'Sullivan and T. Ó Carragáin, *Inishmurray: monks and pilgrims in an Atlantic landscape* (Cork, 2008), pp 70–76.

9.4 Wooden devotional statue of St Molaisse.
© National Museum of Ireland.

Up until 1949, a thirteenth-/fourteenth-century wooden devotional statue of the saint was preserved in Teach Molaisse (Fig. 9.4). Cormac Bourke has proposed that this was likely used to display the saint's relics – a bell and crozier now in the collections of the duke of Northumberland at Alnwick castle.[19] While neither devotional timber statues nor reliquaries survive from Glendalough,[20] it is perhaps noteworthy that the earliest historical reference to a devotional statue of an Irish saint is Gerald of Wales' account of St Kevin, in which he mentions that 'all representations of St Kevin throughout Ireland have a blackbird in the outstretched hand'.[21] Also of note in this context is the so-called 'market' cross from the site, the twelfth-century carved stone cross that Ó Floinn has argued may have been modelled on the miraculous 'speaking crucifix' at Christ Church in Dublin.[22]

While not exclusive to the canons, the 'miraculous' qualities of such objects do seem to have been particularly promoted by the order, and doubtless aided the preservation of earlier art throughout the medieval period. Nearly all of the most celebrated examples of miraculous images in late medieval Ireland are associated with the order. Typically these were associated with Augustinian houses that had been founded on 'green field' sites, i.e., not directly associated with earlier ecclesiastical settlements, so their miraculous quality was most likely a means of creating new foci for pilgrimage. Particularly successful in this context was the abbey of St Mary at Trim, whose miraculous image of Mary was attracting pilgrims, and endowments, to the priory from the late fourteenth century.[23] Other examples included images of Mary at Navan and Kilmore (Roscommon), of St Radegund at Rathkeale and the Holy Cross at Ballyboggan.[24]

19 C. Bourke, 'What the pilgrim saw' in B.S. Turner (ed.), *Down Survey 2000: Yearbook of Down County Museum* (Down, 2000), pp 7–11 at 8; ibid., 'A crozier and bell from Inishmurray island and their place in ninth-century Irish archaeology', *PRIA*, 85C (1985), 145–68.   20 A gilded wooden statue of an unidentified saint from Glendalough that came into the collections of the National Museum of Ireland in 1930 is probably post-medieval. J.K. Cochran, 'Medieval Irish wooden figure sculpture', 2 vols (MLitt, TCD, 2004), i, 166–73, ii, fig. 81.   21 Gerald of Wales, *History and topography*, pp 78–9.   22 R. Ó Floinn, 'The "Market Cross" at Glendalough' in Doherty, Doran and Kelly, *Glendalough*, pp 80–111.   23 M. Potterton, *Medieval Trim: history and archaeology* (Dublin, 2005), pp 306–10.   24 E. Waterton, *Pietas Mariana Britannica: a history of English devotion to the Most Blessed Virgin Mary, Mother of God* (London, 1879), pp 309–10; *AU*, iii, p. 9; *CPL*, 8, p. 603; A. Cogan, *The ecclesiastical history of the diocese of Meath: ancient and modern,*

MATERIAL CULTURE AND THE PROMOTION OF STATUS

The introduction of the mendicant orders to Ireland throughout the thirteenth century led to a decline in the patronage of the Augustinian canons across the country generally. In the largely rural diocese of Clogher, however, mendicant influence was slower to take hold, and houses of the Augustinian canons remained dominant up to the end of the fourteenth century. Canons' houses were located at Lisgoole (Co. Fermanagh), Clones (Co. Monaghan) and Devenish (Co. Fermanagh). At Clogher (Co. Tyrone), the diocesan cathedral was administered by canons, up until the 1260s, and the bishop's palace was located in an enclosure immediately to the south of the priory.[25] Close episcopal links with the canons beyond the cathedral 'city' are indicated by the fact that both Bishops Matthew (1287–1310) and Nicholas (1320–56) Mac Cathsaigh were consecrated not in the cathedral, but at Lisgoole Priory.[26]

This is not an area associated with fine survivals of medieval architecture, and even at the time the poverty of the diocese was acknowledged. The early fourteenth century in particular was a turbulent period in the diocese, with schemes afoot to unite it with the diocese of Armagh. As Brendan Smith has pointed out, one way to avoid this was to exalt the prestige of the bishop, another was to bolster the historical prestige of the area as a whole through the promotion of its saints and its history.[27] As such, the first half of the fourteenth century saw a notable flourishing of creativity, in particular linked to saintly and historical traditions in the area, at least some of which can be directly linked to the canons.[28]

Matthew Mac Cathasaig, a former chancellor of Armagh, was chosen as bishop of Clogher while on a visit to Rome in 1287.[29] He marked his elevation to the see by commissioning new altar plate and vestments, including an altar cross that contained a relic of the patronal saint, Mac Caírthinn's head, and some years later consecrated a new chapel dedicated to him.[30] Around the same time, the relics of another diocesan saint, Constans, were translated from Eoinish, and divided between Mac Cathasaig's home church of Tynan and the Shrine of St MacCairtenn.[31]

In addition to these works, Pádraig Ó Riain has proposed that the collection of saints *Lives* known as the *Codex Salmanticensis* may also have been compiled at Mac Cathasaig's behest.[32] Colophons naming Brother Seán Mac Tighearnáin and Brother

3 vols (Dublin, 1862), i, pp 169–71.   **25** K. Nicholls, 'The register of Clogher', *Clogher Record*, 7:3 (1971–2), 361–431 at 375.   **26** Nicholls, 'Register of Clogher', 389–94.   **27** B. Smith, 'The late medieval diocese of Clogher, *c.*1200–1480' in H.A. Jeffries (ed.), *History of the diocese of Clogher* (Dublin, 2005), pp 70–81 at pp 75–6.   **28** P. Ó Riain, 'Saints in the catalogue of bishops of the lost "Register of Clogher"', *Clogher Record*, 14:2 (1992), 64–7.   **29** Nicholls, 'Register of Clogher', 391, 393.   **30** Nicholls, 'Register of Clogher', 375–8.   **31** Nicholls, 'Register of Clogher', 399.   **32** P. Ó Riain, 'Codex Salmanticensis: a provenance inter Anglos or inter Hibernos' in T. Barnard, D. Ó Cróinín and K. Simms (eds). *'A miracle of learning': studies in manuscripts and Irish learning. Essays in honour of William O'Sullivan* (Aldershot, 1998), pp 91–100; idem, 'The O'Donohue Lives of the Salamancan Codex: the earliest collection of Irish saints' Lives?' in S. Sheehan, J. Findon and W. Follett (eds), *Gablánach in scélaigecht: Celtic studies in honour*

Diarmaid Ó Dúnchadha suggest that it was most likely compiled by canons at the adjacent priory of Clogher.[33] Although executed in 'gothic' or 'English' hand, leading Heist to suggest an origin in a monastery of English or Anglo-Norman monks,[34] the inclusion of the Clogher saints Mac Caírthinn and Tigernach stressed the ancient stature and independence of that diocese, while the text regarding Náile, patron saint of Kinawlely (Co. Fermanagh), emphasized the rise of the local Maguire family.[35] Saints' *Lives* proved a useful means to bolster the status not only of the diocese, but of its local political allies (in this case the Maguires) too. By the end of the fourteenth century many, mostly Gaelic, families had begun to appreciate the power of 'historical' works or *seanchas* in copper-fastening their often shaky claim on territorial rights and privileges.[36]

In pre-Norman Ireland the chronicling of historical events had been undertaken in the old monastic centres, but with the re-organization of the church, this structure of learning changed and passed into the hands of a number of learned families, many of whom remained closely associated with the ancient churches, and, therefore, also with the canons who had taken over their administration. Ádamh Ó Cianáin was described at the time of his death in 1373 as a 'learned historian' and a canon of the Augustinan house at Lisgoole.[37] Taught by poet and scribe Seán Ó Dubhagáin (himself a canon at Holy Island, Lough Ree, by the time of his death), he was a member of the Ó Cianáin scribal family, based in the Cavan–Fermanagh area. Potentially one of the earliest works attributable to Ádamh is a historical miscellany or *seanchas*, NLI MS G 2–3, dated by Kenneth Nicholls to *c.*1328–50 (Plates 9 and 10).[38] This incorporates illuminated components and includes two colophons attributing the work to Ádamh, noting that it was compiled for his own use.[39] The work of Ádamh is of particular significance as it marks what appears to be the first generation of the so-called Gaelic revival, with historical miscellanies and genealogies compiled in a historicist style clearly derived from, and physically emulating, works of the eleventh and twelfth centuries, giving it an additional sense of age and authenticity.[40]

While of great interest to scholars of Irish history, for many years the artistic importance of Ó Cianáin's work was largely passed over. This is perhaps not surprising when it is compared with another almost exactly contemporary Augustinian commission, the lavish psalter made for Stephen de Derby, prior

of Ann Dooley (Dublin, 2013), pp 38–52.   **33** Brussels, Bibliothèque Royale, MSS 7672–4, ff 58r, 96r, 219.   **34** *Vitae sanctorum Hiberniae e codice olim Salmanticensi nunc Bruxellensi*, ed. W.W. Heist, Société des Bollandistes (Brussels, 1965), p. xix.   **35** Ó Riain, 'Codex Salmanticensis', pp 92–94. **36** E. Bhreathnach, 'The Seanchas tradition in late medieval Ireland' in E. Bhreathnach and B. Cunningham (eds), *Writing Irish history: the Four Masters and their world* (Dublin, 2007), pp 18–23. **37** *AFM*, s.a. 1373.   **38** K. Nicholls, 'Genealogy' in N. Buttimer, C. Rynne and H. Guerin (eds), *The heritage of Ireland: natural, man-made and cultural heritage: conservation and interpretation, business and administration* (Cork, 2000), pp 156–61 at 158.   **39** N. Ó Muraile, 'The learned family of Ó Cianáin/Keenan', *Clogher Record*, 18:3 (2005), 397–402. Another surviving work, the first ten pages of Bodl. MS Rawl. B. 506, was compiled for Ádamh by his brother Seán, on condition that he did not share them with anyone else without first getting permission.   **40** J. Carney, 'The Ó Cianáin Miscellany', *Ériu*, 21 (1969), 122–47 at 123.

(1349–82) of Holy Trinity, Dublin (Plates 11 and 12).[41] Made probably in either East Anglia or Oxford, the manuscript includes eight lavishly illuminated historiated initials, each dominated by elegantly delineated figures of holy figures and Augustinian canons, including the donor himself. In comparison, Ádamh Ó Cianáin's manuscript appears naïve and unaccomplished in the extreme, suggestive of a total ignorance of artistic progress abroad. But this is to miss the point. Ó Cianáin was almost certainly familiar with contemporary artistic trends.[42] His was a strategy of total revival, both in content and physical form, which was to be adopted in later centuries by the cultural movement now commonly referred to as the Renaissance.

MATERIAL CULTURE AND THE PROMOTION OF THE ORDER

Though vastly different in their style, Ó Cianáin's contribution to NLI MS G 2–3 and de Derby's psalter share a common feature – a record of the agency under which the work was produced. While members of other religious orders were also responsible for the management and the making of commissions, it is noteworthy that, in an Irish context, it is only the canons who appear to have concerned themselves with imbedding a record of their patronage within the artworks, so preserving a record of their benevolence for future generations.

At the same time that Ádamh was compiling his *seanchas*, and de Derby commissioning his psalter, one of the most precious reliquaries of the diocese of Clogher, the shrine of St Mac Caírthinn, underwent a facelift. Identified since the nineteenth century as the Domhnach Airgid, this reliquary shrine still exists, and is now in the collections of the National Museum of Ireland. It is thought to be the same shrine mentioned in passages in the tenth-century Tripartite Life of St Patrick and the Latin Life of St Mac Caírthinn that recount Patrick's gift to the saint of a 'Domnach Airgid' that contained relics of the holy apostles, Mary's hair, the True Cross, Holy Sepulchre and others. It was presumably also to this shrine that bishop Cathasaig added the relics of Constans referred to above (Plate 13).[43]

The tinned copper alloy plates decorated with incised interlace designs on two of the sides and the top of the shrine represent possibly the earliest decoration, usually dated to the ninth or tenth centuries. A major refurbishment took place in the mid-fourteenth century, replacing the entire front of the object with two registers of *repoussé* figures, and a cast *corpus* of a crucified Christ. Panels of the same

41 L. Dennison, 'Monastic or secular? The artist of the Ramsey Psalter, now at Holkham Hall, Norfolk' in B. Thompson (ed.), *Monasteries and society in early medieval Britain* (Stamford, 1999), pp 223–61; R. Refaussé, 'The Christ Church manuscripts in context' and A.J. Fletcher, 'The de Derby psalter of Christ Church Cathedral' in Gillespie and Refaussé, *Med. MSS*, pp 13–32, 81–102.   **42** For the copying of art styles in English manuscripts at the Augustinian canon's house at Lough Ree, where Ó Cianáin's master worked, see P. Ó Riain, 'Longford priories and their manuscripts: All Saints and Abbeyderg' in M. Morris and F. O'Farrell (eds), *Longford: history and society* (Dublin, 2010), pp 39–50.   **43** E.C.R. Armstrong and H. J. Lawlor, 'The Domnach Airgid', *PRIA*, 34C (1917–19), 96–126; C. Bourke, 'The Domnach Airgid in 2006', *Clogher Record*,

date now on one of the long sides, with images of John the Baptist, St Catherine and Christ in Majesty, may originally have occupied the back of the shrine.[44] An inscription prominently located at the top (though now upside-down) records that John ua Cairbri, successor of St Tigernach, permitted the work (IOHS OKARBRI:COMORBANUS: S : TIG[ER]NACII : P[ER]MISIT). Another, smaller inscription (also upside-down) located above the bottom left hand panel records that it was made by John O Barrdan (IOHANES O BARRDAN FABRICAVIT).[45] John Ua Cairbri, abbot of Clones, died in 1353.[46] There is a later record of a John Ó Bárdáin, goldsmith of Drogheda, and although clearly not the same man, it is suggested that given the unusual name, the shrine's goldsmith may have been a relative also based in that town.[47]

Here, while care has been taken to preserve older elements of the shrine, the updating is international in style, displaying the earliest dateable surviving Irish representation of the *Arma Christi* and of international saints with their attributes. The choice of international saints and holy figures represented in the upper register of the front and the long side may be a reflection of particular devotion of canons – Mary, Peter and Paul, John the Evangelist and John the Baptist all feature in the Drummond martyrology. Figures in the lower register are slightly less recognizable: the mourning figures of Mary and John flank the crucifixion, and to its right, the two ecclesiastical figures have plausibly been identified as Brigid and Patrick. The scene to the left has been the subject of greater debate. It has been variously interpreted as St Patrick giving the shrine to St Mac Caírthinn, and less plausibly as St Columba handing a book or shrine to an unknown ecclesiastic.[48] While the former seems to be the most plausible identification, it is worth noting that the action of who is giving and who is receiving is somewhat ambiguous and that the dress of the two figures is quite distinctive. The seated individual wears a mitre – typical of the manner in which native saints were depicted during the later medieval period.[49] But the latter is tonsured and wears a hooded cope – almost identical dress to the canons depicted in the de Derby psalter.[50] The composition of the piece is very similar to the relatively numerous donor portraits found in English and continental manuscripts, especially popular in the eleventh and twelfth centuries, but also found in later manuscripts. These typically show either the patron in supplication before a saint, presenting the saint with a manuscript by way

20:1 (2006), 31–42.   **44** R. Ó Floinn, 'Domhnach Airgid Shrine' in M. Ryan (ed.), *Treasures of Ireland: Irish art 3000BC–1500AD* (Dublin, 1983), pp 176–7 at 177.   **45** R.A.S. Macalister, *Corpus inscriptionum insularum Celticarum*, 2 vols (Dublin, 1949), ii, p. 126.   **46** *AFM*, s.a. 1353. **47** *Registrum Iohannis Mey: The register of John Mey, archbishop of Armagh, 1443–1456*, ed. W.G.H. Quigley and E.F.D. Roberts (Belfast, 1972), pp 52–4; R. Ó Floinn, 'Goldsmiths' work in Ireland, 1200–1400' in C. Hourihane (ed.), *From Ireland coming* (Princeton, 2001), pp 289–312 at 295. **48** Ó Floinn, 'Domhnach Airgid', p. 177; C. Hourihane, *Gothic art in Ireland, 1169–1550* (London, 2003), p. 130.   **49** R. Moss, 'Permanent expressions of piety: the secular and the sacred in later medieval stone sculpture' in R. Moss, C. Ó Clabaigh and S. Ryan (eds), *Art and devotion in late medieval Ireland* (Dublin, 2006), pp 72–97 at p. 88.   **50** A canon is also shown kneeling in supplication to the figure of St Katherine on the long side of the shrine.

9.5 West doorway, Clontuskert Priory, Co. Galway, with inscription running along the horizontal band at the top. Photo: Rachel Moss.

of commemorating devotion, or the maker supplicating themselves before the donor as they present the fruits of their hard labours.[51] Given the dress of the two, we could be looking at either scenario: either the lower-ranking prior of Clones gifting a refurbishment of the shrine to his superior, the bishop of Clogher (presumably Nicholas Mac Cathasaigh, 1320–56); or a representation of the direct 'gift' of the refurbishment to the saint.

The former interpretation might also help to explain the Clones connection with the shrine, something that has puzzled scholars who identify it as one of the treasured possessions of the church at Clogher. St Tigernach was a follower of St Mac Caírthinn, founding the church at Clones following the latter saint's death. At a time of instability within the diocese, what better way to demonstrate continued allegiances between the churches and canons within the diocese than for the prior of Clones to physically mark it on one of the great diocesan treasures?[52]

The commemoration of interaction between a canon and bishop of his diocese in the commissioning of artwork is not without parallel, and is seen just over a century later in Connacht. The great sculpted portal of the Augustinian priory at Clontuskert is adorned with a similar choice of saints to the Domhnach Airgid, and crowned with an inscription recording that Matthew, bishop of Clonfert, and Patrick O'Naughton, 'canon of this house', commissioned it in AD1471 (MATHEU: DEI:GRA; EPS; CLONFERTENS; ET: PATRE' ONEACDAVAYN: CANONIE' ETS: DOMINE:FI'FECERT: ANO DO:MCCCCLXXI). Although the sculpture of the portal has been covered in some detail, the conspicuous record of its patronage, and involvement by the bishop, has never been questioned (Fig. 9.5).[53]

This is perhaps best understood in conjunction with contemporary work carried out at the nearby cathedral at Clonfert. Extensive works were carried out at Clonfert Cathedral in the late fifteenth century. A new inner order was inserted into the Romanesque doorway, and a new sculpted chancel arch erected. The insertion of the tall western tower may also date to this time, although the lack of sculpted detail makes a precise date harder to pin down. The current chancel is usually dated to thirteenth century, on account of the style of the east window, suggesting, by implication, that the chancel arch was perhaps the replacement of an earlier arch.[54] However, evidence of masons' marks carved so as to overlap the joints of the voussoirs that make up the window arches hint at the possibility that the chancel may only have been added in the fifteenth-century refurbishment, and that the earlier eastern window was carefully dismantled and re-erected as part of the scheme – a deliberate act of preservation (Fig. 9.6).

The prominently placed figures carved onto the inner jamb of the doorway are generally passed over in favour of descriptions of the earlier work. Those who have

51 A. Sand, *Vision, devotion, and self-representation in late medieval art* (Cambridge, 2014), pp 96–8.
52 For comparable motivations in the refurbishment of contemporary Irish reliquaries see R. Moss, 'Substantiating sovereignties: "regal" insignias in Ireland, *c*.1370–1410' in P. Crooks, D. Green and W.M. Ormond (eds), *The Plantagenet empire, 1259–1453* (Donington, 2016), pp 216–31.
53 See, for example, Hourihane, *Gothic art*, pp 72–7.   54 M. Duignan, 'Clonfert Cathedral: a note', *JGAHS*, 26 (1954/5), 29.

9.6 a &b Re-set late 12th-century east window at Clonfert Cathedral, Co. Galway, with rubbings of masons' marks incised across the joins in the window voussoirs to facilitate reassembly. Photo: Rachel Moss; rubbings: Jason Ellis.

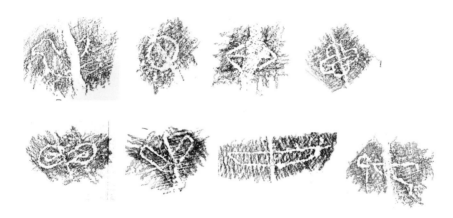

9.7 Figure of a bishop wearing a scholar's cap. South jamb of the west doorway, Clonfert
Cathedral. Photo: Rachel Moss.

attempted identifications have variously suggested that the figure on the south jamb
is St Patrick – on account of the precocious shamrock on his crozier – or St
Brendan, founder of the early church at Clonfert. The figure on the north jamb
has been identified as Petrus Ó Mordha, the twelfth-century Cistercian bishop
sometimes credited with the insertion of the ostentatious Romanesque portal.[55]

55 Hourihane, *Gothic art*, pp 81, 94.

9.8 Figure of an Augustinian canon wearing a rochet and cope. North jamb of the west doorway, Clonfert Cathedral. Photo: Rachel Moss.

The prominent location of the figures at eye level as one enters the building is certainly consistent with the placement of a donor figure; however, they are far more likely to be images of more contemporary donors. The figure on the right holds a crozier, implying a bishop or abbot, but lacks a mitre (Fig. 9.7). The headgear is instead a tight fitting cap of the type worn by academics, commonly depicted, for example, on fifteenth-century brasses at Oxford and Cambridge.[56] Matthew [Mac Craith], bishop of Clonfert (1463–1507), was an Oxford graduate, so it is plausible that this is a representation of him.[57] The figure on the opposite door jamb is tonsured, and wears the distinctive rochet and cloak of an Augustinian canon (Fig. 9.8). Could this be a representation of Patrick O'Naughtan? If so, why was he depicted on the doorway at Clonfert?

The answer may lie just across the Shannon, in the cathedral of the neighbouring diocese of Clonmacnoise. Here, the cathedral had undergone a refurbishment, sensitively maintaining elements of the earlier fabric as at Clonfert, probably during the 1450s.[58] Work coincided with the establishment of a college of priest canons in the cathedral by the then dean, Odo Omolane [O'Malone], whose death is recorded in 1461.[59] His name is inscribed over the north portal (DNS ODO DECANUS CLUAN ME FIERI FECIT). The portal was crowned with carvings of St Dominic (wearing his academic cap, similar to the Clonfert figure), St Patrick and St Francis. The choice of these particular saints can only be speculated upon; however, as suggested by Manning, it may reflect the preponderance of Dominican and Franciscan bishops of the see (including the contemporary incumbent, Seán Ó Dálaigh OFM) – the inclusion of St Patrick a reflection of Clonamcnoise's position in the province of Armagh.[60]

A similar profile could also be seen in the backgrounds of the bishops of Clonfert. Between 1405 and 1534, all bar one were either Dominican or Franciscan, with bishops of Clonfert most frequently cited to execute papal bulls in favour of the mendicants.[61] That one exception was Matthew Mac Craith, an Augustinian canon who had previously served as abbot at Clare Abbey, in Co. Clare. In this context it is tempting to see the works at Clonfert and Clontuskert executed under Mac Craith's watch, with the apparent help of a canon from Clontuskert, as a means of exerting his, and his order's, authority, at a time when, in the face of mendicant success, the majority of houses in the diocese were in decline.

It cannot be said that there was a typical art, or architecture of the Augustinian canons. However, it is clear that they, more than any other order, evoked and preserved the past as a means of self-promotion and ultimately preservation. In so doing, they have left behind a rich legacy of innovative artistic creation, and at the same time proved themselves to be able custodians of the ancient past throughout the tumultuous later Middle Ages.

56 H.W. Mackilin, *Monumental brasses* (London, 1965), pp 48–51.   57 A.B. Emden, *A biographical register of the University of Oxford to AD 1500*, 3 vols (Oxford, 1957–9), ii, p. 1201.   58 C. Manning, 'Clonmacnoise Cathedral' in H. King (ed.), *Clonmacnoise studies 1* (Dublin, 1998), pp 57–86. 59 Manning, 'Clonmacnoise Cathedral', p. 81.   60 Ibid., p. 81.   61 Colmán Ó Clabaigh, 'The mendicant friars in the medieval diocese of Clonfert', *JGAHS*, 59 (2007), 25–36 at 28.

The regular canons and Irish hagiography

PÁDRAIG Ó RIAIN

A new phase in the memorialization of Irish saints began about the middle of the twelfth century in the wake of a number of notable ecclesiastical events. A synod held under the presidency of Malachy of Armagh on St Patrick's Island off Dublin in 1148 enjoined 'rule and good conduct' on laity and clergy.[1] Given its location close to Dublin, we may assume that Gregory, alias Gréne, Hiberno-Norse bishop of Dublin since 1121, was one of the fifteen bishops present at the synod.[2] An entry in the lost Annals of Leinster, which attributes to Malachy and the bishop of the Ostmen, presumably Gregory, the consecration of St Mary's Abbey in Dublin, may also relate to the events of that year.[3] Four years later, at the synod of Kells in 1152, Gregory's new-found status was given final approval in the presence of the papal legate, Cardinal Paparo, when he was elevated to the rank of archbishop.[4]

It was probably during this time of renewal, or correction, as it is now sometimes called, that relics brought from Cologne more than a century earlier by Donatus, alias Dúnán, first abbot of Dublin's Christ Church, were taken from the box in which they had lain and enshrined. This circumstance was duly noted in an entry for 31 July in the Christ Church martyrology, the original of which had also been brought from Cologne.[5] The entry confirms that the enshrinement took place during Gregory's episcopate and, while it mentions no date, the mid-twelfth century is implied by a number of factors. First, by 1162 Gregory was dead.[6] Second, at least one copy of the Christ Church martyrology, if not more, began to circulate about this time. As no other historical martyrology is known from Ireland of this period, the Christ Church copy appears to have been chosen as a useful means of bringing native memorialization of saints into line with universal standards.

First compiled between 853 and 860 by Ado, bishop of Vienne in France, the basic text of the Christ Church martyrology had passed through monasteries associated with Irish Benedictine monks, first in Metz and then in Cologne, before reaching Dublin about 1030.[7] Numerous additions, mostly relating to local feasts,

1 *AFM s.a.* 2 Gregory's episcopate, which began in 1121, lasted until 1161; F.J. Byrne, 'Succession lists: heads of churches to *c.*1200' in T.W. Moody, F.X. Martin and F.J. Byrne (eds), *A new history of Ireland*, ix (Oxford, 1984), pp 237–63, 309. 3 H.J. Lawlor, 'Note on church of St Michan, Dublin', *JRSAI*, 56 (1926), 11–21 at 12; cf. Ó Corráin, 'The Irish church', pp 83, 90. 4 Byrne, 'Succession lists', pp 309, 311. 5 P. Ó Riain, *A martyrology of four cities: Metz, Cologne, Dublin, Lund*, Henry Bradshaw Society 118 (London, 2008), pp 10, 130–1; cf. R. Ó Floinn, 'The foundation relics of Christ Church Cathedral and the origins of the diocese of Dublin' in S. Duffy (ed.), *Medieval Dublin VII* (Dublin, 2006), pp 89–102. 6 *AFM s.a.* 7 J. Dubois and G. Renaud (eds), *Le martyrologe d'Adon: ses deux familles, ses trois recensions: texte et commentaire* (Paris,

but also to a selection of Irish feasts that continued to be commemorated by the Irish monks, were made to the text in both continental centres.[8] Additions were also made to the text after its arrival in Dublin, but not before the middle of the twelfth century, when the martyrology began to circulate.[9] From then on, considering additions made to the Christ Church text itself and additions from it in other texts, there is evidence to show that, while circulating, the martyrology was used mainly by Augustinian canons.

There is no evidence to show that Gregory had planned to introduce the Augustinian Rule to his cathedral in Dublin, but he had surely helped to create an environment conducive to its introduction, which came about after the appointment of his successor Laurence O'Toole in 1162.[10] Laurence's appointment may have taken place, as Marie Therese Flanagan has suggested, at the synod held in that same year at Clane in Co. Kildare under the presidency of Giolla Mic Liag, archbishop of Armagh.[11] This synod, which, according to the annalist, was attended by twenty-six bishops and many abbots, again enjoined 'rule and good conduct' on the Irish church. Furthermore, one of its decrees proclaimed that all future heads of schools in Ireland were to be former pupils of the school at Armagh.[12] Once put into effect, this decree would have given the school in Armagh nominal authority over all ecclesiastical learning in Ireland. Moreover, if the manner in which the Christ Church martyrology circulated is to be our guide, the Armagh school either lay within the Augustinian priory of Ss Peter and Paul or was at least in the care of regular canons.[13]

The earliest evidence for the use of the martyrology outside Christ Church is in the Book of Leinster version of the early ninth-century Martyrology of Tallaght, which was copied, most likely at Terryglass in Co. Tipperary, sometime after 1152.[14] Terryglass is not known to have hosted an Augustinian priory, but the Life written for its patron Colum certainly bears the hallmark of Augustinian authorship.[15] The saint's final miracles were performed on *Inis Erce* (later Enish Sherkey) in the Fergus Estuary, on the River Shannon and close by Canon Island,

1984); Ó Riain, *Four cities*, pp 3–10.   **8** Ó Riain, *Four cities*, pp 5–10; P. Ó Riain, *Feastdays of the saints: a history of Irish martyrologies* (Brussels, 2006), pp 127–39.   **9** The additions made in Dublin before 1200 are discussed in Ó Riain, *Feastdays of the saints*, pp 125–7.   **10** No date is recorded, but the likelihood is that Laurence arranged to have the Augustinian Rule introduced soon after his consecration as archbishop in 1162; *MRHI*, p. 170; Flanagan, *Transformation*, p. 144.   **11** M.T. Flanagan, *Irish royal charters: texts and contexts* (Oxford, 2005), p. 298; cf. Flanagan, *Transformation*, pp 116–17.   **12** *AU* s.a.   **13** The priory of Ss Peter and Paul was one of the earliest to be founded in Ireland; *MRHI*, p. 157.   **14** Some additions to the text show that the copyist was using the Christ Church copy. For example, among seven additions for December/January is the description of Maurus (15 January) as 'discipulus Benedicti', which, although present in both the Christ Church and Tallaght texts, is not in Ado. Ó Riain, *Feastdays of the saints*, p. 142.   **15** P. Ó Riain, *Four Tipperary saints: the lives of Colum of Terryglass, Crónán of Roscrea, Mochaomhóg of Leigh and Ruadhán of Lorrha* (Dublin, 2014), pp 5–8. The exemplar of the Tallaght text used by Aodh may have come from Lorrha, a mere five miles from Terryglass, where already then another Tallaght devotional text, the Stowe Missal, was kept, possibly in the local Augustinian priory, which is thought to have been founded by the 1140s (*MRHI*, pp 155, 185).

from where he was summoned to Clonard, site of an Augustinian priory from about 1144, to perform the last rites for its patron, Finnian.[16] The copyist of the Tallaght martyrology in the Book of Leinster was Aodh Ua Criomhthainn, who is known to have corresponded with a bishop of Kildare named Fionn Ua Gormáin (d. 1160).[17] Fionn had previously been attached to the Cistercian abbey in Newry, but possible leanings towards the regular canons are indicated by the fact that he died at Killeigh, the site of an Augustinian priory at the southern edge of his diocese.[18] Moreover, Fionn was likely a member of a family which included three others with Augustinian associations: Maol Muire Ua Gormáin, abbot of the Augustinian priory of Knock Abbey, Maol Caoimhghin Ua Gormáin (d. 1164), head of school at the Augustinian priory of Louth, and Flann Ua Gormáin (d. 1174), head of school at Armagh, who had studied in England and France.[19] Aodh did not name the sources used for additions to the Tallaght exemplar but, in several cases, the wording of his text shows that he was using a copy of the Christ Church martyrology.[20]

One of Fionn's likely relatives, Flann Ua Gormáin, was at Armagh when preparations began to be made there about 1170 for the provision of a much enlarged commentary to the early ninth-century Martyrology of Óengus.[21] Among the sources used extensively by the commentator was the Christ Church martyrology, which is identified on no fewer than nine occasions by the use of such formulae as *ut Grigorius in Romano marterilogio sapit* (19 Jan.), *in Marti[ro]logio Romano hoc dicit Grigorius* (12 Apr.), or simply *ised atbeir Grigoir* (22 Aug.).[22] The impression is given that the source had been copied by Gregory himself or, at the very least, had been sent to Armagh under the archbishop's name but, setting aside the coincidence that the title anticipated by some 400 years the *Martyrologium Romanum* published in 1583–4 at the behest of Pope Gregory XIII, the Armagh commentator clearly had at his disposal a copy of the Christ Church martyrology.[23]

About the same time, the Christ Church martyrology was used as a source of other martyrologies, of which one was compiled by the previously mentioned Maol Muire Ua Gormáin, abbot of the Augustinian priory of Knock Abbey in Co. Louth.[24] Although mainly drawing his non-Irish saints from a copy of the Martyrology of Usuard, of Winchester origin – possibly obtained through the good offices of Flann Ua Gormáin – Maol Muire included upwards of fifty entries from the Christ Church text.[25] Present among these were feasts of four bishops of Metz, which, as Jacques Dubois pointed out, could only have been drawn from a martyrology completed in Metz.[26] Before arriving in Cologne, from where a copy was brought to Dublin, the text of what was to become the Christ Church martyrology can be shown to have received numerous additions in Metz.[27]

Another martyrology of this period that drew on the Christ Church text forms part of the so-called Drummond Missal. Now preserved in the J.P. Morgan Library

16 W.W. Heist, *Vitae sanctorum Hiberniae* (Brussels, 1965) p. 230, §20; Ó Riain, *Four Tipperary saints*, pp 6–7, 14; *MRHI*, p. 163.   **17** R.I. Best, O. Bergin, M.A. O'Brien and A. O'Sullivan, *The Book of Leinster formerly Lebar na Núachongbála*, 6 vols (Dublin, 1954–83), vol. 1, p. xvi.

in New York, but formerly kept in Drummond castle in Scotland, the missal and martyrology that accompanies it appear to have been first compiled in Armagh, before being taken to Glendalough.[28] Almost all non-native feasts in the text were silently borrowed from a copy of the Christ Church martyrology, and there are indications in both missal and martyrology that the compiler was an Augustinian canon.[29]

It can be seen from the texts of these four late twelfth-century martyrologies that Armagh, under the probable direction of its head of school, Flann Ua Gormáin, occupied a pivotal position in relation to the implementation of the 'rule and good conduct' enjoined at the synods of St Patrick's Island in 1148 and Clane in 1162, at least as far as the commemorative liturgy was concerned. Furthermore, each of the four texts already discussed demonstrably drew on a copy of the Christ Church martyrology, the circulation of which appears to have been largely determined by Augustinian canons. Contemporary documents relating to the introduction of the Augustinian Rule at specific centres may well be lacking – as both Marie Therese Flanagan and Edel Bhreathnach emphasize in this volume – but all locations associated with the above martyrologies were either already then, or were soon to become, sites of priories of regular canons.[30]

Nor is this the sum of the evidence: two other martyrologies from this period – an Irish version of the metrical Martyrology of York and a prose text preserved with it in the Biblioteca Nazionale in Turin – likewise provide internal evidence of provenance in Augustinian houses.[31] The metrical text points to Clonmacnoise, where priories of canons and canonesses were arguably in place by the third quarter of the twelfth century, while entries in the prose text indicate a provenance in the Skreen / Lismullin district of Co. Meath, the location of a priory of canonesses by the 1190s at the latest.[32] The very least that can be said, therefore, is that martyrological memorialization of saints during the second half of the twelfth century appears to have lain primarily in the hands of Augustinian canons and, in one case, canonesses.

A link between the apparently primary Augustinian responsibility for the implementation of the 'rule and good conduct' laid down at various synods and the frequent location of Augustinian priories in close proximity to diocesan cathedrals seems likely. Abbot Gualterus of Arrouaise left an account of how

---

18 *AFM* 1085 (ii, 923); *MRHI*, p. 142; Byrne, 'Succession lists', pp 313, 315. **19** Flanagan, *Transformation*, p. 153n. **20** Ó Riain, *Feastdays of the saints*, pp 116–17. **21** Ibid., pp 173–203. **22** Ibid., pp 188–9; W. Stokes (ed.), *Féilire Oengusso Céli Dé: the martyrology of Oengus the Culdee* (London, 1905; repr. Dublin, 1984), pp 48, 114, 188. **23** J. Hennig, 'The notes on non-Irish saints in the manuscripts of *Félire Oengusso*', *PRIA*, 75C (1975), 119–60 at 125. **24** Stokes, *Félire hÚi Gormáin*; Ó Riain, *Feastdays of the saints*, pp 147–72. **25** Ó Riain, *Feastdays of the saints*, pp 165–9. **26** J. Dubois, 'Les sources continentales du martyrologe irlandais de Gorman', *Analecta Bollandiana*, 100 (1982), 607–17 at 614. **27** Ó Riain, *Feastdays of the saints*, p. 168. **28** Ó Riain, *Four Irish martyrologies*, pp 16–22. The text was copied at Armagh for the use of the Augustinian priory in Glendalough. **29** Ibid., p. 21; Ó Riain, *Feastdays of the saints*, pp 208–11. **30** Cf. Flanagan, *Transformation*, pp 148–9. **31** Ó Riain, *Four Irish martyrologies*, pp 128–30; cf. Ó Riain, *Feastdays of the saints*, pp 214–16, 222–4. **32** Ó Riain, *Four Irish martyrologies*, p. 188; cf. Ó Riain,

Malachy had been so impressed by the customaries of the canons that he induced most of the clergy of cathedral churches in Ireland to adopt their rule and liturgical practices.[33] While this claim cannot be taken at face value, the circumstances that led to a new episcopal appointment in Cork in the 1140s may be seen as a probable example of Malachy's policy being put into action. Following a dispute over the succession to the see of Cork, Malachy nominated, in the words of St Bernard, 'a certain poor man whom he knew to be holy and learned; and he was an outsider'.[34] The outsider was Giolla Aodha Ua Muighin, a saintly man from Errew in the parish of Crossmolina, Co. Mayo, whose influence in Cork was to become so great that the patron of the diocese, St Finbarr, was given a Connacht pedigree in place of the local descent he had previously enjoyed.[35] Indeed, Giolla Aodha's influence became such that the Augustinian priory in Cork, dedicated to John the Evangelist and originally called *Uaimh Bharra*, alias *De Antro Barra*, eventually came to be known by his name as *Mainistear Ghiolla Aodha*, now Gill Abbey, a quite unique phenomenon within the Irish dedicatory pattern.[36] Although Giolla Aodha is nowhere specifically described as a canon, the association of his name with Gill Abbey and the presence in his obit of the phrase *do muntir Airidh*, 'of the community of Errew', indicates that the priory first attested much later for Errew in Co. Mayo was already then in place.[37]

Cork was but one example of probable Augustinian influence on diocesan affairs. No fewer than seventeen of the twenty-four diocesan centres established at Rathbrassil in 1111 became locations of priories in the course of the twelfth century, as did nine of the fifteen new diocesan sees created at, before or after the synod of Kells–Mellifont in 1152.[38] Not surprisingly, therefore, given these circumstances, many pre-1200 bishoprics were occupied either by canons or by clerics from centres that hosted priories. In the case of Armagh, for example, of the nine occupants of the see prior to 1200, two had been abbots at Armagh itself, while the remaining seven were associated with sees from within the northern province that hosted Augustinian priories. In other words, these men are likely, at the very least, to have been influenced by regular canons.[39] As in Louth, therefore, where, as Marie Therese Flanagan has shown on the basis of charter evidence, the community of canons served as the cathedral chapter, many other Irish dioceses

---

Feastdays of the saints, pp 220–2. **33** Cf. Dunning, 'The Arroasian order in medieval Ireland', *IHS*, 4 (1945), 297–315 at 299–300; Flanagan, *Transformation*, p. 136. The text reads: *et fere omnes clericos in episcopalibus sedibus et in multis aliis locis … ordinem nostrum et habitum et maxime divinum in ecclesia officium suscipere et observare praecepit.* **34** H.J. Lawlor, *St Bernard of Clairvaux's Life of St Malachy of Armagh* (London, 1920), pp 92–4, §51; P.-Y. Emery, 'Vie de Saint Malachie' (Paris, 1990), pp 306–9, §51. **35** ATig. 1172; O'Riain et al., *Historical dictionary*, i, 43; Ó Riain, *The making of a saint*, pp 58–61, 64–75. **36** D. Ó Murchadha, 'Gill Abbey and the "Rental of Cong"', *JCHAS*, 90 (1985), 31–45 at 39 (1410 … *St Gillaaeda alias de Antro*). **37** ATig. 1172; *MRHI*, p. 175. **38** The seventeen are: Ardcarn, Armagh, Cong, Connor (*díseart* of, i.e., Kells), Cork, Clogher, Clonard, Clonfert, Derry, Downpatrick, Dublin, Duleek, Ferns, Glendalough, Kilkenny, Leighlin and Tuam. The nine are: Clonmacnoise, Elphin, Kells, Kilmacduagh, Mayo, Roscommon, Roscrea, Trim and Waterford. **39** In addition to Armagh itself, the priories were Derry and Elphin.

are likely to have had chapters composed partly or entirely of regular canons during the latter half of the twelfth century.[40]

Biographical memorialization of Irish saints appears similarly to have lain mainly in Augustinian hands, at least in the period up to 1250 or so, when the Franciscan order began to have an equally important role, especially in Leinster.[41] Three manuscript collections of saints' Lives of the period prior to 1400, or just after that date, were compiled in priories. In two cases, this provenance is certain; the two Rawlinson collections – Bodleian Library manuscripts 485 and 505 – were compiled shortly before and shortly after 1400 in neighbouring Augustinian priories in Co. Longford, namely Saints' Island and Abbeyderg.[42] The provenance of the earliest of the three collections, the possibly early fourteenth-century *Codex Salmanticensis*, is less certain, but, as I have argued elsewhere, some evidence points to the Augustinian priory at Clogher, Co. Tyrone, whose *Register* certainly drew on the collection.[43] Moreover, as Máire Herbert has argued, the Breviary of Aberdeen Office Life of St Colmán of Dromore, which is very close to the *Salmanticensis* version of the Life, probably came from the Augustinian priory at Inchmahome in Perthshire.[44] In other words, later use of the Salamancan collection appears to have been facilitated or managed by canons.

Augustinian involvement is not limited to the collections. I take the view that the greater part of the Irish corpus of hagiography, including the Lives of the so-called O'Donohue group preserved in the *Codex Salmanticensis*, which are assigned a very early date by some scholars, dates to the late twelfth century, or later.[45] Foremost among my reasons for advocating this date is the consistent focus of these texts, as I read them, on centres associated with regular canons. In several previous publications I have drawn attention to O'Donohue Lives that appear to me to reflect Augustinian concerns, those of Fíonán of Kinnitty in Co. Offaly and

---

40 Flanagan, *Transformation*, p. 140; cf. Flanagan, *Irish royal charters*, pp 73–4.   **41** P. Ó Riain, *Beatha Bharra: Saint Finbarr of Cork: the complete life* (Dublin, 1994), pp 101–4.   **42** R. Sharpe, *Medieval Irish saints' Lives: an introduction to Vitae sanctorum Hiberniae* (Oxford, 1991), pp 247–73; Ó Riain, Beatha Bharra, pp 104–13.   **43** P. Ó Riain, 'Codex Salmanticensis: a provenance *inter Anglos* or *inter Hibernos*?' in T. Barnard, D. Ó Cróinín and K. Simms (eds), *A miracle of learning. Essays in honour of William O'Sullivan* (Aldershot, 1997), pp 91–100.   **44** M. Herbert, 'Saint Colmán of Dromore and Inchmahone', *Scottish Gaelic Studies*, 24 (2008), 253–64.   **45** P. Ó Riain, 'The O'Donohue Lives of the Salamancan Codex: the earliest collection of Irish saints' Lives?' in S. Sheehan, J. Findon and W. Follett (eds), *Gablánach in scélaigecht: Celtic studies in honour of Ann Dooley* (Dublin, 2013), pp 38–52; P. Ó Riain, 'Fíonán of Iveragh' in J. Crowley and J. Sheehan (eds), *The Iveragh peninsula: a cultural atlas of the Ring of Kerry* (Cork, 2009), pp 126–8. Some scholars are prepared to assign a date as early as the eighth century to the O'Donohue Lives, either because of the archaic character of the spelling of names in these texts or because of internal evidence deemed to be pointing to an early date (Sharpe, *Medieval Irish saints' Lives*, pp 297–346; M. Herbert, 'Latin and vernacular hagiography of Ireland from the origins to the sixteenth century' in G. Philippart (ed.), *Hagiographies* (Turnhout, 2001), 327–60; M. Herbert, 'The Vita Columbae and Irish hagiography' in J. Carey, M. Herbert and P. Ó Riain (eds), *Studies in Irish hagiography: saints and scholars* (Dublin, 2001), 31–40; M. Herbert, 'Observations on the *Vita* of Bishop Áed mac Bricc' in D. Ó Baoill, D. Ó hAodha and N. Ó Muraíle (eds), *Saltair saíochta, sanasaíochta agus seanchais: a festschrift for Gearóid Mac Eoin* (Dublin, 2013), pp 64–74.

Ruadhán of Lorrha in Co. Tipperary being particular cases in point.[46] Among the Lives most recently examined by me are those of Colmán of Lynally and Ailbhe, patron of the archdiocese of Cashel and Emly, each of which likewise reveals Augustinian influence.[47] In Colmán's case, this is perhaps no more than might be expected of a text relating to a church located within a few miles of Durrow, where an Augustinian priory was founded, possibly already in the 1140s, by Murchadh Ua Maoil Sheachlainn, king of Midhe.[48] By arranging for Laisréan, 'Colum Cille's steward' and superior of Durrow, to accompany Colmán as he chose the location of his church, the author of the saint's Life all but conceded that Lynally was affiliated to the Columban (later Augustinian) church.

Indications of influence on the part of the regular canons are equally prominent in the Life of St Ailbhe of Emly. Although there is no evidence to show that Emly hosted a priory of canons, Ailbhe is said to have been accompanied by a bishop named Cianán when directed by an angel to the place of his resurrection.[49] As no other saint of the name is recorded, Cianán of Duleek is doubtless intended. It bears noting, therefore, that two priories of regular canons were founded at Duleek in the course of the twelfth century.[50] As a prelude to their arrival in Emly, Ailbhe and Cianán are brought together with a saint named Sincheall (Cam), who, as John Colgan also assumed, must have been the patron of Killeigh.[51] Only one other of the name is attested, a younger namesake who was also attached to Killeigh, which is taken to have become home to an Augustinian priory by the middle of the twelfth century.[52] As Emly was the saint's final foundation, it can scarcely be described as a coincidence that the first church to be founded by Ailbhe in Ireland was Kilroot in Co. Antrim, an affiliate of the Augustinian priory of Kells, close by Malachy's diocesan see of Connor.[53]

Among other features of Ailbhe's Life that point to Augustinian authorship is the otherwise unattested visit to Lough Derg attributed to Patrick's predecessor Palladius.[54] This is one of several parallels between Ailbhe's Life and the various Lives written for Patrick, others being a common association with the angel Victor and a prophecy attributed to each saint of the birth of St David of Menevia.[55]

---

46 The primary concern of the author of Fíonán's Life was with Killarney Lower Lake, site of the priory of Inisfallen, and Lough Currane near Waterville, close to the priory in Ballinskelligs, while Ruadhán's biographer attributes to him a role in the founding of Clonfert, an association with Pollrone, and the founding of Shancough and Slanore, all sites with Augustinian or Premonstratensian connections (Ó Riain, 'Fíonán of Iveragh'; idem, 'The O'Donohue Lives'). 47 P. Ó Riain, *Four Offaly saints: the Lives of Ciarán of Clonmacnoise, Ciarán of Seirkieran, Colmán of Lynally and Fíonán of Kinnitty* (Dublin, 2018); Ó Riain, *Beatha Ailbhe*. 48 *MRHI*, pp 174–5. 49 Ó Riain, *Beatha Ailbhe*, p. 78, §34. 50 *MRHI*, p. 173. Duleek was also among the diocesan sees established at Rathbrassil in 1111. 51 Ó Riain, *Beatha Ailbhe*, p. 76, §33; J. Colgan, *Acta sanctorum veteris et majoris scotiae seu Hiberniae … sanctorum Insulae*, I (Louvain, 1645; repr. Dublin, 1947), p. 748; P. Ó Riain, *A dictionary of Irish saints* (Dublin, 2011), pp 562–3. 52 *MRHI*, pp 182–3. 53 W. Reeves, *Ecclesiastical antiquities of Down, Connor and Dromore, consisting of a taxation of those dioceses, compiled in the Year MCCVI* (Dublin, 1847), pp 60n., 95–6. 54 Ó Riain, *Beatha Ailbhe*, p. 60, §3; idem, *A dictionary of Irish saints*, pp 524–5. 55 Ó Riain, *Beatha Ailbhe*, pp 68, §16; 70, §21; K. Mulchrone (ed.), *Bethu Phátraic. The tripartite Life of Patrick* (Dublin & London,

Arguably, therefore, Palladius was brought to Lough Derg because Patrick had come to have a close association with the place, but only from the late twelfth century onwards, when the author of *Tractatus de Purgatorio Sancti Patricii*, followed by Jocelin and Giraldus Cambrensis, bore witness to it.[56] Furthermore, Patrick's association with the place is nowhere attested before the foundation at Lough Derg, perhaps during Malachy's lifetime, of a priory of regular canons dependent on Armagh.[57]

In conclusion, the implementation of what is termed the twelfth-century reform in Ireland arguably followed lines little different from those followed during previous reforms on the Continent and closer to home in England. Commenting on the progress of the Carolingian *reformatio* or *correctio*, as he would prefer to describe it, Rutger Kramer stressed the crucial role played by Benedictine monasteries in the development and propagation of the new ideals, representing themselves in their religious manuscripts as primarily concerned with exemplary lives, such as those of saints.[58] Similarly, the renewal of Benedictine monasticism in England in the late tenth century was followed by a burst of hagiographical activity.[59] So too, it seems to me, the arrival of the external orders in Ireland from the 1130s onwards was arguably a necessary prerequisite for the upsurge in hagiographical activity that followed. Moreover, if any order of religious then introduced to Ireland were to have undertaken the task of compiling saints' Lives and bringing martyrologies up to date, it would have had to be, almost *a fortiori*, the Augustinian canons. A work entitled *A little book about the different orders of the church*, written about 1140 by a man known only by the initial *R-* of his name, stressed that the essential role of canons, as opposed to monks, was teaching.[60] It was no more than might be expected, therefore, that the canons became heavily involved in preparing for and promoting the 'rule and good conduct' enjoined on the clergy of Ireland at the synods held on St Patrick's Island in 1148 and at Clane in 1162. The provision of all necessary liturgical and hagiographical documents would have formed an essential part of their contribution.

1939), ll. pp 214–19, 2330–9; A.W. Wade-Evans (ed.), *Vitae sanctorum Britanniae et genealogiae* (Cardiff, 1944), p. 150, §1.   **56** J. Colgan, *Triadis thaumaturgae seu divorum Patricii, Columbae et Brigidae, trium veteris et maioris Scotiae seu Hiberniae, sanctorum Insulae, communium patronorum acta* (Louvain, 1647; repr. Dublin, 1997), p. 103, §172; J.F. Dimock (ed.), *Giraldi Cambrensis Topographia Hibernica et Expugnatio Hibernica* (London, 1867), p. 82. Cf. Bieler, 'St Patrick's Purgatory'; Flanagan, *Transformation*, p. 136n.   **57** *MRHI*, p. 193.   **58** R. Kramer, 'Teaching emperors: transcending the boundaries of Carolingian monastic communities' in E. Howden, C. Lutter and W. Pohl (eds), *Meanings of community across medieval Eurasia: comparative approaches* (Leiden, 2016), pp 309–37 at pp 309–14.   **59** R.C. Love, *Three eleventh-century Anglo-Latin Lives* (Oxford, 1996), p. xxxiv; R.C. Love, 'Hagiography' in M. Lapidge, J. Blair, S. Keynes and D. Scragg (eds), *The Blackwell encyclopaedia of Anglo-Saxon England* (London, 2001), pp 226–8.   **60** J.A. Franklin, 'Augustinian and other canons' churches in Romanesque Europe: the significance of the aisleless cruciform plan' in J.A. Franklin, T.A. Heslop and C. Stevenson (eds), *Architecture and interpretation: essays for Eric Fernie* (Woodbridge, 2012), pp 78–98 at p. 87.

The Augustinian canons and the development of late medieval Irish pilgrimage

LOUISE NUGENT

INTRODUCTION

Reconstructing the pilgrim landscape of medieval Ireland is a daunting task. While it is possible to identify some destinations frequented by Irish pilgrims many more remain unknown. It is also difficult to gain a clear picture even of known sites as the surviving sources are fragmentary and often span several centuries.[1] Whereas historians and archaeologists have only recently engaged with this subject, the surviving evidence indicates that religious orders played a key role in shaping and sustaining the medieval pilgrimage landscape and this paper provides a preliminary assessment of the Augustinian canons' role in the development of Irish pilgrimage.[2]

THE DIFFICULTIES OF ANALYSING THE LATE MEDIEVAL PILGRIM LANDSCAPE

Across the Christian world the pilgrim landscape consisted of a vast network of holy places of local, regional, national and international importance radiating from Jerusalem – the most sacred and important place in Christendom. A similar hierarchy of pilgrim sites also existed in medieval Ireland. With the exception of St Patrick's Purgatory at Lough Derg in Co. Donegal, no other Irish pilgrimage site had a truly international appeal.[3] Of the other known Irish sites it is difficult to establish if any had a truly national appeal although it is possible some did, many certainly had at the least a regional importance. Some shrines within the Pale such as that of Our Lady of Trim and Christ Church Cathedral attracted pilgrims from

---

[1] The limitations of the Irish sources on pilgrimage are shared with other European countries. See J. Stopford, 'Some approaches to the archaeology of Christian pilgrimage', *World Archaeology*, 26:1 (1994), 57–9; D. Webb, *Pilgrimage in medieval England* (London, 2000). [2] Reports on some excavated early medieval pilgrim sites include J. O'Sullivan and T. Ó Carragáin, *Inishmurray: archaeological survey and excavations 1997–2000* (Cork, 2008); J. White Marshall and G.D. Rourke, *High Island: an Irish monastery in the Atlantic* (Dublin, 2000); J. White Marshall and C. Walsh, *Illaunloughan Island: an early medieval monastery in County Kerry* (Bray, 2005); P. Harbison, *Pilgrimage in Ireland: the monuments and the people* (London, 1995). Many important excavated pilgrim sites such as Ballintubber Abbey, Co. Mayo, and Holycross Abbey remain unpublished. For Irish pilgrimage to foreign shrines see B. Cunningham, *Medieval Irish pilgrims to Santiago di Compostela* (Dublin, 2018). [3] M. Haren and Y. de Pontfarcy, *The medieval pilgrimage to St Patrick's Purgatory: Lough Derg and the European tradition* (Enniskillen, 1988); D. Webb, *Medieval European pilgrimage*,

Gaelic areas, while Lough Derg located in Gaelic Ulster also attracted pilgrims from Anglo-Irish territories in addition to its foreign visitors.

Literary evidence for Irish pilgrimage predominantly concerns individuals' pilgrimages to specific shrines and seldom provides more information than the name of the pilgrim, the date of the pilgrimage and its destination. This means that while one may identify active places of pilgrimage at a particular period, one cannot accurately assess their popularity over the *longue durée* and so map the ebb and flow of devotion. It is also difficult to establish the extent of each shrine's hinterland. Medieval Irish pilgrimage sites also lack sources like *miracula* – collections of miracle tales – whose study allows the researcher to build profiles of pilgrims, establish their origins and demographic profiles and analyse their interactions with the shrine and its custodians.[4] The only surviving Irish *miracula* dates to the seventeenth century and relates to the Cistercian Abbey of Holycross, Co. Tipperary.[5] Despite these shortcomings sufficient material remains to catch glimpses of medieval Irish pilgrims and their destinations.

RELIGIOUS ORDERS AND PILGRIMAGE

Although there has been little study of how Irish religious orders engaged with pilgrimage, even a cursory glance of all known late medieval pilgrim sites shows that a significant number were located at or controlled by religious houses, of which majority were communities of Augustinian canons.[6] As a primarily clerical order the canons were ideally suited for this role as their priest members were qualified to attend to the pastoral and sacramental needs of pilgrims coming to the shrines. The presence of a well-disciplined religious community also meant that pilgrimage centres enjoyed a higher standard of liturgy than was available elsewhere, something that would have been attractive to pilgrims. The canons' reputation for scholarship meant that pilgrims could also expect a better standard of preaching and religious instruction.

For religious communities involvement with a shrine or pilgrimage could be financially lucrative. Pilgrim offerings provided an additional income stream that could be put towards essential expenses such as building and maintenance projects. In addition, the fame of the shrine fostered the cult of the saint and encouraged

c.700–c.1500 (Basingstoke, 2002).   **4** S.S. Morrison, *Women pilgrims in late medieval England* (London, 2002); R.C. Finucane, *Miracles and pilgrims: popular beliefs in medieval England* (Macmillan, 1995); J. Bugslag, 'Local pilgrimages and their shrines in pre-modern Europe', *Pereginations: The Journal of the International Society for the Study of Pilgrimage Art*, 2:1 (2005), 1–26.   **5** M. Harty, *Triumphalia Chronologica Monasterii Sanctae Crucis in Hibernia. De Cisterciensium Hibernorum viris illustribus. Edited, with a translation, notes, and illustrations, by the Rev. Denis Murphy* (Dublin, 1893). **6** Pilgrimage and the Augustinian order is briefly discussed in S.M. Preston, 'The canons regular of St Augustine in medieval Ireland: an overview' (PhD, TCD, 1996), pp 152, 164, 181–8. See also Cunningham, *Medieval Irish pilgrims*, pp 24, 88, 101–4. Pilgrimage at Glendalough is discussed in R. Moss, 'Architectural sculpture at Glendalough' in C. Doherty, L. Doran and M. Kelly (eds),

ongoing support from powerful benefactors. Indulgences also played a key role in fostering medieval pilgrimage. Many religious houses, including Augustinian foundations, offered indulgences to those who supported building projects and the upkeep of the shrine. Even churches that were not pilgrimage sites themselves offered indulgences in return for material support or on specific feast days or anniversaries. These also attracted pilgrims on the occasions on which the indulgence was offered.[7]

AUGUSTINIAN RE-USE AND RE-BRANDING

As Bhreathnach and Moss have noted above, when the continental orders arrived in Ireland in the twelfth century a mature pilgrim landscape already existed.[8] This consisted of pre-existing monastic and ecclesiastical settlements centred on the corporeal or associative relics of Irish saints. Elements of the natural landscape such as holy wells, trees, mountain tops and caves sanctified by their saintly associations also attracted pilgrims. These sacralized landscapes could occur independently or in association with an individual shrine.

These existing cults and established pilgrimage sites clearly played a part in the choice of location for post-twelfth-century foundations and many Augustinian foundations were located on the sites of older foundations.[9] Examples include the important ecclesiastical sites at Kilmacduagh, Clonmacnoise, Glendalough, Devenish and Armagh, all places of pilgrimage associated with early Irish medieval saints.[10] As Ó Riain and Cunniffe demonstrate elsewhere in this volume, such sites were frequently chosen in the hope that their long history could be re-written and manipulated for the benefit of the new order. The Augustinian foundation at Aughris, Co. Sligo, assumed responsibility for the pilgrimage at the early medieval monastic site on the island of Inishmurray. Archaeological surveying and excavation on the island have shown they continued to invest in the existing landscape by maintaining and rebuilding structures during the later medieval period as well as adding new devotional points in the landscape, such as the statute of St Molaise and the creation of an artificial cave built in imitation of St Patrick's Purgatory, Lough Derg.[11]

Some new foundations were established beside busy pilgrim roads, as for example at Ballintubber Abbey, Co. Mayo. Here the abbey was built on a nodal

Glendalough: city of God (Dublin, 2011), pp 278–301.   **7** An in-depth study of indulgences in medieval Ireland is long overdue. For a preliminary overview see L. Nugent, 'Pilgrimage in medieval Ireland, AD 600–1600' (PhD, UCD, 2009), vol. ii, appendix viv.   **8** Nugent, 'Pilgrimage in medieval Ireland'; L. Nugent, 'Gathering of faith: pilgrimage in early medieval Ireland' in Fiona Beglane (ed.), *Proceedings of the conference of the archaeology of gatherings of Sligo IT* (Oxford, 2016), 20–30.   **9** P. Ó Riain, *Four Offaly saints: the Lives of St Ciarán of Clonmacnoise, Ciarán of Seir, Colmán of Lynally and Fíonán of Kinnitty* (Dublin, 2018), p. 30; *MRHI*, pp 157–200.   **10** Other examples include Saul, Co. Down, Clonfert, Co. Galway, Lorrha and Roscrea, Co. Tipperary, and Mothel, Co. Waterford; see *MRHI*, pp 148–152.   **11** O'Sullivan and Ó Carragáin,

point of the Tóchar Phádraig, a medieval pilgrim road leading to the penitential mountain-top site of Croagh Patrick.[12] Its location made it accessible to passing travellers and pilgrims. The monastery of St John the Evangelist, also known as Gill Abbey, in Cork, a daughter house of the Augustinian abbey of Cong, Co. Mayo, was founded to cater for pilgrims from Connacht.[13] Occasionally, foundations established at new sites, like the monasteries dedicated to St Mary at Navan and Trim in County Meath and at Mullingar, Co. Westmeath, subsequently developed into pilgrimage centres or hospices in their own right.

TYPES OF PILGRIMAGE SITES

The pilgrim centres operated by the Augustinian canons took a variety of forms. Some functioned primarily as penitential sites, others were associated with miracles and healing, while others were visited by those in search of indulgences. A number combined all elements. Some sites fostered devotion to existing Irish saints, while others promoted universal cults like that of the Blessed Virgin or introduced foreign cults like that of St Radegund at Rathkeale, Co. Limerick or St Edmund at Athassel, Co. Tipperary.[14]

PENITENTIAL SITES

From the eleventh and twelfth centuries the expiation of sin and guilt became one of the primary motives for going on pilgrimage,[15] coinciding with an 'increasing definition and popularity of the doctrine of Purgatory' and the rise in private penance and concern for expiation of sin.[16] Penitential pilgrimage had a long history in Ireland, having been first introduced in the sixth century as a penance for 'offences against the moral and spiritual code' of the church.[17] While penance could be performed anywhere, certain holy places emerged as more suited to penitential pilgrimage, with Jerusalem and Rome being pre-eminent.

In Ireland the Augustinians controlled several penitential sites including the island sanctuary of St Patrick's Purgatory, Lough Derg (Fig. 11.1). The shrine, an artificial cave, akin to a souterrain, was believed to allow the pilgrim enter

---

Inishmurray, pp 346–8.   **12** Nugent, 'Pilgrimage in medieval Ireland, AD 600–1600', pp 194–5, 242–3. The Augustinian foundation at Devenish Abbey, established on an existing pilgrim site, also catered for pilgrims travelling to Lough Derg. See C. Foley, R. McHugh and B. Scott, *An archaeological survey of County Fermanagh* (Newtownards, 2014), pp 663–65.   **13** *MRHI*, p. 167.   **14** Preston, 'The canons regular of St Augustine in medieval Ireland', 184; Thomas Arnold, *Memorials of St Edmund's Abbey*, vol. 3 (London, 1967), pp 347–8.   **15** J. Sumption, *Pilgrimage: an image of mediaeval religion* (London, 1975), pp 102–3.   **16** J. Bird, 'Penance' in *Encyclopedia of medieval pilgrimage*, ed. L. Taylor (Leiden, 2010), p. 500.   **17** L. Bieler, *The Irish penitentials* (Dublin, 1963); Sumption, *Pilgrimage*, p. 98.

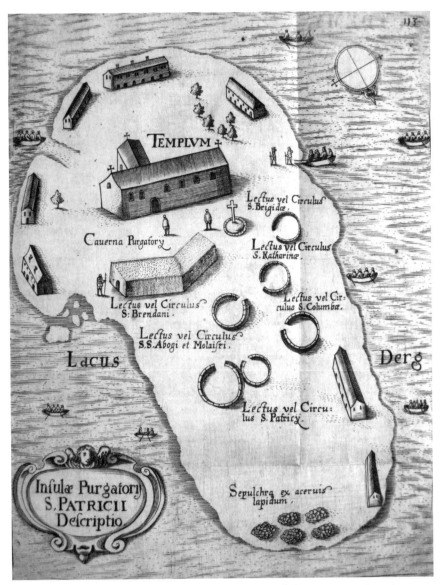

11.1 St Patrick's Purgatory, Lough Derg, Co. Donegal, from T. Carve, *Lyra, sive Anacephalaeosis Hibernica* (Sulzbach, 1666), plate 113.

purgatory and experience its pains while on earth. Those who entered the cave in a spirit of penance, it was believed, would not suffer the pains of hell.[18] The earliest account of the cave is found in *De Purgatorio Patritii*, written *c.*1120 by David Scottus of Würzburg,[19] before the establishment at Lough Derg in the 1130s of a priory

18 M. Dowd, *The archaeology of caves in Ireland* (Oxford, 2015), pp 217–21.   **19** J. Hennig, 'Irish saints in early German literature', *Speculum*, 22:3 (1947), 364.

dependent on the Augustinian Abbey of Ss Peter and Paul, Armagh. The cave was located on Station Island, a short distance from the Augustinian priory at Saints' Island. The site is unique as several literary accounts of the experiences and rituals undertaken by pilgrims survive dating from the twelfth to the sixteenth centuries. International visitors included pilgrims from France, Hungary, Catalonia, Italy, Switzerland, the Netherlands and England.[20] The canons used their own networks to promote knowledge of the site. The *Liber Niger* of Christ Church, Dublin, a composite manuscript containing material dating from the early fourteenth to sixteeth centuries, contains a fragment of one of the earliest descriptions of Lough Derg pilgrimage, that of the Knight Owein who visited there in the early twelfth century. This particular account enjoyed widespread circulation and a version of the text was included in the library of the Augustinan canons in Leicester.[21] The Lough Derg pilgrimage drew on wider European practice and the universal belief in purgatory, but it was also influenced by Irish traditions. The act of being enclosed in a cave as penance is attested in the Lives of the Irish saints. St Brendan of Clonfert was made to spend the night in a cave by Bishop Erc as a punishment for striking a girl.[22] The Irish Life of St Ruadhán reports that the saint dug a cave within his oratory, which was located at his monastery of *Poll Ruadháin*, and the Latin Life of St Rúadán states that the cave was dug to hide or punish the king of Connacht.[23] Haren and de Pontfarcy suggest that the Lough Derg pilgrimage echoed elements of the anchoritic life, whereby the pilgrim temporarily experienced this lifestyle.[24] 'In this perspective, the entering into the cave appears to be a dramatization of the symbolic death that the recluse goes through, and the specified time of a day and a night to be spent in the cave can be understood as a metaphor of totality.'[25]

The widespread circulation of accounts of St Patrick's Purgatory meant that it attracted pilgrims from all over Europe, many of whom were from the upper echelons of society. Not all had happy or uplifiting spiritual experiences. A Dutch monk from Eymstadt, who made the pilgrimage in the 1490s, bemoaned the fact that money was demanded of him along the route by the archbishop of Armagh, local rulers such as the O'Neills and the prior of Lough Derg. His experience suggests that the pilgrimage was a lucrative business, and not just for the Augustinians. To add salt to the wound, the monk failed to experience the pains of purgatory when he entered the cave and was so angry over his experience that he complained to Pope Alexander V, who in 1497 ordered the closure of the cave, although it reopened shortly afterwards.[26]

20 For a discussion of foreign pilgrims at Lough Derg see Haren and de Pontfarcy, *The medieval pilgrimage to St Patrick's Purgatory*.   **21** C. Ó Clabaigh, 'The *Liber Niger* of Christ Church Cathedral, Dublin' in Gillespie and Refaussé, *Med. MSS*, pp 60–80, at p. 65. This section of the manuscript dates to the early fourteenth century.   **22** Haren and de Pontfarcy, *Medieval pilgrimage*, p. 9; Charles Plummer, *Bethada náem nÉrenn*, vol. 2 (Oxford, 1922), p. 46.   **23** Haren and de Pontfarcy, *Medieval pilgrimage*, p. 10. For discussion of caves at Irish religious sites see Dowd, *Archaeology of caves*, pp 215–17; C. Manning, 'Rock shelters and caves associated with Irish saints' in *Above and beyond: essays in honour of Leo Swan*, ed. T. Condit and C. Corlett (Bray, 2005), pp 109–20.   **24** Haren and de Pontfarcy, *Medieval pilgrimage*, p. 14.   **25** Ibid.   **26** Ibid., pp 190–2.

11.2 St Kevin's Cave, Glendalough, Co. Wicklow. Photo © Christiaan Corlett, courtesy of Culture Stock.

Lough Derg was also recorded on a list of pilgrim destinations to which the secular court of Antwerp sentenced criminals in the early fifteenth century.[27] The identities of a small number of Irish pilgrims have also been preserved. These included John Bonham and Guidu Cissy who travelled there in 1366,[28] the priest Thomas O'Callachan who made the journey in 1470[29] and Nylanus O'Ledan, another priest, who made the pilgrimage in 1507.[30] St Patrick's Purgatory also features prominently in late medieval Gaelic poetry.[31]

27 D. Webb, *Pilgrims and pilgrimage in medieval Europe* (London, 1999), 225–6; Maggioni, 'The tradition of Saint Patrick's Purgatory between visionary literature and pilgrimage reports', *Studia Aurea*, 11 (2017): 161; J. Van Herwaarden, *Between Saint James and Erasmus: studies in late-medieval religious life: devotions and pilgrimages in the Netherlands* (Leiden, 2003), p. 177.   **28** H.J. Lawlor, 'A calendar of the register of Archbishop Sweteman', *PRIA*, 29C (1911), 272, no. 193.   **29** A. Lynch, 'A calendar of the reassembled register of John Bole, archbishop of Armagh, 1457–71', *Seanchas Ard Mhacha*, 15:1 (1992), 148.   **30** L. Bieler, 'Letter of credence by Donatus Magrahe, prior of Lough Derg, for Nylanus O Ledan, priest and pilgrim', *Clogher Record*, 2:2 (1958), 257–9.   **31** S. Ó Dufaigh, 'Two poems on St Patrick's Purgatory' in H.A. Jefferies (ed.), *History of the diocese of Clogher* (Dublin, 2005), 108–33; S. Leslie, *Saint Patrick's Purgatory, a record from history and literature* (London, 1932), pp 163–82.

St Patrick's Purgatory may also have influenced the development of the ritual landscape at other Augustinian sites. Excavations at the island pilgrim site at Inishmurray, Co. Sligo, uncovered a stone-built, souterrain-like passage within the main enclosure close to the early medieval shrine chapel known as *Tech Molaise*.[32] The passage extends from the church of Templeatinney to *Tech Molaise* and access to it could be gained from near the doors of both buildings, making it possible to creep between the two.[33] The excavators interpreted the feature as having a similar function to the cave at St Patrick's Purgatory and suggest 'that the mortification suffered by pilgrims who were entombed in this structure would prepare them for the apotheosis of their visit to Inishmurray – the privilege of access to Tech Molaise and the relics of the saint'.[34] At the Upper Lake at Glendalough, Co. Wicklow, a manmade cave known as St Kevin's Bed was hewn out of the rock face some time in the twelfth century and this also may have been a response to the holy cave at Lough Derg (Fig. 11.2; Plate 3).[35]

The extent of Augustinian involvement with both penitential pilgrimage and pilgrimage sites is demonstrated in an early sixteenth-century account from Armagh.[36] In 1544 or 1545 Heneas MacNichaill completed a penitential pilgrimage imposed on him in 1543 by Edmund MacCawell, dean of Armagh Cathedral, for having strangled his son.[37] MacNichaill was ordered to visit eighteen holy places around Ireland, of which only sixteen can now be identified with certainty. The itinerary was designed to take over a year to complete and to equate in length and duress to a pilgrimage to an international shrine such as Rome or the Holy Land. The destinations are spread over a wide geographic area with a cluster of sites in Cos. Down, Donegal and Tipperary and along the western seaboard. There is a marked absence of sites in the centre of Ireland.

Perhaps influenced by Ss Peter and Paul's in Armagh, many of the sites listed were controlled by Augustinian houses. Given its prominence, it is not surprising that MacNichaill's pilgrimage also included a visit to Lough Derg. At Glendalough, Co. Wicklow, St Kevin's Bed (*Lectum Cayn*) was near two Augustinian foundations, one at the site of St Kevin's Monastery, the other at St Saviour's Priory, approximately half a mile east of Glendalough Cathedral.[38] The Patrician site of Saul, Co. Down, was an Augustinian house from the 1140s.[39] Of the sites visited by MacNichaill along the west coast, the island sanctuaries of Skellig Michael, Co. Kerry, and *Inishglora* near Erris, Co. Mayo, were also in the care of the canons.[40]

---

32 O'Sullivan and Ó Carragáin, *Inishmurray*, p. 342. **33** Ibid. **34** O'Sullivan and Ó Carragáin, *Inishmurray*, p. 346. **35** A. Mac Shamhráin, *Church and polity in pre-Norman Ireland: the case of Glendalough* (Maynooth, 1996), p. 5; C. Plummer, 'Vie et miracles de S. Laurent archevêque de Dublin', *Analecta Bollandiana*, 33 (1919), 141–2; C. Plummer, *Bethada náem nÉrenn*, vol. 2, p. 121; Dowd, *Archaeology of caves*, p. 216; Manning, 'Rock shelters and caves', p. 117. **36** *MRHI*, p. 194. **37** L.P. Murray, 'A calendar of the register of Primate George Dowdall, commonly called the "Liber Niger" or "Black Book" (Continued)', *Journal of the County Louth Archaeological Society*, 6:3 (1927), 152, no. 71. **38** *MRHI*, pp 176–7. **39** *MRHI*, p. 198. **40** For discussion of the pilgrim landscape of Inishglora see M. Gibbons and M. Gibbons, 'Inishglora – the western threshold between land and wave' in *Recent explorations and discoveries in Irish heritage*, ed. Jim

Both originated as early medieval eremitic foundations, whose communities had transferred to the mainland by the twelfth century when they became Augustinian foundations. Skellig Michael was dedicated to St Michael the Archangel and was controlled by the Augustinian priory at Ballinskelligs, Co. Kerry. *Inishglora* was administered by the canons of Cross Abbey, Co. Mayo.[41] In both cases the communities fulfilled a role similar to that of their confreres at Aughris Priory and Inishmurray, acting as caretakers and controlling pilgrims' access to the sites.

MacNichaill also made pilgrimage to Cill Chraobh Íosa or 'church of the branch/tree of Jesus'. This has been identified as the townland of Killavees in Co. Down. There is no known church in the townland, so perhaps the site was a holy tree as referred to in the townland name. Some holy trees did attract medieval pilgrims and are mentioned in a number of medieval Lives of Irish saints.[43] In medieval times, Killavees was the property of 'the Priory of St Thomas the Martyr, otherwise called the Priory of Toberglory (the Spring of Glory)', an Augustinian priory founded before 1183 by John de Courcy, granted by him to the prior and canons of Carlisle. It gets its name from an adjacent well, at which St Patrick is said to have had a vision of angels.[44]

Other sites listed included the Benedictine foundations of Downpatrick Cathedral, Co. Down and Ross, Co. Cork.[45] MacNichaill also visited the Cistercian foundation at Holycross Abbey and the cathedral church at the Rock of Cashel, both in Co. Tipperary.[46]

SHRINES AND RELICS

In keeping with trends of devotion in the rest of Europe a number of the Irish Augustinian pilgrim sites were associated with the cults of Christ, Mary and the saints.[47]

Relics of Christ

The veneration of relics and images of Christ such as miraculous crosses, bleeding hosts, fragments of the True Cross and the Holy Blood was characteristic of late

Higgins (Galway, 2017), pp 24–40.   **41** A. O'Sullivan, J. Sheehan and South West Kerry Archaeological Survey, *The Iveragh peninsula: an archaeological survey of south Kerry* (Cork, 1996), p. 346; *MRHI*, pp 168, 192.   **43** P. Ó Riain, *Four Tipperary saints: the Lives of Colum of Terryglass, Crónán of Roscrea, Mochaomhóg of Leigh and Ruadhán of Lorrha* (Dublin, 2014), pp 12, 53; J. O'Hanlon (ed.), *Life of St Brigid, Virgin: first abbess of Kildare* (Dublin, 1877), p. 97.   **44** James O'Laverty, *An historical account of the diocese of Down and Connor, ancient and modern* (Dublin, 1878), 254. The priory site 'seems to have stood about two miles north of Grangicam, on the south-east side of Downpatrick town and close to the ruined cromlech known as Sampson's Stone in the townland of Demesne of Down', see http://www.placenamesni.org/ resultdetails.Php?Entry =17506', accessed 12 July 2018.   **45** *MRHI*, pp 105–8.   **46** *MRHI*, pp 62–3, 134–5.   **47** C. Walker Bynum, *Wonderful blood: theology and practice in late medieval northern Germany and beyond* (Philadephia, 2007); H. Klein, 'Relics of the passion' in L. Taylor (ed.), *Encyclopedia of medieval*

medieval piety, so it is not surprising to find such relics at Augustinian houses in Ireland.

Of the relics preserved by the canons in Dublin's Christ Church Cathedral, two had particular Christological significance. These were the *Bacall Íosa* or the Staff of Jesus and the miraculous 'speaking crucifix'. The *Bacall Íosa* was believed to be the pastoral staff or crozier given to St Patrick by Christ himself. Originally kept at Armagh, it came into the possession of Christ Church Cathedral during the twelfth century and was venerated there until its destruction in 1538.[48] It was repeatedly mentioned in the annals and credited with numerous miracles and oaths were frequently validated before it. Its popularity was such that in 1493 offerings made to it by pilgrims were used to support the choirboys at Christ Church (Fig. 11.3).[49]

The other star of the collection was the miracle-working 'speaking crucifix'.[50] This was not listed among the relics enshrined by Bishop Gréne (1121–61), being obtained by the cathedral after 1161.[51] Gerald of Wales noted that the cross 'earned everywhere respect and veneration' and listed four miracles associated with it.[52] The English chronicler Roger of Howden described the cross as having 'a life-sized image of Christ',[53] which was the focus of a liturgical clamour ordered by Archbishop John Cumin in 1197.[54]

> There was in the cathedral-church of Dublin a certain cross on which a rather expressive figure of Christ was carved (*incisa*): all the Irish, and other people as well, held this cross in the greatest veneration. Now, while this image of the crucified one lay prostrate on the floor surrounded by thorns, it went into agony on the sixth day. Its face reddened vehemently as if it were close to a roaring fire, and it perspired freely. Drops fell from its eyes as if it were weeping.[55]

The clergy present reportedly collected this holy liquid and asked the archbishop to inform the pope.[56] This liquid became an additional relic in the Cathedral's

pilgrimage (Leiden, 2010), pp 599–601; J. Bugslag, 'Relics of the Virgin Mary' in Taylor (ed.), *Encyclopedia of medieval pilgrimage*, pp 603–10. For devotion to the Blessed Virgin and relics of Christ see J. Bugslag, 'Material and theological identities: a historical discourse of constructions of the Virgin Mary', *Théologiques*, 17:2 (2009), 19–67.   **48** A. Lucas, 'The social role of relics and reliquaries in ancient Ireland', *JRSAI*, 116 (1986), 9; C. Bourke, *Patrick: the archaeology of a saint* (Belfast, 1993), pp 18–20, 49.   **49** B. Boydell, 'The establishment of the choral tradition, 1480–1647' in Milne, *CCCD*, p. 238; R. Gillespie, 'The crisis of reform, 1625–60' in Milne, *CCCD*, p. 160.   **50** J. Lydon, 'The text and its context' in J. Mills (ed.), *The account roll of the priory of the Holy Trinity, Dublin, 1337–1346* (Dublin, 1996), p. xvi; J. Lydon, 'Christ Church in the later medieval world, 1300–1500' in Milne, *CCCD*, p. 93.   **51** R. Refaussé, 'Introduction' in Milne, *CCCD*, p. 15; Flanagan, *Transformation*, p. 233.   **52** S. Kinsella, 'From Hiberno-Norse to Anglo-Norman, c.1030–1300' in Milne, *CCCD*, p. 46; T. Wright (ed.), *Giraldus Cambrensis. The Topography of Ireland* (Cambridge, 2000), p. 58.   **53** R. Stalley, 'The architecture of the cathedral and priory buildings, 1250–1530' in Milne, *CCCD*, p. 108.   **54** Flanagan, *Transformation*, p. 234.   **55** Ibid., p. 234; W. Stubbs (ed.), *Chronica Roger de Houedone*, vol. iv (London, 1868), pp 29–30.   **56** Flanagan, *Transformation*, p. 234. For discussion of the clamour and tradition of ritual

11.3 Christ Church Cathedral, Dublin.

collection. The Christ Church cross was not the only Irish cross to miraculously exude liquid. The Annals of the Four Masters record that in 1411: 'The Holy Crucifix of Raphoe poured out blood from its wounds. Many distempers and diseases were healed by that blood.'

In the West of Ireland a prominent relic of the True Cross was the focus of pilgrimage at Cong Abbey in Co. Mayo. Originally a seventh-century foundation associated with St Fechin, the Annals of the Four Masters record that it was burnt in 1114 and 1137 and re-founded by Turlough O'Connor, king of Connacht (d. 1156). Later, his son Rory built a new monastery and it became an Augustinian foundation.[57] The abbey's relic of the True Cross was housed in an elaborate shrine now known as the Cross of Cong. This took the form of a processional cross and was commissioned by Turlough O'Connor in 1123 to house the relic he had received from the pope the previous year. Originally donated to the cathedral church at Tuam, Co. Galway, it was later transferred to Cong, where it remained in the possession of the Augustinian canons of St Mary's Abbey until the nineteenth century.

The cross was designed for processional use but also functioned as an altar cross.[58] There are nineteenth-century references to it being 'placed upon the altar of Cong chapel at Christmas and Easter'.[59] Regarded as one of the masterpieces of medieval Irish metalwork, it consists of an oak core covered by plates of cast bronze. A large polished rock crystal is positioned at the front of the cross at the junction of the four arms. The crystal is in turn set in a conical mount surrounded by a collar of gold filigree panels, blue and white glass studs, set over an internal cavity where the relic was housed. The bronze plates on the surfaces of the cross are cast openwork, decorated with ribbon-shaped intertwined zoomorphic animals in the Scandinavian-derived Urnes style.[60] The earliest reference to pilgrimage to Cong occurs in 1168, when the Annals of Ulster recorded the death of the bishop of Elphin while on pilgrimage there. Indulgences granted in 1428 and 1425 for repairs to the monastery refer to multitudes arriving at the church, indicating it remained an active pilgrimage centre.[61]

The priory of the Holy Trinity, Ballyboggan, Co. Meath, also known as *De Laude Dei*, likewise possessed a miraculous crucifix. Although founded in the twelfth century by Jordan Comin, little is known about its early history but it was burned in 1446 and rebuilt soon after.[62] The earliest evidence of the cross and its cult occurs in the records of the priory's dissolution in 1537, when the monastic buildings and over 5,000 acres of its land were granted to Sir William Bermingham.[63] The following year, the Annals of Ulster record the destruction of the cross of Ballyboggan along with other prominent relics: 'The image of Mary

humiliation of relics in Gaelic Ireland see pp 235–7. **57** *MRHI*, p. 166. **58** G. Murray, *The Cross of Cong: a masterpiece of medieval Irish art* (Dublin, 2014), p. 189. **59** Ibid. **60** Ibid., pp 67–111, 202–4. **61** Preston, 'The canons regular of St Augustine in medieval Ireland', 184; *CPL*, 8, p. 21; *CPL*, 8, p. 530. **62** *MRHI*, pp 159–60. **63** *EIMP*, pp 311–13; S. Lewis, *A topographical dictionary of Ireland*, 2 vols (London, 1837), vol. 1, p. 123.

of the town of Ath-truim and the Holy Cross of Baile-Ui-Bogain and the Staff of Jesus were burned by the Saxons this year.'[64] No description of the Ballyboggan cross survives but the fact that it was destroyed with the image of St Mary of Trim and the *Bacall Íosa* suggests that it was a significant artefact. The lack of historical references makes it difficult to ascertain if the cult and pilgrimage was ever more then a local phenomenon.[65]

Marian shrines and the cult of the Saints

The late Middle Ages saw a proliferation of images and relics of the saints, with the cult of the Virgin Mary being particularly popular.[66] The motives for Marian pilgrimages were manifold. Some sought healing from sickness and fertility issues. Others resorted to her as an intercessor, seeking her protection on the high seas, or relief from drought and in innumerable other situations.[67] Over time some images were regarded in much the same light as relics and from the beginnings of Marian devotion in Western Europe, both relics and images played central roles.[68] As Marian shrines proliferated in Western Europe, faith in Mary's intercessory powers became more localized and her devotees knew her by 'diversity of advocations', for example, 'Our Lady of Chartres', 'Our Lady of Soissons', 'Our Lady of Walsingham' and so forth.[69]

At least three significant Marian shrines existed at Irish Augustinian houses. Unfortunately, there is no clear indication of when these became centres of pilgrimage. The earliest reference relates to the statue of Our Lady of Kilmore, kept at an Augustinian priory in Co. Roscommon, established *c.*1232.[70] Like many other Augustinian houses, the priory was re-established on the site of an earlier monastery.[71] The fortunes of the community were mixed. Although Fedhlim Ua Conchobhair, son of Cathal Craobhderg, king of Connacht, increased the initial endowments of the priory in 1248, by 1412 the priory was so poor that the numbers of its canons could not be maintained, and a vicarage was granted *in commendam* when it was transformed into a parish church.[72] The financial difficulties experienced by the priory may have inspired a miraculous event in 1381, when the Annals of Ulster record that 'The image of Mary in Cell-mor in Tir-Briuin spoke miraculously this year'.[73] This wondrous act resulted in pilgrimage at least at a local level and it was reported in 1412 that 'innumerable miracles were wrought there', with pilgrims arriving 'from divers parts of the world'.[74] One could surmise that the canons instigated and used the pilgrimage to attempt to address their financial woes. Despite what appears to be at least a vibrant local pilgrimage, the income

64 *AU* 1538.   **65** A. Cogan, *The diocese of Meath: ancient and modern*, vol. 1 (Dublin, 1862), pp 169–70.   **66** Bugslag, 'Material and theological identities', p. 37.   **67** Ibid., p. 43.   **68** Ibid., p. 35.   **69** Ibid., pp 35–6.   **70** *MRHI*, p. 183.   **71** *MRHI*, p. 183.   **72** *MRHI*, p. 183; Preston, 'The canons regular of St Augustine in medieval Ireland', 66.   **73** B. Mac Carthy (ed.), *Annala Uladh. Annals of Ulster, otherwise, Annala Senait, Annals of Senait; a chronicle of Irish affairs A.D. 1379–1541* (Dublin, 1895).   **74** *CPL*, 6, p. 309.

11.4 Yellow Steeple, St Mary's Abbey, Trim.

was not sufficient to secure the community's finances and references to the statue and pilgrimage subsequently disappear from the historical record.

Another miraculous statue was venerated at St Mary's Augustinian Abbey, Trim, Co. Meath (Fig. 11.4). The early history of the priory is obscure and it seems to have been a pre-Anglo-Norman foundation that by the 1140s had become Augustinian.[75] St Mary's became one of the wealthiest religious houses in Ireland, receiving grants from Henry VII in 1485 and from the duke of York in 1495.[76] It also hosted parliament on at least three occasions between 1484 and 1491.[77] When the abbey was suppressed in 1539 it held over 800 acres, along with the churches of Kildalkey and Clonard and had a total value of £125 14s. 1½d.[78] The sale of chattels from the abbey raised £206 15s. 2d., while four bells remained unsold. This sum was higher than that raised at any other Augustinian house in Ireland.[79]

75 M. Potterton, *Medieval Trim: history and archaeology* (Dublin, 2005), pp 294–5; *MRHI*, pp 195–6. **76** M. Potterton, 'The archaeology and history of medieval Trim, County Meath' (PhD, NUI, Maynooth, 2003), p. 64; Potterton, *Medieval Trim*, p. 302. **77** Potterton, *Medieval Trim*, p. 303; *MRHI*, p. 196. **78** *EIMP*, pp 303–5. On 15 May 1539, St Mary's was surrendered to Henry VIII's commissioners and dissolved. The community included Abbot Dardis and eight canons who all received pensions in July 1539. **79** C. McNeill, 'Accounts of sums realized by sales of

The buildings of the priory, 'the church, bell tower, cemetery, cloister, and dormitory', were still intact in 1565, but by 1649 only the tower survived.[80] Like many monastic churches, Trim accommodated several chapels. One chapel, dedicated to St George the Martyr, is mentioned in the register of the archbishop of Armagh in 1484, while another housed the miraculous statue of Our Lady, which is first mentioned in the late fourteenth century.[81] In 1397, Hugh Mac Mahon recovered his sight by fasting before the statue and at the relic of the True Cross at Raphoe, Co. Donegal. In 1412, the Annals of the Four Masters recorded: 'The image of [the Blessed Virgin] Mary of Ath-Trim wrought many miracles'.

The number of pilgrims would have increased dramatically in the year 1423, when the pope granted an indulgence of ten years to visitors to the shrine 'in which by the merits of the Virgin, the Lord works many miracles'[82] In 1444, further miracles were reported when the statue allegedly restored sight to a blind man, speech to a dumb man, the use of his feet to a cripple, stretched out the hand of a person to whose side it had been fastened and caused a pregnant woman to deliver cats.[83] The statue remained popular and in 1462 King Edward IV made special grants to the abbot of Trim for the 'renewal and perpetual continuance of a wax candle continually from day to day and from night to night burning before the image of Our Blessed Lady'.[84] The grant also stipulated that four other wax candles continually burn before the image at the Mass of St Mary, to petition the 'the good estate' of the king and his family and the souls of his ancestors. A sixteenth-century reference indicates the continuance of pilgrimage to Trim. In 1529, the Ecclesiastical Court of Armagh imposed a penance on Karulus O Rayly (Cathal O'Reilly), the lord of east Breifne, after he was absolved by the archbishop of Armagh from the censures and excommunications incurred by his invasion of Julianstown, Co. Meath. In addition to making restitution to the injured villagers, he had to donate two cows towards the support of the cathedral of Armagh and undertake a pilgrimage to either St Patrick's Purgatory or to the statue of Our Lady of Trim.[85] The inclusion of Trim shows it was still an important and active pilgrim site and was regarded as being of equal status to Lough Derg. The statue was burned by the reformers in 1538[86] although some claimed that it survived until 1641 when it was destroyed.[87]

The statue of Our Lady at St Mary's Abbey, Navan, was another site of Marian devotion in late medieval Ireland.[88] The Anglo-Irish lord, John de Courcy,

chattels of some suppressed Irish monasteries', *JRSAI*, 12:1 (1922), 17.   **80** Potterton, *Medieval Trim*, pp 305–6.   **81** Potterton, 'The archaeology and history of medieval Trim, County Meath', p. 85.   **82** *CPL*, 7, pp 254–55.   **83** D. Hall, *Women and the church in medieval Ireland, c.1140–1540* (Dublin, 2003), p. 29, fn. 58; Potterton, *Medieval Trim*, p. 305, fn.17.   **84** J. Hardiman (ed.), *A statute of the fortieth year of King Edward III: enacted in a parliament held in Kilkenny, AD 1367, before Lionel duke of Clarence*, vol. 2 (Dublin, 1843), p. 51.   **85** L.P. Murray, 'A calendar of the register of Primate George Dowdall, commonly called the "Liber Niger" or "Black Book" (Continued)', *Journal of the County Louth Archaeological Society*, 6:3 (1927), 38; Potterton, *Medieval Trim*, p. 308.   **86** Potterton, *Medieval Trim*, pp 306–10; J. Clarke Crosthwaite, *The book of obits and martyrology of the Cathedral Church of the Holy Trinity, commonly called Christ Church. Dublin* (Dublin 1844), p. xviii.   **87** C. MacLeod, 'Some late medieval wood sculptures in Ireland', *JRSAI*, 77 (1947), 54.   **88** For a detailed

confirmed the church of St Mary's to the Augustinian canons in 1189, and abbots are mentioned sporadically thereafter.[89] Pilgrimage and devotion to the statue was first recorded in 1453, when Abbot John Bole persuaded Pope Nicholas V to grant a rare plenary indulgence to all pilgrims undertaking pilgrimage to the shrine.[90] This was available to pilgrims on Pentecost Sunday and on the three days that followed. As with all such indulgences the pilgrims were required to confess their sins and to give alms for the much-needed repair and conservation of the abbey and its buildings, before the indulgence could be granted.[91] Two years later the event was recorded in the Annals of Ulster.[92] The inclusion in the annals of a site located in Anglo-Irish controlled lands in the Pale shows that pilgrimage at Navan crossed Irish cultural divides and that the Navan indulgence appealed to Gaelic as well as Anglo-Irish pilgrims. One of the miracles attributed to the statue involved the restoration to health of a Dr Stackbolle, a member of the Navan community whose eyes had been put out and tongue removed by the instruction of Thomas Bathe, with whom he had a long-running feud; 'Dr Stackbolle was carried back to the abbey, and cast before the image of the Blessed Virgin, and by her grace, mediation, and miraculous power, he was restored to his sight and speech'.[93] The statue was also destroyed at the Reformation.

The cult of the saints

Like many other medieval cathedrals, Christ Church Cathedral Dublin, possessed an extensive collection of relics. The initial collection was assembled by Dúnán, bishop of Dublin sometime before 1074, and was later enshrined in a reliquary between 1121 and 1161. It is thought they were kept in a feretory or shrine positioned behind the cathedral's high altar.[94] The collection is remarkable both for its size and its range. The relics of Christ included a portion of the True Cross, fragments of the Holy Sepulchre and a thorn from the Crown of Thorns. Marian devotion was represented by a phial of the Virgin Mary's milk and her belt. Apostolic relics included those of Ss Paul and Andrew, along with the Cross and chains of St Peter. Relics of Ss Sylvester and Catherine of Alexandria, the vestments of St Olaf of Norway and of St Herbert of Cologne and relics of the

---

discussion of the abbey and its history see Clare Ryan, 'The town walls of medieval Navan, Co. Meath' in C. Corlett and M. Potterton (eds), *Towns in medieval Ireland in the light of recent archaeological excavations* (forthcoming, Dublin, 2019).   **89** Tentative evidence suggests the abbey was founded before the Anglo-Norman settlement of Meath, as one of its abbots witnessed a charter dated to 1174–84, suggesting it was well established by then. *MRHI*, p. 189. See also Clare Ryan, 'The town walls of medieval Navan, Co. Meath'.   **90** A. Lynch, 'A calendar of the reassembled register of John Bole, archbishop of Armagh, 1457–71', *Seanchas Ard Mhacha*, 15:1 (1992), 42–3; Anthony Cogan, *The diocese of Meath: ancient and modern*, 2 vols (Dublin, 1862), vol. 2, p. 224.   **91** Anthony Lynch, 'The administration of John Bole, archbishop of Armagh, 1457–71', *Seanchas Ard Mhacha*, 14:2 (1991), 42–3; Cogan, *The diocese of Meath*, vol. 2, p. 224.   **92** Lynch, 'Administration of John Bole', 43; *AU* 1455.   **93** Cogan, *The diocese of Meath*, vol. 2, pp 225–6; Hardiman, *A statute of the fortieth year of King Edward III*, 2, p. 25.   **94** R. Ó Floinn, 'The foundation relics of Christ Church Cathedral and the origins of the diocese of Dublin' in Seán

English and Welsh saints David, Oswald, Wolfstan and Edward the Confessor were also included in the collection.[95] Irish saints were represented by relics of Ss Patrick, Brigid, Laurence O'Toole and Brendan, as well as by a portable marble altar associated with St Patrick.

Devotion to foreign saints was also evident at Augustinian foundations elsewhere in Ireland. In 1435, the priory of Rathkeale, Co. Limerick, was recorded as being the site of 'manifest miracles' by the 'merits of St Mary the Virgin and the devotion of a venerable image' of the French saint Radegund.[96] Athassel Priory, Co. Tipperary, discussed above by Tadhg O'Keeffe, possessed an image of its patron saint, the Anglo-Saxon king and martyr Edmund of East Anglia, which stood next to the high altar with the saint holding a lance in his right hand. The monastery was founded at the turn of the thirteenth century as the mausoleum of the de Burgh family and the statue was said to throw the lance along the choir of the church every time the head of the Clanwilliam Burkes died. St Edmund was also said to protect sheep grazing near the abbey from attacks by wolves.[97]

PROTECTION OF PILGRIMS

In addition to its spiritual significance, pilgrimage was a lucrative business and many communities depended on pilgrim offerings to meet their expenses or to pay for repairs and renovation to the buildings.[98] Pilgrim offering to the relics of the True Cross probably financed the fifteenth-century rebuilding of the Cistercian house of Holycross Abbey, Co. Tipperary.[99] It was therefore in the interest of communities to secure the protection and free movement of pilgrims, particularly during periods of political unrest. This concern overrode the ethnic divisions within medieval Irish society and although located within the Pale, the Augustinian communities at Holy Trinity Priory, Dublin, Navan and Trim all appealed for royal protection of pilgrims coming from Gaelic areas.

In the early fifteenth century a spate of arrests of pilgrims accused of 'rebellious sentiment' caused much concern to the abbot of Trim, who feared such acts would have a deleterious effect on pilgrim numbers at his shrine. The situation prompted him to write to the king stating that pilgrims had long enjoyed the privilege of protection for their journey to and from the shrine and for the duration of their stay there.[100] The recent arrests and imprisonment of certain pilgrims had been to the detriment of the abbot and the convent, who depended on the oblations made by such pilgrims as their primary source of income. King Henry IV responded by granting protection to all people, Irish rebel or liege subject, going on pilgrimage

Duffy (ed.), *Medieval Dublin VI* (Dublin, 2006), 89–102.   **95** J. Lydon, 'Christ Church in the later medieval world, 1300–1500' in Milne, *CCCD*, p. 93.   **96** Preston, 'The canons regular of St Augustine in medieval Ireland', 184.   **97** Arnold, *Memorials of St Edmund's Abbey*, 3:347–8.   **98** J. Lydon, 'The text and its context', p. xvii; J. Davies, *Pilgrimage yesterday and today: Why? Where? How?* (London, 1988), p. 57; B. Nilson, *Cathedral shrines of medieval Europe* (Woodbridge, 1988), p. 105.   **99** Harbison, *Pilgrimage in Ireland*, p. 305.   **100** Potterton, *Medieval Trim*, p. 306.

to St Mary's at Trim. The grant was confirmed in 1402 and again in 1414.[101] In 1450, Henry VI issued an additional order to ensure the protection of all pilgrims travelling to and from Trim.[102] In 1472/3, parliament extended the protection granted to pilgrims to Trim by Henry VI and '... enacted that anyone despoiling or robbing any pilgrim ... should be stained as a felon.'[103]

Similar efforts were made to protect pilgrims visiting the miraculous statue at the Augustinian Abbey in Navan. In 1454, the parliament of Dublin enacted: '... that letters patent of the King be made (in the form laid down) for taking into protection all people, whether rebel or other, who shall go in pilgrimage to the convent of the Blessed Virgin of Navan'.[104]

The dependence of the canons of Holy Trinity, Dublin, on pilgrimage became starkly clear in 1461 when the east window at Christ Church Cathedral was destroyed by a storm and the repairs were financed from the votive offerings of pilgrims.[105] The damage caused by the falling window was very costly to repair. A letter states, 'the destruction of the two chief windows, commonly called Gabilles, cannot be restored without the aid of Christians and oblations of pilgrims'.[106] Legislation was also issued for the protection of pilgrims visiting Christ Church Cathedral on 26 October 1462, when a royal warrant issued by the king, with the assent of the acting chief governor of Ireland, 'takes into his protection all who shall come to the said church [Christ Church], as well English rebels as Irish enemies in time of war or peace for the sake of pilgrimage or presenting alms'.[107]

Further legislation was issued in 1491 and was confirmed by a provincial council of the archdiocese of Dublin in 1495 when it was decreed that 'offenders' who harassed pilgrims 'are to be liable to the greater excommunication'. This was also confirmed in similar terms by an Armagh synod in the same year'.[108] The efforts by Christ Church to protect Irish pilgrims and the potential revenue that they brought to the monastery is very interesting in light of attempts by the Dublin municipal assembly to drive all Irish men and women from the city.[109] The Augustinians at St Patrick's Purgatory were likewise concerned about the safety and well-being of their pilgrims. In 1507, Donatus Magrahe, prior of St Patrick's Purgatory, issued a letter of credence to Nylanus O'Ledan, stating he had completed his pilgrimage and asking for safe passage and shelter in the lands he travelled through and offering those who provided alms an indulgence, stating they were to 'share in all the indulgences of divers Roman pontiffs and other bishops granted to our place,

101 Ibid. 102 Ibid., p. 307; P. Connolly, *Statute rolls of the Irish parliament, Richard III to Henry VIII* (Dublin, 2000), p. 176. 103 Potterton, *Medieval Trim*, p. 307. 104 Cogan, *The diocese of Meath*, vol. 2, p. 225; Hardiman, *A statute of the fortieth year of King Edward III*, 2, p. 51. 105 McEnery and Refaussé, *Christ Church deeds*, p. 90, no. 297. 106 Stalley, 'Architecture of the cathedral and priory buildings, 1250–1530' in Milne, *CCCD*, p. 100. 107 Lydon, 'Christ Church in the later medieval world, 1300–1500', p. 86; McEnery and Refaussé, *Christ Church deeds*, p. 90, no. 297. 108 Lydon, 'Christ Church in the later medieval world, 1300–1500', p. 86 fn. 69; Lydon, 'The text and its context', pp xvi–xvii; H.J. Lawlor, 'A calendar of the *Liber Niger* and *Liber Albus* of Christ Church, Dublin', *PRIA*, 27C (1908): 25–6. 109 Lydon, 'Christ Church in the later medieval world, 1300–1500', p. 86.

which sum up to ten thousand six hundred and seven years, and also of the suffrages of our Order in masses, psalmody, prayers, stations and other pious works as best we can'.[110]

THE CANONS AS PILGRIMS

From their emergence in Ireland in the twelfth century the Augustinian canons played a key role in the development of pilgrimage in medieval Ireland and not only as curators of old and newly established pilgrim shrines. Many of their members, like those of other Irish religious orders, also undertook pilgrimages themselves to holy places within and outside of Ireland.[111] In 1470, for example, Archbishop John Bole of Armagh (1457–71) granted licence to Brother Patrick O Segill (or O'Fegill), priest and canon of the monastery of Ss Peter and Paul, Armagh, to go on pilgrimage, and be absent from his monastery for seven years.[112] Likewise, in 1485 Abbot John Purcell of St Thomas the Martyr in Dublin petitioned parliament to go to the shrine of St Thomas Becket at Canterbury.[113]

Evidence for pilgrimage to the shrine of St James at Santiago de Compostela comes from archaeological excavations at various Augustinian sites. At the abbey of St Thomas the Martyr in Dublin, two thirteenth-century pilgrim burials were uncovered during recent excavations. Each contained a single scallop shell, the characteristic emblem of the Compostela pilgrimage.[114] Both burials were adult males aged approximately 30 years at time of death and it is not certain that they were canons, as the graveyard was also used for lay burials. The abbey was located close to the pilgrim hostel at St James's Gate and it may have taken responsibility for the burial of unfortunate pilgrims who died while resident there. The remains of two pilgrims were found during excavations at the Augustinian priory of *Domus Dei* in Mullingar, Co. Westmeath, in the 1990s. One burial had a perforated scallop shell under its chin. The second burial had a perforated scallop shell on the left arm and the excavator suggests that these were members of the monastic community.[115]

CONCLUSION

At the onset of the religious and social upheavals of the sixteenth century the Augustinian canons controlled more pilgrim sites than any other order in Ireland. It is not surprising that during the first wave of iconoclasm in Ireland, the shrines

110 L. Bieler. 'Letter of credence by Donatus Magrahe, prior of Lough Derg, for Nylanus O Ledan, priest and pilgrim', *Clogher Record*, 2:2 (1958), 257–9.   111 The remains of a Dominican pilgrim to Santiago were uncovered during excavations at Tralee. See Michael Connolly, 'Investigations in the Abbey, Tannery & Tesco Car Parks, Tralee, Co. Kerry', Excavations carried out in 2000 under License 00E0433. Unpublished Excavation Report, 2000. For pilgrimages undertaken by Augustinian friars see C. Ó Clabaigh, *The friars in Ireland, 1224–1540* (Dublin, 2012), p. 198.   112 A. Lynch, 'Register of John Bole', 152.   113 P. Connolly (ed.), *Statute rolls of the Irish parliament, Richard III–Henry VIII* (Dublin, 2002), p. 53.   114 Paul Duffy, pers. comm. 115 Michael Gibbons, pers. comm. See also B. Cunningham, *Medieval Irish pilgrims*, pp 101–5 for

and relics they had so carefully guarded were among the first to be targeted and destroyed. In 1538, Archbishop George Browne of Dublin ordered the destruction of the relics of Christ Church, along with the *Bacall Íosa* and the Holy Cross of Ballyboggan.[116] The burning of the images of Our Lady of Trim and of Navan soon followed and the Annals of Loch Ce for the same year noted:

> The very miraculous image of Mary which was in the town of Ath-Truim, in which all the people of Erinn believed for a long time previously, which healed the blind, and deaf and lame, and every other ailment, was burnt by Saxons; and the Bachall-Isa, which was in the town of Ath-Cliath, ... and not alone this, but there was not in Erinn a holy cross, or a figure of Mary, or an illustrious image, over which their power reached, that was not burned.[117]

The Tudor Reformation and the dissolution of the monasteries brought the Augustinian involvement with medieval Irish pilgrimage to an end, but despite this disconnect and the destruction of many of their holy relics, some of the monasteries, especially those that developed from early medieval foundations, functioned as centres of devotion up to the nineteenth century, with sites such as Lough Derg and St Mullins in Carlow continuing as active places of pilgrimage to the present day. Although bereft of the canons' services, pilgrims now interact with these pilgrimage landscapes on their own terms, an enduring testimony to the capacity of these holy sites to speak with their own authority.

the canons' role in maitaining an infrastructure catering to the needs of pilgrims and travellers throughout Ireland.   **116** *State papers, Henry VIII*, 1515–38, ii, pt III, p. 35.   **117** The Annals of the Four Masters record the event in the year 1537. It is possible that the *Bachall Íosa* survived this destruction, as in 1561 it was reported that men were going around the countryside and using it to assist women in childbirth; see R. Gillespie, *Devoted people: belief and religion in early modern Ireland* (Manchester, 1997), p. 161.

Community, commemoration and confraternity: the chapter office and chapter books in Irish Augustinian foundations*

COLMÁN Ó CLABAIGH OSB

The chapter office or daily gathering of medieval religious communities was central to their discipline and self-identity. Although its origins are obscure, by the eleventh century it was a universal feature of Western monastic communities and had given rise to a distinctive architectural space – the chapter room – and a body of texts known as *libri capituli* or chapter books. This essay assesses the evidence for the chapter office in the Irish Augustinian foundations, analyses the surviving *libri capituli* from Dublin and Navan and demonstrates how the gathering shaped the regular canons' articulation of their vocation to themselves, to their novices and to their benefactors in medieval Ireland.

THE CHAPTER OFFICE

Although the sixth-century Rule of St Benedict envisaged abbots consulting and instructing their communities and provided for a daily assignment of manual labour at certain times of the year, it made no provision for a formal daily gathering or chapter office.[1] The earliest legislation for this emerged in the eighth century and envisaged the recitation of certain prayers, the reading of the day's martyrology, confession of faults and assignment of daily tasks. With the Carolingian monastic reforms undertaken by the synods of Aachen (816–19) the basic outline of the office with its reading of the calendar, martyrology, monastic rule and scripture lesson, followed by the transaction of business and the confession of faults became established and, subject to embellishments, remained the norm for the rest of the Middle Ages.[2]

The significance of this daily gathering led to the emergence of a designated space known as the *domus capituli*, the chapter room or chapter house.[3] This was

---

* For Dom Anton Höslinger, Can. Reg. **1** *Regula S. Benedicti* 3:48. **2** For the development of the chapter office see Jean-Loup Lemaître, '*Libri Capituli*: Le Livre du Chapitre, des origines au XVI siècle. L'exemple Français' in K. Schmid and J. Wollasch (eds), *Memoria: der geschichtliche Zeugniswert des liturgischen Gedenkens im Mittelalter* (Munich, 1984), pp 625–48. See also J.T. Sorrentino, 'The chapter office in the Gilbertine order' in Burton and Stöber, *Canons*, pp 173–89 at 181–4 for its development in an English Augustinian milieu. **3** The role of the chapter house in shaping Cistercian identity is discussed by Meghan Cassidy-Welch, *Monastic spaces and*

12.1 Chapter house entrance, St Mary's Abbey, Cong, Co. Mayo. Photo: Rachel Moss.

normally situated in the east range of the claustral complex and took its designation from the reading of a section or a 'chapter' of the monastic rule that formed an integral part of the proceedings. Although the chapter house became a routine feature of monastic architecture, not every community possessed one and many smaller foundations may have used other locations for their meetings. With the exception of the Augustinian nunnery at Killone, Co. Clare, for instance, none of the Irish Augustinian nunneries have readily identifiable chapter houses.[4] The spiritual significance of the chapter room was reflected in its architecture, which often referenced that of the church.[5] The entrance doorway was frequently ornamented with elaborate mouldings, as is still evident at Ballintubber Abbey, Co. Mayo; Ballybeg Priory, Co. Cork; Holy Trinity Priory, Dublin and Newtown Trim priory, Co. Meath. Sometimes, as at Kells Priory, Co. Kilkenny; Holy Trinity, Dublin and Cong, Co. Mayo, the doorway was flanked by ornate windows that provided additional illumination and allowed latecomers to follow its proceedings externally (Fig. 12.1).

their meaning: thirteenth century English Cistercian houses (Turnhout, 2001), pp 105–32.   **4** See the contribution by T. Collins above, pp 97–100.   **5** T. O'Keeffe, *Medieval Irish buildings, 1100–1600*

12.2 The chapter house, Holy Trinity Priory, Dublin. Photo: Rachel Moss.

In smaller communities, the chapter room extended the breadth of the east range, but at Athassel, Co. Tipperary, Canon Island, Co. Clare and Holy Trinity, Dublin it extended beyond the line of the range, an arrangement more frequently found in Cistercian foundations.[6] Relatively few Augustinian chapter houses had stone vaults, with evidence surviving at Athassel and Holy Trinity, Dublin. At the east end of the room two or three large windows illuminated the space and provided an architectural frame for the superior's seat, which often stood on a dais and was surmounted by a cross or crucifix. This orientation had symbolic resonance as the superior was believed to hold the place of Christ in the community and the early morning scheduling of the meeting meant that the rising sun, another Christological symbol, illuminated the proceedings. The community sat on stone or wooden benches flanking the north and south walls of the room and these still survive at Holy Trinity Priory, Dublin (Fig. 12.2). The chapter room routinely functioned as a mausoleum for deceased superiors. At the Cistercian abbeys of Fountains and Byland in Yorkshire these abbatial burials were clustered around the abbot's seat, symbolically underpinning his authority by linking him spatially with his deceased predecessors.[7] Miriam Clyne suggests that this arrangement explains

(Dublin, 2015), pp 148–53, 160–4.   **6** R. Stalley, *The Cistercian monasteries of Ireland* (New Haven, 1987), pp 162–6.   **7** Cassidy-Welch, *Monastic spaces*, pp 113–16.

the pattern of burials in the chapter house of the Premonstratensian foundation at Lough Key, Co. Roscommon.[8]

Given its importance, the rituals governing the chapter meeting received detailed instructions in monastic customaries.[9] The constitutions of the Arrouaisian canons and the *Liber ordinis* of the Victorines illustrate how, ideally, the daily chapter meeting was conducted, though factors like the size of the communities and fluctuating levels of observance were likely influential factors. As both Scott and Galban demonstrate below, at the dissolution most Irish Augustinian communities were tiny, with some having only one, two or five members, while Dublin's largest houses, St Thomas's Abbey and Holy Trinity Priory, hosted nine and twelve canons respectively. Nor was this a sixteenth-century aberration. In 1468, Archbishop Michael Tregury conducted a visitation of the Dublin houses. At Holy Trinity, there were eight canons; at Holmpatrick, four; at All Hallows, six and at St Thomas's, twelve. The female communities at St Mary de Hogges and Grace Dieu respectively housed four and six nuns.[10] For such communities the elaborate ritual prescribed must have been more honoured in the breach than in the observance. Nevertheless, they represented a standard to which they could aspire and of which some of them were demonstrably aware.

Early each morning in both Arrouaisian and Victorine houses, the community assembled in the cloister walk after the office of Prime where, when instructed by the abbot, the canon responsible for timekeeping gave the signal, possibly by beating the *tabula lignea* or wooden percussion board in the corner of the cloister, and the entire community processed to the chapter room in pairs. Members observed the same conventual order that they did in church, with the seniors leading the procession and the juniors at the end. On entering the chapter room, they proceeded as far as the central pulpit or lectern and bowed to venerate the crucifix over the superior's seat. They then assembled next to the benches that flanked the walls, each bowing to the abbot as he processed to his seat. When he sat down, each canon did likewise and the door of the chapter house was closed. Latecomers were instructed not to disrupt proceedings by knocking, but to remain seated in the cloister near the door of the parlour.

Once assembled, the canon appointed to read at the chapter sought a blessing from the superior and commenced reading from the chapter book on the lectern. He first announced the calends (a dating system based on the phases of the moon and varying from month to month), before reading the relevant entry from the martyrology commemorating the saints or liturgical celebrations that occurred on that day. This was followed by a reading of a section from the Rule of St Augustine and, if it was a Sunday, solemn feast day or during the octaves of Easter and

---

8 See above, pp 80–2. **9** See L. Jocqué and L. Milis, *Liber ordinis Santi Victoris Parisiensis* (Turnhout, 1984), pp 153–63 and L. Milis, *Constitutiones canonicorum regularium ordinis Arroasiensis* (Turnhout, 1990), pp 37–43. For an overview of Victorine practice see J. Mousseau, 'Daily life at the abbey of Saint Victor' in Feiss and Mousseau, *Saint Victor*, pp 55–78 at pp 72–3. **10** H.F. Berry, *Register of the wills and inventories of the diocese of Dublin* (Dublin, 1898), pp 172–8.

Pentecost, by the gospel reading from that day's Mass. He then read from the necrology, the book listing the anniversaries of those who had been granted a share in the suffrages of the community. When the customary prayers for the dead had been recited, the *armarius* or librarian announced the liturgical duties that each member was to perform until the time of the next chapter meeting. Each canon was urged to listen diligently to this and to indicate by a sign to the superior if he foresaw any difficulty in discharging his assignment. After this, the abbot or another delegated by him might preach a sermon to the chapter, following which the lay brothers, visiting religious and other guests were led out before the chapter of faults began.

The chapter of faults was integral to the maintenance of discipline within medieval monasteries, although participants sometimes viewed it with trepidation.[11] In Victorine and Arrouaisian houses it began with an invitation from the abbot or, in his absence the prior or subprior, to 'speak of the things of our order', after which individual canons stood or prostrated themselves before him and accused themselves of any infractions of monastic observance that they had committed. Participants were warned that matters of conscience and sinful behaviour were reserved for private sacramental confession, which was available at the end of the meeting. In Victorine communities, the abbot then invited an official known as the *circator* to speak.[12] His function was to circumambulate the monastery in the course of the day and observe what the brethren were doing. If he spotted any misbehaviour he was not to comment on it immediately, but to wait until the following chapter to make it known. This official is the subject of a detailed section of the *Liber ordinis* and was warned not to let ties of friendship interfere with his duties.[13] After this the canons could accuse their confreres of faults or transgressions that they had omitted to declare or had forgotten. Accusations were to be made against individuals rather than against the whole community or a section thereof and had to concern something that had been witnessed rather than grounded on hearsay. The accused was urged not to dispute the charge but to seek pardon and promise amendment. Canons were also forbidden to denounce their accuser of any fault during the same chapter. If the superior determined that the transgression warranted a beating, the accused stripped to the waist and was whipped by a confrere. Among the Victorines, this punishment was administered by one of equal or superior rank to the miscreant rather than by a junior canon.[14] Perhaps significantly, at this stage both the Arrouaisian constitutions and the Victorine *Liber ordinis* forbid, in almost identical terms, any canon from revealing what has been disclosed at the chapter of faults or any other confidential matters discussed at the meeting.[15] In the Victorine customary, provision was made at this juncture for the abbot to assign or dismiss canons from various assignments.

11 For Premonstratensian attitudes to the chapter of faults see M. Clyne above, p. 80. 12 Jocqué and Milis, *Liber ordinis*, p. 158. 13 Jocqué and Milis, *Liber ordinis*, pp 194–6. See also H. Feiss, '*Circatores*: From Benedict of Nursia to Humbert of Romans', *The American Benedictine Review*, 40:4 (1989), 346–79, particularly 357–8 and 363–4. 14 Jocqué and Milis, *Liber ordinis*, p. 161. 15 Jocqué and Milis, *Liber ordinis*, p. 161; Milis, *Constitutiones*, p. 41.

The chapter meeting was also the forum at which the community interacted formally with representatives of other religious communities and with high-ranking benefactors and patrons and the constitutions contain detailed instructions regarding how such visitors were to be received.[16] Frequently, such visitors sought a share in the prayers, penances and spiritual exercises of the community. In acceding to these requests the canons were themselves to ask for a similar remembrance in the prayers of the visitors and of their respective communities and, as shown below, such spiritual networks existed in Ireland. These interactions provided an opportunity for benefactors to endow the community and the canons were instructed to request such support from visiting bishops and rulers. Once this had concluded, a designated canon conducted the visitors from the chapter room. Appropriate behaviour was expected at all times during the chapter meeting and young Victorine canons were sternly warned against any inclination to levity.[17] Having concluded the day's business, the presider recited a prayer, the community turned towards the east and bowed and then withdrew to continue the day's work, with the exception of those who remained behind either to confess their sins or to consult the abbot. The final collect of the chapter book of Holy Trinity Priory in Dublin is probably representative of how the chapter meeting in most Irish Augustinian houses concluded and demonstrates how it set the tone for the brethren as they set about their daily tasks:

> May the glory of the Lord be upon us and direct the work of our hands. Let us pray: Holy Lord, Father all-powerful, eternal God, deign to direct, bless and rule today and every day our hearts and our bodies by your holy law and in the works of your commandments so that now and forever, by your aid, we may merit to be saved, safe and free.[18]

IRISH CHAPTER BOOKS

The various elements in the daily chapter office led to the emergence of a distinctive body of monastic literature known as *libri capituli* or chapter books. Although subject to local variations, these included the texts necessary for the celebration of the office: the martyrology, lectionary, monastic rule and necrology. They might also include commentaries on the rule, customaries, didactic texts and legislative and devotional material.

The earliest Irish chapter literature to survive is contained in TCD MS 576 from the Augustinian priory of Holy Trinity, Dublin. It consists of two separate parts, a calendar and martyrology compiled in the mid-thirteenth century and discussed above and elsewhere by Pádraig Ó Riain, and the early sixteenth-century list of

---

16 Jocqué and Milis, *Liber ordinis*, pp 161–2; Milis, *Constitutiones*, pp 41–2.   **17** Jocqué and Milis, *Liber ordinis*, p. 162.   **18** J.C. Crosthwaite and H.H. Todd, *The book of obits and the martyrology of the Cathedral Church of the Holy Trinity, commonly called Christ Church, Dublin* (Dublin, 1844) p. 240.

the cathedral's relics and the community's necrology or Book of Obits. It is not clear when the two texts were bound together, but an inscription by Archbishop James Ussher suggests that this had occurred by the early seventeenth century. The volume may have passed with the rest of Ussher's manuscripts to the library of Trinity College in 1661. In 1844, the Irish Archaeological Society published an edition of the complete text prepared by J.C. Crosthwaite with an introduction by J.H. Todd.[19]

TCD MS 97, from St Thomas's Abbey in Dublin, is a composite volume of 297 vellum leaves containing texts transcribed by various scribes in the late thirteenth and early fourteenth centuries. In addition to a calendar (incomplete) and martyrology, it contains a wide range of theological, devotional and didactic material designed to complement the texts required for the chapter office and constituting a 'handbook' that elucidated the canonical vocation and fostered a sense of corporate identity. The penultimate folio bears the signature of the last abbot, Henry Duff, who surrendered the house in 1538. This codex also belonged to Archbishop Ussher and in 1661 passed to the library of Trinity College, Dublin.[20] The material from St Mary's Abbey in Navan is fragmentary and consists of two elements now bound together in Oxford Bodleian Library MS Rawlinson B. 486, a miscellany of texts assembled by Sir James Ware. These consist of the first four chapters of the commentary on the Rule of St Augustine attributed to Hugh of St Victor and a portion of a fifteenth-century martyrology.[21]

CALENDARS, COMPUTUS AND MARTYROLOGIES

The initial texts in both the Christ Church and the St Thomas's volumes are calendars listing the feast days and celebrations of the liturgical year. As is customary with such documents each month is assigned a separate page and each entry consists of a single line indicating the saint or celebration. The rank of each holy day is designated by the use of black, blue or red ink for the entries, with initials after each entry indicating the degree of solemnity with which it was celebrated. As the liturgical year contained both fixed and movable celebrations, the calendars also contain the complex astronomical and mathematical tables necessary to compute the moveable feasts. In the Holy Trinity volume an introductory page consisting of four tabular columns with computational data, followed by nineteen columns giving sample reckonings for random years between

19 Colker, *Latin MSS*, pp 1038–40. See also R. Refaussé, 'The Christ Church manuscripts in context' in Gillespie & Refaussé, *Med. MSS*, pp 13–32 at pp 22–4. **20** Colker, *Latin MSS*, pp 187–95. See also C. Ó Clabaigh, 'Formed by word and example: the training of novices in fourteenth-century Dublin' in K. Stöber et al. (eds), *Monastic life in the medieval British Isles: essays in honour of Janet Burton* (Cardiff, 2018), pp 41–52. I am grateful to Dom Clemens Galban Can. Reg., for his observations on this point. **21** Oxford, Bodl. MS B. 486, ff 4–15, 16–22; D. Ó Corráin, *Clavis litterarum Hibernensium* (3 vols, Turnhout, 2017), vol. 3, p. 1718; J.H. Todd, 'Obits of eminent individuals and other notices connected with Navan and its neighbourhood', *PRIA,*

1167 and 1620, precedes the calendar, while in both manuscripts each page of the calendar contains three columns, containing the necessary aids for computation. These consisted of the 'golden numbers' (1–19), which facilitated calculation of the position of the moon; the 'dominical' or 'Sunday letters' (A–G), which determined the day of the week on which a feast might fall and the Roman calendar giving the calends, nones and ides of each month (Plate 14). Both texts indicate when the sun rose in each house of the zodiac and in the St Thomas's calendar the astrological symbol for each month is incorporated into the marginal decoration of the page. This information facilitated the calculation of horoscopes, a routine feature of medieval life.[22] Both texts also include marginalia and calendar verses, short rhyming phrases and mnemonic devices that conveyed liturgical and astrological information. Thus verses in the Holy Trinity calendar give the lunar formulas indicating the beginning of Lent and the end of Rogationtide, the dates of Easter and Pentecost and when to cease singing 'alleluia' in the liturgy.[23] Both calendars also included verses indicating when the 'Egyptian days' occurred in each month. These were also known as the dismal days (dies mali) on which it was inauspicious to start a journey, initiate a project or undergo procedures like bloodletting or surgery.[24]

The ability to determine the variable elements of the calendar was known as computus, proficiency in which was a fundamental requirement of clerical education. This gave rise to a body of specialist literature that is well represented in the St Thomas's volume. In addition to the marginalia in the calendar, it also includes more advanced computistical literature including the Doctrina tabularum, attributed to the English friar-philosopher Roger Bacon (d. 1292) and the Massa compoti (ff 7–32) of the French Franciscan mathematician Alexander of Villedieu.[25] This latter text was composed in verse and was one of the most widely consulted works in the field.

As Pádraig Ó Riain has noted above, the regular canons played a pivotal role in the production of liturgical books and the writing of hagiography in twelfth- and thirteenth-century Ireland. The martyrologies that survive from Dublin and Navan corroborate this and demonstrate the different influences to which the canons were susceptible. As the title suggests, a martyrology initially consisted of a daily listing of martyrs, indicating the dates and places of their deaths. Over time this expanded to include other significant commemorations: events in the life of Christ and the Blessed Virgin; feast days of the apostles, patriarchs, confessors and virgins, the translations of relics and the anniversaries of church dedications. The earliest martyrology, spuriously attributed to St Jerome (d. 420), was compiled in either Gaul or Italy in the late sixth or seventh century and provided the basis for all subsequent texts. These included the so-called historical martyrologies that emerged from the early eighth century, which consisted of short summaries of the

7C (1861), 367.   **22** P. Ó Riain, 'The calendar and martyology of Christ Church' in Gillespie and Refaussé, Med. MSS, pp 33–76 at p. 39.   **23** Crostwhaite and Todd, Book of obits, pp 61–5. **24** J. Hennig, 'Versus de mensibus', Traditio, 11 (1955), 65–90 at 84.   **25** TCD MS 97, ff 5–6v; ff 7–32. Roger Bacon, Opera Hactenus Inedita VI (Oxford, 1926), ed. R. Steele, pp 284–9; 268–89.

saints' lives arranged calendrically. The text composed by the Northumbrian monk Bede the Venerable (d. 735) was an influential exemplar of this format and was subsequently expanded by three ninth-century writers from Gaul: Florus of Lyon (d. 860), Ado of Vienne (d. 875) and Usuard of St Germain des Prés (d. *c.*877). Of these texts the work of Ado and Usuard proved most influential in Irish Augustinian circles.[26]

The transmission history of the version of Ado's martyrology in the Holy Trinity codex sheds fascinating light on both the life of the priory and the origins of the diocese of Dublin.[27] Whereas the present text dates to the mid-thirteenth century, it derives from an exemplar that was transmitted to Dublin via Irish Benedictine circles in Germany *c.*1028/30. At each stage of transmission it acquired local accretions that enable its trajectory to be traced. Once in Ireland the text circulated in Augustinian circles from the middle of the twelfth century and Ó Riain argues that this occurred in the context of liturgical reforms promoted by Bishop Gregory (Gréne) who was elevated to archiepiscopal rank in 1152. The addition of various English feast days is indicative of Anglo-Norman influence after 1169, while the thirteenth-century mendicant commemorations including the Dominican St Peter of Vercelli (d. 1252, canonized 1253) give a *terminus ad quem* for the production of the text.

The martyrology used by the canons of St Thomas was an adaptation of that of Usuard of St Germain-des-Prés.[28] This was the most popular of the medieval martyrologies and its influence in Irish Augustinian circles is evident from the late twelfth century when Máel Muire Ua Gormáin, abbot of Knock, Co. Louth, used it as a source for the vernacular, versified martyrology he composed between 1168 and 1170. The text was adapted for use at St Thomas's sometime after 1253, as it also includes an entry for St Peter of Vercelli, who was canonized in that year. The monastery's dedication to St Thomas Becket accounts for the lengthy entry commemorating his martyrdom (29 December) and the commemoration of the translation of his relics in Canterbury in 1220 (7 July). The community's devotion to St Augustine is evident in the commemoration of his feast day (28 August), along with that of the translation of his relics (11 October). The text is noteworthy for the relatively few Irish commemorations that it includes.[29] Sir James Ware attributed the disarranged, fragmentary, fifteenth-century copy of Usuard's martyrology preserved in Oxford Bodleian Library Rawlinson MS 486 to St Mary's Abbey, Navan. Ó Riain notes its similarities with a characteristically Franciscan version of Usuard's text that circulated in Ireland, most notably the surviving late medieval exemplar from the friary in Youghal. The Navan text contains out of sequence entries for forty-one feast days between May and July.[30]

---

26 See above, pp 207–10. Also Ó Riain, 'Calendar and martyrology', pp 41–4 and P. Ó Riain, *Feastdays of the saints: a history of Irish martyrologies* (Brussels, 2006), pp 119–46. 27 P. Ó Riain, 'Dublin's oldest book? A list of saints "made in Germany"' in S. Duffy (ed.), *Medieval Dublin V* (Dublin, 2004), pp 52–72. 28 TCD MS 97, ff 36v–72v. See also J. Dubois, *Le Martyrologe d'Usuard* (Brussels, 1965). 29 Ó Riain, *Feastdays of the saints*, pp 247–66 at pp 250–4. 30 Ó Riain, *Feastdays of the saints*, pp 261–2.

FORGING A CANONICAL IDENTITY

The reading of a section of the monastic rule formed an integral part of the daily chapter meeting. Given the complex textual history of the dossier of fifth-century texts that constitute the Rule of St Augustine, it is fortunate that the version used at Holy Trinity Priory survives. It provides a unique witness to what the community (and presumably other Irish Arrouaisian houses) heard in chapter on a daily basis.[31] The document consists of the first four chapters of the version known as the *Praeceptum*, divided into sections for daily reading from Monday to Saturday. This textual arrangement is almost identical to that used by the order of Sempringham, an indigenous English religious order whose clerical members also followed the Rule of St Augustine.[32] Although the decision to read only a portion of the Rule was criticized by the nineteenth-century editors of the Book of Obits, the passages selected indicate what elements the community considered important, thereby giving an insight into its *mentalité*.[33] Thus, on Monday, the canons were urged to live in harmony, possessing all things in common and being content with whatever they received from the superior. On Tuesday, members who came from a lower social background were urged not to covet possessions that would previously have been beyond their means or to become proud because they now associated with those of higher status. Conversely, on Wednesday, canons from higher social positions were warned not to despise poorer confreres or to think the community beholden to them if they had contributed some resources to it. All members were urged to live in harmony and concord, to be assiduous in prayer at the appointed times, thereby giving honour to God. On Thursday, attention turned to more practical matters. The canons were admonished to honour the monastery oratory as a place of prayer and not to conduct any business there. They were urged to fast if their strength allowed it, while those who couldn't were instructed to at least refrain from eating between meals and to listen attentively to the devotional reading that accompanied dining. On Friday, the community members were instructed not to disparage those who received concessions concerning food or clothing but instead to give thanks for their own ability to bear the burdens that others could not. Care of the sick and decorous behaviour was dealt with on Saturday. Convalescent brethren were to be given whatever treatment they needed but were warned not to let dietary dispensations become a 'pleasure that ensnares them'.[34] Likewise the canons were encouraged to be modest in their dress and to edify people by their behaviour rather than their appearance. They were not to leave the monastery without a companion and in their

---

31 The standard account of the evolution of the Augustinian Rule remains L. Verheijen (ed.), *La Règle de St Augustin*, 2 vols (Paris, 1967). See also G. Lawless, *Augustine of Hippo and his monastic Rule* (Oxford, 1987), pp 65–154. TCD MS 347, a late thirteenth-century Franciscan *vademecum*, contains a copy of the Rule along with an anonymous commentary. See Colker, *Latin MSS*, p. 736. **32** Sorrentino, 'Chapter office', p. 186. The female branch of the Gilbertines followed the Rule of St Benedict. **33** Crosthwaite and Todd, *Book of obits*, p. lxxxviii. **34** Ibid., p. 240.

deportment and bearing were to act at all times in a manner appropriate to their calling.[35]

The brevity of the Rule of St Augustine made it adaptable to a wide variety of needs and circumstances. Unlike the Rule of St Benedict, it contains relatively few prescriptive elements governing the practical aspects of communal living. These were supplied by the various commentaries and constitutions that proliferated as part of the canonical revival in the eleventh and twelfth centuries. Of these, the works produced by the canons of St Victor in Paris enjoyed widespread circulation and several were included in the St Thomas's codex. These provide an invaluable insight into how the Dublin community sought to foster an *esprit de corps* and to convey this to its members, particularly novices in the initial phases of formation.[36]

Included among these texts was the influential *Expositio in Regulam S. Augustini.*[37] Long attributed to the pre-eminent Victorine theologian, Hugh of St Victor (d. 1141), this pseudonymous work circulated widely and became the standard commentary on the Augustinian Rule. The library of the Augustinian canons in Leicester, for instance, possessed seven copies of the work.[38] The text consists of a commentary on discrete sections of each of the rule's twelve chapters. In the St Thomas's codex, the text of the Rule is written in a large-format centrally placed script, while the commentary takes the form of marginal notes written in a smaller hand (Plate 15). In the Navan text, where only the first four chapters of the work survive, the commentary occurs directly after each section of the Rule.[39] The St Thomas's manuscript also contains the unique copy of the *De quaestionibus Regulae S. Augustini* by Richard of St Victor (d. 1173), a Scottish canon who served as subprior of St Victor from 1159 to 1162 and as prior from 1162 to 1173.[40] The commentary takes the form of responses to twenty practical questions on Augustinian life and observance posed by a Br Simon.[41] These included the reasons why a canon could legitimately withdraw from the monastery of his profession, what elements of the Rule of Augustine were universally binding, what the commitment to living without personal property entailed, how the canons were to conduct the liturgy and what obligations they had regarding fasting and abstinence. Other issues addressed include how they were to guard chastity, engage in spiritual reading and an instruction that they travel in pairs when engaged in business outside the monastery.

In addition to the rule of St Augustine, two other texts were of seminal importance in shaping the lives of Victorine communities and both are included in the St Thomas's codex. These were the customary of the abbey of St Victor in

35 Ibid., pp 235–40. **36** What follows summarizes Ó Clabaigh, 'Formed by word and example'. **37** TCD MS 97, ff 73–95. **38** T. Webber and A.G. Watson (eds), *The libraries of the Augustinian canons* (London, 1998), pp 161, 182, 399. **39** Hugo de S. Victore, *Expositio in Regulam S. Augustini* (Paris: *Patrologia Latina* 176, 1854), pp 881–924. See also the translation by A. Smith, *Explanation of the Rule of St Augustine by Hugh of St Victor, canon regular* (London, 1911). **40** TCD MS 97, ff 95–102. **41** M.L. Colker, 'Richard of St Victor and the Anonymous of Bridlington', *Traditio*, 18 (1962), 201–23. Colker suggests that this may be Abbot Simon of St Albans, who corresponded with Richard and who had a great interest in the work of Hugh of St Victor.

Paris – the *Liber ordinis S. Victoris* – and Hugh of St Victor's *De institutione nouiciorum*, a treatise on the training of novices. The *Liber ordinis* was compiled *c.*1116 by Gilduin, the first abbot of St Victor, and although initially intended as the customary for the Parisian house, it became normative for houses that adopted the Victorine reform.[42] Divided into ninety chapters, it supplemented the Rule of St Augustine and gave detailed instruction on the practical aspects of cenobitic life, including a detailed description of the Victorine liturgy and an elaborate system of sign language.[43] Whereas customaries were routine features of monastic communities, the degree to which the ritual of Victorine life was prescribed is remarkable even in the context of other contemporary reformed groups. External deportment became an indication of a serene inner life and a means of edifying those who interacted with the canons. This began at the very gates of the monastery where the porter was instructed to receive visitors with 'great kindness and humanity from the first moment of reception … so that from their first impressions of the exterior they may form an estimate of the things concealed within.'[44]

A similar attitude is evident in the reception and training of novices and newcomers to the life and this is reflected in Hugh of St Victor's *De institutione nouiciorum*.[45] Compiled in the early decades of the twelfth century, this proved one of the most widely read of his works and was hugely influential in the formation literature of other religious orders, especially the mendicant friars. It was also quarried by writers of secular courtesy books. Although ostensibly a work about the cultivation of virtue, it lays particular emphasis on the importance of deportment and bearing. As the candidate mastered his external bearing, his inner life would be transformed and he would advance in virtue. An elegant bearing betokened a virtuous mind and the well-ordered functioning of the members of the body produced a harmony of the whole being.[46] As a cleric the canon was to be gracious in all his actions, not just as an expression of self-control but also as a means of edifying others. He was called to instruct both by word and example – *docere verbo et exemplo*.[47]

This emphasis on external deportment and courtliness contextualizes some of the other texts included in TCD MS 97. These include an anonymous, unique text, the *Contra religionis simulatores*. This takes the form of a highly entertaining dialogue between the exemplary Gregory and Romanus, a negligent religious who

---

42 TCD MS 97, ff 102–47. Lucas Jocqué & Ludovicus Milis (eds), *Liber ordinis Sancti Victoris Parisiensis* (Turnhout, 1984). The Dublin text is an early witness to the text and was used in this edition.   **43** H.F. Berry, 'On the use of signs in the ancient monasteries, with special reference to a code used by the Victorine canons of St Thomas's Abbey, Dublin', *JRSAI*, 2:2 (1892), 107–25. **44** *Liber ordinis*, 15, lines 55–6. Cited in C. Stephen Jaeger, 'Victorine humanism' in Feiss and Mosseau, *Saint Victor*, pp 79–112 at p. 90.   **45** TCD MS 97, ff 219–27. H. Feiss and P. Sicard, *L'oeuvre de Hugues de Saint-Victor*, 2 vols (Turnhout, 1997), I, pp 8–114.   **46** Jaeger, 'Victorine humanism', pp 98–9.   **47** C.W. Bynum, 'The spirituality of regular canons in the twelfth century' in C.W. Bynum, *Jesus as mother: studies in the spirituality of the high Middle Ages* (Berkeley, 1982), pp 22–58.

nevertheless believed himself a paragon of monastic observance.[48] It also accounts for the presence of secular courtesy texts for the training of squires. The first of these, the short poem *Facetus*, was composed in the twelfth century and became a staple of the English school curriculum by the fourteenth century. It was loosely modelled on the third-century *Distichs of Cato* and gave advice on courtly conduct in a wide range of social situations, including conversation, interaction with social superiors and table manners.[49] Another work, *Urbanus Magnus*, is the earliest English courtesy book to survive and was composed at the end of the twelfth century by Daniel of Beccles, a courtier who had been in the service of Henry II.[50] It consists of 2,835 lines of Latin verse presented in the form of an instruction from a father to his son. Its intended audience was junior members of aristocratic households who had to interact appropriately with both social superiors and inferiors. The range of situations covered was comprehensive and unflinching and ranged from instructions on how to behave at table to the etiquette of killing one's enemy. Presumably, some of these were superfluous in a monastic context but, nevertheless, the text is heavily annotated and was obviously read carefully.

Although Victorines had a distinctive approach to monastic life and religious formation, they did not forego the insights available in other rules and observances. Consequently, the St Thomas's manuscript provides the earliest witness to the circulation of several other monastic texts in medieval Ireland. These include the earliest Irish copy of the Rule of St Benedict, with extensive marginal annotations; the Rule of the Friars Minor and other foundational Franciscan texts along with the Dublin Anchorites' Rule and another text relating to the reclusive life. The Cistercian tradition is represented by the *Speculum monachorum* of Arnulf de Boeriis (d. 1149), while the inclusion of the *Sententiae ex operibus S. Augustini* by the fifth-century writer Prosper of Aquitaine honours the Augustinian tradition. Noteworthy too is the inclusion of numerous excerpts from patristic sources including the works of Ss Bede, Gregory the Great and Jerome. Likewise, the presence of the influential text *De contemptu mundi* of Innocent III (d. 1216) situates the devotional outlook of the St Thomas's community within the broad current of late medieval spirituality. Combined, all this material articulated a distinctive spiritual tradition that combined clerical and monastic elements. Daily exposure to readings from the Rule of St Augustine and its commentaries re-enforced their self-perception as regular canons while the *Liber ordinis*, with its detailed prescriptions on lifestyle, gestures and conduct, consolidated their identity as Victorines.

48 TCD MS 97, ff 227v–38v. M.L. Colker (ed.), *Analecta Dublinensia: three medieval Latin texts in the library of Trinity College Dublin* (Cambridge, MA, 1975), pp 2–62.   **49** TCD MS 97, ff 253–4; C. Schroeder (ed.), 'Facetus', *Palestra*, 86 (1911), 14–28.   **50** TCD MS 97, ff 254–72v; J. Gilbart Smyly (ed.), *Urbanus Magnus Danielis Becclesiensis* (Dublin, 1939).

COMMEMORATION AND CONFRATERNITY

The expansion of the concept of Purgatory from the tenth century onwards meant that intercessory prayer for the dead became almost the *raison d'être* for medieval monasticism. Benefactors received a share of the merits gained by religious communities through their liturgical, spiritual and ascetic exercises.[51] In an age preoccupied with the post-mortem welfare of the soul and in which prayer was a negotiable commodity, such transactions formed an essential component of a monastery's economy and social networks. Consequently, religious communities assiduously recorded the names of those for whom they owed suffrages. They also promoted various ways in which living benefactors could be admitted to confraternity or enlisted as associates of the community. As both the commemoration of the dead and admission to confraternity took place during the chapter office the formulas for both rituals were included in each orders' customaries.[52]

Initially, obits and anniversaries were entered in the margins of calendars and martyrologies next to the appropriate date. The St Thomas's calendar contains several marginal entries from the thirteenth, fifteenth and sixteenth centuries recording the obits of canons and their relatives along with a 1478 memorandum concerning a property transaction.[53] The Holy Trinity calendar similarly records the death of Thomas FitzGerald, earl of Desmond.[54] Likewise, marginal entries in the Navan martyrology record the anniversaries of Abbots Thomas Devenys (d. 1370) and Patrick Cantwell (d. 1436) along with Master Martin White, rector of Lascartan (d. 1338), who bequeathed a bible and a canon law text to the community. Also recorded are the community's commemoration of deceased parents on 20 June and the admission to confraternity and a share of the community's prayers of seven men and four women from prominent local families.[55]

As the number of anniversaries increased specially dedicated volumes developed to record them. Variously described as *Libri vitae, libri memoriales, libri benefactorum,* necrologies or obituary books, these texts played a central role in commemorations at Mass and in the chapter office. Entries in *Libri vitae* and *Libri benefactorum* were generally not listed in calendrical order. Examples from English Benedictine houses such as the *Liber vitae* of Durham cathedral priory contain the names of several thousand benefactors entered by contemporary hands between the ninth and sixteenth centuries.[56] From 1077 to 1500, the *Liber benefactorum* of St Alban's Abbey

---

51 J. Le Goff, *The birth of Purgatory* (Chicago, 1984). **52** For the relevant texts from the Cluniac, Cistercian, Arrouaisian, Victorine and Premonstatenian statutes see A.-J.A. Bijsterveld, 'Looking for common ground: from monastic *fraternitas* to lay confraternity in the southern Low Countries in the tenth to twelfth centuries' in E. Jamroziak and J. Burton (eds), *Religious and laity in Western Europe, 1000–1400* (Turnhout, 2006), pp 287–314 at pp 311–13. For mendicant confraternity in Ireland see Ó Clabaigh, *Friars in Ireland*, pp 302–4. **53** TCD MS 97, f. 1v. **54** Crosthwaite and Todd, *Book of obits*, p. 61. **55** Todd, 'Obits of eminent individuals', 367. James Butler, earl of Ormond, was among those granted confraternity and another entry records the killing of Barnabas Nangle, Baron Navan, in 1435. **56** D. Rollason, A.J. Piper and M. Harvey, *The*

enlisted over 600 of the community's benefactors including approximately 300 recipients of spiritual confraternity. Lavishly decorated with miniature depictions of various benefactors, it is likely that as with the Durham volume, it reposed on the high altar of the monastery church thereby linking benefactors with the community's celebration of the Eucharist.[57]

Although nothing comparable to the St Alban's volume survives from Ireland, the Book of Obits or necrology of Holy Trinity Priory illustrates the intercessory role of the community and the extent of its networks.[58] Compiled in the early sixteenth century, probably by the community's subprior Thomas Fyche (d. 1518), the volume drew on earlier sources dating back to the foundation of the cathedral. It comprises forty-six vellum folios with each side containing headings for four days of the year. The heading of each entry gives the golden number, the Sunday letter, the date according to the Roman calendar and, where applicable, the feast day or liturgical commemoration. There then follows the names of the deceased with sporadic references to their benefactions and occasionally to the year of their death. In all approximately 1,000 people are commemorated with obits ranging from the eleventh to the mid-sixteenth centuries and with only seven of the 365 days having no entries.

The list constitutes a roll call of the ecclesiastical, political and mercantile elite of medieval Dublin with occasional glimpses of the canons' servants and lay associates. Not surprisingly, the largest group commemorated are the canons themselves with over 133 obits listed. The names of almost two dozen of the thirty-six priors and seven of the subpriors who governed the community are also recorded.[59] Most of these are described as 'our canon and priest', but a minority are described as *conversus*, the term used for a lay brother or non-clerical member of a monastic institute. There is even one reference to Eva, a *conversa*, or female religious who may have lived as an anchoress or vowess attached to the community.[60] There are some five references to *canonici* or *fratres ad succurendum*, men who were received into the community on their deathbeds.[61] Of particular interest are the twenty-nine religious from other communities included in the necrology. This entitled them to the same suffrages as a member of Holy Trinity community and such networks of commemoration were very common. These included canons from St Thomas's Abbey, All Hallows and Holmpatrick priories; canonesses from the priories at Grace Dieu and St Mary de Hogges, Cistercians from St Mary's Abbey and Hospitallers from Kilmainham. Also commemorated are canons from Llanthony Secunda near Gloucester, Cartmel Priory, Cumbria, and a Benedictine monk from St Werburgh's Abbey, Chester, all of whom

Durham Liber vitae and its context (Martlesham, 2004).   **57** J. Clarke, 'Monastic confraternity in medieval England: the evidence from St Alban's Abbey *Liber benefactorum*' in E. Jamroziak and J. Burton (eds), *Religious and laity in Western Europe, 1000–1400* (Turnhout, 2006), pp 315–31. **58** What follows largely summarizes C. Lennon, 'The book of obits of Christ Church Cathedral, Dublin' in Gillespie and Refaussé, *Med. MSS*, pp 163–82.   **59** Lennon, 'Book of obits', p. 168. **60** Crosthwaite and Todd, *Book of obits*, p. 21.   **61** Ibid., pp 9, 10, 30, 52, 53.

presumably came to know the Holy Trinity community as representatives of their own houses' economic interests in Ireland. Significantly, the Book of Obits contains no reference to any members of the city's friaries, an indication that the mendicants were perceived as belonging to another category of religious life and perhaps of low-level antipathy between the various orders.[62]

Given the close association between the canons and the cathedral it is not surprising that prelates and secular clergy from Dublin feature prominently in the Book of Obits. In all thirteen bishops or archbishops of the see are commemorated starting with Bishop Donatus or Dúnán (d. 1074), the first bishop of Dublin, and ending with Archbishop Hugh Yng (d. 1528). A touching inclusion is that of Mabilia, mother of Archbishop Luke, whose own death in 1255 is also recorded.[63] The cathedral's role as a centre of civic religion accounts for the presence of several royal and aristocratic entries. Three kings of England, Edward IV (d. 1483), Henry VIII (d. 1547) and Edward VI (d. 1553), are included as are Richard de Clare 'Strangewyll' or Strongbow (d. 1176) and William Marshal (d. 1219). Members of the Butler family including James, earl of Ormond (d. 1452), and Elizabeth his countess (d. 1451) are also enrolled as are a number of the earls of Kildare. The most fulsome entry relates to Garret *Mór* Fitzgerald (d. 1513), the eighth earl, who granted the community the village of Great Corporan to fund a chantry for his soul, for that of Thomas Plunkett (d. 1519), chief justice of the common pleas, and for all the faithful departed. He also presented one set of cloth-of-gold vestments and donated his purple robe to make another.[64]

The majority of those commemorated belonged to lower social orders, particularly to the mercantile and gentry class. The chantry chapel of the Holy Trinity guild, the city's principal merchants' guild, was located in the cathedral's south aisle. The close connection between the canons and the merchants ensured that thirty-six of the mayors who governed Dublin between 1367 and 1539 are listed in the Book of Obits as are several other prominent officials. Women also figure prominently with over 220 being recorded as benefactors or members of the confraternity.[65] A glimpse of the canons' mundane relationships is evident in the record of the tradesmen and servants who enjoyed confraternity with them. These included a barber, a bellfounder, a blacksmith, a carpenter, a gardener, two goldsmiths and a tiler.[66] No fewer than three of the community's cooks are memorialized including Walter Sennot whose death on Christmas Eve must have been particularly inconvenient.[67]

For the regular canons of St Thomas's Abbey, Holy Trinity Priory and St Mary's Abbey the chapter office played an essential role in establishing their self-identity. Gathered in the chapter room each morning to hear a chapter of the Rule, they constituted the chapter of the monastery, the corporate body that was the community. Repeated exposure to the Rule and its commentators reaffirmed their

---

62 C. Ó Clabaigh, *The friars in Ireland* (Dublin, 2012), pp 143–68.   63 Crosthwaite and Todd, *Book of obits*, pp 23, 35, 53, 54.   64 Lennon, 'Book of Obits', pp 170–1.   65 Ibid., pp 176–9. 66 Crosthwaite and Todd, *Book of obits*, pp 7, 8, 15, 25, 26, 33, 36.   67 Ibid., pp 33, 55.

commitment. The confession and correction of faults reiterated their values and the reception and instruction of novices allowed all to reflect on their vocation and its obligations. This corporate identity transcended time and space. Assembled with the abbot as the representative of Christ, the community's commemoration of the dead united them with the saints in heaven and the souls in purgatory. Through confraternity, they drew their benefactors into a spiritual communion that held the promise of perpetual intercession. This outlook was articulated in the texts that comprised the *Libri capituli*. With the dissolution of the monasteries and the theological upheaval of the Reformation, this worldview shattered and the chapter books passed into desuetude and antiquarianism. Viewed in this light the signature of Henry Duff on the penultimate folio of TCD MS 97 becomes particularly poignant: faced with the collapse of his world, the last abbot of St Thomas's Abbey chose as his memento the volume that for four centuries had articulated all that he and his community had believed in and hoped for.

The dissolution of the Augustinian communities in the Pale during the Henrician period*

BRENDAN SCOTT

Of all of the religious reforms and changes attempted during the Henrician Reformation, the dissolution process was really the only aspect of the early Reformation campaign that actually worked, and probably because of the large amounts of money and property involved. Religious communities certainly occupied an ambiguous position in Henrician Ireland. Eyeing possible material gains for himself, William Brabazon, the notoriously corrupt vice-treasurer, stated that religious houses should be suppressed on the grounds that 'they nourish rebels'.[1] In 1536, Robert Cowley, the chief solicitor, possibly spotting an opportunity to benefit from a dissolution campaign in Ireland similar to that already underway in England, informed Thomas Cromwell that 'the abbayes here doo not kepe soo good Divine Service, as the abbayes in England, being suppressed, did kepe; the religious personages here lesse continent or virtuous, keeping no hospitalitie, saving to theyme silves, theire concubynes [and] childerne'.[2]

But that same year, attempts to dissolve eight small houses were rejected by the parliament (although the Irish property of English houses was confiscated), and opposition, led by a group of Pale families headed by the lawyer Patrick Barnewall, also made clear the unhappiness of some at the threatened closures. They soon began to support the dissolutions, however, once it became clear that they would be beneficiaries in the process and in May 1537, some smaller communities were closed. By September 1538, Henry VIII had decided on total suppression in Ireland, a policy issued formally in April 1539. That same year, it was declared that all religious houses in Ireland 'are at present in such a state that in them the praise of God and the welfare of man are next to nothing regarded'.[3] Of course it was in the interests of those hoping to benefit from the land grab that would follow the dissolutions to paint the communities in as bad a light as possible. The activities of the so-called 'Geraldine League' held up the work of the suppression commission, but by late 1539, most of the Pale houses had surrendered, with more closing in 1540. The dissolution of the Pale's religious communities altered radically the fabric of society, education, religion and charity at that time.

---

*In memoriam Brendan Bradshaw, whose pioneering work on the monastic dissolutions has proved so influential. **1** *State papers, Hen VIII*, ii, 212–13. **2** Ibid., 371. **3** *Cal. pat. rolls Ire., Hen. VIII–Eliz.*, p. 55. For more on this process, see B. Bradshaw, *The dissolution of the religious*

This chapter is concerned with Augustinian religious communities of the Pale (Dublin, Meath and Kildare),[4] and will examine those who benefitted from the closures as well as the fate of the religious who occupied these sites and their properties. This is in many ways a sordid tale, in which few of the participants acquit themselves honourably. The dissolution process forever changed society and the landscape of the Pale.

DUBLIN

The priory of Holmpatrick near Skerries in Co. Dublin was probably dissolved in May 1537. The church there had also served as the parish church 'from time immemorial', so remained open for that purpose. By the time the three acre site was valued on 29 October 1540 it was in a ruinous state and 'worth nothing above repairs'.[5] The prior, Philip Corr, was granted a pension of £8 for life, or until his promotion to a benefice worth £13 6s. 8d., indicating his active participation in the process there.[6] Robert Cowley, Master of the Rolls, had been agitating for this site since at least early October 1536[7] and was leased the site in February 1538 for twenty-one years, but was dead by the time the estate was valued in 1540. It was then granted to John Parker, secretary to Lord Deputy Anthony St Leger, in 1545, although he had an interest in the site since at least 1540.[8]

The next wave of monastic closures in Dublin came in late 1538, when the priory of All Hallows on the outskirts of the city was dissolved on 16 September.[9] All Hallows was an unusual case in the dissolution process. It was granted to the city of Dublin in recognition of the 'siege, famine, miseries, wounds, and loss of blood suffered by the citizens, and their chivalrous service in defending the city against the rebellion of Thomas Fitzgerald'.[10] This case and how it benefitted the city of Dublin demonstrate the reasons why there was not as much outrage as there may otherwise have been in relation to the dissolution programme. In fact, the city had lobbied in 1536 to receive either All Hallows (reckoned to be worth about eighty-four marks a year) or the hospital of St John's, Newgate, in 'consideration of the ruin and decay sustained by the city in the late siege'.[11] Bowing to the inevitable and probably not wishing to make enemies of the local populace, the five-man community led by Prior Walter Hancoke surrendered All Hallows and its possession on 16 November 1538, according to themselves, 'purely of their own volition "for certain just and reasonable causes which prompted their minds and consciences"'.[12] It was granted on 4 February 1539 to the corporation. But as a later

orders in Ireland under Henry VIII (Cambridge, 1974). **4** Four of these communities were held by overseas priories such as Llanthony and Cartmel and will not be discussed here for reasons of space. See A. Hogan, *The priory of Llanthony Prima and Secunda in Ireland, 1172–1541: lands, patronage and politics* (Dublin, 2008). **5** *EIMP*, p. 49. **6** *EIMP*, p. 52. **7** *State papers, Hen. VIII*, ii, pp 370–2; S.G. Ellis and J. Murray (eds), *Calendar of state papers, Ireland, 1509–1547* (Dublin, 2017), pp 102–3. **8** *EIMP*, p. 53; *Fiants Ire., Hen. VIII*, no. 447. **9** *EIMP*, p. 122. **10** *Cal. pat. rolls Ire., Hen. VIII–Eliz.*, p. 48. **11** Ellis and Murray (eds), *Calendar of state papers, Ireland, 1509–1547*, p. 80. **12** *Cal.*

inquisition informs us, Hancoke made sure that before this happened, 'knowing the house to have been suppressed and dissolved, [he] made grants to various persons in fraud & deceit of the king & by coveri & collusion'.[13]

Much of this property seems to have been leased to family members.[14] This was a common move by which religious communities, aware of their impending closures, would sell, lease and grant as many assets as possible before their dissolution, in order to gain something from the property before its confiscation. The authorities were aware of this and Thomas Cusack, one of the commissioners involved in the dissolution process, in a note dated to *c*.1537–8 stated that if the communities of the Pale were suppressed suddenly their goods would amount to £3000, but if they were not suppressed suddenly, the king could expect to receive £1000 less than that amount.[15] A letter from Gerald Aylmer and John Alen to Anthony St Leger in 1538 also noted a rumour in Ireland regarding the suppressions, which was leading the heads of houses to grant 'out their lands and rents'.[16] Brabazon also advised Cromwell to consider waiting until the communities had sown their corn before dissolving them.[17] In any case, the act of suppression in 1537 declared such property transactions in the run up to dissolution null and void, but actions aimed at reversing such grants or sales were rarely taken. The unusual case of All Hallows was concluded in January 1539, when the house and its holdings were granted to the city of Dublin.[18] It later became the site for Trinity College in 1591.

Another unusual case in Dublin was the Augustinian priory of Holy Trinity or Christ Church. Having the double function of monastic house as well as cathedral, in 1537, William Hassard, the prior there, resigned. There were normally eleven or twelve canons in the priory before its dissolution, higher than was the norm at the time. By the dissolution, only the Cistercian houses of St Mary's in Dublin and Mellifont had higher numbers residing within their walls. Judging by the surnames, the overwhelming majority of canons there were English or Anglo-Irish in origin.[19] There was also a number of canons who joined the Christ Church community when their own establishments were closed in England. Most of the canons came from prominent Dublin families, such as the Balls and Stanihursts. In reality, Christ Church carried out a threefold function – the Irish parliament also met in the refectory of Christ Church, giving it an important civic role function also.[20] Christ Church, like Trim, also held two famous relics – the *baculus Jhesu* (or Staff of Jesus) and a 'speaking crucifix', along with less important relics as well.[21] These would have generated a steady revenue stream for Christ Church, as did ringing of bells for monthly and yearly minds (£1 12*s*. 2*d*.), funerals (15*s*.) and other small offerings,

---

pat. rolls Ire., *Hen. VIII–Eliz.*, p. 47; *Fiants Ire.*, *Hen. VIII*, no. 70; Bradshaw, *The dissolution of the religious orders in Ireland*, p. 99.   **13** M.C. Griffith (ed.), *Calendar of inquisitions formerly in the office of the chief remembrance of the exchequer prepared from the MSS of the Irish Record Commission* (Dublin, 1991), p. 74.   **14** Ibid., pp 71–4.   **15** Ellis and Murray (eds), *Calendar of state papers, Ireland, 1509–1547*, p. 111.   **16** Ibid., p. 195.   **17** Ibid., p. 102.   **18** *Cal. pat. rolls Ire.*, *Hen. VIII–Eliz.*, pp 47–8; *Fiants Ire.*, *Hen. VIII*, no. 70.   **19** R. Gillespie, 'The coming of reform, 1500–58' in Milne, *CCCD*, pp 151–73 at p. 154.   **20** Ibid., p. 157.   **21** *MRHI*, p. 171.

which amounted to the not inconsiderable sum of £26 6s. 8d. Indeed, proceeds from the offerings to the Staff of Jesus were enough to support the maintenance of the singing boys.[22] Despite this, Christ Church was not the wealthiest community in Ireland – it was valued at £100 in 1536 and £160 in 1544, much less than other Dublin establishments such as St Mary's and St Thomas's.[23]

Hassard resigned in 1537, which was an unusual move prior to the dissolution. Perhaps he saw the fate of All Hallows being granted to the corporation of the city and felt there would be no support for Christ Church from the city. An old man at this stage (he died in early 1538), Hassard possibly felt that this was one headache too many for him. Perhaps he did not see eye to eye with George Browne, the former Augustinian friar who was now archbishop of Dublin. Browne was pressurising Dean Fich of St Patrick's Cathedral to step down around this time.[24] In any case, Browne refused to accept Christ Church's nomination of Hassard's successor, and installed an English Augustinian called Robert Castle. Castle was unhappy in Dublin and in 1542 pleaded for an English benefice worth £50 in order to leave Ireland. He never did leave Ireland, however, and died the following year, in 1543.[25]

Despite Hassard's fears of a lack of support in Dublin for the community, its civic importance did ensure it some measure of support in the city. In the late 1530s, the mayor and aldermen of Dublin wrote to Thomas Cromwell, stating that any such dissolution of Christ Church would be 'a great comfort and encouraging of our sovereign lord the king's Irish enemies', as Christ Church was viewed by Dubliners as their version of St Paul's, as Lord Deputy Grey put it.[26] Not only that, but the council and lord deputy also defended Christ Church, citing its civic role and use as a parliament and council meeting place. Faced with this resistance, the commissioners yielded and a compromise was struck. Instead, the monastic house was converted into a secular cathedral and from January 1540 the prior and convent styled themselves a dean and chapter instead.[27] It was secularized in 1541 and reformed as a secular chapter with a dean and nine canons in May 1542. Some issues arose, but by 1544 Christ Church's future as a new secular cathedral was secure. Interestingly, the former Augustinian canons of Christ Church Cathedral produced pre-Reformation vestments for use at the accession of Queen Mary in 1553.[28] So they had obviously been holding on to these items, as many churches did, in the hopes of a return to the old faith, as Bishop John Bale reported in Ossory.[29] The fate and experience of Christ Church does show what compromises could have been struck and how houses could have reorganized and saved themselves had there

22 Gillespie, 'The coming of reform, 1500–58', p. 160. **23** *L. & P. Hen. VIII*, xi, no. 564; *State papers, Hen. VIII*, iii, 489; Gillespie, 'The coming of reform, 1500–58', p. 161. **24** Gillespie, 'The coming of reform, 1500–58', p. 163. **25** *L. & P. Hen. VIII*, xvii, no. 382. **26** Following the precedent of the earlier state papers, recent editors have dated these letters to January 1538, but Bradshaw contends that this dating is incorrect: Ellis & Murray (eds), *Calendar of state papers, Ireland, 1509–1547*, p. 169; *State papers, Hen. VIII*, ii, pp 544–5; Bradshaw, *The dissolution of the religious orders in Ireland*, p. 118, fn. 2. **27** Bradshaw, *The dissolution of the religious orders in Ireland*, p. 118; Gillespie, 'The coming of reform, 1500–58', p. 165. **28** Gillespie, 'The coming of reform, 1500–58', pp 166–7, 171. **29** S.G. Ellis, 'John Bale, bishop of Ossory, 1552–3', *Journal*

been a groundswell of support and political backing for the deal. But for most communities, those who could have saved the house were often the ones to benefit most from its dissolution.

The abbey of St Thomas the Martyr in Dublin (Thomas Court) was dissolved by the surrender of the last abbot, Henry Duff, on 25 July 1539.[30] He was granted a pension of £42, while the previous abbot, James Coterel, and seven other canons received smaller pensions.[31] On 3 October 1540, the jurors reported that the hall, with a tower, a chamber, an upper room and other buildings, called the king's lodging, were suitable for the lord deputy and commissioners, while the remaining buildings were needed by the farmer.[32] The possessions included at least 2,300 acres of land, with two manors, three castles, numerous cottages, five mills and an interest in forty-six rectories. This property was spread out around the counties of Dublin, Meath, Kilkenny, Tipperary, Louth, Cork, Waterford and Wexford, and the total value was recorded as £452 1s. 2d. gross. However, much of the property was unvalued, being in ruin or unoccupied, particularly outside the Pale – unsurprising given the recent violent events of the Kildare rebellion.[33] Duff also leased out lands into secular hands in the run-up to dissolution, but it has been suggested that two silver crosses known as the 'holye crossys' held by the community contained relics of the True Cross, which perhaps indicates the origin of Duff's high pension.[34] The receiver was Barnaby King at £419 18s. 4d.[35]

The convent of Grace Dieu in north County Dublin, which also doubled as a girls' school, was surrendered by its prioress, Alison White, on 28 October 1539, who received a pension of £6 in March 1540. Four other nuns – Margaret Coscrowe, Thomasina Dermyn, Katherine Eustace and Alison FitzSimon – received pensions of 50s. each at the same time.[36] When the site was valued on 25 October 1540, it was noted that the 'house, church and other buildings on the site are in good repair for the use and accommodation of the farmer and parishioners'. Its church also functioned as the parish church, 'from time immemorial'.[37] Much of the lands were in Swords and Lusk, and the total value of the site was then estimated at £70 12s. 10d. gross and £60 12s. 10d. net; although when it was valued again in June 1541, the site was said to be worth £112 2s.[38] The site was granted to Patrick Barnewall in July 1541,[39] despite the hopes of Archbishop George Browne that he might be the recipient, but Barnewall supported the community when they

of the Butler Society, 3:2 (1984), 283–93.   **30** *Cal. pat. rolls Ire., Hen. VIII–Eliz.*, p. 56; *EIMP*, p. 47. See also J.T. Gilbert (ed.), *Register of the abbey of St Thomas, Dublin* (London, 1889); C. Walsh, 'Archaeological excavations at the abbey of St Thomas the Martyr, Dublin' in S. Duffy (ed.), *Medieval Dublin I* (Dublin, 2000), pp 185–202 and M.T. Flanagan in this volume.   **31** *MRHI*, p. 172.   **32** *EIMP*, p. 26.   **33** *EIMP*, pp 25–48. St Thomas's was reckoned by Thomas Cusack to be worth £300 annually: *L. & P. Hen. VIII*, xi (ii), no. 1416; Ellis and Murray (eds), *Calendar of state papers, Ireland, 1509–1547*, p. 111.   **34** M.V. Ronan, *The reformation in Dublin, 1536–1558* (London, 1926), p. 145.   **35** *EIMP*, p. 47. William Brabazon had recommended the closure of this site in 1536, reckoning its worth to be 700 to 800 marks: Ellis and Murray (eds), *Calendar of state papers, Ireland, 1509–1547*, p. 102.   **36** Not 26 October as stated in *MRHI*, p. 317. *EIMP*, p. 77; *Fiants Ire., Hen. VIII*, nos 96, 102; Bradshaw, *The dissolution of the religious orders in Ireland*, p. 115.   **37** *EIMP*, p. 73.   **38** *EIMP*, p. 77; *MRHI*, p. 317.   **39** *Fiants Ire., Hen. VIII*, no. 235;

moved into a small house close to Grace Dieu. They remained living there until 1577.[40]

The nunnery of St Mary of Hogges was likely dissolved in 1536 or early 1537 as it was not named in the undated list of Irish religious communities from that time.[41] This early suppression was possibly due to the fact that seemingly only one nun, Margaret Gaydon, actually lived there. Indeed, some years previously in 1530, John Alen, archbishop of Dublin, compared the present state of Hogges unfavourably with its former glories.[42] Gaydon had, like other religious, pre-empted the dissolution and granted all of the nunnery's possessions in Rathgar to James Rochford, a Dublin merchant, for forty-one years.[43] As the prioress, Gaydon was granted in December 1537 a pension of £6 to be backdated to the previous Easter, indicating the likely date of Hogges' closure to be 1537.[44] The sum of £8 5s. 4d. was raised from the sale of goods and chattels on the site, noted when it was surveyed on 8 November 1540.[45] Much of the complex was dismantled earlier by William Brabazon, who robbed out the building materials (stone, tiles and timber) for use in repairing Dublin Castle. It is not said when exactly this happened, but it was noted in the report that the materials were still lying unused at Dublin Castle when the report was made.[46] The convent held property in places such as Dublin city, Crumlin, Meath and Kildare (which was at that time worthless).[47] Parts of the property were leased to Francis Cosby, who was possibly a soldier, and Robert Lyens.[48] One Robert Jans received in 1551 a lease of possessions in Dublin and Meath belonging to Hogges.[49] The following year a Dublin merchant named James Sedgrave was granted the site and its possessions, only to alienate this property to two separate groups of people the following year.[50]

KILDARE

The convent at Graney, Kildare's third-most valuable independent house, was one of the first in Ireland to be dissolved, although the route to full suppression was a tortuous one.[51] Lying on the border between Kildare and Carlow (and occasionally

Cal. pat. rolls Ire., Hen. VIII–Eliz., pp 12, 73–4; Bradshaw, *The dissolution of the religious orders in Ireland*, p. 239. Barnewall is noted to have been living there in 1545 and 1546: *Fiants Ire., Hen. VIII*, nos 469, 510.   **40** *State papers, Hen. VIII*, iii, 10; *MRHI*, p. 317; D. Hall, *Women and the church in medieval Ireland, c.1140–1540* (Dublin, 2003), p. 205.   **41** *MRHI*, p. 316; Ellis and Murray (eds), *Calendar of state papers, Ireland, 1509–1547*, p. 111. See Bradshaw, *The dissolution of the religious orders in Ireland*, p. 81, for a reappraisal of the dating.   **42** Bradshaw, *The dissolution of the religious orders in Ireland*, p. 36.   **43** M.C. Griffith (ed.), *Calendar of inquisitions formerly in the office of the chief remembrancer of the exchequer* (Dublin, 1991), pp 98, 119.   **44** *EIMP*, p. 73. Gaydon had been superior there since at least 1522: B. Scott, 'The religious houses of Tudor Dublin: their communities and resistance to the dissolution, 1537–41' in S. Duffy (ed.), *Medieval Dublin VII* (Dublin, 2006), pp 214–32 at p. 219, fn. 39.   **45** *EIMP*, pp 69, 72.   **46** *EIMP*, p. 69.   **47** *EIMP*, pp 69–72.   **48** Bradshaw, *The dissolution of the religious orders in Ireland*, pp 75, 233, 235.   **49** *Fiants Ire., Edward VI*, no. 859.   **50** *Cal. pat. rolls Ire., Hen. VIII–Eliz.*, pp 268, 281, 292; *Fiants Ire., Edward VI*, nos 1189, 1997.   **51** M.A. Lyons, *Church and society in County Kildare, c.1470–1547* (Dublin, 2000), p. 115.

referred to as being in Carlow),[52] its position made it an attractive site for strategic reasons in the wake of the Kildare rebellion. The nunnery had been highlighted in 1534 as being a monastic community which had supported Kildare during his rebellion. The following year, a commission for the suppression of Graney was granted to Leonard Grey, then marshal of the army. It stated that the site was the property of the king and that the community of nuns should be transferred to other houses. Upon payment of a fine, however, the nuns survived a short period longer.[53] But the inevitable occurred eventually in May 1537, when Graney was listed in a new suppression bill.[54] Although dissolved formally as part of this bill, the revenues from it were still being withheld by the wily abbess there, Aegidia Wale. She managed to qualify for her pension, receiving a grant of £4 from 14 January 1539, even though she had granted much of her convent's properties out before their confiscation.[55] On 7 February that same year, Leonard Grey, now lord deputy of Ireland, was granted the site.[56] Its strategic importance to the Dublin government is obvious given that the convent was also granted to the next lord deputy of Ireland, Anthony St Leger, following the fall of Grey and his execution in June 1541.[57]

The case of St Wolstan's Priory, near Celbridge in Co. Kildare, was another unusual one in the dissolution story. Provision for its suppression came in an individual commission in December 1536 and by an act of parliament in 1537. Although its dissolution coincided roughly with the first wave of suppressions under the May 1536 commission, St Wolstan's dissolution remained an entirely separate business. In Easter 1536, the crown was in receipt of St Wolstan's revenues and in May, John Alen, Master of the Rolls, received a promise from the king of a grant of the priory. News of the intended closure spread like wildfire around the Pale and on 26 June 1536, the prior of the abbey, Richard Weston, and his community wrote to Thomas Cromwell to let him know that they were aware of this fact. They supplicated the king to remain open and sought Cromwell's support in this action. Weston wrote that the suppression of St Wolstan's 'would be greatly to the decay and hinderance of the common weale, the decrease of English order and speech, good hospitality, and divine service there well and truly kept'. They also asked that Alen be rewarded with a grant of lands elsewhere.[58] This was ignored and the suppression was authorized on 15 September 1536 and on 28 October 1536, Weston was seized of all of the priory's possessions, although he was not officially granted the site until 1 December 1536.[59] The community held over 1,000 acres, which contained over twenty-four cottages – the property was valued at around £41, with some of the possessions not valued as they were in a wasted state, probably as a result of the Geraldine rebellion.[60]

52 *Fiants Ire., Hen. VIII*, no. 71.   53 Lyons, *Church and society in County Kildare*, p. 116; Bradshaw, *The dissolution of the religious orders in Ireland*, p. 66.   54 Bradshaw, *The dissolution of the religious orders in Ireland*, p. 73.   55 *Fiants Ire., Hen. VIII*, no. 69; Bradshaw, *The dissolution of the religious orders in Ireland*, p. 73.   56 *Fiants Ire., Hen. VIII*, no. 71.   57 Ibid., no. 304.   58 *L. & P. Hen. VIII*, x, no. 1211; Ellis and Murray (eds), *Calendar of state papers, Ireland, 1509–1547*, p. 90.   59 *Fiants Ire., Hen. VIII*, no. 57; *EIMP*, p. 176; *MRHI*, p. 193; Lyons, *Church and society in County Kildare*, p. 118.   60 *MRHI*,

Weston was to be looked after, however. In a most unusual step, an act of parliament was passed that gave the former prior the right to continue to live in the dissolved priory for the remainder of his life. He was to be provided with a decent chamber with a chimney, along with a supply of wood and other necessities for his fire. A proper diet, both food and drink, and all of his provisions to the value of £6 annually were to be provided. The act also decreed that Gerald Aylmer and Thomas Luttrell were to reserve to themselves and their heirs an annual sum of £4 from the dissolved priory lands for Weston's personal use. This requirement would cease upon Weston's death.[61] John Alen immediately took up residence in St Wolstan's and renamed it Alenscourt.[62] As Marian Lyons has noted, the conferring of patronage on a loyal servant of the crown was the major motivation behind the grant to Alen.[63]

Of the three religious communities in Naas, the Augustinian hospital of St John was the largest. On 26 July 1539, the last prior there, Thomas Possick, surrendered the property and all of its possessions.[64] On 20 April 1540, Thomas Alen, its occupant, and a brother of the lord chancellor, received a lease for a term of twenty-one years for the site of the former hospital, along with lands elsewhere and affiliated rectories of St John's that it held in Naas and Whitechurch, which lay nearby. It was obviously a wealthy property, with Alen charged a rent of over £35 18s. 2d. (Irish) for the property.[65] The community were also catered for, with Possick receiving a pension of £9, and another member, Laurence Birely, receiving a pension of £2, to be funded from the revenues of Whitechurch rectory. It was granted to a Richard Mannering in 1553 at a value of £35 18s. 2d. and was valued again at £40 in 1568 when leased to Roger Finglas.[66] Interestingly, this was another community which at the time of its dissolution hid property that it owned, as a later inquisition revealed five acres and a mill which had not been mentioned at the time of dissolution.[67]

MEATH

Two, and possibly three, Augustinian houses in Meath – Duleek, Ss Peter and Paul's at Newtown near Trim, and possibly Ballyboggan – were included in the first wave of dissolutions in the summer of 1537.[68] In Ballyboggan, William Bermingham, who eventually received the property in 1541 and became baron of Carbery, had been one of the jurors appraising the abbey, and was possibly related to the prior there, Thomas Bermingham, who received a pension of 100s. (Irish) upon the dissolution of the site.[69] That family members, often related to the head

p. 193; Lyons, *Church and society in County Kildare*, p. 118.   **61** Lyons, *Church and society in County Kildare*, p. 118; *MRHI*, p. 193.   **62** *Fiants Ire., Hen. VIII*, no. 57.   **63** Lyons, *Church and society in County Kildare*, p. 119.   **64** *EIMP*, p. 156.   **65** *MRHI*, p. 189; *EIMP*, p. 156.   **66** *Cal. pat. rolls Ire., Hen. VIII–Eliz.*, p. 301, 507; *MRHI*, p. 189.   **67** *MRHI*, p. 189.   **68** For the dissolution process in Meath, see B. Scott, 'The dissolution of the religious houses in the Tudor diocese of Meath', *Archivium Hibernicum*, 59 (2005), 260–76.   **69** *Fiants Ire., Hen. VIII*, nos 191,

of the community, frequently benefitted from the dissolution, probably went some way to explaining the lack of major protests at the dissolution policy in Ireland. There is no record as to when this priory was dissolved – it was leased to Lord Deputy Grey for twenty-one years on 12 March 1538, so it seems likely that it was dissolved in the summer of 1537.[70] The house, situated on the Meath–Kildare border, was in quite a ruinous state when surveyed on 14 October 1540, with only the church, which doubled as the parish church, in good condition – indeed, the site's value was entered as £21 13s. 4d., as much of the property was ruined through raids and wars.[71] Only the paltry sum of 26s. could be raised through the sale of goods and chattels from Ballyboggan, which is surprising given that it was the site of a famous cross, the destruction of which in 1538 was bemoaned in the Annals of Ulster.[72] It could have been supposed that the crucifix would have been a popular attraction, which may have helped the community financially. There was also a cemetery, cloister, hall and other chambers in a state of ruination, along with other unnamed buildings which were stated to be necessary for the farmer, as well as an orchard and garden. They also held the advowson for the parish.

St Mary's Abbey in Duleek was dissolved in early 1537.[73] On 13 December that year a pension of £10 from the previous Easter was granted to Edmund Anger, the former abbot. The total value of the site was given as £29 9s. 11d., although some possessions were apparently omitted from this valuation.[74] The abbey and possessions were granted on 28 January 1538 to Edward Becke, an English merchant, for twenty-one years at £43.[75] Following Becke's death a few years later, Henry Draycott, remembrancer of the exchequer, was granted the property in 1554, and was recorded as paying a rent of £40 17s. 7d. in 1559.[76]

The priory of Ss Peter and Paul in Newtown Trim functioned as the cathedral in Meath. There is some confusion as to when this community closed, but it was in either 1536 or 1537. Certainly, on 1 December 1537, the site and some of the possessions were granted to Robert Dillon, the attorney general. In October 1540, the jurors found that there were no superfluous buildings except for a part of the church, which was still standing and suitable to be repaired as chancel of Newtown's parish church. Other parts of the church and buildings had been demolished and sold off (sometimes for unspecified sums, such as in the case of parts of the cloister and timber from a roof which were sold to Thomas Agard for a 'price not known').[77] There was also a hall and other buildings with three acres of gardens, which had been leased by Dillon – none of which were valued. The possessions included over 650 acres, two castles, a large number of cottages, tenements and gardens, two watermills, twelve appropriated rectories and five

197; *EIMP*, pp 310, 313.   **70** *Cal. pat. rolls Ire., Hen. VIII–Eliz.*, p. 55; *EIMP*, p. 313.   **71** *EIMP*, pp 311–12.   **72** C. McNeill (ed.), 'Accounts of sums realized by sales of chattels of some suppressed Irish monasteries', *JRSAI*, 52 (1922), 11–37 at 15; *AU, s.a.* 1538. See the chapter by Louise Nugent in this volume.   **73** *Cal. pat. rolls Ire., Hen. VIII–Eliz.*, p. 55; *EIMP*, p. 318.   **74** *EIMP*, p. 318.   **75** The National Archives, Kew, State papers 65/4/14.   **76** *Fiants Ire., Philip & Mary*, no. 20; *Fiants Ire., Eliz.*, no. 163.   **77** *EIMP*, p. 292.

chapels, with a gross value of £94 9s. 1d. and a net of £83 9s. 9d., some of the property being undervalued.[78]

Leasing property to family members or anyone who would take it before the dissolution was a common practice and it was no different in Navan, where Thomas Wafre, abbot of the abbey of the Blessed Virgin Mary in Navan, leased a castle belonging to the community, to a relative of his, Nicholas Wafre. Although the site was in a ruinous state when surveyed in 1540, due to Gaelic raids, it held extensive properties in Meath and Louth. Bishop Edward Staples of Meath also held the tithes and profits from a number of sites owned by the monastery.[79] Despite Wafre's selling of property before its dissolution on 19 July 1538, he co-operated when the commissioners arrived at the site, assisting them with the valuation.[80] The abbey church was parochial and so was saved for their use, while the house and other buildings were ruinous and required immediate attention if they were to be saved. John Brokes, a servant of Thomas Cromwell's, was the occupier in 1540–1.[81] Wafre was rewarded with a pension of £13 and two new positions worth £3, including that of canon at St Patrick's Cathedral in Dublin. Four other canons also received smaller pensions.[82]

On 15 May 1539, with the 'surrender' of the Augustinian abbey of the Blessed Virgin Mary in Trim, Geoffrey Dardice, the abbot in Trim, received a pension of £15 and also seems to have held on to a breviary from the site following its closure. Eight other canons from this community were also granted pensions.[83] The abbey was also the site of a famous wooden statue of the Blessed Virgin, discussed elsewhere in this volume, which had long been held in great reverence until its supposed destruction in 1539. The church attached to this property was not closed, as it had been used 'since time immemorial' as the local parish church, so it remained open to fulfil that function. The other buildings on this site were also kept in good repair to be used by the lord deputy when he was in the area. It lay on the periphery of the Pale and was occasionally the victim of Gaelic raids, which resulted in the destruction of some of its property. Thomas Agard, an assistant of Brabazon's, who was listed as the occupier and farmer of the lands in the valuation undertaken in 1540 was confirmed in his title to the property in 1542. Agard received this lease at £16 lower than the valuation and the sale of goods and chattels from the site raised the sum of £40 (the highest sum raised in this way in Ireland – perhaps suggestive of items or relics associated with the shrine of the Blessed Virgin), with further sales raising £206 15s. 2d., the highest such figure of any Irish Augustinian house.[84] Lord Deputy Anthony St Leger also received property from here, being granted two watermills in 1542.[85]

78 *EIMP*, pp 292–8. **79** *EIMP*, p. 254. **80** Ibid. **81** *MRHI*, p. 190; *EIMP*, p. 250; Bradshaw, *The dissolution of the religious orders in Ireland*, p. 238. **82** *Fiants Ire., Hen. VIII*, no. 76. **83** *Cal. pat. rolls Ire., Hen. VIII–Eliz.*, pp 67, 64, 136; *Fiants Ire., Hen. VIII*, no. 75; *EIMP*, p. 305; M. Potterton, *Medieval Trim: history and archaeology* (Dublin, 2005), p. 303. **84** McNeill (ed.), 'Accounts of sums realized', 14. Although Bradshaw believed that much of the valuables may have been hidden by custodians of the shrines prior to their visitation by the commission authorized to enquire into relics: Bradshaw, *The dissolution of the religious orders in Ireland*, p. 106. **85** *Fiants*

St Mary's Abbey in Kells, lying as it did in a marcher region, often had Gaelic members in its community; indeed, members of the O'Reilly family served as abbot in the late fifteenth and early sixteenth centuries. Kells had further close links with Kilmore as it had links with Drumlane Abbey, which were not always appreciated either by the bishop of Kilmore or Drumlane itself.[86] The abbey was dissolved by the surrender of the last abbot, Richard Plunkett, on 18 November 1539.[87] He was also one of the jurors who reported on 3 October 1540 that the monastic church was now used as a granary, and other buildings, not valued, were occupied by the farmer, William Dormer. The possessions included *c*.200 acres, much unmeasured land, some tenements and the tithes for seven rectories, valued at £42 15*s*. 4*d*. gross.[88] Plunkett and two canons were granted pensions, the abbot received £10, with the canons receiving 20*s*. each.[89] In 1541 the property was granted to Sir Gerald Fleming, with nearly 400 acres. Later inquisitions, however, gave a total acreage of over 600 acres.[90]

The canons of the priory of St Mary, Mullingar, conscious of their precarious position, sold the tithes attached to the rectory of Dunboyne to a merchant named John Stephens for £41, even though they were valued in 1540 at £61. It was surrendered on 28 November 1539.[91] The prior there, John Petit, managed to reserve the only local rectory belonging to the monastery by leasing it along with Edward Petit and Thomas Casey in 1540; he also received a pension of £20. One other canon received a pension of 26*s*. 8*d*.[92] The large sum granted to Petit might be explained by the high opinion which Thomas Cusack had of the community (or perhaps rather the site) – referring to St Mary's in the late 1530s, Cusack reported that there was 'no good in all that quarters but itself'.[93] In October 1540, the jurors reported that the church, belfry, house and other buildings were needed for the entertainment of the lord deputy when he was in the area and for the defence of the region. They held over 630 acres, as well as several unmeasured holdings, a watermill and an interest in five rectories.[94]

The priory of the Blessed Virgin Mary in Tristernagh surrendered on 30 November 1539. When the site was surveyed the following year, there were still a number of stone buildings and stone walls standing and in good condition. It was recommended that these be kept as the site was important for the protection of the region from Gaelic raids, lying as it did in a marcher region. There were at least five members of this community and possibly six when it was dissolved, which was quite large for the time, and the lands were reckoned to be worth about £100, despite their lying 'mostly among the wild Irish'.[95]

An interesting point about this house was that Edmund Nugent, bishop of Kilmore, was also the commendator at Tristernagh.[96] He claimed that he was

Ire., Hen. VIII, no. 392; *EIMP*, pp 302–3.   **86** Liam Kelly, *The diocese of Kilmore, c.1100–1800* (Dublin, 2017), pp 123, 131, 149–52.   **87** *EIMP*, p. 264.   **88** *EIMP*, p. 263.   **89** *Fiants Ire., Hen. VIII*, no. 87.   **90** *MRHI*, p. 181.   **91** *EIMP*, p. 290.   **92** *Cal. pat. rolls Ire., Hen. VIII–Eliz.*, p. 65; *Fiants Ire., Hen. VIII*, no. 106; *EIMP*, p. 290.   **93** *L. & P. Hen. VIII*, xi (ii), no. 1416; Ellis and Murray (eds), *Calendar of state papers, Ireland, 1509–1547*, p. 111.   **94** *EIMP*, pp 286–90.   **95** *Fiants Ire., Hen. VIII*, no. 105; *EIMP*, p. 280.   **96** Scott, 'The dissolution of the religious

deeply in debt to various creditors as a result of buying goods for the community there. So large were these debts that even if everything was sold on the site, his costs would still not be covered. So it was agreed that Nugent should receive most of the goods of the monastery to pay off creditors in order to exonerate the king from the debt which he would owe when the ownership of the monastery passed into his hands.[97] The site was leased for twenty-one years to Robert Delman, a Dublin merchant, in 1539 and when the commissioners visited the site in 1540, some of the superfluous buildings on the site which Nugent was expected to sell remained unsold, and no records appear of Nugent paying off these debts, perhaps indicating the nature of transactions relating to this site.[98] It is possible that Robert Nugent, who was a juror at Tristernagh, was related to Edmund Nugent, and he did receive a pension from the monastery. Incidentally, Thomas Cusack, one of the commissioners, believed that the Augustinian houses at Mullingar and Tristernagh should remain open, as they were the only religious houses in that area fit to receive the lord deputy and able to keep good residence, a recommendation which was ignored.[99]

There next came a number of communities that the commissioners had to survey at a distance for fear of the wild Irish. It is not known exactly when these were suppressed, and whether in some cases the suppression was in name only and had no real standing in fact. According to Thomas Cusack in 1538, the only occupant at Loughsewdy (also known as Ballymore) was the prior, Thomas Tuit, and 'no divine service or hospitality kept'.[100] The previous prior, a man called Richard Walshe, had been a close supporter and advisor of Thomas Fitzgerald during the Kildare rebellion and his name litters the state papers during that period. Indeed, he travelled to Spain to seek aid for the rebels.[101] The church was reported to be in ruins on 8 October 1540 when the commissioners reported on statements made by Tuit, unable as they were to visit the one-acre site. But in 1539 Tuit surrendered his house for a pension of £4 and in 1542 the property was leased to a Dublin merchant named Walter Tirrell for twenty-one years.[102] Its total value was recorded in 1540 as being £26 12s. but in 1548 it was being farmed at £24 16s. 4d. by Tirrell, who was over £49 in arrears. In 1566, the property was granted to Thomas Le Strange for twenty-one years. He had this renewed ten years later in 1576 for a further twenty-one years and again in 1580 for thirty-one years, a lease which would only come into force in 1608. Le Strange was right to be worried about the security of his title as it was leased again to Francis Shane in 1593 for forty-five years, and had it regranted again in 1597. One Edmund Barett had

houses in the Tudor diocese of Meath', 268. See also C. Lennon, 'The Nugent family and the diocese of Kilmore in the sixteenth and early seventeenth centuries', *Breifne*, 37 (2001), 360–74 at 362–7. **97** McNeill (ed.), 'Accounts of sums realized', 19; *EIMP*, p. 280. **98** *Fiants Ire., Hen. VIII*, no. 79; McNeill (ed.), 'Accounts of sums realized', p. 19; *EIMP*, p. 280. **99** *L. & P. Hen. VIII*, xi (ii), no. 1416; Ellis & Murray (eds), *Calendar of state papers, Ireland, 1509–1547*, p. 111. **100** Ibid. **101** See, for example, Ellis and Murray (eds), *Calendar of state papers, Ireland, 1509–1547*, pp 47, 58, 77. **102** *Cal. pat. rolls Ire., Hen. VIII–Eliz.*, p. 63; *EIMP*, pp 283–4; *Fiants Ire., Hen. VIII*, no. 326; *L. & P. Hen. VIII*, xi (ii), no. 1416. A Hugh Dale, described as a 'conventual person' claimed that the monastery had contained concealed lands and so should be granted to him. Indeed, a fiant from Elizabeth's reign granted a commission powers to retrieve hidden church lands,[103] and a rectory of Rathreagh belonging to Loughsewdy had indeed been 'discovered' and was granted to John Lye in 1594 for sixty years.[104]

Abbeyderg and Inchmore seem to have had no viable communities residing within their walls at all. The houses were dissolved through the surrender of their respective heads but really they were held by the O'Farrell family, who had taken these houses and their contents for their own use long before the dissolutions ever occured.[105]

Again, there is evidence of corruption here, no doubt aided by the fact that an extent of these houses was impossible due to their location 'among the Irish, for fear of whom it was not safe to approach thither for the purpose of making extents'.[106] No real information was available on Inchmore, yet it was held by Thomas Cusack, one of the commissioners – it is puzzling that he was not able to provide some detail regarding this site. Moreover, it was recorded that no account could be made of goods and chattels from Inchmore as 'long before the dissolution these goods were carried off and consumed' by the O'Farrells, 'so that nothing of them came into the hands of the accounting officer', save an old pair of vestments and a leaden chalice, both reckoned to be worthless.[107] Was this further evidence of properties and goods being sold before dissolution in order to circumvent the stripping of these communities? These properties were formally surrendered and were regranted to the O'Farrells at a nominal rent, which was never paid.[108]

According to Bradshaw, the abbey of Ss John and Peter at Clonard was never actually dissolved, due to the uncertainty regarding under whose jurisdiction it fell in the church, *inter Anglicos* or *inter Hibernicos*. The death of the abbot, Gerald Walshe, in May 1540, however, meant that the crown could claim it without opposition. The site and its buildings were in ruins due to the 'war and rebellion of the O'Connor and other Irish'.[109] There do not appear to have been any other members of the community. There was something especially suspicious going on at this site – when Walshe died in May 1540, he was seized of 2,968 acres. Yet a few months later, on 25 November, only 272 acres were mentioned – a massive discrepancy, and there were other discrepancies also. Either way, it was leased to William Bermingham, who was one of those who evaluated the site, in 1541, and was still there in 1548. In 1553, the monastery and *c*.260 acres were leased to Thomas Cusack.[110]

The dissolution story is a sordid one – supposedly intended to wipe out corrupt practices and the like, it became instead the means for many of Ireland's richest and most powerful men further to line their pockets. It shows many of the players in

---

of Loughsewdy, received in 1543 a pension of 26s. 8d. No other records known to me indicate his presence in Loughsewdy: *Fiants Ire., Hen. VIII*, no. 344.   **103** *Fiants Ire., Eliz.*, no. 2906. **104** Ibid., no. 5878.   **105** *MRHI*, p. 156; *EIMP*, p. 283.   **106** *EIMP*, p. 283.   **107** *EIMP*, p. 284.   **108** Bradshaw, *The dissolution of the religious orders in Ireland*, p. 117.   **109** *EIMP*, p. 309. **110** *Cal. pat. rolls Ire., Hen. VIII–Eliz.*, p. 85; *MRHI*, p. 164.

this saga in the worst light possible – as avaricious land grabbers unconcerned with the social vacuum left in the wake of the monastic closures. Although mostly small communities, the Augustinians of the Pale had played an important role in the life of the region and their dissolution were to create much wealth for those in a position to exploit the situation. There is also considerable evidence pointing to corrupt practices on the part of those leasing properties, with large discrepancies often manifest. Eager to prevent a total loss of all of their properties, many of the houses, and not just the Augustinians, began to lease and sell what they could in order to keep it out of the hands of the king. It could also be that people bought lands with a view to holding them for the communities, a practice not unknown even to this day. Either way, the Augustinians in the Pale during the 1530s did what they could to hinder the progress of the dissolution, but no matter how they attempted, they could not halt the process, and the Augustinian order had disappeared from the Pale landscape by the early 1540s.

The regular canons in early modern Ireland*

CLEMENS GALBAN, CAN. REG.

The dissolution of the Irish monasteries in the Tudor period was a piecemeal event and largely depended on the strength of the English crown to impose its will on any given area of Ireland at any one time. But whatever 'fits and starts' it may have had, it was an unrelenting process. Nevertheless, the crown's inability to assert its programme of secularization wholesale throughout the island allowed numerous religious orders to continue in existence. It is probable that many religious, like their counterparts in England, thought that this was to be a temporary situation, and that eventually things with Rome would be righted and they would be permitted to resume their religious lives as heretofore. But as Brendan Scott points out in the previous chapter, it was not a noble story on either side.[1] In the end, only the larger canonical houses had any semblance of conventual life left by the time of the suppression. Many had already been reduced to one or two members before the Reformation, and these served largely to hold the property titles. Even the larger canonries had small communities and these accepted the new order without undue qualms of conscience. The prior and convent of Holy Trinity Priory, Dublin, became the dean and chapter of Christ Church Cathedral, while others were content to accept whatever pensions and appointments were on offer.[2] Some may even have been swayed by Reformation ideals. John Bradley notes that in 1551 John Bicton, a former canon of St John's Priory, Kilkenny, was commended as one who had done most within the realm to further the king's cause. The preamble to his 1552 will, with its absence of any invocation of the Virgin Mary and the saints, indicates that he possessed at least a moderate reforming outlook.[3]

The piecemeal progress of the Tudor conquest and of the Reformation meant that many religious communities outside the Pale and areas of royal authority survived unmolested. This was particularly true of the mendicant friars, who maintained an active presence in Gaelic territories and whose well-established continental contacts provided a lifeline that facilitated the establishment of numerous seventeenth-century continental foundations that ensured their survival.[4]

Likewise, what subsisted of canonical life in Ireland also depended on the location and the degree of English authority there. There were probably a few,

* I am grateful to Colmán Ó Clabaigh OSB for advice on Irish historical sources and for his comments on this chapter.

1 See above, pp 252–65. See also B. Bradshaw, *The dissolution of the religious orders in Ireland* (Cambridge, 1974). **2** R. Gillespie, 'The coming of reform, 1500–58' in Milne, *CCCD*, pp 151–73. **3** J. Bradley, 'The precinct of St John's Priory, Kilkenny at the close of the Middle Ages', *Peritia*, 22–3 (2011–12), 317–45 at 323–4. **4** For the Franciscan experience see C. Lennon, 'The dissolution to the foundation of St Anthony's College, Louvain, 1534–1607'

small houses which persisted. At Lisgoole, Co. Fermanagh, for instance, the community had some form of attenuated existence until *c.*1580–83, when the abbot, Cathal Mac Brian, agreed to repair the building and cede it to the Franciscans.[5] The Premonstratensians at Lough Key, Co. Roscommon, continued in possession of their monastery until 1585 and possibly even until 1608.[6] Such foundations presumably recruited the occasional novice, but there are few records. Whatever the case, Aloysius Smith points to the tenuous connections and subsistence of the regular canons in Ireland:

> Thus in 1594, Robert Fleming was collated as prior of Holmpatrick, and he was succeeded in 1608 by Patrick Duff. In 1620 Donal O'Gryphy, or Griffin, appears as precentor of Killaloe and prior of Lorrha, and on May 16, 1625, he was provided by the pope as commendatory abbot of Corcomroe.[7]

This gives a picture of the haphazard existence of the once-great order in her now downtrodden circumstances. Benefices and titles were still being assigned and fought over which, while not an edifying thing, does indicate that there was personnel to support. What sort of classical, canonical or conventual life they might have led, however, is unknown and, indeed, extremely doubtful. More likely was that individual vocations accrued to the order in an individual way and engaged in pastoral ministry in a hostile environment. Lacking the centralized structures of the mendicant orders and their extensive continental network, the Irish canons were forced to struggle on as best they could without great support from any bases on the Continent, at least not until the mid-seventeenth century. When it occurred, the revival of the canonical life coincided with renewed Catholic hopes in Ireland and a vigorous reform of the regular canons on the Continent.

In Ireland, the 1641 Rising and the period of self-government that followed under the aegis of the Irish Catholic Confederation (1642–9) fanned the hopes of the Catholic community and of the religious orders in particular. The mendicant friars, already securely established, were particularly influential, but smaller groups like the Benedictines and Cistercians sought opportunities to reclaim some of their ancient properties and to re-establish conventual life.[8] Although numerically the smallest of all the religious orders, the memory of the extensive rights, privileges

and M.A. Lyons, 'The role of St Anthony's College, Louvain in establishing the Irish Franciscan college network, 1607–60' both in E. Bhreathnach, J. MacMahon and J. McCafferty (eds), *The Irish Franciscans, 1534–1990* (Dublin, 2009), pp 2–26 and 27–44. **5** *MRHI*, p. 185. See also K. Nicholls, 'The Lisgoole agreement of 1580', *Clogher Record*, 7:1 (1969), 27–33. **6** *MRHI*, p. 205. See also M. Clyne, 'The rental of Holy Trinity Abbey, Lough Cé' in T. Finan (ed.), *Medieval Lough Cé: history, archaeology and landscape* (Dublin, 2010), pp 67–96 and her contribution to this volume. **7** A. Smith, 'The Lateran canons and Ireland', *The Dublin Review* 175:351 (1924), 280. **8** R. Gillespie, 'The Irish Franciscans, 1600–1700' in Bhreathnach et al., *The Irish Franciscans*, pp 45–76; C. Ó Clabaigh, 'The Benedictines in medieval and early modern Ireland' in M. Browne and C. Ó Clabaigh (eds), *The Irish Benedictines: a history* (Dublin, 2005), pp 79–121 at pp 118–20; C. Ó Conbhuidhe, *Studies in Irish Cistercian history* (Dublin, 1998), pp 121–235.

and properties that their pre-Reformation foundations possessed galvanized the canons into action. Their demands for the restitution of their estates would have dispossessed numerous Catholic landowners who had enjoyed possession of them for nigh on a century and who resisted them vigorously. The dispute proved particularly contentious during the mission to Ireland of the papal nuncio Giovanni Battista Rinuccini (1645–9) and posed a serious threat to the unity of the Confederated Catholics. Ultimately, Rinuccini was forced to accept the status quo and canons' claims went unheeded, but they remained a recurring source of tension with the hierarchy and the secular clergy throughout the seventeenth and eighteenth centuries.[9]

Rinuccini's mission also saw the rise to prominence of Dom James Lynch as the regular canons' representative in Ireland. His surname suggests a western origin and he proved a staunch ally of the nuncio. On 24 January 1646, he secured papal appointment as abbot of Cong, Co. Mayo, and about six months later he received powers through the procurator general of the Lateran canons in Rome to appoint Dom Andrew Nugent, abbot of St Thomas's Abbey, Dublin, as visitor for the whole of Ireland, with faculties to clothe and profess novices. This development sought to establish the canons on a secure organizational footing in Ireland, as well as developing links with their continental confreres. It also established the abbot of Cong as the pre-eminent figure in the movement and the monastery there would remain the canons' principal foundation throughout the seventeenth and eighteenth centuries. Simultaneously, Bishop Francis Kirwan (1589–1661) of Killala took steps to replant the order on Irish soil. An avid admirer of the regular canons, Kirwan took advantage of the lull to take young men to France with the intent of forming them as regular canons for the Irish mission. His intention itself already shows the change which had come about in the church since the reforms of the Council of Trent. The view of religious life had changed considerably, especially with the emergence of the Jesuit model, with its new structures and forms of piety. The medieval model of religious life had been replaced with something new.

Kirwan's first two attempts failed, but they brought him to Paris and into contact with the great French canonical reformer, Dom Charles Faure. Faure, originally professed at the Abbey of St Vincent de Senlis, became superior general of St Geneviève in Paris. St Geneviève was an ancient and venerable house of regular canons in Paris and had become the centre and seat of the new reform. Faure was the mastermind behind the newly-formed Congregation of France, a centralized congregation of regular canons championed by Cardinal Francis de la Rochefoucauld (d. 1645).[10] De la Rochefoucauld enjoyed the favour of both King Henri IV and King Louis XIII, who supported his reform attempts – an indispensable element in Gallican France. King Louis XIII named him his grand almoner in 1618. The cardinal and Faure had met in Senlis, where the former was

---

9 T. Ó hAnnracháin, *Catholic reformation in Ireland: the mission of Rinuccini, 1645–1649* (Oxford, 2002) pp 68–81. I am grateful to Dr Pádraig Lenihan for this reference and for advice on this point.   10 Smith, 'Lateran canons and Ireland', 283.

bishop. An ardent reformer, he was also titular abbot of St Geneviève, so when he was charged with the reform of all the religious orders in the kingdom of France by Pope Gregory XV in 1622, he began with his own monastery of regular canons.[11] When Faure met Kirwan, Faure was seeking to aggregate as many canonical houses and congregations to the Congregation of France as was possible. His absolute belief in a united, national system would eventually lead to a break with de la Rochefoucauld, who was more inclined to divide such a large enterprise into provinces or separate congregations.

The regular canons of the Congregation of France were very much in the 'modern style' of religious orders that emerged after the Council of Trent. They had a superior general and common novitiate houses. As they took over more and more canonries, the resident religious were given the choice to accept the reform or leave. Those who accepted had to repeat their novitiate and profess their vows anew. Their constitutions were drawn up to reflect the new reality presented by the post-Tridentine church. The ancient tradition of independent abbeys and priories was supplanted by this new structure and it was this structure which Kirwan and his Irish vocations encountered when Kirwan met Faure in Paris. The latter was more than willing to give the young Irishmen formation in his congregation according to the reform he was carrying out.[12] Under his aegis, this congregation would also be a national congregation, like that of France. Here we see the first clear example of the Irish canons having some sort of foothold on the Continent, though they had no house of their own. It also gives us insight into the structure of the new congregation.

The Congregation of St Patrick was called into being by Pope Innocent X in 1646 and aimed at uniting all the regular canons working in Ireland under a single, national congregation. The members of the new congregation were spread throughout the island with others doubtless still in France. The inescapable conclusion is that they were living individually, though they still sought the titles, honours and benefices of their predecessors. The reasons behind this were many, including the desire to preserve titles for a future revival, as well as simple survival. Abbot James Lynch of Cong was appointed the commissary general of the congregation by the Holy See and sought to restore some level of conventual life to at least part of the congregation in Ireland. The canons who had sought and been granted canonical titles were instructed by Nuncio Rinuccini in 1648 to pay Lynch a fee to support houses of common life wheresoever they could be erected. He also gave permission for the erection of a house in Galway and the restoration of other houses of the order. This should have provided some economic basis for the restoration of the conventual life and the renewal of the order in Ireland. There is even some evidence that the important canonry of Christ Church in Dublin was returned to the canons during the period that James II spent in Ireland in Ireland in 1689–90.[13]

11 M. Schmid and S. Diermeier, 'Kurzgefaßte Geschichte der Augustiner-Chorherren. Heft 4: Die nachtridentinische Zeit bis zur Aufklärung', *In Unum Congregati*, 7 (1962), 14. **12** Ibid., 15. **13** Ibid.

These years of the seventeenth century saw much litigation between the regular canons and bishops with regard to titles and benefices. Smith points out that the courts and the Holy See usually sided with the canons.[14] This litigious situation was not unique to the regular canons, but was part of a widespread rivalry between the secular and regular clergy. The dispute could be manipulated by the crown authorities to destabilize the Irish Catholic clergy, at times to good effect, as under Lord Deputy Sir Thomas Wentworth (1632–40). At the heart of the conflict lay questions of the limited resources available to the clergy due to the dissolution and prohibitions laid on the Catholic church, as well as the issues surrounding ecclesiastical authority.[15]

It may have been with the motive of strengthening their hand in these disputes that the members of the Congregation of St Patrick sought union with the canonical Congregation of the Lateran at the end of the seventeenth century. This congregation originated as the Congregation of Fregionaia in the beginning of the fifteenth century. Its original statutes, approved by Pope Martin V in 1421, were a noted departure from the 'classical' structures of the regular canons. From the beginning they had a superior general and abolished lifetime abbacies and the vow of stability. In this they resembled other reformed monastic orders including the Benedictine Congregation of Santa Giustina of Padua. Interestingly, the reforms enacted there began with Ludovico Barbo, a canon regular of San Giorgio in Alga, appointed by Pope Gregory XII as abbot of Santa Giustina in 1408. In 1439, Pope Eugene IV called for a community of thirty canons to be sent from Fregionaia to take up the common life at the Lateran basilica in Rome, replacing the secular chapter there. The latter did not take kindly to being supplanted and riled the citizenry to bodily remove the regular canons three times in the following years; once in 1440, again in 1455, and for the last time in 1471, after which, Pope Sixtus IV left the basilica in the hands of the secular clergy. In 1445, Pope Eugene IV renamed the Congregation of Fregionaia as the Congregation of the Lateran and granted them all the rights and privileges of the Lateran canons even after they were forced out and had retired to the church of Santa Maria della Pace in central Rome.[16] The popes continued to favour the congregation and bestowed on it numerous privileges, dispensations and indulgences. Its relationship to the papacy gave it a position of singular honour among the canonical congregations, though it was only an Italian phenomenon, despite the aggregations of other groups.

The union of the Irish canons was effected by the general chapter of the Lateran Congregation and confirmed by Pope Innocent XII in 1699 in the brief, *Exponi nuper*. In this, the pope prescribed for the Irish canons the statutes of the Lateran Congregation. In Smith's words, 'Since in course of time and through many

---

14 Ibid., 288.   **15** For a comprehensive insight into this dispute, especially during Wentworth's term of office, see M. Empey, 'State intervention in disputes between secular and regular clergy in early seventeenth-century Ireland', *British Catholic History* 34: 2 (2018), 304–26.   **16** M. Schmid and S Diermeier, 'Kurzgefaßte Geschichte der Augustiner-Chorherren. Heft 3: Die Zeit von Benedikt XII. bis zur Glaubensspaltung', *Unum Congregati*, 7 (1961), 30–2.

calamities many of their customs and constitutions had perished, the constitutions of the Lateran Congregation were now prescribed for them – though adapted so as to suit their particular needs – in the same way as they had been given to regular canons in Poland and Moravia'.[17]

It should be stated that seeking this union with the Lateran Congregation was not a phenomenon unique to the Irish canons, but was rather a widespread movement among several branches of regular canons at the time, including the Austrian monasteries. Floridus Röhrig points out that the union sought was not a full one, but rather union in the privileges and rights that had been richly bestowed upon the Lateran Congregation by the papacy through the centuries. This is echoed by Pietro Guglielmi in his work on the history of the Lateran canons. He adds that the Lateran Congregation also benefitted from the aggregation, as it allowed a declining congregation to appear flourishing and it gained in prestige as the 'head of a fictitious multitude'.[18] The greatest prize for the aggregated congregation was, of course, exemption from episcopal jurisdiction. But it was just this prize which was most illusory.[19] Smith also points to the possibility that they were seeking a greater foothold on the Continent, especially for the training of their candidates, as Ireland was becoming untenable for recruitment and formation during the reigns of William and Mary, and of Anne (d. 1714). Despite the essentially superficial nature of the union of the two congregations, the adoption of the Lateran Constitutions is an indication of the dire straits in which the Congregation of St Patrick found itself.

The political situation at the end of the seventeenth century was extremely precarious for the religious orders in Ireland, and the Irish regular canons were not alone in seeking shelter abroad. In 1698 the government banished the bishops and regular clergy from Ireland and 444 religious departed for destinations in France and Belgium, with approximately 200 remaining in hiding in Ireland.[20] It was in this context that an attempt was made to set up the first house for Irish canons on the Continent. Dom William Henegan, originally a canon of Cong Abbey, found refuge in the abbey of Arrouaise and in 1700 he petitioned the abbot there to concede the abbey of Beaulieu in the diocese of Boulogne to the Irish canons so that they might pursue the conventual life there. The project failed due to suits by commendatory abbots in the civil courts.[21] There is no other known attempt at an Irish canonical foundation on the Continent, similar to those established by the friars or by male and female members of the English Benedictine congregation. Gradually, the religious drifted back to Ireland and in 1737 Bernard O'Gara, archbishop of Tuam, reported that there were eleven canons in Ireland, most

17 Smith, 'Lateran canons'. Smith mentions a copy of said statutes can be found in the archives of St Pietro in Vincoli in Rome.   **18** Pietro Guglielmi, *La Vita Comune nel Clero: i canonici regolari Lateranensi* (Rome, 2010), p. 255 [own translation].   **19** Floridus Röhrig, 'Die Augustiner-Chorherren in Österreich' in by Floridus Röhrig (ed.), *Die Stifte der Augustiner-Chorherren in Österreich, Südtirol und Polen* (Klosterneuburg-Wien, 1997), p. 22.   **20** H. Fenning, *The undoing of the friars of Ireland* (Louvain, 1972), p. 44.   **21** Smith, 'Lateran canons', 291.

based in Cong. By 1750, Fenning estimates that the regular canons numbered approximately sixteen members.[22]

Despite their contemporary travails in Ireland, knowledge of the history and importance of the canonical tradition in Ireland remained strong in continental circles in the early modern period. In the late seventeenth century, the Augustinian canons of St Dorothea in Vienna commissioned a series of full-length pictures depicting saints associated with the order as a way of emphasizing its antiquity and significance in a Counter-Reformation context. Now preserved in Stift Klosterneuburg near Vienna, the series includes images of Saints Patrick and Malachy. The latter's role as the putative founder of the order in Ireland is underlined by his depiction in the habit of a regular canon (Plate 16).

In Ireland, the canons' insistence on asserting their claims to properties and privileges means that the history of the Congregation of St Patrick in the eighteenth and early nineteenth centuries is one of more and more litigation. Although their attempts at reasserting their rights during the Confederation of Kilkenny had been rebuffed, they marshalled sufficient energy to renew their efforts in the early eighteenth century. In this case, recognizing the political realities, their efforts focused less on reclaiming properties and more on asserting their right to exercise pastoral ministry in their former churches and parishes. In this, Dom Thomas O'Kelly proved indefatigable. Sent to study in Rome in 1728, he spent the next fourteen years canvassing the Holy See on behalf of his brethren. In 1729, he successfully petitioned Pope Benedict XIII to appoint four members of the congregation as abbots in Ireland. He himself became abbot of St Colman's Abbey in Mayo and prior of the ancient pilgrimage site at Lough Derg, Co. Fermanagh. Dom Mark Kenny became abbot of Cong; Dom Andrew Quirke, abbot of Annaghdown; and Dom Henry O'Kelly, abbot of St Thomas, St Catherine and St James in Dublin. In each case, each 'abbey' claimed jurisdiction over three or four parishes that were listed by name in the papal bull. Not surprisingly, the bishops of Clogher, Tuam and Dublin, in whose dioceses the parishes lay, contested these claims and protracted litigation ensued. Eventually a compromise was reached in September 1737, whereby Abbot Kenny was confirmed as abbot of Cong and in the possession of its annexed parishes, but the claims of the other three abbots were set aside. The bishops were ordered to find parishes for all members of the congregation and the canons were ordered not to accept any more novices until all canons had secured an appointment. Thomas O'Kelly contested the ban on recruitment but this was ultimately upheld in 1742.[23]

The dispute shone a spotlight on the activities and lifestyle of the order in Ireland and the survival of a report on the community at Cong dating to 1740 is therefore of particular interest. The community was resident in a house adjacent to the ruins of the medieval abbey and consisted of the abbot, Mark Kenny, the abbot of Annaghdown, Andrew Quirke and six other priests. It also included three novices and observed a reasonable standard of conventual life. The canons had

---

22 Fenning, *Undoing of the friars*, pp 44, 86.   **23** Fenning, *Undoing of the friars*, pp 117–22.

constructed an oratory within the ruins of the medieval church that contained a choir and pulpit. The sacristy possessed sufficient vestments to ensure dignified worship and the community also owned two silver and two pewter chalices.

The description of the novitiate regime gives a unique insight into the process of recruiting and training new members. The abbot and two senior priests interviewed each candidate to ascertain his background and motives. Once admitted to the novitiate, the novices were trained in the obligations of their vocation as well as the necessity of observing their vows, particularly that of obedience. Their spiritual formation included instruction in the methods of meditation and mental prayer, examination of conscience and emphasized the necessity for frequent confession and the reception of the Eucharist. When the novitiate was complete, the abbot consulted the chapter of the house and a secret ballot was taken on their suitability. Successful candidates were admitted to profession, which took place during Mass. A register of professions was kept, which each candidate signed, along with two witnesses.[24]

The dispute between the canons and the bishops was but one of many that exacerbated tensions between the regular clergy and the hierarchy and secular clergy in Ireland. If one reads between the lines of all the litigation, it is far from a black-and-white story. The bishops of Ireland were struggling to provide for a large flock and needed to be able to grant livings to their priests and provide for good ecclesiastical governance in a changed time. To constantly have the medieval rights of religious reasserted over benefices and properties was a serious aggravation and even a detriment to the Catholic cause in Ireland. This was the case all the more so when the English government proved adept at fomenting discord between the various branches of the Catholic church in Ireland. In addition, the Roman authorities were increasingly concerned about the standard of formation and training that religious in Ireland received. Whereas concern focused primarily on the mendicant friars, who were by far the most numerous of the regulars, the canons also provided a convenient *causus belli* and were the first in the firing line. Whereas episcopal attempts at reining in religious had been a perennial feature of church life in early modern Ireland, it became more pronounced in the 1730s, as a succession of reports and visitations presented a very bleak picture of standards of religious observance and formation in Irish religious houses. The closure of the regular canons' novitiate in Cong in 1742 was but the opening salvo that would end with the suppression of the novitiates of all the religious orders in Ireland by order of the Congregation of Propaganda Fide in July 1751. Henceforth, all candidates for religious life would have to be admitted in continental houses of formation where they could be trained to the standard required by Tridentine Catholicism. The impact in Ireland was immediate and catastrophic. For the friars, their continental foundation provided a lifeline until they were permitted to reopen some novitiates in Ireland in 1775. The regular canons, however, were condemned to a slow and inexorable decline. Even the relaxation granted in 1766 that allowed

---

24 Fenning, *Undoing of the friars*, p. 84.

them to receive six new candidates was not sufficient to avoid extinction.[25] By 1800, only seven canons were mentioned among the 400 religious listed in Ireland.[26]

In the course of their long history, the regular canons in Ireland underwent many changes in their religious life. In the seventeenth century the traditional medieval form of canonical life was extinguished in favour of the new, centralized structures favoured after Trent. For the Irish Congregation of St Patrick, the influence of Charles Faure and the Congregation of France would have been decisive. Since the Lateran Congregation was already centralized, aggregation to it and the adoption of its statutes would not have involved any great changes. This newer structure was also better suited to the smaller Irish communities or even to isolated canons working in parishes. And yet without the common life, the canonical life would have ceased to have real meaning, so it is all the more remarkable that the Congregation of St Patrick persisted as long as it did. Despite this, the memory of their past achievements and the hope of a better future continued to inspire a small number of Irishmen to adopt this way of life. The last of these, Patrick Prendergast, abbot of Cong, died in 1829, the year in which Catholic Emancipation removed the remaining penal restrictions on Catholics in Ireland. He is buried at the east end of the ruined chancel at St Mary's Abbey and among his possessions he preserved the magnificent twelfth-century Cross of Cong. Commissioned in 1123 by Turlough O'Connor to enshrine a relic of the True Cross and long venerated by the community at Cong, it remains a potent witness to the transformation of Irish church and society in which the regular canons and canonesses of St Augustine and of Prémontré played such a vital, integral and enduring part.[27]

25 Fenning, *The undoing of the friars*, p. 384.   **26** Smith, 'Lateran canons', 295.   **27** G. Murray, *The Cross of Cong* (Dublin, 2014), pp 2–14.

Bibliography

MANUSCRIPT SOURCES

Belgium
Brussels, Bibliothèque Royale
MSS 7672–4, *Codex Salmanticensis*

England
London

British Library
Additional MS 4787, Sir James Ware, manuscript
Additional MS 24,198, Missal, St Thomas's Abbey, Dublin
Lansdowne MS 418, Sir James Ware, manuscript

Kew, National Archives
C 143/202/21, Chancery: Inquisitions ad quod damnum, Henry III to Richard III, 1329
DL 25/535/453, Athassel deed, 1335
DL 25/284/230, Athassel deed, 1336
MS C.115/75, Llanthony cartulary
MS C115/80, Llanthony cartulary
RCH 179/22, s.a. 1405
RCH 191/110, s.a. 1408
SC 1/35/91 Richard de Burgh, earl of Ulster, to the bishop of Worcester, 1310

Oxford

Bodleian Library
MS Bodl. 240 Life, passion & miracles of St Edmund
MS Rawlinson B. 486 St Mary's Abbey, Navan: martyrology and rule commentary
MS Rawlinson B. 499, Register of St Thomas's Abbey, Dublin
MS Rawlinson B. 500, Register of St Thomas's Abbey, Dublin
MS Rawlinson G. 185, Psalter of Prior Stephen de Derby

Ireland
Dublin

National Library of Ireland
NLI MS 13, transcripts by Walter Harris
NLI MS G 2–3, Ó Cianáin miscellany
NLI MS 700, Gerald of Wales' *Topography of Ireland*

Royal Irish Academy
MS 12 D 2 (olim MS 98), Register of St Thomas's Abbey, Dublin

Trinity College
MS 97, Chapter book, St Thomas's Abbey, Dublin
MS 347, Franciscan *vademecum*
TCD MS 576, Chapter book of Holy Trinity Priory, Dublin
TCD MS 4877 (2), Image of St Catherine's Priory, Waterford

PRINTED SOURCES*

Abram, Andrew, 'Augustinian canons and the survival of cult centres in medieval England' in Burton and Stöber (eds), *The regular canons* (2011), pp 79–95.

Adam Scot, *De ordine*, in Jacques-Paul Migne (ed.), *Patrologiae cursus completus*, series Latina, 221 vols (Paris, 1841–64), cxcviii, cols 443–610.

Adam Scot, *De instructione animae*, in Jacques-Paul Migne (ed.), *Patrologiae cursus completus*, series Latina, 221 vols (Paris, 1841–64), cxcviii, cols 843–72.*

Alemand, Louis-Augustin, *Monasticon Hibernicum: or, The monastical history of Ireland* (London, 1722).*

Anstruther, Robert (ed.), *Radulphi Nigri chronica: the chronicles of Ralph Niger*, Caxton Society, 13 (London, 1851).*

Appleby, J.T., 'The ecclesiastical foundations of Henry II', *Catholic Historical Review*, 48 (1962), 205–15.

Archdall, Mervyn, *Monasticon Hibernicum* (Dublin, 1786).

Archdall, Mervyn, *Monasticon Hibernicum*, ed. P.F. Moran, 2 vols (Dublin, 1873–6).

Armstrong, E.C.R., and H.J. Lawlor, 'The Domnach Airgid', *PRIA*, 34C (1917–19), 96–126.

Arnold, Thomas (ed.), *Memorials of St Edmund's Abbey* (London, 1900).*

Bacon, Roger, *Opera Hactenus Inedita VI* (Oxford, 1926), ed. R. Steele, pp 268–9; 284–9.*

Barlow, Frank, *Thomas Becket* (London, 1986).

Barry, Terence B., *The archaeology of medieval Ireland* (London & New York, 1987).

Bartlett, Robert, 'Colonial aristocracies of the high Middle Ages' in Robert Bartlett and Angus Mackay (eds), *Medieval frontier societies* (Oxford, 1989), pp 23–47.

Bartlett, Robert, 'Gerald of Wales' (*c.*1146–1220×23) in *ODNB*, ed. H.C.G. Matthew and B. Harrison, 60 vols (Oxford, 2004), 21.

Bartlett, Robert, *Gerald of Wales, 1146–1223* (Oxford, 1982).

Bartlett, Robert, *Why can the dead do such great things? Saints and worshippers from the martyrs to the Reformation* (Princeton, NJ, 2013).

Beechcroft, Gwen, and Arthur Sabin (eds), *Two computus rolls of St Augustine's Abbey, Bristol from 1491–2 and 1511–12*, Bristol Record Society, 9 (1938).*

Berger, Rainer, 'Radiocarbon dating of early medieval Irish monuments', *PRIA*, 95C (1995), 159–74.

Bermingham, Helen, 'Priests' residences in later medieval Ireland' in Elizabeth FitzPatrick and Raymond Gillespie (eds), *The parish in medieval and early modern Ireland* (Dublin, 2006).

---

* Primary printed sources have been marked with an asterisk

Berry, Henry F., 'On the use of signs in the ancient monasteries, with special reference to a code used by the Victorine canons of St Thomas's Abbey, Dublin', *JRSAI*, 2:2 (1892), 107–25.*

Berry, Henry F., 'Notes on a statement dated 1634, regarding St Thomas' Court and St Katherine's churchyard, Dublin', *JRSAI*, ser. 5, 37 (1907), 393–6.*

Berry, Henry F., 'Proceedings in the matter of the custom called tolboll, 1308 and 1385', *PRIA*, 28C (1910), 169–73.*

Berry, Henry F., *Register of the wills and inventories of the diocese of Dublin* (Dublin, 1898).*

Bertram, Jerome, *The Chrodegang rules: the rules for the common life of the secular clergy from the eighth and ninth centuries. Critical texts from the eighth and ninth centuries* (Farnham, 2005).*

Best, Richard I., O. Bergin, M.A. O'Brien and A. O'Sullivan (eds), *The Book of Leinster formerly Lebar na Núachongbála*, 6 vols (Dublin, 1954–83).*

Bhreathnach, Edel, 'Abbesses, minor dynasties and kings *in clericatu*: perspectives of Ireland, 700–850' in M.P. Brown and C.A. Fahr (eds), *Mercia: an Anglo-Saxon kingdom in Europe*, Studies in the Early History of Europe (Leicester, 2001), pp 113–25.

Bhreathnach, Edel, 'The Seanchas tradition in late medieval Ireland' in Edel Bhreathnach and Bernadette Cunningham (eds), *Writing Irish history: the Four Masters and their world* (Dublin, 2007), pp 18–23.

Bhreathnach, Edel, and Ger Dowling, 'The lands and settlements of Augustinian canons, bishops and lords of medieval Ferns, Co. Wexford', *Medieval Archaeology* (forthcoming).

Bhreathnach, Edel, Joseph MacMahon & John McCafferty (eds), *The Irish Franciscans, 1534–1990* (Dublin, 2009).

Bieler, Ludwig, 'Letter of credence by Donatus Magrahe, prior of Lough Derg, for Nylanus O Ledan, priest and pilgrim', *Clogher Record*, 2:2 (1958), 257–9.*

Bieler, Ludwig, 'St Patrick's Purgatory: contributions towards an historical topography', *Irish Ecclesiastical Record*, 93 (1960), 137–44.

Bieler, Ludwig, *The Irish penitentials* (Dublin, 1963).

Bigger, Francis Joseph, 'Inis Chlothrann (Inis Cleraun), Lough Ree: its history and antiquities', *JRSAI*, 10 (1900), 69–90.

Bijsterveld, A.-J.A., 'Looking for common ground: from monastic *fraternitas* to lay confraternity in the southern Low Countries in the tenth to twelfth centuries' in Jamroziak and Burton, *Religious and laity* (2006), pp 287–314.

Binns, Alison M., *Dedications of monastic houses in England and Wales, 1066–1216* (Woodbridge, 1989).

Bird, Jessalyn, 'Penance' in Larissa Taylor (ed.), *Encyclopedia of medieval pilgrimage* (Leiden, 2010), pp 498–501.

Blair, John, 'Debate: ecclesiastical organization and pastoral care in Anglo-Saxon England', *Early Medieval Europe*, 4:2 (1995), 193–212.

Blake, Martin J., 'A note on Roland de Burgo alias Burke, bishop of Clonfert and the monastery "De Portu Puro" at Clonfert', *JGAHS*, 4 (1905–6), 230–2.

Bond, James, 'Medieval nunneries in England and Wales: buildings, precincts and estates' in Diana Wood (ed.), *Women and religion in medieval England* (Oxford, 2003), pp 46–90.

Bosl, Karl, *Regularkanoniker (Augustinerchorherren) und Seelsorge in Kirche und Gesellschaft der europäischen 12. Jahrhunderts* (Munich, 1979).

Bourke, Cormac, 'A crozier and bell from Inishmurray island and their place in ninth-century Irish archaeology', *PRIA*, 85C (1985), 145–68.

Bourke, Cormac, 'What the pilgrim saw' in Brian S. Turner (ed.), *Down Survey 2000. Yearbook of Down County Museum* (Down, 2000), 7–11.

Bourke, Cormac, 'The Domnach Airgid in 2006', *Clogher Record*, 20:1 (2006), 31–42.

Bourke, Cormac, *Patrick: the archaeology of a saint* (Belfast, 1993).

Boydell, Barra, 'The establishment of the choral tradition, 1480–1647' in Milne (ed.), *Christ Church Cathedral Dublin* (2000), pp 237–51.

Bracken, Damien, and Dagmar Ó Riain-Raedel (eds), *Ireland and Europe in the twelfth century: reform and renewal* (Dublin, 2006).

Bradley, John, 'St Patrick's Church, Duleek', *Ríocht na Midhe*, 7:4 (1980–1), 40–51.

Bradley, John, 'Archaeological remains of the Llanthony granges at Duleek and Colpe' in John Bradley (ed.), *Settlement and society in medieval Ireland: studies presented to Francis Xavier Martin* (Kilkenny, 1988), pp 291–326.

Bradley, John, 'A tale of three cities: Bristol, Chester, Dublin and "the coming of the Normans"' in Howard B. Clarke and J.R.S. Phillips (eds), *Ireland, England and the Continent in the Middle Ages and beyond: essays in memory of a turbulent friar, F.X. Martin, OSA* (Dublin, 2006), pp 51–66.

Bradley, John, 'The precinct of St John's Priory, Kilkenny at the close of the Middle Ages', *Peritia*, 22–3 (2011–12), 317–45.

Bradley, John, Alan J. Fletcher and Anngret Simms (eds), *Dublin in the medieval world: studies in honour of Howard B. Clarke* (Dublin, 2009).

Bradshaw, Brendan, *The dissolution of the religious orders in Ireland* (Cambridge, 1974).

Brady, John, 'The nunnery at Clonard', *Ríocht na Midhe*, 2 (1960), 4–7.

Bray, Gerald (ed.), *Records of convocation XVI: Ireland 1101–1690*, Church of England Record Society (Woodbridge, 2006).*

Brewer, J.S., J.F. Dimock and G.F. Warner (eds), *Giraldi Cambrensis opera*, 8 vols, Rolls Series (London, 1862–91).*

Britnell, R.H., 'The proliferation of markets in England, 1200–1349', *Economic History Review*, 34:1 (1998), 209–21.

Brookes, Eric St John (ed.), *Register of the hospital of St John the Baptist without the Newgate, Dublin* (IMC, Dublin, 1936).*

Brooks, Eric St John, *Knights' fees in counties Wexford, Carlow and Kilkenny* (IMC, Dublin, 1950).*

Brooks, Eric St John (ed.), *The Irish cartularies of Llanthony Prima and Secunda* (IMC, Dublin, 1953).*

Brooks, Eric St John, 'The early Irish Comyns', *JRSAI*, 86 (1956), 170–86.

Brundage, James A. (ed.), *The chronicle of Henry of Livonia* (New York, 2003).

Bruzelius, Caroline, and Constance Berman, 'Introduction', *Gesta: monastic architecture for women*, 31:2 (1992), 73–75.

Bruzelius, Caroline, 'The architecture of the mendicant orders in the Middle Ages: an overview of recent literature', *Perspective*, 2 (2012), 365–86.

Buckley, Victor M., *Archaeological inventory of County Louth* (Dublin, 1986).

Bugslag, James, 'Local pilgrimages and their shrines in pre-modern Europe', *Peregrinations*, 2:1 (2005), 1–26.

Bugslag, James, 'Relics of the Virgin Mary', in Taylor (ed.), *Encyclopedia of medieval pilgrimage* (2010), 603–10.

Bugslag, James, 'Material and theological identities: a historical discourse of constructions of the Virgin Mary', *Théologiques*, 17:2 (2014), 19–67.

Buldorini, Chiara, 'Drogheda as a case study of Anglo-Norman town foundation in Ireland, 1194–1412' (PhD, TCD, 2009).

Bull, Marcus, 'Criticism of Henry II's expedition to Ireland in William of Canterbury's miracles of St Thomas Becket', *Journal of Medieval History*, 33 (2007), 108–29.

Burton, Janet, 'Les chanoines réguliers en Grande-Bretagne' in Michel Parisse (ed.), *Les chanoines réguliers. Émergence et expansion (XIe-XIIIe siècles)* (Publications de l'Université de Sainte-Étienne, 2009), pp 477–98.

Burton, Janet, *Monastic and religious houses in Britain, 1000–1300* (Cambridge, 1994).

Burton, Janet, 'The regular canons and diocesan reform in northern England' in J. Burton and K. Stöber (eds), *The regular canons* (2011), pp 41–58.

Burton, Janet, and Karen Stöber (eds), *The regular canons in the medieval British Isles* (Turnhout, 2011).

Butler, Richard (ed.), *Jacobi Grace Kilkenniensis Annales Hiberniae* (Dublin, 1842).*

Bynum, Caroline W., 'The spirituality of regular canons in the twelfth century' in Caroline W. Bynum, *Jesus as mother: studies in the spirituality of the high Middle Ages* (Berkeley, 1982), pp 22–58.

Bynum, Caroline W., *Wonderful blood: theology and practice in late medieval northern Germany and beyond* (Philadelphia, 2007).

Byrne, Francis J., 'Succession lists. Heads of churches to c.1200', in T.W. Moody, F.X. Martin and F.J. Byrne (eds), *A new history of Ireland*, ix (Oxford, 1984), pp 237–63.

Calendar of charter rolls, 1257–1300 (London, 1906).*

Calendar of charter rolls, 1327–41 (London, 1912).*

Calendar of entries in the papal registers relating to Great Britain and Ireland: papal letters, 20 vols (London, 1893–1960; Dublin, IMC, 1978–2008).*

Calendar of the close rolls, 1272–1509, 47 vols (HMSO, London, 1892–1963).*

Calendar of patent rolls, Edward III, 1361–1364 (London, 1912).*

Calender of patent rolls, Richard II, 1377–81 (London, 1895).*

Carey Bates, Rhiannon, and Tadhg O'Keeffe, 'Colonial monasticism, the politics of patronage, and the beginnings of Gothic in Ireland: the Victorine cathedral priory of Newtown Trim, Co. Meath', *Journal of Medieval Monastic Studies*, 6 (2017), 51–76.

Carney, James, 'The Ó Cianáin Miscellany', *Ériu*, 21 (1969), 122–47.

Carter, Michael, 'Silk purse or sow's ear? The art and architecture of the Cistercian nunnery of Swine, Yorkshire' in Janet Burton and Karen Stöber (eds), *Women in the medieval monastic world* (Turnhout, 2015), pp 253–78.

Casey, Christine, and Alistair Rowan, *The buildings of Ireland. North Leinster* (London, 1993).

Cassidy-Welch, Meghan, *Monastic spaces and their meaning: thirteenth-century English Cistercian houses* (Turnhout, 2001).

Catalogue of additions to the manuscripts in the British Museum (London, 1877).

Cavero Domínguez, Gregoria, 'Spanish female monasticism: "family" monasteries and their transformation (eleventh to twelfth centuries)' in J. Burton and K. Stöber (eds), *Women in the medieval world* (Turnhout, 2015), pp 15–52.

Charles-Edwards, Thomas, 'The pastoral role of the church in early Irish laws' in John Blair and Richard Sharpe (eds), *Pastoral care before the parish* (Leicester, 1992), pp 63–80.

Chartae, privilegia et immunitates (printed for the Irish Record Commission, Dublin, 1829–30, published 1889).*

Chibnall, Marjorie, 'Aspects of knighthood: knights and monks' in Ripyard (ed.), *Chivalry, knighthood, and war* (1999), pp 99–109.

Chibnall, Marjorie, 'Aspects of knighthood: the knight and his horse' in Ripyard (ed.), *Chivalry, knighthood, and war* (1999), pp 5–27.

Chibnall, Marjorie, 'Changing expectations of a royal benefactor: the religious patronage of Henry II' in E. Jamroziak and J. Burton (eds), *Religious and laity* (2006), pp 8–21.

Chibnall, Marjorie, *The Empress Matilda: queen consort, queen mother and lady of the English* (Oxford, 1991).

Chibnall, Marjorie, *The Normans* (Oxford, 2000).

Childs, Wendy, and T. O'Neill (eds), 'Overseas trade' in *NHI*, ii, pp 492–532.

Choy, Renie, 'Praying by the rules: legislating intercessory prayer in Carolingian monastic reform' in Krijn Pansters and Abraham Plunkett-Latimer, *Shaping stability: the normation and formation of religious life in the Middle Ages* (Turnhout, 2016), pp 69–87.

Christie, R.C. (ed.), *Annales Cestrienses or chronicle of the abbey of St Werburg at Chester*; Lancashire and Cheshire Record Society Publications, 14 (1886).*

Clapham, Alfred, 'The priory and manor house of Dartford', *Archaeological Journal*, 83 (1926), 67–85.

Clarke, Howard B. (ed.), *Medieval Dublin: the living city* (Dublin, 1990).

Clarke, Howard B., 'The 1192 charter of liberties and the beginnings of Dublin's municipal life', *Dublin Historical Record*, 46 (1993), 5–14.

Clarke, Howard B., '*Urbs et suburbium*: beyond the walls of medieval Dublin' in Conleth Manning (ed.), *Dublin and beyond the Pale: studies in honour of Patrick Healy* (Bray 1998), pp 45–58.

Clarke, Howard B., 'Cult, church and collegiate church before *c.*1220' in John Crawford and Raymond Gillespie (eds), *St Patrick's Cathedral, Dublin: a history* (Dublin, 2009), pp 23–44.

Clarke, Howard B., *The four parts of the city: high life and low life in the suburbs of medieval Dublin*, The Sir John T. Gilbert commemorative lecture, 2001 (Dublin, 2003).

Clarke, James, 'Monastic confraternity in medieval England: the evidence from St Alban's Abbey *Liber benefactorum*' in E. Jamroziak and J. Burton (eds), *Religious and laity* (2006), pp 315–31.

Clarke, Maude V., *Register of the priory of the Blessed Virgin Mary at Tristernagh* (Dublin, 1941).*

Claussen, Martin Allen, 'Practical exegesis: the Acts of the Apostles, Chrodegang's *Regula canonicorum*, and the early Carolingian reform' in David Blanks, Michael

Frasetto and Amy Livingstone (eds), *Medieval monks and their world: ideas and realities. Studies in honor of Richard E. Sullivan* (Leiden & Boston, 2006), pp 119–46.

Close rolls of the reign of Henry III, 1237–1242 (London, 1911).*

Clyne, Miriam, 'Archaeological excavations at Holy Trinity Abbey, Lough Key, Co. Roscommon', *PRIA*, 105C (2005), 23–98.

Clyne, Miriam, 'The founders and patrons of Premonstratensian houses in Ireland' in J. Burton and K. Stöber (eds), *The regular canons* (2011), pp 145–76.

Clyne, Miriam, 'The rental of Holy Trinity Abbey, Lough Cé' in Thomas Finan (ed.), *Medieval Lough Cé: history, archaeology and landscape* (Dublin, 2010), pp 67–96.

Clyne, Miriam, *Kells Priory, Co. Kilkenny: archaeological excavations by T. Fanning & M. Clyne* (Dublin, 2007).

Cochran, Jennifer K., 'Medieval Irish wooden figure sculpture' (MLitt, TCD, 2004).

Cochrane, Robert, 'Notes on the Augustinian priory of Athassel, Co. Tipperary', *JRSAI*, 39 (1909), 279–89.

Cogan, Anthony, *The ecclesiastical history of the diocese of Meath: ancient and modern*, 3 vols (Dublin, 1862).

Coleman, Ambrose, 'Regestum Monasterii Fratrum Praedicatorum de Athenry', *Archivium Hibernicum*, 1 (1912), 201–21.*

Colfer, Billy, *Arrogant trespass: Anglo-Norman Wexford, 1169–1400* (Enniscorthy, 2002).

Colgan, John, *Acta sanctorum veteris et majoris Scotiae seu Hiberniae … sanctorum Insulae* I (Louvain, 1645; repr. Dublin, 1947).*

Colgan, John, *Triadis thaumaturgae seu divorum Patricii, Columbae et Brigidae, trium veteris et maioris Scotiae seu Hiberniae, sanctorum Insulae, communium patronorum acta* (Louvain, 1647; repr. Dublin, 1997).*

Colker, Marvin L., 'Richard of St Victor and the Anonymous of Bridlington', *Traditio*, 18 (1962), 201–23.*

Colker, Marvin L. (ed.), *Analecta Dublinensia: three medieval Latin texts in the library of Trinity College Dublin* (Cambridge, MA, 1975), pp 2–62.*

Colker, Marvin L., *Trinity College Library Dublin: descriptive catalogue of the mediaeval and Renaissance Latin manuscripts*, 2 vols (Aldershot, 1991).

Colvin, Howard M., *The white canons in England* (Oxford, 1951).

Colvin, Howard M., *The history of the king's works*, 8 vols (London, 1963–82).

Connolly, Philomena, 'Irish material in the class of ancient petitions', *Anal. Hib.*, 34 (Dublin 1987), 1–106.*

Connolly, Philomena, *Statute rolls of the Irish parliament: Richard III to Henry VIII* (Dublin, 2000).*

Constable, Giles, *Monastic tithes from their origins to the twelfth century* (Cambridge, 1964).

Coppack, Glyn, 'Thornholme Priory: the development of a monastic outer court' in R. Gilchrist and H. Mytum (eds), *The archaeology of rural monasteries* (1989), pp 185–222.

Coppack, Glyn, *Abbeys and priories* (Stroud, 2006).

Cosgrove, Art (ed.), *A new history of Ireland*, ii: *medieval Ireland, 1169–1534* (Oxford, 1987).

Cotter, Eamonn (ed.), *Buttevant: a medieval Anglo-French town in Ireland* (Rathcormac, 2013).

Crooks, Peter, 'Mac Murchada, Diarmait' in Seán Duffy (ed.), *Medieval Ireland: an encyclopedia* (New York, 2005), pp 299–302.

Crosthwaite, John C., and James H. Todd (eds), *The book of obits and the martyrology of the Cathedral Church of the Holy Trinity, commonly called Christ Church, Dublin* (Dublin, 1844).*

Currie, Christopher K., 'The role of fishponds in the monastic economy' in R. Gilchrist and H. Mytum (eds), *The archaeology of rural monasteries* (1989), pp 147–72.

Curtis, Edmund (ed.), *Calendar of Ormond deeds, 1172–1350*, 6 vols (IMC, Dublin, 1932).*

Davies, John, *Pilgrimage yesterday and today. Why? Where? How?* (London, 1988).

Davies, Oliver, 'The churches of County Cavan', *JRSAI*, 78 (1948), 73–118.

Davies, Wendy, 'Local priests in Iberia', in Steffen Patzold and A. Carine van Rhijn (eds), *Local priests in early medieval Europe* (Berlin, 2016), pp 125–44.

Davis, Virginia, 'Relations between the abbey of St Thomas the Martyr and the municipality of Dublin, *c.*1176–1527, *Dublin Historical Record*, 40:2 (1987), 57–65.

De Certeau, Michel, *The practice of everyday life* (Berkley, 1984).

De Paermentier, Els, 'Experiencing space through women's convent rules: the Rich Clares in medieval Ghent (thirteenth to fourteenth centuries)', *Medieval Feminist Forum*, 44:1 (2008), 53–68.

Delisle, Léopold, and Elie Berger (eds), *Recueil des actes de Henri II*, 4 vols (Paris, 1909–27).*

Dennison, Linda, 'Monastic or secular?: the artist of the Ramsey Psalter, now at Holkham Hall, Norfolk' in Benjamin Thompson (ed.), *Monasteries and society in early medieval Britain* (Stamford, 1999), pp 223–61.

Dickinson, John C., 'English regular canons and the Continent in the twelfth century', *Transactions of the Royal Historical Society*, 1 (1951), 71–89.

Dickinson, John C., 'The origins of St Augustine's, Bristol' in Patrick McGrath and John Cannon (eds), *Essays in Bristol and Gloucestershire history* (Bristol, 1976), pp 109–26.

Dickinson, John C., *The origin of the Austin canons and their introduction into England* (London, 1950).

Dimock, James F. (ed.), *Itinerarium Kambriæ et descriptio Kambriæ. Giraldi Cambrensis opera*, vol. 6 (London, 1868).*

Dobbs, Margaret E. (ed.), 'The Ban-shenchus', *Revue celtique*, 48 (1931), 163–234.*

Dodsworth, Roger, and William Dugdale (eds), *Monasticon Anglicanum*, 3 vols (London, 1655–73).*

Doggett, Dermot, 'The medieval monasteries of the Augustinian canons regular', *Archaeology Ireland*, 10:2 (1996), 31–3.

Doherty, Charles, 'The transmission of the cult of St Máedhóg' in Proinséas Ní Chatháin and Michael Richter (eds), *Ireland and Europe in the early Middle Ages: texts and transmission* (Dublin, 2002), pp 268–83.

Doherty, Charles, Linda Doran and Mary Kelly (eds), *Glendalough: city of God* (Dublin, 2011).

Dowd, Marion, *The archaeology of caves in Ireland* (Oxford, 2015).

Dubois, Jacques, 'Les sources continentales du martyrologe irlandais de Gorman', *Analecta Bollandiana*, 100 (1982), 607–17.

Dubois, Jacques and Geneviève Renaud (eds) *Le martyrologe d'Adon: ses deux familles, ses trois recensions: textes et commentaire* (Paris, 1984).*

Dubois, Jacques, *Le martyrologe d'Usuard* (Brussels, 1965).*

Duddy, Cathal, 'The western suburb of medieval Dublin: its first century', *Irish Geography*, 34 (2001), 157–75.

Duddy, Cathal, 'The role of St Thomas's Abbey in the early development of Dublin's western suburb' in Seán Duffy (ed.), *Medieval Dublin IV* (Dublin, 2003), pp 79–97.

Duffy, Paul and Tadhg O'Keeffe, 'A stone shrine for a relic of Thomas Becket in Dublin?', *Archaeology Ireland*, 31:4 (2017), 18–23.

Duffy, Seán, *Ireland in the Middle Ages* (Dublin, 1997).

Duffy, Seán (ed.), *Medieval Ireland: an encyclopedia* (New York, 2005).

Dugdale, William, *Monasticon Anglicanum*, ed. J. Caley, H. Ellis and B. Bandinel (8 vols, London, 1817–30, reprint [6 vols] 1846).*

Dugdale, William and Roger Dodsworth, *Monasticon Anglicanum*, new edition; ed. J. Caley, H. Ellis and B. Bandinel, 6 vols in 8 (London, 1817–30).*

Duggan, Anne J., 'The cult of St Thomas Becket in the thirteenth century' in Meryl Jancey (ed.), *St Thomas Cantilupe, bishop of Hereford: essays in his honour* ([Hereford], 1982), pp 21–44.

Duggan, Anne J., 'Diplomacy, status, and conscience: Henry II's penance for Becket's murder' in Karl Borchardt and Enno Bünz (eds), *Forschungen zur Reichs- Papst- und Landesgeschichte: Peter Herde zum 65. Geburtstag von Freunden, Schülern und Kollegen dargebracht*, 2 vols (Stuttgart, 1998), i, pp 265–90.

Duggan, Anne J., *Thomas Becket* (London, 2004).

Duggan, Anne J., *Thomas Becket: friends, networks, texts and cult* (London, 2007).

Duignan, Michael, 'Clonfert Cathedral: a note', *JGAHS*, 26 (1954/1955), 29.

Dunning, P.J., 'The Arroasian order in medieval Ireland', *IHS*, 4 (1945), 297–315.

Egan, Patrick K., 'The Carmelite cell of Bealaneny', *JGAHS*, 26 (1956).

Egan, Patrick K., 'The convent of St Mary's Oghill', *Past and present, Lawrencetown community hall* (1995).

Egan, Patrick K., *Parish of Ballinasloe* (1994).

Elkins, S.K., *Holy women of twelfth-century England* (Carolina, 1988).

Ellis, Clarence, *Hubert de Burgh: a study in constancy* (London, 1952).

Ellis, Steven G., and James Murray (eds), *Calendar of state papers, Ireland, Tudor period, 1509–1547* (Dublin, 2017).*

Emden, A.B., *A biographical register of the University of Oxford to AD 1500*, 3 vols (Oxford, 1957–9).

Emery, P.-Y., 'Vie de Saint Malachie', *Sources Chrétiennes*, 367 (Paris, 1990), pp 137–377.*

Empey, Adrian, 'The settlement of the kingdom of Limerick' in James Lydon (ed.), *England and Ireland in the later Middle Ages* (Dublin, 1981), pp 1–25.

Empey, Adrian, 'The sacred and the secular: the Augustinian priory of Kells in Ossory, 1193–1541', *IHS*, 24 (1984), 131–51.

Empey, Adrian, 'Inistioge in the Middle Ages' in John Kirwan (ed.), *Kilkenny: studies in honour of Margaret M. Phelan* (Kilkenny, 1997), pp 9–15.

Empey, Adrian, 'Introduction' in Kinsella (ed.), *Augustinians at Christ Church* (2000), pp 3–8.

Empey, Adrian, 'The origins of the medieval parish revisited' in Howard B. Clarke and J.R.S. Phillips (eds), *Ireland, England and the Continent in the Middle Ages and beyond: essays in memory of a turbulent friar, F.X. Martin OSA* (Dublin, 2006), pp 29–50.

Empey, Adrian, 'The Augustinian priory of Kells: an historical introduction' in Clyne (ed.), *Kells Priory* (2007), pp 1–11.

Empey, Mark, 'State intervention in disputes between secular and regular clergy in early seventeenth-century Ireland', *British Catholic History*, 34: 2 (2018), 304–26.

Esposito, Mario, 'The sources of Conchubranus' Life of St Monenna', *EHR*, 35 (1920), 71–8.

Etchingham, Colmán, *Church organisation in Ireland, AD 650 to 1000* (Maynooth, 1999).

Eyton, Robert W., *Court, household and itinerary of King Henry II* (London, 1878).

Fassler, Margaret E., *Gothic song: Victorine sequences and Augustinian reform in twelfth-century Paris* (2nd ed., Notre Dame, IN, 2011).

Fawtier, Robert, and Ferdinand Lot (eds), *Histoire des institutions françaises au moyen age: tome III, institutions ecclésiastiques* (Paris, 1962).

Feehan, John, and Grace O'Donovan, *The bogs of Ireland: an introduction to the natural, cultural and environmental heritage of Irish peatland* (Dublin, 1996).

Feiss, Hugh, 'The order of St Victor in Ireland' in *Ordo canonicus: studia canonicalia cura confoederationis canonicorum regularium S. Augustini edita*, series altera, 4 (1988), pp 56–87.

Feiss, Hugh, '*Circatores*: from Benedict of Nursia to Humbert of Romans', *The American Benedictine Review*, 40:4 (1989), 346–79.

Feiss, Hugh, and Patrice Sicard, *L'oeuvre de Hugues de Saint-Victor*, 2 vols (Turnhout, 1997).*

Feiss, Hugh, and Juliet Mousseau (eds), *A companion to the abbey of Saint Victor in Paris* (Leiden, 2018).

Feiss, Hugh, 'Pastoral ministry: preaching and confession' in H. Feiss and J. Mousseau (eds), *Companion to the abbey of Saint Victor* (2018), pp 147–86.

Fenning, Hugh, *The undoing of the friars of Ireland* (Louvain, 1972).

Finucane, Ronald C., *Miracles and pilgrims: popular beliefs in medieval England* (London, 1995).

FitzPatrick, Elizabeth, and Raymond Gillespie (eds), *The parish in medieval and early modern Ireland: community, territory and building* (Dublin, 2006).

Flanagan, Marie Therese, 'St Mary's Abbey Louth and the introduction of the Arrouaisian observance into Ireland', *Clogher Record*, 10 (1980), 223–34.

Flanagan, Marie Therese, 'Devotional images and their uses in the twelfth-century Irish church: the crucifix of Holy Trinity Dublin and Archbishop John Cumin' in Howard B. Clarke and J.R.S. Philips (eds), *Ireland, England and the Continent in the Middle Ages and beyond: essays in memory of a turbulent friar, F.X. Martin OSA* (Dublin, 2006), pp 67–87.

Flanagan, Marie Therese, '*Conquestus* and *adquisicio*: some early charters relating to St Thomas' Abbey, Dublin' in Emer Purcell et al. (eds), *Clerics, kings and vikings: essays on medieval Ireland in honour of Donnchadh Ó Corráin* (Dublin, 2014), pp 127–46.

Flanagan, Marie Therese, 'High-kings with opposition, 1072–1166' in *NHI*, i, pp 899–933.

Flanagan, Marie Therese, *Irish royal charters: texts and contexts* (Oxford, 2005).*

Flanagan, Marie Therese, *The transformation of the Irish church in the twelfth century* (Woodbridge, 2010).

Fleming, John, *Gille of Limerick c.1070–1145: architect of a medieval church* (Dublin, 2001).

Fletcher, Alan J., 'The de Derby psalter of Christ Church Cathedral' in R. Gillespie and R. Refaussé (eds), *Medieval manuscripts* (2006), pp 81–102.

Foley, Áine, *The abbey of St Thomas the Martyr, Dublin* (Dublin, 2017).

Foley, Clare, Ronan McHugh and Brian Scott (eds), *An archaeological survey of County Fermanagh*, 2 vols (Northern Ireland Environment Agency, Newtownards, 2014).

Follett, Westley, *Céli Dé in Ireland: monastic writing and identity in the early Middle Ages* (Woodbridge, 2006).

Foot, Sarah, *Veiled women: female religious communities in England, 871–1066* (Aldershot, 2000).

Foot, Sarah, *Veiled women: the disappearance of nuns from Anglo-Saxon England* (Aldershot, 2000).

Foot, Sarah, *Monastic life in Anglo-Saxon England, c.600–900* (Cambridge, 2006).

Frame, Robin, 'The immediate effect and interpretation of the 1331 ordinance "Una et eadem lex"': some evidence', *Irish Jurist*, 7 (1972), 109–14.

Frame, Robin, 'Power and society in the lordship of Ireland' in Frame (ed.), *Ireland and Britain, 1170–1450* (1998), pp 191–220.

Frame, Robin (ed.), *Ireland and Britain, 1170–1450* (London, 1998).

Franklin, Jill A., 'Augustinian and other canons' churches in Romanesque Europe: the significance of the aisleless cruciform plan' in Jill A. Franklin, T.A. Heslop and Christine Stevenson (eds), *Architecture and interpretation: essays for Eric Fernie* (Woodbridge, 2012), pp 8–98.

Freeman, A. Martin (ed.), 'The Annals in Cotton MS Titus A. XXV', *Revue Celtique*, 41 (1924), 301–30; 42 (1925), 283–305; 43 (1926), 358–84; 44 (1927), 336–61.*

Freeman, A. Martin (ed.), *Annála Connacht: The Annals of Connacht (AD 1224–1544)* (Dublin, 1944).*

Gallwey, Hubert, 'The Cusack family of Counties Meath and Dublin', *Irish Genealogist*, 5 (London, 1974–5), 298–313.

Gibbons, Michael, and Myles Gibbons, 'Inishglora – "The western threshold between land and wave"' in Jim Higgins (ed.), *Recent explorations and discoveries in Irish heritage* (Galway, 2017).

Gilbert, John T., *Historical and municipal documents of Ireland, AD 1170–1320*, Rolls Series (London, 1870).*

Gilbert, John T., *Facsimiles of national manuscripts of Ireland*, 4 vols, Public Record Office of Ireland (Dublin, 1874–84).*

Gilbert, John T. (ed.), *Chartularies of St Mary's Abbey, Dublin: with the register of its house at Dunbrody, and the Annals of Ireland*, 2 vols, Rolls Series (London 1884–6).*

Gilbert, John T. (ed.), *Register of the abbey of St Thomas, Dublin*, Rolls Series (London, 1889).*

Gilbert, John T. (ed.), *Calendar of ancient records of Dublin*, 18 vols (Dublin, 1889–1944).*

Gilbert, John T. (ed.), *Crede Mihi: the most ancient register book of the archbishops of Dublin before the Reformation* (Dublin, 1892).*

Gilchrist, Roberta, 'Unsexing the body: the interior sexuality of medieval religious women' in Robert A. Schmidt and Barbara L. Voss (eds), *Archaeologies of sexuality* (London & New York, 2000).

Gilchrist, Roberta and Harold Mytum (eds), *The archaeology of rural monasteries* (Oxford, 1989).

Gilchrist, Roberta, *Gender and material culture: the archaeology of religious women* (London, 1994).

Gillespie, Raymond, 'The coming of reform, 1500–58' in Milne (ed.), *Christ Church Cathedral, Dublin* (2000), pp 151–73.

Gillespie, Raymond, 'The crisis of Reform, 1625–60' in Milne (ed.), *Christ Church Cathedral, Dublin* (2000), pp 195–217.

Gillespie, Raymond, 'The Irish Franciscans, 1600–1700' in E. Bhreathnach et al. (eds), *The Irish Franciscans* (2007), pp 45–76.

Gillespie, Raymond, and Raymond Refaussé (eds), *The medieval manuscripts of Christ Church Cathedral, Dublin* (Dublin, 2006).

Giroud, Charles, *L'Ordre des chanoines réguliers de Saint-Augustin et ses diverses formes de régime interne* (Martigny, 1961).

Golding, Brian, *Gilbert of Sempringham and the Gilbertine order, c.1130–c.1300* (Oxford, 1995).

Gourlay, Andrew, 'Things left behind: matter, narrative and the cult of St Edmund of East Anglia' (PhD, University of Glasgow, 2017).

Grélois, Alexis, 'Les chanoines réguliers et la conversion des femmes au XIIe siècle' in Parisse (ed.), *Les chanoines réguliers*, pp 233–63.

Green, Lauryl B., 'Unveiling the cloisters: Augustinian nunneries in twelfth-century Ireland', *History Studies*, 2 (2000), 37–49.

Greene, J. Patrick, 'Methods of interpretation of monastic sites' in R. Gilchrist and H. Mytum (eds), *The archaeology of rural monasteries* (1989).

Greene, J. Patrick, *Medieval monasteries* (London & New York, 1995).

Griffith, Margaret C. (ed.), *Irish patent rolls of James I: facsimile of the Irish record commissioners' calendar prepared prior to 1830* (IMC, Dublin, 1966).*

Griffith, Margaret C. (ed.), *Calendar of inquisitions formerly in the office of the chief remembrancer of the exchequer prepared from the MSS of the Irish Record Commission* (Dublin, 1991).*

Griffiths, Fiona, 'Canonesses' in Margaret Schaus (ed.), *Women and gender in medieval Europe: an encyclopedia* (New York, 2006), pp 106–7.

Grose, Daniel C., 'Shrine of the Holy Trinity, in the monastery of the Holy Trinity, Lough Kee, or Rockingham Lake, County of Roscommon', *The Irish Penny Magazine*, I (1833), 357–8.

Grose, Francis, *The antiquities of Ireland*, 2 vols (London, 1795).

Guglielmi, Pietro, *La Vita Comune nel Clero: i canonici regolari Lateranensi* (Rome, 2010).

Gwynn, Aubrey, 'Some unpublished texts from the Black Book of Christ Church', *Anal. Hib.*, 16 (1946), pp 281–337.*

Gwynn, Aubrey, 'Medieval Bristol and Dublin', *IHS*, 5 (1947), 275–86.

Gwynn, Aubrey, 'The early history of St Thomas's Abbey, Dublin', *JRSAI*, 84 (1954), 1–35.

Gwynn, Aubrey, *The Irish church in the eleventh and twelfth centuries*, Gerard O'Brien (ed.) (Dublin, 1992).

Gwynn, Edward (ed.), 'The Rule of Tallaght', *Hermathena 44, supplemental volume* (Dublin and London, 1927).*

Hadcock, R. Neville, 'The origin of the Augustinian order in Meath', *Ríocht na Midhe*, 3 (1964), 124–31.

Hagger, Mark S., *The fortunes of a Norman family: the de Verduns in England, Ireland and Wales, 1066–1316* (Dublin, 2001).

Hall, Diane, 'Towards a prosopography of nuns in medieval Ireland', *AH*, 53 (1999), 3–15.

Hall, Dianne, *Women and the church in medieval Ireland, c.1140–1540* (Dublin, 2003).

Hallam, Elizabeth M., 'Henry II as a founder of monasteries', *Journal of Ecclesiastical History*, 28 (1977), 113–32.

Hand, Geoffrey J., 'The rivalry of the cathedral chapters in medieval Dublin', *JRSAI*, 92 (1962), 193–206.

Hand, Geoffrey J., 'The status of the native Irish in the lordship of Ireland, 1272–1331', *Irish Jurist*, 1 (1966), 93–115.

Harbison, Peter, *Pilgrimage in Ireland: the monuments and the people* (London, 1995).

Hardiman, James (ed.), *A statute of the fortieth year of King Edward III: enacted in a parliament held in Kilkenny, AD 1367, before Lionel duke of Clarence* (Dublin, 1843).*

Hardy, Thomas D. (ed.), *Rotuli litterarum clausarum in turri Londinensi asservati*, 2 vols (London, 1833–44).*

Hardy, Thomas D. (ed.), *Rotuli de oblatis et finibus* (London, 1835).*

Haren, Michael, 'St Victor, Richard of (d. 1173?)' in *ODNB*, 48, pp 672–4.

Haren, Michael, and Yolande de Pontfarcy, *The medieval pilgrimage to St Patrick's Purgatory: Lough Derg and the European tradition* (Enniskillen, 1988).

Harrington, Christina, *Women in a Celtic Church: Ireland* (Oxford, 2002).

Hart, W.H. (ed.), *Historia et cartularium Monasterii Sancti Petri Gloucestriae* (London, 1863).*

Hawkes, William, 'The liturgy in Dublin, 1200–1500', *Reportorium Novum*, 2 (1958), 33–67.

Heist, William Watts (ed.), *Vitae sanctorum Hiberniae: ex codice olim Salmanticensi, nunc Bruxellensi. Lives of the saints of Ireland, from the Salamanca manuscript now of Brussels*, Subsidia Hagiographica 28. Société des Bollandistes (Brussels, 1965).*

Helbig, Herbert, and L.Weinrich (eds), *Urkunden und erzählende Quellen zur deutschen Ostsiedlung im Mittelalter* (Darmstadt, 1975).*

Hennessy, Mark, 'Manorial organization in early thirteenth-century Tipperary', *Irish Geography*, 29:2 (1996), 116–25.

Hennig, John, 'Irish saints in early German literature', *Speculum* 22: 3 (1947), 358–74.

Hennig, John, 'Versus de mensibus', *Traditio*, 11 (1955), 65–90.*

Hennig, John, 'The notes on non-Irish saints in the manuscripts of the *Féilire Oengusso*', *PRIA*, 75C (1975), 119–60.*

Herbert, Máire, 'Latin and vernacular hagiography of Ireland from the origins to the sixteenth century' in Guy Philippart (ed.), *Hagiographies* (Turnhout, 2001), pp 327–60.

Herbert, Máire, 'Saint Colmán of Dromore and Inchmahone', *Scottish Gaelic Studies*, 24 (2008), 253–64.

Herbert, Máire, 'The *Vita Columbae* and Irish hagiography' in John Carey, Máire Herbert and Pádraig Ó Riain (eds), *Studies in Irish hagiography: saints and scholars* (Dublin, 2011), pp 31–40.

Herbert, Máire, 'Observations on the *Vita* of Bishop Áed mac Bricc' in Dónall Ó Baoill, Donncha Ó hAodha and Nollaig Ó Muraíle (eds), *Saltair saíochta, sanasaíochta agus seanchais: a festschrift for Gearóid Mac Eoin* (Dublin, 2013), pp 64–74.

Herwaarden, J. Van, *Between Saint James and Erasmus: studies in late-medieval religious life: devotions and pilgrimages in the Netherlands* (Leiden/Boston, 2003).

Hicks, Leonie, V., *Religious life in Normandy, 1050–1300: space, gender and social pressure* (Woodbridge, 2007).

Hill, Rosalind, 'A letter-book of S. Augustine's Bristol', *Transactions of the Bristol and Gloucestershire Archaeological Society*, 65 (1944), 141–56.*

Hill, Rosalind, 'Ecclesiastical letter books of the thirteenth century' (MLitt, Oxford, 1936).

Hogan, Arlene, *Killmallock Dominican Priory: an architectural perspective, 1291–1991* (Limerick, 1991).

Hogan, Arlene, *The priory of Llanthony Prima and Secunda in Ireland, 1172–1541: lands, patronage and politics* (Dublin, 2008).*

Hogan, Edmund, *Onomasticon Goedelicum* (Dublin, 1910).

Holden, Brock, 'King John, the Braoses, and the Celtic fringe', *Albion*, 33 (2001), 1–23.

Holland, Martin, 'Malachy (Máel Máedóc)' in Seán Duffy (ed.), *Medieval Ireland: an encyclopedia* (New York, 2005), pp 312–14.

Horn, Walter, and Ernest Born, *The plan of St Gall* (Berkeley, 1979).

Hourihane, Colum, *Gothic art in Ireland, 1169–1550* (London and New Haven, 2003).

Hudson, Benjamin T., 'The changing economy of the Irish Sea province: AD 900–1300' in Smith (ed.), *Britain and Ireland* (1999), pp 39–66

Hughes, Kathleen, *The church in early Irish society* (London, 1966).

Hugo, Charles Louis (ed.), *Sacrae antiquitatis monumenta historica, dogmatica, diplomatica*, 2 vols (Stivagii (Étival), 1725–31).*

Hugo de S. Victore, *Expositio in Regulam S. Augustini: Patrologia Latina* 176 (Paris, 1854) pp 881–924.*

Irish fiants of the Tudor sovereigns: during the reigns of Henry VIII, Edward VI, Philip and Mary, and Elizabeth I, 4 vols (Dublin, 1994).*

Irish patent rolls of James I: facsimile of the Irish Record Commission's calendar prepared prior to 1830 (Dublin, 1966).*

Jaeger, C. Stephen, 'Victorine humanism' in H. Feiss and J. Mousseau (eds), *Companion to the abbey of Saint Victor* (2018), pp 79–112.

Jamroziak, Emilia, and Janet Burton (eds), *Religious and laity in Western Europe, 1000–1400* (Turnhout, 2006).

Jefferies, Henry A., 'Mac Carthaig (Mac Carthy)' in Seán Duffy (ed.), *Medieval Ireland: an encyclopedia* (New York, 2005), pp 289–90.

Jocqué, Lucas, 'Les structures de la population claustrale dans l'ordre de Saint-Victor au xiie siècle: un essai d'analyse du *Liber ordinis*' in Longère (ed.), *L'abbaye Parisienne de Saint-Victor*, pp 53–95.

Jocqué, Lucas, and Ludovicus Milis (eds), *Liber ordinis Sancti Victoris Parisiensis*, Corpus Christianorum Continatio Mediaevalis (Turnhout, 1984).*

Joyce, P.W., *Irish place names* (Belfast, 1984).

Kalkreuter, Britta, *Boyle Abbey and the School of the West* (Bray, 2001).

Kelly, Liam, *The diocese of Kilmore, c.1100–1800* (Dublin, 2017).

Kenney, J.F., *The sources for the early history of Ireland (ecclesiastical)* (New York, 1929; repr. Dublin, 1997).

Kinsella, Stuart, 'From Hiberno-Norse to Anglo-Norman, c.1030–1300' in Milne (ed.), *Christ Church Cathedral, Dublin* (2000), pp 25–52.

Kinsella, Stuart, 'Mapping Christ Church Cathedral, Dublin, c.1028–1608: an examination of the western cloister' in John Bradley et al. (eds), *Dublin in the medieval world* (2009), pp 143–6.

Kinsella, Stuart (ed.), *Augustinians at Christ Church: the canons regular of the cathedral priory of Holy Trinity, Dublin* (Dublin, 2000).

Klein, Holger, 'Relics of the Passion' in Larissa Taylor (ed.), *Encyclopedia of medieval pilgrimage* (2010), pp 599–601.

Knowles, David, and R. Neville Hadcock, *Medieval religious houses: England and Wales* (London, 1953).

Knowles, David, Christopher N.L. Brooke and Vera C.M. London (eds), *Heads of religious houses, 940–1216* (2nd ed., Cambridge 2001).

Knox, Hubert T., *Notes on the early history of the diocese of Tuam, Killala and Achonry* (Dublin, 1904).

Koopmans, Rachel, *Wonderful to relate: miracles stories and miracle collecting in high medieval England* (Philadelphia, 2011).

Kramer, Rutger, 'Teaching emperors: transcending the boundaries of Carolingian monastic communities' in Eirik Howden, Christian Lutter and Walter Pohl (eds), *Meanings of community across medieval Eurasia: comparative approaches* (Leiden & Boston, 2016), pp 309–37.

Krings, Bruno (ed.), 'Das Ordensrecht der Prämonstratenser vom späten 12. Jahrhundert bis zum Jahr 1227. Der Liber consuetudinum und die Dekrete des Generalkapitels', *Analecta Praemonstratensia*, 69 (1993), 108–242.*

Langston, J.N., 'Priors of Llanthony by Gloucester', *Transactions of the Bristol and Gloucestershire Archaeological Society*, 63 (1942), 1–143.

Larkin, Patrick, *A calendar of papal registers relating to Clonfert diocese* (2016).*

Lawless, George, *Augustine of Hippo and his monastic Rule* (Oxford, 1987).*

Lawlor, Hugh J., 'A calendar of the *Liber Niger* and *Liber Albus* of Christ Church, Dublin', *PRIA*, 27C (1908), 1–93.*

Lawlor, Henry J., 'A calendar of the register of Archbishop Sweteman', *PRIA*, 29C (1911), 213–310.*

Lawlor, Hugh J., 'A charter of Cristin, bishop of Louth', *PRIA*, 32C (1914–61), 28–40.*

Lawlor, Hugh J. (ed.), *St Bernard of Clairvaux's Life of St Malachy of Armagh* (London, 1920).*

Lawlor, Hugh J., 'Note on the church of St Michan, Dublin', *JRSAI*, 56 (1926), 11–21.

Lawrence, C.H., *Medieval monasticism: forms of religious life in Western Europe in the Middle Ages* (3rd ed., London & New York, 2001).

Le Goff, Jacques, *The birth of Purgatory* (Chicago and London, 1984).

Leask, Harold G., *Irish churches and monastic buildings II: Gothic architecture to AD 1400* (Dundalk, 1966).

Lee, Gerard A., *Leper hospitals in medieval Ireland* (Dublin, 1996).

Lefèvre, Placide F. (ed.), *L'ordinaire de Prémontré, d'après des manuscrits du XIIe et du XIIIe siècle*, Bibliothèque de la Revue d'Histoire Ecclésiastique, 22 (Louvain, 1941).*

Lefèvre, Placide F. (ed.), *Les statuts de Prémontré réformés sur les ordres de Grégoire IX et d'Innocent IV au XIIIe siècle*, Bibliothèque de la Revue d'Histoire Ecclésiastique, 23 (Louvain, 1946).*

Lefèvre, Placide F. (ed.), *Coutumiers liturgiques de Prémontré du XIIIe et du XIVe siècle*, Bibliothèque de la Revue d'Histoire Ecclésiastique, 27 (Louvain, 1953).*

Lefèvre, Placide F., and Wilfried M. Grauwen (eds), *Les statuts de Prémontré au milieu du XIIe siècle*, Bibliotecheca Analectorum Praemonstratensium, 12 (Averbode, 1978).*

Le Paige, Joannes, *Bibliotheca Praemonstratensis ordinis*, Instrumenta Praemonstratensia, 3 (Averbode, 1998; facs. repr. of orig. publ. Paris, 1633).*

Lemaître, Jean-Loup, '*Libri Capituli*: Le Livre du Chapitre, des origines au XVI siècle. L'exemple Français' in Karl Schmid and Joachim Wollasch (eds), *Memoria: der geschichtliche Zeugniswert des liturgischen Gedenkens im Mittelalter* (Munich, 1984), pp 625–48.

Lennon, Colm, 'The Nugent family and the diocese of Kilmore in the sixteenth and early seventeenth centuries', *Breifne*, 37 (2001), 360–74.

Lennon, Colm, 'The book of obits of Christ Church Cathedral, Dublin' in Gillespie & Refaussé (eds), *Medieval manuscripts* (2006), pp 163–82.

Lennon, Colm, 'The dissolution to the foundation of St Anthony's College, Louvain, 1534–1607' in Bhreathnach et al. (eds), *The Irish Franciscans* (2009), pp 2–26.

Lewis, Samuel, *A topographical dictionary of Ireland* (London, 1837).

Little, Bryan, *Abbeys and priories in England and Wales* (London, 1979).

Löffler, A., and B. Gebert (eds), *Legitur in necrologio Victorino: studien zum Nekrolog von Sankt Viktor*, Corpus Victorinum, Instrumenta, 3 (Münster, 2015).

Longère, Jean (ed.), *L'abbaye Parisienne de Saint-Victor au moyen âge: communications présentés au XIIIe colloque d'humanisme médiéval de Paris (1986–1988)*, Bibliotheca Victorina, 1 (Paris, Turnhout, 1991).

Love, R.C., 'Hagiography' in Michael Lapidge, John Blair, Simon Keynes and Donald Scragg (eds), *The Blackwell encyclopedia of Anglo-Saxon England* (London, 2001), pp 226–8.

Love, R.C., *Three eleventh-century Anglo-Latin Lives* (Oxford, 1996).*

Luard, Henry R. (ed.), *Annales monastici*, 4 vols, Rolls Series (London, 1864–9).*

Lucas, A.T., 'The social role of relics and reliquaries in ancient Ireland, *JRSAI*, 116 (1986), 5–37.

Luxford, Julian, 'The idol of origins: retrospection in Augustinian art during the later Middle Ages' in Burton and Stöber (eds), *The regular canons* (2011), pp 417–42.

Lydon, James, 'The text and its context' in James Mills (ed.), *The account roll of the priory of the Holy Trinity, Dublin, 1337–1346* (repr. Dublin, 1996), pp ix–xxii.

Lydon, James, 'Christ Church in the later medieval world, 1300–1500' in Milne (ed.), *Christ Church Cathedral, Dublin* (2000), pp 75–94.

Lynch, Anthony, 'The administration of John Bole, archbishop of Armagh, 1457–71', *Seanchas Ard Mhacha*, 14:2 (1991), 39–108.

Lynch, Anthony, 'A calendar of the reassembled register of John Bole, archbishop of Armagh, 1457–71', *Seanchas Ard Mhacha*, 15:1 (1992), 113–85.*

Lyons, Mary Ann, 'Manorial administration and the manorial economy in Ireland, *c*.1200–*c*.1377' (PhD, TCD, 1984).

Lyons, Mary Ann, 'The role of St Anthony's College, Louvain in establishing the Irish Franciscan college network, 1607–60' in E. Breathnach et al. (eds), *The Irish Franciscans* (2009), pp 27–44.

Lyons, Mary Ann, *Church and society in County Kildare, c.1470–1547* (Dublin, 2000).

Lyttelton, George, *History of the life of King Henry II*, 6 vols (3rd ed., London, 1773).

Mac Airt, Seán, *The annals of Inisfallen: MS Rawlinson B. 503* (Dublin, 1951).*

Macalister, R.A.S., *Corpus inscriptionum insularum Celticarum*, 2 vols (Dublin, 1949).*

MacCaffrey, James (ed.), *The Black Book of Limerick* (Dublin, 1907).*

MacCotter, Paul, *Medieval Ireland: territorial, political and economic divisions* (Dublin, 2008).

MacCotter, Paul, *A history of the medieval diocese of Cloyne* (Dublin, 2013).

MacCurtain, Margaret, 'Late medieval nunneries of the Irish Pale' in Howard B. Clarke, Jacinta Prunty and Mark Hennessy (eds), *Surveying Ireland's past: multidisciplinary essays in honour of Anngret Simms* (Dublin, 2004), pp 129–44.

Mackilin, Herbert W., *Monumental brasses* (London, 1965).

MacLeod, Caitriona, 'Some late medieval wood sculptures in Ireland', *JRSAI*, 77 (1947), 53–62.

Mac Mahon, Michael, 'The charter of Clare Abbey', *The Other Clare*, 17 (1993), 21–8.*

MacNeill, Charles, and A.J. Otway-Ruthven (eds), *Dowdall deeds* (IMC, Dublin, 1960).*

Mac Niocaill, Gearóid (ed.), 'Dán do Chormac Mág Shamhradháin Easpag Ardachaidh 1444–?1476', *Seanchas Ard Mhacha*, 4 (1960–1), 141–6.*

Mac Niocaill, Gearóid, *Notitiæ as Leabhar Cheanannais 1033–1161* (Cló Morainn, 1961), pp 24–6 (VII).*

Mac Niocaill, Gearóid, 'Cartae Dunenses: 12ú–13u céad', *Seanchas Ard Mhacha*, 5 (1970), 418–28.*

Mac Niocaill, Gearóid, *Na Buirgéisí, XII–XV aois* (2 vols, Dublin, 1964).*

Mac Niocaill, Gearóid (ed.), *Crown surveys of lands, 1540–41, with the Kildare rental begun in 1518* (IMC, Dublin, 1992).*

Mac Shamhráin, Ailbhe, *Church and polity in pre-Norman Ireland: the case of Glendalough* (Maynooth, 1996).

Maggioni, Giovanni Paolo, 'The tradition of Saint Patrick's Purgatory between visionary literature and pilgrimage reports', *Studia Aurea*, 11 (2017), 151–77.

Mahaffy, R.P., *Calendar of state papers relating to Ireland preserved in the Public Record Office, 1647–1660* (London, 1903).*

Makowski, Elizabeth, *'A pernicious sort of woman': quasi-religious women and canon lawyers in the later Middle Ages* (Washington, DC, 2005).

Manning, Conleth, 'Clonmacnoise Cathedral' in Heather King (ed.), *Clonmacnoise studies 1* (Dublin, 1998), pp 57–86.

Manning, Conleth, 'Rock shelters and caves associated with Irish saints' in Tom Condit and Christiaan Corlett (eds), *Above and beyond: essays in honour of Leo Swan* (Bray, 2005), pp 109–20.

Manning, Conleth, 'The Athassel tomb', *Irish Arts Review*, 22:4 (2005), 132–5.

Manning, Conleth, 'Remains of a second pre-Romanesque church at Inchcleraun on Lough Ree', *Archaeology Ireland*, 26 (Summer 2012), 28–9.

Margaret Quinlan Architects, *Conservation plan: Athassel Augustinian Priory, County Tipperary* (Dublin, 2009).

Marks, Richard, *Image and devotion in late medieval England* (Stroud, 2004).

Marshall, Jenny White, and Grellan D. Rourke. *High Island: an Irish monastery in the Atlantic* (Dublin, 2000).

Marshall, Jenny White, and Claire Walsh, *Illaunloughan Island: an early medieval monastery in County Kerry* (Bray, 2005).

Martin, Charles T., *The record interpreter* (Guilford, 1982).

Marx, Richard, 'Framing the rood in medieval England and Wales' in Spike Buckelow, Richard Marks and Lucy Wrapson (eds), *The art and science of the church screen in medieval Europe: making, meaning, preserving* (Woodbridge, 2017), pp 7–29.

Massari, Dionysius, 'My Irish campaign', *The Catholic Bulletin*, 7 (1917), 111–14, 179–82, 246–9, 295–6.*

Masterson, Rory, *Medieval Fore, County Westmeath* (Dublin, 2014).

Matter, E. Ann, and Lesley Smith (eds), *From knowledge to beatitude: St Victor, twelfth-century scholars and beyond: essays in honour of Grover A. Zinn Jr* (Notre Dame, IN, 2013).

McCullough, Catherine, and W.H. Crawford, *Irish historic towns atlas no. 18: Armagh* (Dublin, 2007).

McEnery, M.J., and Raymond Refaussé (eds), *Christ Church deeds* (Dublin, 2001).*

McKeown, L., 'The abbey of Muckamore', *Down and Connor Historical Society's Journal*, 9 (1938), 63–70.

McNamara, Jo Ann Kay, *Sisters in arms: Catholic nuns through two millennia* (Harvard, 1996).

McNeill, Charles, 'Accounts of sums realised by sales of chattels of some suppressed Irish monasteries', *JRSAI*, 12 (1922), 11–37.*

McNeill, Charles, 'Rawlinson manuscripts, class B', *Anal. Hib.*, 1 (1930), 111–78.

McNeill, Charles, 'Harris: collectanea de rebus Hibernicis', *Anal. Hib.*, 6 (1934), 248–450.

McNeill, Charles (ed.), *Calendar of Archbishop Alen's register c.1172–1534* (Dublin, 1950).*

McNeill, Charles, and A.J. Otway-Ruthven, *Dowdall deeds* (IMC, Dublin, 1960).*

Meijns, Brigitte, 'Les chanoines réguliers dans l'espace flamand' in Parisse, *Les chanoines réguliers*, pp 456–76.

Meyer, Kuno, 'The Laud genealogies and tribal histories', *Zeitschrift für celtische Philologie*, 8/9 (1911), 291–338.*

Milis, Ludo, *L'ordre des chanoines reguliers d'Arrouaise: son histoire et son organisation de la fondation de l'abbaye-mère (vers 1090) à la fin des chapitres annuels (1471)* (Brugge, 1969).

Milis, Ludo, *Angelic monks and earthly men: monasticism and its meaning to medieval society* (Woodbridge, 1992).

Milis, Ludovicus (ed.), *Constitutiones canonicorum regularium ordinis Arroasiensis* (Turnhout, 1970).*

Mills, James (ed.), *Account roll of the priory of the Holy Trinity, Dublin, 1337–1346*, with an introduction by James Lydon and Alan J. Fletcher (Dublin, 1996).*

Milne, Kenneth (ed.), *Christ Church Cathedral, Dublin: a history* (Dublin, 2000).

Mohn, Claudia, *Mittelalterliche Klosteranlagen der Zisterzienserinnen: Architektur der Frauenklöster im mitteldeutschen Raum. Berliner Beiträge zu Bauforschung und Denkmalpflege 4* (Petersberg, 2006).

Moorman, John, *Church life in England in the thirteenth century* (Cambridge, 1945).

Morant, Roland, *The monastic gatehouse* (Lewes, 1995).

Morrin, James (ed.), *Calendar of patent and close rolls of chancery in Ireland, from the reigns of Henry VIII, Edward VI, Mary, and Elizabeth*, 3 vols (Dublin, 1861–3).*

Morris, Colin, *The papal monarchy: the Western church from 1050 to 1250* (Oxford, 1991).

Morrison, Susan S., *Women pilgrims in late medieval England* (London, 2002).

Moss, Rachel, 'Permanent expressions of piety: the secular and the sacred in later medieval stone sculpture' in Rachel Moss, Colmán Ó Clabaigh and Salvador Ryan (eds), *Art and devotion in late medieval Ireland* (Dublin, 2006), pp 72–97.

Moss, Rachel, 'Architectural sculpture at Glendalough' in C. Doherty et al. (eds), *Glendalough: city of God* (2011), pp 278–301.

Moss, Rachel, 'Athassel, Augustinian Priory, Co. Tipperary' in Rachel Moss (ed.), *Art and architecture of Ireland, volume 1: medieval, c.400–c.1600* (Dublin, 2014), 193–4.

Moss, Rachel, 'Devotional images' in Rachel Moss (ed.), *Art and architecture of Ireland, volume 1: medieval, c.400–c.1600* (Dublin, 2014), pp 280–82.

Moss, Rachel, 'Substantiating sovereignties: "regal" insignias in Ireland, c.1370–1410' in Peter Crooks, David Green and W. Mark Ormrod (eds), *The Plantagenet empire, 1259–1453* (Donington, 2016), pp 216–31.

Mousseau, Juliet, 'Daily life at the abbey of Saint Victor' in H. Feiss and J. Mousseau (eds), *Companion to the abbey of Saint Victor* (2018), pp 55–78.

Mulchrone, Kathleen (ed.), *Bethu Phátraic. The tripartite Life of Patrick* (Dublin & London, 1939).*

Mullally, Evelyn, *The deeds of the Normans in Ireland: la geste des Engleis en Yrlande* (Dublin, 2002).*

Müller, Anne, 'Presenting identity in the cloister, remarks on Benedictine and mendicant concepts of space' in Anne Müller and Karen Stöber (eds), *Self-representation of medieval religious communities: the British Isles in context* (Berlin, 2009), pp 167–87.

Murphy, Deidre, 'Recent archaeological discoveries in Drogheda', *Old Drogheda Society Journal*, 11 (1998), 6–17.

Murphy, Margaret, 'Cumin, John' in Seán Duffy (ed.), *Medieval Ireland: an encyclopedia* (New York, 2005), pp 118–20.

Murray, Griffin, 'The Breac Maodhóg: a unique Irish medieval reliquary' in Jonathan Cherry and Brendan Scott (eds), *Cavan: history and society* (Dublin, 2014), pp 83–125.

Murray, Griffin, *The Cross of Cong* (Dublin, 2014).

Murray, Laurence P., 'The register of Archbishop Cromer, 1521–1542', *Journal of the County Louth Archaeological Society*, vols 7–10 (1929–44).*

Murray, Laurence P., 'A calendar of the register of Primate George Dowdall, commonly called the "Liber Niger" or "Black Book"', *Journal of the County Louth Archaeological Society*, vols 7–10 (1929–44).*

Ní Ghrádaigh, Jenifer, ' "But what exactly did she give?": Derbforgaill and the Nuns' Church at Clonmacnoise' in H. King (ed.), *Clonmacnoise studies 2* (Dublin, 2003), pp 175–207.

Nicholls, Kenneth, 'The Lisgoole agreement of 1580', *Clogher Record*, 7:1 (1969), 27–33.

Nicholls, Kenneth, 'Visitations of the dioceses of Clonfert, Tuam and Kilmacduagh, c.1565–1567', *Anal. Hib.*, 26 (1970).*

Nicholls, Kenneth, 'The register of Clogher', *Clogher Record*, 7:3 (1971/1972), 361–431.*

Nicholls, Kenneth, 'Mediæval Irish cathedral chapters', *AH*, 31 (1973), 102–11.

Nicholls, Kenneth, 'Gaelic society and economy in the high Middle Ages' in A. Cosgrove (ed.), *A new history of Ireland*, ii (1987), pp 399–438.

Nicholls, Kenneth, 'Genealogy' in Niall Buttimer, Colin Rynne and Helen Guerin (eds), *The heritage of Ireland: natural, man-made and cultural heritage: conservation and interpretation, business and administration* (Cork, 2000), pp 156–61.

Nichols, Nick, 'The Augustinian canons and their parish churches: a key to their identity' in J. Burton and K. Stöber, *The regular canons* (2011), pp 313–37.

Nilson, Ben, *Cathedral shrines of medieval Europe* (Woodbridge, 1988).

Nugent, Louise, 'Gathering of faith: pilgrimage in early medieval Ireland' in Fiona Beglane (ed.), *Gatherings: past and present. Proceedings of the conference of the archaeology of gatherings of Sligo IT* (Dublin, 2016), pp 20–30.

Nugent, Louise, 'Pilgrimage in medieval Ireland, AD 600–1600' (PhD, UCD, 2009).

O'Brien, M.A. (ed.), *Corpus genealogiarum Hiberniae* (Dublin repr. 1976)★

Ó Carragáin, Tomás, 'Recluses, relics and corpses: interpreting St Kevin's House' in C. Doherty et al. (eds), *Glendalough* (2011), pp 64–79.

Ó Carragáin, Tomás, *Churches in early medieval Ireland* (New Haven & London, 2010).

O'Carroll, Gerald, *The earls of Desmond: the rise and fall of a Munster lordship* (Limerick, 2013).

Ó Clabaigh, Colmán, 'The Benedictines in medieval and early modern Ireland' in Martin Browne and Colmán Ó Clabaigh (eds), *The Irish Benedictines: a history* (Dublin, 2005), pp 79–121.

Ó Clabaigh, Colmán 'The mendicant friars in the medieval diocese of Clonfert', *JGAHS*, 59 (2007), 25–36.

Ó Clabaigh, Colmán, 'Anchorites in late medieval Ireland' in Liz Herbert McAvoy (ed.), *Anchoritic traditions of medieval Europe* (Woodbridge, 2010), pp 153–77.

Ó Clabaigh, Colmán, and Michael Staunton, 'Thomas Becket and Ireland' in Elizabeth Mullins and Diarmuid Scully (eds), *Listen, O Isles unto me: studies in medieval word and image in honour of Jennifer O'Reilly* (Cork, 2011), pp 87–101.

Ó Clabaigh, Colmán, 'Formed by word and example: the training of novices in fourteenth-century Dublin' in Karen Stöber, Julie Kerr and Emilia Jamroziak (eds), *Monastic life in the medieval British Isles: essays in honour of Janet Burton* (Cardiff, 2018), pp 41–52.

Ó Clabaigh, Colmán, *The friars in Ireland, 1224–1540* (Dublin, 2012).

Ó Conbhuidhe, Colmcille, *Studies in Irish Cistercian history* (Dublin, 1998).

Ó Corráin, Donnchadh, 'Mael Muire Ua Dúnáin (1040–1117), reformer' in P. de Brún, S. Ó Coileáin and P. Ó Riain (eds), *Folia Gadelica; essays presented by former students to R.A. Breatnach* (Cork, 1983), pp 47–53.

Ó Corráin, Donnchadh, *Clavis litterarum Hibernensium*, 3 vols (Turnhout, 2017).

Ó Corráin, Donnchadh, *The Irish church, its reform and the English invasion* (Dublin, 2017)

Ó Cuív, Brian (ed.), 'In praise of Ragnall king of Man', *Éigse*, 8 (1956–7), 283–301.*

O'Donovan, John (ed. and trans.), *Annála ríoghachta Eireann: annals of the kingdom of Ireland by the Four Masters from the earliest period to the year 1616*, 7 vols (Dublin, 1848–51).*

O'Donovan, Patrick F., *Archaeological inventory of County Cavan* (Dublin, 1995).

O'Dwyer, Peter, *Mary: a history of devotion in Ireland* (Dublin, 1988).

O'Flanagan, Michael, *Letters containing information relative to the antiquities of the County of Galway collected during the progress of the Ordnance Survey in 1839* (Bray, 1928).*

Ó Floinn, Raghnall, 'Domhnach Airgid shrine' in Michael Ryan (ed.), *Treasures of Ireland: Irish art 3000BC–1500AD* (Dublin, 1983), pp 176–7.

Ó Floinn, Raghnall, 'Goldsmiths' work in Ireland 1200–1400' in Colum Hourihane (ed.), *From Ireland coming* (Princeton, 2001), pp 289–312.

Ó Floinn, Raghnall, 'The "Market Cross" at Glendalough' in C. Doherty et al. (eds), *Glendalough* (2011), pp 80–111.

Ó Floinn, Raghnall, 'The foundation relics of Christ Church Cathedral and the origins of the diocese of Dublin' in Seán Duffy (ed.), *Medieval Dublin VII* (Dublin, 2006).

Ó Floinn, Raghnall, 'The late-medieval relics of Holy Trinity Church, Dublin' in J. Bradley et al. (eds), *Dublin in the medieval world* (2009), pp 369–89.

Ó hAnnracháin, Tadhg, *Catholic reformation in Ireland: the mission of Rinuccini, 1645–1649* (Oxford, 2002).

O'Keefe, J.G., 'The ancient territory of Fermoy', *Ériu*, 10 (1926), 179–89.

O'Keeffe, Grace, 'The merchant conquistadors: medieval Bristolians in Dublin' in Seán Duffy (ed.), *Medieval Dublin XIII* (Dublin, 2013), pp 116–38.

O'Keeffe, Peter, and Tom Simington, *Irish stone bridges* (Dublin, 1991).

O'Keeffe, Tadhg, 'Architecture and regular life in Holy Trinity Cathedral, 1150–1350' in S. Kinsella (ed.), *Augustinians at Christ Church* (2000), pp 23–40.

O'Keeffe, Tadhg, 'Augustinian regular canons in twelfth- and thirteenth-century Ireland: history, architecture and identity' in J. Burton and K. Stöber (eds), *The regular canons* (2011), pp 469–84.

O'Keeffe, Tadhg, and Rhiannon Carey Bates, 'The abbey and cathedral of Ferns, 1111–1253' in Ian Doyle and Bernard Browne (eds), *Medieval Wexford: essays in memory of Billy Colfer* (Dublin, 2016), pp 73–96.

O'Keeffe, Tadhg, 'A cryptic puzzle from medieval Dublin', *Archaeology Ireland*, 31:2 (2017), 39–43.

O'Keeffe, Tadhg, 'Trim before 1224: new thoughts on the caput of the de Lacy lordship in Ireland' in Paul Duffy, Tadhg O'Keeffe and Jean-Michel Picard (eds), *From Carrickfergus to Carcassonne: the epic deeds of Hugh de Lacy during the Albigensian Crusade* (Turnhout, 2017), 31–56.

O'Keeffe, Tadhg, 'The design of the early thirteenth-century cathedral church of Newtown Trim, Co. Meath', *Ríocht na Midhe*, 29 (2018), 14–26.

O'Keeffe, Tadhg, *An Anglo-Norman monastery: Bridgetown Priory and the architecture of the Augustinian canons regular in Ireland* (Cork, 1999).

O'Keeffe, Tadhg, *Medieval Irish buildings, 1100–1600* (Dublin, 2015).

O'Keeffe, Tadhg, *Tristernagh Priory, Co. Westmeath: colonial monasticism in medieval Ireland* (Dublin, 2018).

O'Meara, John (ed. and trans.) Gerald of Wales, *The history and topography of Ireland* (London, 1982).*

Ó Muraíle, Nollaig, 'The learned family of Ó Cianáin/Keenan', *Clogher Record*, 18:3 (2005), 397–402.

Ó Murchadha, Diarmaid, 'Gill Abbey and the "Rental of Cong"', *JCAHS*, 90 (1985), 31–45.

O'Neill, Michael, 'Christ Church Cathedral as a blueprint for other Augustinian buildings in Ireland' in J. Bradley et al. (eds), *Dublin in the medieval world* (2009), pp 168–87.

O'Neill, Timothy, *Merchants and mariners in medieval Ireland* (Dublin, 1987).

Ó Riain, Pádraig, 'Saints in the catalogue of bishops of the lost "Register of Clogher"', *Clogher Record*, 14:2 (1992), 64–7.

Ó Riain, Pádraig, '*Codex Salmanticensis*: a provenance *inter Anglos* or *inter Hibernos*?' in Toby Barnard, Dáibhí Ó Cróinín and Katharine Simms (eds), *A miracle of learning: essays in honour of William O'Sullivan* (Aldershot, 1997), pp 91–100.

Ó Riain, Pádraig, 'Dublin's oldest book? A list of saints "made in Germany"' in Seán Duffy (ed.), *Medieval Dublin V* (Dublin, 2004), pp 52–72.

Ó Riain, Pádraig, 'The calendar and martyrology of Christ Church' in R. Gillespie and R. Refaussé (eds), *Medieval manuscripts* (2006), pp 33–76.

Ó Riain, Pádraig, 'Fionán of Iveragh' in John Crowley and John Sheehan (eds), *The Iveragh peninsula: a cultural history of the Ring of Kerry* (Cork, 2009), pp 126–8.

Ó Riain, Pádraig, 'Longford priories and their manuscripts: All Saints and Abbeyderg' in Martin Morris and Fergus O'Farrell (eds), *Longford: history and society* (Dublin, 2010), pp 39–50.

Ó Riain, Pádraig, *Corpus genealogiarum sanctorum Hiberniae* (Dublin, 1985).*

Ó Riain, Pádraig, *Beatha Bharra: Saint Finbarr of Cork. The complete life*, Irish Texts Society, 57 (Dublin, 1994).*

Ó Riain, Pádraig, *Four Irish martyrologies: Drummond, Turin, Cashel, York*, Henry Bradshaw Society, 115 (London, 2002).*

Ó Riain, Pádraig, Diarmuid Ó Murchadha and Kevin Murray, *Historical dictionary of Gaelic placenames: Foclóir stairiúil áitainmneacha na Gaeilge*, i, Irish Texts Society (London, 2003).

Ó Riain, Pádraig, *Feastdays of the saints: a history of Irish martyrologies*, Subsidia Hagiographica, 86 (Brussels, 2006).

Ó Riain, Pádraig, *A martyrology of four cities: Metz, Cologne, Dublin, Lund* (London, 2008).*

Ó Riain, Pádraig, 'The Lives of Kevin (Caoimhghin) of Glendalough' in C. Doherty et al. (eds), *Glendalough* (2011), pp 137–44.*

Ó Riain, Pádraig, *A dictionary of Irish saints* (Dublin, 2011).

Ó Riain, Pádraig, 'The O'Donohoe Lives of the Salamancan Codex: the earliest collection of Irish saints' Lives?' in Sarah Sheehan, Joanne Findon and Westley Follett (eds), *Gablánach in scélaighecht: Celtic studies in honour of Ann Dooley* (Dublin, 2013), pp 38–52.

Ó Riain, Pádraig, *Beatha Ailbhe: the Life of Saint Ailbhe of Cashel and Emly*, Irish Texts Society, 67 (Dublin, 2017).*

Ó Riain, Pádraig, *Four Offaly saints: the Lives of Ciarán of Clonmacnoise, Ciarán of Seirkieran, Colmán of Lynally and Fíonán of Kinnitty* (Dublin, 2018).*

O'Sullivan, Ann, John Sheehan, and South West Kerry archaeological survey, *The Iveragh peninsula: an archaeological survey of south Kerry* (Cork, 1996).

O'Sullivan, Jerry, and Tomás Ó Carragáin, *Inishmurray: monks and pilgrims in an Atlantic landscape* (Cork, 2008).

O'Sullivan, Jerry, and Tomás Ó Carragáin, *Inishmurray: archaeological survey and excavations 1997–2000* (Cork, 2008).

Orme, Nicholas, 'The Augustinian canons and education' in J. Burton and K. Stöber (eds), *The regular canons* (2011), pp 213–32.

Orpen, Goddard Henry (ed.), *The song of Dermot and the Earl* (Oxford, 1892).*

Orpen, Goddard Henry, *Ireland under the Normans, 1169–1333*, 4 vols (Oxford, 1911–20).

Oschinsky, Dorothea, *Walter of Henley and other treatises on estate management and accounting* (Oxford, 1971).*

Otway-Ruthven, A. Jocelyn, 'The mediaeval church lands of Co. Dublin' in John A. Watt, John B. Morrall and Francis X. Martin (eds), *Medieval studies presented to Aubrey Gwynn S.J.* (Dublin, 1961), pp 54–73.

Otway-Ruthven, A. Jocelyn, 'Parochial development in the rural deanery of Skreen', *JRSAI*, 94, Part 2 (1964), 111–22.

Page, William (ed.), *The Victoria history of the county of Gloucester* (London, 1907).

Patterson, Robert B., 'Robert fitz Harding of Bristol: profile of an early Angevin burgess-baron patrician and his family's urban involvement', *Haskins Society Journal*, 1 (1989), 109–22.

Patterson, Robert B., 'Bristol: an Angevin baronial caput under royal siege', *Haskins Society Journal*, 3 (1991), 171–81.

Patterson, Robert B., 'Robert fitz Harding' in *ODNB*, 47, p. 119.

Philip of Bonne Espérance, *De institutione clericorum*, in Jacques-Paul Migne (ed.), *Patrologiae cursus completus*, series Latina, 221 vols (Paris, 1841–64), cciii.*

Picard, Jean-Michel, and Yolande de Pontfarcy, *Saint Patrick's Purgatory: a twelfth-century tale of a journey to the other world* (Dublin, 1985).*

Picard, Jean-Michel, and Yolande de Pontfarcy, *The vision of Tnugdal* (Dublin, 1989).*

Pinner, Rachel, *The cult of St Edmund in medieval East Anglia* (Woodbridge, 2015).

Pipe roll 23 Henry II, 1176–1177, Pipe Roll Society, 26 (London 1905).*

Pipe roll 33 Henry II, 1186–1187, Pipe Roll Society, 37 (London, 1915).*

Plummer, Charles (ed.), 'Vie et miracles de S. Laurent, archevêque de Dublin', *Analecta Bollandiana*, 33 (1914), 121–86.*

Plummer, Charles, *Bethada náem nÉrenn*, 2 vols (Oxford, 1922).*

Potterton, Michael, *Medieval Trim: history and archaeology* (Dublin, 2005).

Potterton, Michael, 'The archaeology and history of medieval Trim, County Meath' (PhD, NUI Maynooth, 2003).

Power, Eileen E., *Medieval English nunneries, c.1275–1535* (Cambridge, 1922).

Prendergast, J.P., 'An ancient record relating to the families into which were married the co-heiresses of Thomas fitz Anthony, seneschal of Leinster', *Journal of the Kilkenny and South-East of Ireland Archaeological Society*, 5 (1864), 139–53.*

Preston, Sarah Marya, 'The canons regular of St Augustine in medieval Ireland: an overview' (PhD, TCD, 1996).

Preston, Sarah, 'The canons regular of St Augustine: the twelfth-century reform in action' in S. Kinsella (ed.), *Augustinians at Christ Church* (2000), pp 23–40.

Price, Liam, *Place-names of Co. Wicklow*, 7 vols (Dublin, 1945–67).

Quentin, Henri, *Les martyrologies historiques du Moyen Âge. Étude sur la formation du martyrologe romain* (Rome, 1908; repr. Spoleto, 2002).

Quigley, W.G.H., and E.F.D. Roberts (eds), *Registrum Iohannis Mey: the register of John Mey, archbishop of Armagh, 1443–1456* (Belfast, 1972).*

Rasche, Ulrich, 'The early phase of appropriation of parish churches in medieval England', *Journal of Medieval History*, 26 (2000), 213–37.

Reeves, William, *Ecclesiastical antiquities of Down, Connor and Dromore, consisting of a taxation of those dioceses, compiled in the year MCCVI* (Dublin, 1847).*

Refaussé, Raymond, 'Introduction' in Milne (ed.), *Christ Church Cathedral, Dublin* (2000), pp 1–22.

Refaussé, Raymond, 'The Christ Church manuscripts in context' in R. Gillespie and R. Refaussé, *Medieval manuscripts* (2006), pp 13–32.

Rhodes, John, 'Llanthony Priory', *Glevensis*, 23 (1989), 16–30.

Richter, Michael, 'Procedural aspects of the canonisation of Lorcán Ua Tuathail' in Gábor Klaniczay (ed.), *Procès de canonisation au moyen âge: aspects juridiques et religieux / Medieval canonization processes: legal and religious aspects*, Collection de l'école française de Rome, 340 (Rome, 2004), pp 53–65.

Ripyard, Susan J. (ed.), *Chivalry, knighthood, and war in the Middle Ages* (Sewanee, 1999).

Robertson, J.C., and J.B. Sheppard (eds), William of Canterbury, 'Miracula S. Thomae' in *Materials for the history of Thomas Becket*, 7 vols, Rolls Series (London, 1875–85), i, pp 487–8.*

Robinson, David, 'The Augustinian canons in England and Wales: architecture, archaeology and liturgy 1100-1540', *Monastic Research Bulletin*, 18 (2012), 2–29.

Robinson, David, *The geography of Augustinian settlement in medieval England and Wales* (Oxford, 1980).

Roe, Helen M., 'Illustrations of the Holy Trinity in Ireland: 13th to 17th centuries', *JRSAI*, 109 (1979), 101–50.

Röhrig, Floridus, 'Die Augustiner-Chorherren in Österreich' in Floridus Röhrig (ed.), *Die Stifte der Augustiner-Chorherren in Österreich, Südtirol und Polen* (Klosterneuburg-Wien, 1997), pp 9–28.

Rollason, David, A.J. Piper and Margaret Harvey, *The Durham Liber Vitae and its context* (Martlesham, 2004).

Ronan, Myles V., 'St Laurentius, archbishop of Dublin: original testimonies for canonization', *Irish Ecclesiastical Record*, series 5, 27 (1926), 347–64; 28 (1926), 247–56, 467–80.*

Ronan, Myles V., 'St Laurentius, archbishop of Dublin – lessons, hymns, litanies and prayers', *Irish Ecclesiastical Record*, series 5, 28 (1926), 596–612.*

Ronan, Myles V., *The Reformation in Dublin, 1536–1558* (London, 1926).

Schmid, M., and S. Diermeier, 'Kurzgefaßte Geschichte der Augustiner-Chorherren. Heft 3: Die Zeit von Benedikt XII. bis zur Glaubensspaltung', *In Unum Congregati*, 7 (1961), 30–2.

Sand, Alexa, *Vision, devotion, and self-representation in late medieval art* (Cambridge, 2014).

Schmid, M., and S. Diermeier, 'Kurzgefaßte Geschichte der Augustiner-Chorherren. Heft 4: Die nachtridentinische Zeit bis zur Aufklärung', *In Unum Congregati*, 8 (1962), 14.

Schroeder, Carl (ed.), 'Facetus', *Palestra*, 86 (1911), 14–28.*

Schweitzer, Holger, 'Drogheda boat: a story to tell', *Proceedings from the twelfth symposium on boat and ship archaeology*, ed. Nergis Gunsenin (Istanbul, 2009), pp 225–31.

Scott, A.B., and F.X. Martin (eds), *Expugnatio Hibernica: the conquest of Ireland by Giraldus Cambrensis* (Dublin, 1978).*

Scott, Brendan, 'The Dissolution of the religious houses in the Tudor diocese of Meath', *AH*, 59 (2005), 260–76.

Scott, Brendan, 'The religious houses of Tudor Dublin: their communities and resistance to the dissolution, 1537–41' in Seán Duffy (ed.), *Medieval Dublin VII* (Dublin, 2006), pp 214–32.

Scott, Brendan, *Religion and reformation in the Tudor diocese of Meath* (Dublin, 2006).

Seymour, St. John D., 'The coarb in the medieval Irish church (circa 1200–1550)', *PRIA*, 41C (1932–4), 219–31.

Sharpe, Richard, 'Quattuor sanctissimi episcopi: Irish saints before St Patrick' in Donnchadh Ó Corráin, Liam Breatnach and Kim McCone (eds), *Sages, saints and story-tellers: Celtic studies in honour of Professor James Carney* (Maynooth, 1989), pp 376–99.

Sharpe, Richard, 'Churches and communities in early medieval Ireland: towards a pastoral model' in John Blair and Richard Sharpe (eds), *Pastoral care before the parish* (Leicester, 1992), pp 81–109.

Sharpe, Richard, *Medieval Irish saints' Lives: an introduction to the Vitae sanctorum Hiberniae* (Oxford, 1991).

Sharpe, Richard, Review of Ó Riain, *Four Tipperary saints*, *Studia Hibernica*, 22–3 (2016), 204–7.

Sheehy, Maurice P. (ed.), *Pontificia Hibernica: medieval papal chancery documents concerning Ireland, 640–1261*, 2 vols (Dublin, 1962–5).*

Simms, Anngret, 'The geography of Irish manors: the example of the Llanthony cells of Duleek and Colp, Co. Meath' (with appendix by John Bradley), in John Bradley (ed.), *Settlement and society in medieval Ireland* (Kilkenny, 1988), pp 291–326.

Simpson, Linzi, *Excavations at Isolda's tower* (1994) in Seán Duffy (ed.), *Medieval Dublin I* (Dublin, 2000), pp 11–68.

Smith, Aloysius, 'The Lateran canons and Ireland', *The Dublin Review* (October 1924), 278–95.

Smith, Aloysius, *Explanation of the Rule of St Augustine by Hugh of St Victor, canon regular* (London, 1911).*

Smith, Brendan, 'The late medieval diocese of Clogher, c.1200–1480' in Henry A. Jeffries (ed.), *History of the diocese of Clogher* (Dublin, 2005), pp 70–81.

Smith, Brendan, 'Late medieval Ireland and the English connection: Waterford and Bristol c.1360–1460', *Journal of British Studies*, 50 (2011), 546–65.

Smith, Brendan (ed.), *Britain and Ireland, 900–1300: insular responses to medieval European change* (Cambridge, 1999).

Smith, Brendan (ed.), *The Cambridge history of Ireland*, vol. i (Cambridge, 2018).

Smith, Julie Ann, *Ordering women's lives: penitentials and nunnery rules in the early medieval west* (Aldershot, 2001).

Smyly, J. Gilbart (ed.), *Urbanus Magnus Danielis Becclesiensis* (Dublin, 1939).*

Sorrentino, J.T., 'The chapter office in the Gilbertine order' in J. Burton and K. Stöber (eds), *The regular canons* (2011), pp 173–89.

Spencer, Brian, 'Pilgrim souvenirs' in Patrick F. Wallace (ed.), *Miscellanea I: medieval Dublin excavations, 1962–1981*, ser. B, 2, fasc. 1–5 (Dublin, 1988), pp 33–48.

St John Brooks, Eric, 'A charter of John de Courcy to the abbey of Navan', *JRSAI*, 63 (1933), 38–45.*

Stalley, Roger, *Architecture and sculpture in Ireland, 1150–1350* (Dublin, 1971).

Stalley, Roger, 'The medieval sculpture of Christ Church Cathedral, Dublin', *Archaeologia*, 106 (1979), 107–22.

Stalley, Roger, 'Athassel (Tipperary), Augustinian Priory', *Archaeological Journal*, 153 (1996), 315–20.

Stalley, Roger, 'The construction of the medieval cathedral, *c.*1030–1250' in K. Milne (ed.), *Christ Church Cathedral, Dublin* (2000), pp 53–74.

Stalley, Roger. 'The architecture of the cathedral and priory buildings, 1250–1530' in K. Milne (ed.), *Christ Church Cathedral, Dublin* (2000), pp 95–128.

Stalley, Roger, 'The construction of Cashel Cathedral' in Roger Stalley (ed.), *Irish Gothic architecture: construction, decay and reinvention* (Dublin, 2012), pp 55–98.

Stalley, Roger, *The Cistercian monasteries of Ireland: an account of the history, art and architecture of the white monks in Ireland from 1142 to 1540* (New Haven, 1987).

Staunton, Michael, *The historians of Angevin England* (Oxford, 2017).

Stöber, Karen, 'The regular canons in Wales' in J. Burton and K. Stöber, *The regular canons* (2011), pp 97–113.

Stöber, Karen, and David Austin, 'Culdees to canons: the Augustinian houses of north Wales' in Janet Burton & Karen Stöber (eds), *Monastic Wales, new approaches* (Cardiff, 2013), pp 41–54.

Stokes, Whitley (ed.), *Féilire Oengusso Céili Dé: The martyrology of Oengus the Culdee*, Henry Bradshaw Society 29 (London, 1905; repr., Dublin, 1984).*

Stokes, Whitley (ed.), *Félire hÚi Gormáin: The martyrology of Gorman*, Henry Bradshaw Society 9 (London, 1895).*

Stopford, Jennie, 'Some approaches to the archaeology of Christian pilgrimage', *World Archaeology* 26:1 (1994), 57–72.

Stubbs, William (ed.), *Gesta Henrici secundi Benedicti abbatis*, 2 vols, Rolls Series (London, 1867).*

Stubbs, William (ed.), Gervase of Canterbury, *Historical works*, 2 vols, Rolls Series (London, 1879–80).*

Stubbs, William (ed.), *Chronica Magistri Rogeri de Houedone*, 4 vols, Rolls Series (London, 1868–1).*

Stubbs, William (ed.), *Radulfi de Diceto opera*, 2 vols, Rolls Series (London, 1876).*

Sughi, Mario (ed.), *Registrum Octaviani alias Liber Niger: the register of Octavian de Palatio, archbishop of Armagh (1478–1513)*, 2 vols (Dublin, 1998).*

Summerson, Henry, and Stuart Harrison, *Lanercost Priory, Cumbria: a survey and documentary history* (Kendal, 2000).

Sumption, Jonathan, *Pilgrimage: an image of mediaeval religion* (London, 1975).

Sweetman, H.S. (ed.), *Calendar of documents relating to Ireland, 1171–1307*, 5 vols (HMSO, London, 1875–86).*

Swift, Cathy, 'Early Irish priests within their own localities' in Fiona Edmonds and Paul Russell (eds), *Tome: studies in medieval Celtic history and law in honour of Thomas Charles-Edwards* (Woodbridge, 2011), pp 29–40.

Tanner, Norman (ed.), *Decrees of the Ecumenical councils*, 2 vols (Washington and London, 1990).*

Thompson, Sally, *Women religious: the founding of English nunneries after the Norman conquest* (Oxford, 1991).

Thorpe, Lewis (ed.), *Gerald of Wales: The journey through Wales and description of Wales* (London, 1978).*

Todd, John H., 'Obits of eminent individuals and other notices connected with Navan and its neighbourhood', *PRIA*, 7 (1861), 367.*

Tommasini, Anselmo, *Irish saints in Italy* (London, 1937).

Tresham, Edward (ed.), *Rotulorum patentium et clausorum cancellariae Hiberniae calendarium* (Dublin, 1828).*

Valvekens, J.B. (ed.), 'Acta et decreta capitulorum generalium ordinis Preaemonstratensis', vol. 1, *Analecta Praemonstratensia*, 42 (Averbode, 1944).*

Van Waefelghem, Raphaël (ed.), *Les premiers statuts de l'Ordre de Prémontré. Le Clm 17174 (XIIᵉ)* (Louvain, 1913).*

Vanderputten, Steven, *Dark age nunneries: the ambiguous identity of female monasticism, 800–1050* (Ithaca, NY, 2018).

Veitch, Kenneth, *A study of the extent to which existing native religious society helped to shape Scotland's monastic community, 1070–1286* (PhD, Edinburgh, 1999)

Venarde, Bruce L., *Women's monasticism and medieval society: nunneries in France and England 890–1215* (London, 1997).

Verheijen, Luc (ed.), *La Règle de St Augustin*, 2 vols (Paris, 1967).*

Verstraten, Freya, 'Ua Conchobair' in Seán Duffy (ed.), *Medieval Ireland: an encyclopedia* (New York, 2005), pp 464–6.

Veyrenche, Yannick, '*Quia vos estis qui sanctorum patrum vitam probabilem renovatis ...* naissance des chanoines réguliers, jusqu'à Urbain II' in M. Parisse (ed.), *Les chanoines réguliers. Émergence et expansion (XIᵉ–XIIIᵉ siècles)* (Publications de l'Université de Sainte-Étienne, 2009), pp 29–70.

Vincent, Nicholas, 'The early years of Keynsham Abbey', *Transactions of the Bristol and Gloucestershire Archaeological Society*, 111 (1993), 95–113.

Vincent, Nicholas, 'Pilgrimages of the Angevin kings of England' in Colin Morris (ed.), *Pilgrimage: the English experience from Becket to Bunyan* (Cambridge, 2002), pp 12–45.

Vita Sancti Norberti, in Jacques-Paul Migne (ed.), *Patrologiae cursus completus*, series Latina, 221 vols (Paris, 1841–64), clxx, cols 1253–1350.*

Vones-Liebenstein, Ursula, M. Seifert and R. Berndt (eds), *Necrologium abbatiae Sancti Victoris Parisiensis*, Corpus Victorinum, Opera ad fidem codicum recollecta, 1 (Münster, 2012).*

Wade-Evans, A.W. (ed.), *Vitae sanctorum Britanniae et genealogiae*, History and Law Series 9 (Cardiff, 1944).*

Walker, David (ed.), *The cartulary of St Augustine's Abbey, Bristol*, Gloucestershire Record Series, 10 (Bristol, 1998).*

Walsh, Claire, 'Archaeological excavations at the abbey of St Thomas the Martyr, Dublin' in Seán Duffy (ed.), *Medieval Dublin I* (Dublin, 2000), pp 185–202.

Ware, James, *The antiquities and history of Ireland* (Dublin, 1705).

Warren, Wilfred L., *Henry II* (2nd ed., London, 2000).

Waterton, Edmund, *Pietas Mariana Britannica: a history of English devotion to the Most Blessed Virgin Mary, Mother of God* (London, 1879).

Webb, Diana, *Pilgrims and pilgrimage in medieval Europe* (London, 1999).

Webb, Diana, *Pilgrimage in medieval England* (London, 2000).

Webb, Diana, *Medieval European pilgrimage, c.700–c.1500* (Basingstoke, 2002).

Webber, Teresa, and A.G. Watson (eds), *The libraries of the Augustinian canons* (London, 1998).*

Webster, Paul, and Marie-Pierre Gelin, *The cult of St Thomas Becket in the Plantagenet world, c.1170–c.1220* (Woodbridge, 2016).

Wemple, Susan Fonay, *Women in Frankish society: marriage and the cloister, 500–900* (Philadelphia, 1981).

Went, A.E., 'Fisheries on the River Liffey' in Howard Clarke (ed.), *Medieval Dublin: the living city* (Dublin, 1990), pp 132–91.

White, Newport B., *Irish monastic and episcopal deeds A.D. 1200–1600* (IMC, Dublin, 1936).*

White, Newport B., *Extents of Irish monastic possessions, 1540–41* (IMC, Dublin, 1943).*

Wilkins, David, *Concilia Magnae Britanniae et Hiberniae*, 4 vols (London, 1737).*

Williams, Bernadette, 'The Dominican annals of Dublin' in Seán Duffy (ed.), *Medieval Dublin II* (Dublin, 2001), pp 142–68.

Williams, Bernadette (ed.), *Annals of Ireland: by Friar John Clyn* (Dublin, 2007).*

Wilmans, Roger (ed.), *Vita Norberti archiepiscopi Magdeburgensis*, in Georg Pertz et al. (eds), *Monumenta Germaniae historica*, scriptores, 30 vols (Hanover, 1826–92), xii, 670–703.*

ONLINE SOURCES

ACS-Projects http://www.acsltd.ie/project6.html.

Archaelogical survey of Ireland: www.archaeology.ie

BHO: British History Online: www.british-history.ac.uk

CELT, Corpus of Electronic Texts: www.ucc.ie/celt

CIRCLE: A calendar of Irish Chancery Letters, c.1244–1509: chancery.tcd.ie

Place Names NI: www.Placenamesni.Org

Index